Models of
Urban and Regional Systems
in Developing Countries:

Some Theories and
Their Application in Physical Planning

Models of Urban and Regional Systems in Developing Countries:

Some Theories and Their Application in Physical Planning

by

GEORGE CHADWICK

PERGAMON PRESS

OXFORD · NEW YORK · BEIJING · FRANKFURT
SÃO PAULO · SYDNEY · TOKYO · TORONTO

U.K.	Pergamon Press, Headington Hill Hall, Oxford OX3 0BW, England
U.S.A.	Pergamon Press, Maxwell House, Fairview Park, Elmsford, New York 10523, U.S.A.
PEOPLE'S REPUBLIC OF CHINA	Pergamon Press, Quianmen Hotel, Beijing, People's Republic of China
FEDERAL REPUBLIC OF GERMANY	Pergamon Press, Hammerweg 6, D-6242 Kronberg, Federal Republic of Germany
BRAZIL	Pergamon Editora, Rua Eça de Queiros, 346, CEP 04011, São Paulo, Brazil
AUSTRALIA	Pergamon Press Australia, P.O. Box 544, Potts Point; N.S.W. 2011, Australia
JAPAN	Pergamon Press, 8th Floor, Matsuoka Central Building, 1-7-1 Nishishinjuku, Shinjuku, Tokyo 160, Japan
CANADA	Pergamon Press Canada, Suite 104, 150 Consumers Road, Willowdale, Ontario M2J 1P9, Canada

Copyright © 1987 George Chadwick

First edition 1987   1560182

Library of Congress Cataloging in Publication Data
Chadwick, George F.
Models of urban and regional systems in developing countries.
(Urban and regional planning series; v. 36)
Bibliography: p.
1. Sociology, Urban. 2. City planning—Developing countries.
3. Regional planning—Developing countries. 4. Urban policy—
Developing countries.
I. Title. II. Series.

HT149.5.C43   1986   307.7′6   86-17080

British Library Cataloguing in Publication Data
Chadwick, George
Models of urban and regional systems in developing countries: some theories and their application in physical planning. (Urban and regional planning series; v.36)
1. Urban policy—Developing countries
I. Title II. Series
307′.12′091724   HT149.5

ISBN 0-08-023000-8 (Hardcover)
ISBN 0-08-022999-9 (Flexicover)

Printed in Great Britain by A. Wheaton & Co. Ltd., Exeter

To Doreen and in memory of J. C. and D. E. C.

Essentia non sunt multiplicanda praeter necessitatem.

("Hypotheses are not to be multiplied without necessity": Occam's Razor)

Foreword

This study has taken a long time to appear: its roots go back to 1972, although formally it was begun in 1973, having been crystallized one hot day on the road to Mrewa. A rather simple comparative study of models in developing countries seemed to be indicated at that time, but subsequent travel to various countries gradually resulted in some changes of view. To experience of Southern Africa and Mauritius was added brief experience of Ghana, Egypt, Morocco and Australia, whilst longer stays in Bahrain and Hong Kong were helpful: to these were added kind invitations to visit Costa Rica and Brazil, whilst lengthy recent stays in Korea and Saudi Arabia have been influential. These working travels, added to shorter visits elsewhere, have both prolonged the study, and, hopefully, directed its aim more usefully.

Amongst the many very kind people and institutions I must thank for help, hospitality and stimulus on the way are: the Central Office of Statistics at Rose Hill, Mauritius; Denis Fair, John Lea, John Muller, Nic Patricios and Joan Verster at the University of the Witwatersrand; the City Engineer of Salisbury, Rhodesia; the Colegio Federado de Arquitectos y de Engenieros de Costa Rica, and Esther Salas de Weiss in San José; the Universidade de São Paulo and its Escola de Engenharia de São Carlos, and FAPESP for their support through Professor Romeu Corsini, Professor Azevedo and EMPLASA in São Paulo, and especially in São Carlos, Dante and Julieta Martinelli and José Savério Lia and other friends in CPD; and the Korea Research Institute for Human Settlements and Dr. W. Y. Kwon in Seoul.

For helpful assistance in securing reference material, the County Libraries of Cheshire and Buckinghamshire, and through them the National Lending Library, must be thanked once again. Acknowledgement is expressed also to the various authors quoted herein and their publishers, and perhaps especially those whose models are cited: though some criticism of their models is made, no one should doubt the pioneering nature of much of this work.

Finally, as always, I must thank my wife for bearing with kindness and affection the many long absences and absentmindednesses that a work like this entails.

GEORGE CHADWICK

Halton, Buckinghamshire, England

Contents

List of Figures and Tables

1. Developing Countries: A Perspective

This work is concerned with the understanding of the structure and behaviour of urban and regional systems in developing countries. By "urban and regional systems" we mean socio-economic relationships and their physical expression in towns and associated rural areas.

A second purpose of the study is to consider not only how such systems change, but also how they might be changed by some kind of manipulation; the primary kind of manipulation considered here is via physical, rather than economic planning.

Both of these purposes necessarily involve the activity of the modelling of the systems concerned, simply because modelling is an appropriate way in which to summarize the complexity of often very complex systems: modelling of any such systems has the objective of making them more accessible to understanding, and afterwards to the possibility of their manipulation.

No exact definition of the term "developing country" is attempted in this work: it does not need to be, for the purpose is a broad one. In a real sense, of course, all countries are developing, i.e. in a state of change, moving hopefully onward towards some—even if unstated—goal. However, the use of "developing country", or "undeveloped", or "less-developed", terminology is primarily in the sense of economic development; in the League Tables of organizations like the World Bank, the countries viewed as more successful are those whose rate of increase of total Gross National Product, or GNP per capita, are highest: "growth" is the word used as implying the most desirable state of affairs. The question: "Growth for what?" is rarely asked, and rarely answered, although growth in any economy cannot be an end in itself: other purposes, other needs, lie beyond this means to those ends, whatever they may be.

Alternatively, attempts may be made to distinguish poor countries from those not-so-poor; World Bank statistics, in fact, are often organized in this way, i.e. as low-income, middle-income and industrialized countries. Generalizations, however, are always unsatisfactory, for few countries are exactly like other ones: the same "low-income" bracket covers Burundi with 4.1 million people on 28,000 km^2 of land, and India with 673 million on 3,288,000 km^2; the GNP per capita of Kenya with 15.9 million people is within 3% of that of Indonesia with 147 million. Undoubtedly, a clearer picture of each country is given by a series of indicators, and the World Bank compiles such statistics

1

annually; Table 1.1, taken from the World Development Report 1984 (World Bank, 1984), gives such an overall comparison, ranked by GNP per capita. (Other data, e.g. on energy consumption per capita, population growth, labour force, health, education, is published annually by the Bank.)

It must always be borne in mind that figures of this kind, i.e. averages over populations numbered in millions, are most likely to cover a very wide range of personal incomes, living conditions, and life-styles. The more-developed "core" of a country's major city or cities, and the less-developed "periphery" of its rural areas is a frequent phenomenon; the range may be from western-style affluence in city suburbs to deep poverty in the "bundu" areas a few hours away; it may also occur within the same city; with both *favelas* and high-rise apartments not very far from each other. Again, generalizations must be seen as unsatisfactory, unless supported by hard evidence.

However, whilst generalizations as to the *current state* of the national systems of developing countries may be inappropriate, it is conceivable that the *underlying mechanisms* of these systems may show certain similarities, especially at the urban and regional levels. This is not to say that such systems are necessarily like those of the now-"developed" or industrialized countries, either now, or at the time of their earlier development: indeed, there is evidence to show that at least the factors affecting the trajectories of change of the first country to industrialize, i.e. Britain, were considerably different from those in currently-industrializing countries like Brazil or Korea.

There are two ways in which one might proceed to examine the possibilities of developing a body of theory relating to developing countries, of course. It may be possible to extend theories developed from the economics and sociology of more-developed or industrialized countries; or it may be feasible to proceed via case-studies from developing countries themselves, thus deducing directly-relevant theories. It is probable that an amalgam of both approaches may be necessary—and, certainly in the field of direct concern in this work, what may be termed (now) "conventional" urban and regional theory has already played a dominant (possibly too-dominant) role. Also, the practical application of such theory is highly relevant: the focus in this exercise is one of hoped-for utility in aiding decision-making in practice.

A glance at any of the tables in the World Bank's *Development Report* will suggest that even measuring the current, or future, state of a developing country is a multi-dimensional business: many indicators (Drewnowski, 1970; UNESCO, 1976) are needed. The construction of even a small series of such indicators may be a difficult business, but the attempt to compress a number of these indicators into one, rather like a benefit/cost ratio is supremely difficult. It is, of course, the problem of the social welfare function (Arrow, 1951): the business of synthesis is usually more difficult than that of analysis. Fortunately, human beings are capable of overcoming this difficulty, though not always with complete rationality. By way of example, Table 1.2 shows indicators used in the Mesarovic/Pestel World Model commented on later in

TABLE 1.1. *World Basic Indicators for 1980 (from World Development Report 1984, OUP for World Bank)*

	Population (millions) mid-1982	Area (thousands of square kilometres)	GNP per capita[a] Dollars 1982	GNP per capita[a] Average annual growth rate (%) 1960-82[b]	Average annual rate of inflation[a] (%) 1960-70[c]	Average annual rate of inflation[a] (%) 1970-82[d]	Life expectancy at birth (years) 1982
Low-income economies	**2,266.5 t**	**29,097 t**	**280 w**	**3.0 w**	**3.2 m**	**11.5 m**	**59 w**
China and India	**1,725.2 t**	**12,849 t**	**290 w**	**3.5 w**	**3.2 m**	**11.7 m**	**62 w**
Other low-income	**541.3 t**	**16,248 t**	**250 w**	**1.1 w**	**3.2 m**	**11.7 m**	**51 w**
1 Chad	4.6	1,284	80	-2.8	4.6	7.8	44
2 Bangladesh	92.9	144	140	0.3	3.7	14.9	48
3 Ethiopia	32.9	1,222	140	1.4	2.1	4.0	47
4 Nepal	15.4	141	170	-0.1	7.7	8.9	46
5 Mali	7.1	1,240	180	1.6	5.0	9.8	45
6 Burma	34.9	677	190	1.3	2.7	9.7	55
7 Zaire	30.7	2,345	190	-0.3	29.9	35.3	50
8 Malawi	6.5	118	210	2.6	2.4	9.5	44
9 Upper Volta	6.5	274	210	1.1	1.3	9.7	44
10 Uganda	13.5	236	230	-1.1	3.2	47.4	47
11 India	717.0	3,288	260	1.3	7.1	8.4	55
12 Rwanda	5.5	26	260	1.7	13.1	13.4	46
13 Burundi	4.3	28	280	2.5	2.8	12.5	47
14 Tanzania	19.8	945	280	1.9	1.8	11.9	52
15 Somalia	4.5	638	290	-0.1	4.5	12.6	39
16 Haiti	5.2	28	300	0.6	4.0	9.2	54
17 Benin	3.7	113	310	0.6	1.9	9.6	48
18 Central African Rep.	2.4	623	310	0.6	4.1	12.6	48
19 China	1,008.2	9,561	310	5.0	—	—	67
20 Guinea	5.7	246	310	1.5	1.5	3.3	38
21 Niger	5.9	1,267	310	-1.5	2.1	12.1	45

Table 1.1—continued

	Population (millions) mid-1982	Area (thousands of square kilometres)	GNP per capita[a]		Average annual rate of inflation (%)		Life expectancy at birth (years) 1982
			Dollars 1982	Average annual growth (%) 1960–82[b]	1960–70[c]	1970–82[d]	
22 Madagascar	9.2	587	320	−0.5	3.2	11.5	48
23 Sri Lanka	15.2	66	320	2.6	1.8	13.3	69
24 Togo	2.8	57	340	2.3	1.3	8.8	47
25 Ghana	12.2	239	360	−1.3	7.5	39.5	55
26 Pakistan	87.1	804	380	2.8	3.3	12.7	50
27 Kenya	18.1	583	390	2.8	1.6	10.1	57
28 Sierra Leone	3.2	72	390	0.9			38
29 Afghanistan	16.8	648	—	—	11.9	12.2	36
30 Bhutan	1.2	47	—	—			43
31 Kampuchea, Dem.	—	181	—	—			—
32 Lao PDR	3.6	237	—	—			43
33 Mozambique	12.9	802	—	—			51
34 Viet Nam	57.0	330	—	—			64
Middle-income economies	1,158.3 t	43,031 t	1,520 w	3.6 w	3.0 m	12.8 m	60 w
Oil exporters	519.5 t	15,036 t	1,260 w	3.6 w	3.0 m	13.9 m	57 w
Oil importers	638.8 t	27,995 t	1,710 w	3.5 w	3.0 m	12.7 m	63 w
Lower middle-income	669.6 t	20,952 t	840 w	3.2 w	2.9 m	11.7 m	56 w
35 Sudan	20.2	2,506	440	−0.4	3.9	15.2	47
36 Mauritania	1.6	1,031	470	1.4	2.1	8.7	45
37 Yemen, PDR	2.0	333	470	6.4	—	—	46
38 Liberia	2.0	111	490	0.9	1.9	8.5	54
39 Senegal	6.0	196	490	(.)	1.8	7.9	44
40 Yemen Arab Rep.	7.5	195	500	5¢l	—	15.0	44
41 Lesotho	1.4	30	510	6.5	2.7	11.4	53

42 Bolivia	5.9	1,099	570	1.7	3.5	25.9	51
43 Indonesia	152.6	1,919	580	4.2	—	19.9	53
44 Zambia	6.0	753	640	−0.1	7.6	8.7	51
45 Honduras	4.0	112	660	1.0	2.9	8.7	60
46 Egypt, Arab Rep.	44.3	1,001	690	3.6	2.6	11.9	57
47 El Salvador	5.1	21	700	0.9	0.5	10.8	63
48 Thailand	48.5	514	790	4.5	1.8	9.7	63
49 Papua New Guinea	3.1	462	820	2.1	4.0	8.1	53
50 Philippines	50.7	300	820	2.8	5.8	12.8	64
51 Zimbabwe	7.5	391	850	1.5	1.1	8.4	56
52 Nigeria	90.6	924	860	3.3	4.0	14.4	50
53 Morocco	20.3	447	870	2.6	2.0	8.3	52
54 Cameroon	9.3	475	890	2.6	4.2	10.7	53
55 Nicaragua	2.9	130	920	0.2	1.8	14.3	58
56 Ivory Coast	8.9	322	950	2.1	2.8	12.4	47
57 Guatemala	7.7	109	1,130	2.4	0.3	10.1	60
58 Congo, People's Rep.	1.7	342	1,180	2.7	4.7	10.8	60
59 Costa Rica	2.3	51	1,430	2.8	1.9	18.4	74
60 Peru	17.4	1,285	1,310	1.0	10.4	37.0	58
61 Dominican Rep.	5.7	49	1,330	3.2	2.1	8.8	62
62 Jamaica	2.2	11	1,330	0.7	4.0	16.2	73
63 Ecuador	8.0	284	1,350	4.8	6.1	14.5	63
64 Turkey	46.5	781	1,370	3.4	5.6	34.4	63
65 Tunisia	6.7	164	1,390	4.7	3.6	8.7	61
66 Colombia	27.0	1,139	1,460	3.1	11.9	22.7	64
67 Paraguay	3.1	407	1,610	3.7	3.1	12.7	65
68 *Angola*	8.0	1,247	—	—	—	—	43
69 *Cuba*	9.8	115	—	—	—	—	75
70 *Korea, Dem. Rep.*	18.7	121	—	—	—	—	64
71 *Lebanon*	2.6	10	—	—	1.4	—	65
72 *Mongolia*	1.8	1,565	—	—	—	—	65

Table 1.1—*continued*

	Population (millions) mid-1982	Area (thousands of square kilometres)	GNP per capita[a] Dollars 1982	GNP per capita[a] Average annual growth rate (%) 1960-82[b]	Average annual rate of inflation[a] (%) 1960-70[c]	Average annual rate of inflation[a] (%) 1970-82[d]	Life expectancy at birth (years) 1982
			2,490 w	**4.1 w**	**3.0 m**	**16.4 m**	**65 w**
Upper middle-income	**488.7 t**	**22,079 t**					
73 Syrian Arab Rep.	9.5	185	1,680	4.0	2.6	12.2	66
74 Jordan	3.1	98	1,690	6.9	—	9.6	64
74 Malaysia	14.5	330	1,860	4.3	-0.3	7.2	67
76 Korea, Rep. of	39.3	98	1,910	6.6	17.5	19.3	67
77 Panama	1.9	77	2,120	3.4	1.5	7.5	71
78 Chile	11.5	757	2,210	0.6	33.0	144.3	70
79 Brazil	126.8	8,512	2,240	4.8	46.1	42.1	64
80 Mexico	73.1	1,973	2,270	3.7	3.5	20.9	65
81 Algeria	19.9	2,382	2,350	3.2	2.7	13.9	57
82 Portugal	10.1	92	2,450	4.8	3.0	17.4	71
83 Argentina	28.4	2,767	2,520	1.6	21.4	136.0	70
84 Uruguay	2.9	176	2,650	1.7	50.2	59.3	73
85 South Africa	30.4	1,221	2,670	2.1	3.0	12.8	63
86 Yugoslavia	22.6	256	2,800	4.9	12.6	20.0	71
87 Venezuela	16.7	912	4,140	1.9	1.3	12.4	68
88 Greece	9.8	132	4,290	5.2	3.2	15.4	74
89 Israel	4.0	21	5,090	3.2	6.4	52.3	74
90 Hong Kong	5.2	1	5,340	7.0	2.4	8.6	75
91 Singapore	2.5	1	5,910	7.4	1.1	5.4	72
92 Trinidad and Tobago	1.1	5	6,840	3.1	3.2	17.8	68
93 *Iran, Islamic Rep.*	41.2	1,648	—	—	-0.5	—	60
94 *Iraq*	14.2	435	—	—	1.7	—	59

High-income oil exporters	**17.0 *t***	**4,312 *t***	**14,820 *w***	**5.6 *w***	—	**16.0 *m***	**58 *w***
95 Oman	1.1	300	6,090	7.4	—	—	52
96 Libya	3.2	1,760	8,510	4.1	5.2	16.0	57
97 Saudi Arabia	10.0	2,150	16,000	*7.5*	—	22.5	56
98 Kuwait	1.6	18	19,870	*−0.1*	—	15.6	71
99 United Arab Emirates	1.1	84	23,770	*−0.7*	—	—	71
Industrial market economies	**722.9 *t***	**30,935 *t***	**11,070 *w***	**3.3 *w***	**4.3 *m***	**9.9 *m***	**75 *w***
100 Ireland	3.5	70	5,150	2.9	5.2	14.3	73
101 Spain	37.9	505	5,430	4.0	6.8	16.0	74
102 Italy	56.3	301	6,840	3.4	4.4	16.0	74
103 New Zealand	3.2	269	7,920	1.5	3.6	13.1	73
104 United Kingdom	55.8	245	9,660	2.0	4.1	14.2	74
105 Austria	7.6	84	9,880	3.9	3.7	6.1	73
106 Japan	118.4	372	10,080	6.1	5.1	6.9	77
107 Belgium	9.9	31	10,760	3.6	3.6	7.1	73
108 Finland	4.8	337	10,870	3.6	6.0	11.7	73
109 Netherlands	14.3	41	10,930	2.9	5.4	7.4	76
110 Australia	15.2	7,687	11,140	2.4	3.1	11.4	74
111 Canada	24.6	9,976	11,320	3.1	3.1	9.3	75
112 France	54.4	547	11,680	3.7	4.2	10.1	75
113 Germany, Fed. Rep.	61.6	249	12,460	3.1	3.2	4.9	73
114 Denmark	5.1	43	12,470	2.5	6.4	9.9	75
115 United States	231.5	9,363	13,160	2.2	2.9	7.3	75
116 Sweden	8.3	450	14,040	2.4	4.3	9.9	77
117 Norway	4.1	324	14,280	3.4	4.4	9.0	76
118 Switzerland	6.4	41	17,010	1.9	4.4	4.8	79
East European nonmarket economies	**383.3 *t***	**23,422 *t***	—	—	—	—	**79 *w***
119 Hungary	10.7	93	2,270	6.3	—	3.2	71
120 Romania	22.5	238	2,560	*5.1*	—	—	71
121 Albania	2.9	29	—	—	—	—	72
122 Bulgaria	8.9	111	—	—	—	—	72
123 Czechoslovakia	15.4	128	—	—	—	—	72

Table 1.1—continued

| | Population (millions) mid-1982 | Area (thousands of square kilometres) | GNP per capita[6] | | Average annual rate of inflation[a] (%) | | Life expectancy at birth (years) 1982 |
			Dollars 1982	Average annual growth rate (%) 1960–82[b]	1960–70[c]	1970[d]	
124 German Dem. Rep.	16.7	108	—	—	—	—	73
125 Poland	36.2	313	—	—	—	—	72
126 USSR	270.0	22,402	—	—	—	—	69
Populations less than 1 million:							
Guinea-Bissau	0.8	36	170	-1.7	—	7.1	38
Comoros	0.4	2	340	0.9	3.4	11.7	48
Cape Verde	0.3	4	350	—	—	11.9	61
Gambia, The	0.7	11	360	2.5	2.2	9.7	36
Sao Tome and Principe	0.1	1	370	1.2	—	7.5	62
St. Vincent and the Grenadines	0.1	(.)	620	0.6	4.0	12.9	—
Solomon Islands	0.2	28	660	1.3	3.0	8.3	—
Guyana	0.8	215	670	1.7	2.4	9.9	68
Dominica	0.1	1	710	-0.8	3.8	16.5	58
St. Lucia	0.1	1	720	3.4	3.6	11.0	—
St. Kitts-Nevis	0.1	(.)	750	1.1	5.5	9.8	—
Grenada	0.1	(.)	760	1.6	3.4	15.0	69
Botswana	0.9	600	900	6.8	2.4	11.5	60
Swaziland	0.7	17	940	4.2	2.4	12.8	54
Belize	0.2	23	1,080	3.4	3.4	9.5	—
Mauritius	0.9	2	1,240	2.1	2.2	15.0	66
Antigua and Barbuda	0.1	(.)	1,740	-0.2	3.1	14.0	—
Fiji	0.7	18	1,950	3.2	2.5	11.7	68
Barbados	0.3	(.)	2,900	4.5	2.3	13.8	72
Malta	0.4	(.)	3,800	8.0	1.5	4.9	72

Bahamas	0.2	14	−0.4	3,830	3.4	7.4	69
Cyprus	0.6	9	5.9	3,840	1.3	7.3	74
Gabon	0.7	268	4.4	4,000	5.4	19.5	49
Bahrain	0.4	1	—	9,280	—	—	68
Iceland	0.2	103	3.2	12,150	12.2	38.2	77
Luxembourg	0.4	3	4.0	14,340	3.7	6.8	73
Qatar	0.3	11	—	21,880	2.6	29.4	71
Djibouti	0.4	22	—	—	—	—	50
Equatorial Guinea	0.4	28	—	—	3.4	—	43
Maldives	0.2	(.)	—	—	1.0	—	47
Seychelles	0.1	(.)	—	—	—	—	66
Suriname	0.4	163	—	—	—	—	65
Vanuatu	0.1	15	—	—	—	—	—
Western Samoa	0.2	3	—	—	—	—	65

Note: For data comparability and coverage see the technical notes in Report.

a See the technical notes.

b Because data for the early 1960s are not always available, figures in italics are for periods other than that specified.

c Figures in italics are for 1961–70, not 1960–70.

d Figures in italics are for 1970–81, not 1970–82.

e Because data for the early 1960s are not available, figures in italics are for periods other than that specified.

f Figures in italics are for 1970–81, not 1970–82.

g Figures in italics are for years other than 1982. See the technical notes in Report.

TABLE 1.2. *Example Values and Indicators*

Values	Indicators
Food	Calories per capita
	Protein per capita
	Animal fats per capita
	Distribution of calories
	Distribution of protein
	Distribution of animal fats
Shelter	Metres^2 per capita of housing
	Rooms per capita
	Bathrooms per capita
	Heated metres^2 per capita of housing
Medical care	Doctors per 1000
	Hospital beds per 1000
	Distribution of doctors
Environmental quality	ppm CO_x
	ppm NO^x
	ppm dust
	Park area per capita
	Water quality
	Exposure to noise
	Radioactivity above background
	Probabilistic safety hazard of nuclear plants
	Thermal pollution
Material well-being	Income per capita above food, shelter expenses
Physical security	Percentage of GRP on defence
	Crimes per 1000
	Policemen per 1000
Family	Abandoned children per 1000
	Child abuse incidence per 1000
	Hours of family member contact per week
	Subjective question
Non-family social	Average group memberships per capita
	Distribution of group memberships
	Hours per month of non-job social contact
Formal education	Average years of schooling
	Distribution of formal education
Self-improvement opportunity	Annual travel days per capita
	Library volumes per capita
	Leisure hours weekly
When used in place of material well-being, shelter, and medical care:	
Economy	GRP per capita
	Distribution of GRP
	Probabilistic GRP cost of energy imports

Source: Mesarovic and Pestel, IAASA.

this study. (See also Fig. 1.3 for an example of the spatial variation of a number of indicators.)

Whilst an over-focus on economic growth may be criticized, there is no doubt that low incomes are one of the major criteria, and difficulties, of many developing countries; the attempt to relieve, to eradicate poverty is the real purpose of economic development, for with higher incomes the other needful

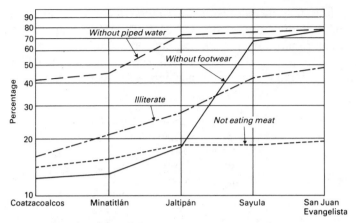

FIG. 1.3. Decline of living standards with increasing distance from a large city, Isthmus region, Mexico, 1970. *Source:* 1970 census (Scott, 1982).

criteria, or indicators of a reasonably satisfactory life, can be satisfied: food, housing, sanitation, education, health care, and so on, can be bought. However, there is the great difficulty, already commented on, that success in development is largely measured by averages—usually Gross Domestic Product per capita—and averages may conceal quite extreme conditions. Thus, the distribution of incomes (and of other indexed criteria) is of fundamental importance: the problem in many developing countries is to provide the lower precentiles of the income distribution with employment and income opportunities and with essential services (food, housing, water, sanitation). Poverty is a negative feedback situation: lack of income (whether monetary or exchangeable produce or goods), means a lack of opportunity to create income by taking up employment or self-employment by reason of malnutrition, illhealth, or immobility, the lack of education, homelessness. Growth of income, i.e. the positive feedback situation, requires savings or available money beyond some subsistence threshold to invest in job-seeking or one's own enterprise, in a personal condition which can meet the requirements likely to obtain in the employment situation, e.g. ability to walk to work, to meet the demands of the working day without distress, to have adequate nourishment, to be able to perform satisfactorily.

A major factor in the continuation of poverty—and it is increasing in many countries despite some degree of economic development having occurred—is population growth. Developing countries are characterized by fast rates of population growth, especially of their lower-income groups. Thus numbers of people living in poverty in many countries are increasing: low incomes and low literacy levels are not conducive to family planning. The pressure of numbers is felt overall in these countries, however: more mouths to feed, more demands on services of all kinds, more jobs required; the faster the pace of population increase, the faster jobs and services are required to stay in the same place, as it were—and the more money that is needed, whilst the new population added, by definition, cannot earn its own keep for some longish time.

The economic trap resulting from such fast population growth relates to the difficulty of providing many more new jobs each year for a very long time

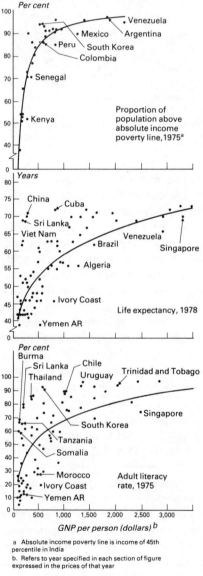

Fig. 1.4. National income and national poverty. *Source:* World Bank Development Report, 1980.

ahead: there is a growing mismatch between the size of the potential labour force and potential jobs, which is exacerbated by the growing tendency of individual and service processes to become mechanized, to require fewer pairs of hands to operate—and skilled hands at that.

The result of population growth and lack of employment opportunities appears in the migratory flows—sometimes based on earlier agricultural or traditional practices—which lead to urbanization on a massive scale in many developing countries, with the larger cities (perhaps existing from earlier or colonial times) being the receiving focus. Very high rates of urbanization thus occur, with consequent pressures on housing, including the rise of self-built suburbs, on water and sanitation services, on environmental health services, on transport facilities, education, and indeed all normal urban services. However, at the same time, these large—some hold, overgrown—cities are at the same time the locus of whatever economic development "growth" is taking place: indeed, it can be held that the large, possibly primate city, is the engine *par excellence* of economic growth. Large cities, large economic focii, require large numbers of people to keep them in motion. Urbanization creates the myriad relationships, the networks of complex interactions, which are the basis of such economic development, notwithstanding those nugatory factors: unemployment, overcrowding, pollution, crime, etc., which also seem to characterize large cities.

Meanwhile, back in the rural areas, the rural-based population may still be growing: agriculture may have become more productive with development, probably resulting also in rural unemployment and under-employment, pressure on minimal facilities and services, and continuing low incomes. In some countries, prone to natural disasters such as floods or droughts, even the subsistence basis of rural life may be threatened at times, the normal possibilities of survival through available food, water, and shelter disappearing. Rural areas are also subject to change during the process of development.

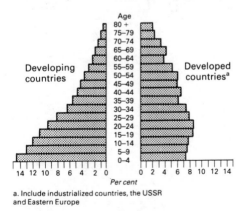

a. Include industrialized countries, the USSR and Eastern Europe

FIG. 1.5. Population distribution by age, 1980. *Source:* World Bank Development Report, 1980.

TABLE 1.6. *Real growth of GNP and GNP per capita, 1966–80*

	GNP					GNP per capita				
	1966–76	1977	1978	1979	1980ª	1966–76	1977	1978	1979	1980ᶜ
All developing regionsᵇ	6.1	5.8	5.2	5.2	4.6	3.6	3.5	2.8	2.7	2.3
Africa south of the Sahara	5.0	2.9	3.4	3.3	2.3	2.3	0.3	0.7	0.6	–0.4
East Africa and Pacific	8.1	8.4	9.4	6.6	3.9	5.5	5.9	6.9	4.3	1.6
Latin America and the Caribbean	5.9	4.8	3.9	5.5	5.4	3.2	2.5	1.6	3.1	3.1
North Africa and Middle East	8.1	10.0	6.0	14.6	7.5	5.1	6.6	2.7	11.1	4.2
South Asia	1.7	7.1	7.0	–2.6	7.4	1.4	4.9	4.8	–4.9	5.0
More advanced Mediterranean countries	6.0	4.0	4.1	2.6	1.4	4.5	2.5	2.6	1.1	–0.1
Industrial countries	4.2	3.8	4.0	3.5	1.3	3.3	3.2	3.3	2.8	0.6

ª Preliminary.

ᵇ For country coverage, see General Notes to Annex Tables and footnote to Statistical Annex Table 1. Note that all developing country and exporters, as well as the sum capital-surplus and exporters are included.

ᶜ For country coverage, see footnote to Statistical Annex Table 1. The growth rates for industrial countries refer to GDP rather than GNP.

Source: World Bank Annual Report 1981.

The process briefly sketched above is much more complex, of course, in reality. A major point of consideration is the interlocking nature of what are often seen as rather separate facets of development situations. It is believed that a systems viewpoint will help to illuminate the theoretical issues which are involved—as well as assist materially in the fabrication of models of various kinds. (Reference may be made to the author's: *A Systems View of Planning* (1971, 1978), which applies systems theory to the physical planning process). As an appendage to this introductory chapter, a number of tables published by the World Bank are included. They give an overall view of world development (Fig.. 1.1); graphs showing relationships between GNP per person and population in poverty, life expectancy, and adult literacy rates, for selected countries (Fig. 1.4); and population distribution by age for developed and developing countries, for 1980 (Fig. 1.5).

Figure 1.6 shows real growth of GNP and GNP per capita for various groups of countries; the generally low rate of increase of GNP per capita, and its recent decrease, for Africa south of the Sahara should be noted. The critical situation in Africa is also pointed up by Fig. 1.7, showing life expectancy in relation to income per person at 1978. Figure 1.8 depicts clearly the wide differences in productivity between the various sectors in Latin America (from Roberts, 1978).

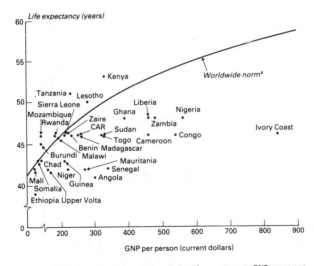

a. Derived from cross-country equation relating life expectancy to GNP per person

FIG. 1.7. Sub-Saharan Africa: life expectancy in relation to income per person, 1978.

TABLE 1.8. *Latin America: Average Productivity per Employed Person by Strata within Each Sector and Population Percentages at End of 1960*

	Total		Modern		Intermediate		Primitive		
	Percentage of employment	Average productivity in dollars at 1960 prices	Percentage of employment	Average productivity in dollars at 1960 prices	Percentage of employment	Average productivity in dollars at 1960 prices	Percentage of employment	Average productivity in dollars at 1960 prices	Ratio of productivity in modern productivity in primitive stratum
Total	100.0	1371	12.4	5,909	47.7	1194	34.3	203	29
Agriculture	42.4	694	6.8	4,830	27.7	830	65.5	205	24
Mining	1.0	6484	38.0	15,606	34.2	1420	27.8	246	63
Manufacturing	13.8	2517	17.5	8,938	64.9	1400	17.6	220	41
(a) Industrial	7.7	4168	28.1	9,800	71.9	1960	—	—	—
(b) Artisan-type	6.1	419	4.1	1,760	55.9	470	40.0	220	8
Construction	4.5	1116	24.8	2,322	64.9	800	10.3	203	11
Basic services	5.5	2174	25.0	4,276	71.6	1530	3.4	220	19
Trade	10.1	2731	14.0	8,990	76.1	1990	9.9	340	26
Other services	17.3	1283	16.2	2,713	70.5	940	13.3	160	17

Source: Estimates taken from ECLA, *La mano de obra y el desarrollo económico de América Latina en los últimos años*, E/CN.12/L.1 (Annex) (Roberts, 1978).

2. Population, Urbanization, and Migration

The three topics of population, urbanization, and migration are obviously interlinked: one cannot consider any one of the three without bringing in the others. Migration is an element in population change, and urbanization occurs initially through migration; urbanization in turn provides a further basis for natural population change. We begin with urbanization, to which we return after a consideration of population change and migration.

Urbanization

To urbanize means to render urban (OED), to remove the rural character of a district or a population; urban means of, or living or situated in, a city or a town; whilst urbanity generally means of the city, but can also mean refined or polished in style of manner. Urbanization is thus the process of becoming urban—and hence of ceasing to be rural. There is also a close correlation between urbanization and civilization, for both processes share a root word meaning town or city: this is a fundamental point, for civilization, seen as a fundamental cultural process in essence is the process of founding and enhancing the growth of cities. Urbanization and civilization are also very definite economic and technological processes, and this suggests that "development", i.e. *economic* (and thus technological) development, implies urbanization or changing, by and large, from a rural to an urban way of life.

The preconditions for life in cities have been summarized by Sjöberg (1960), using Gordon Childe's analysis as:

(1) a favourable "ecological" base,
(2) an advanced technology (relative to the pre-urban form), and
(3) a complex social organization—above all, a well-developed power structure.

Such prerequisites led, in Childe's own words (1957), to ". . . the aggregation of large populations in cities; the differentiation within these of primary producers (fishers, farmers, etc.), full-time specialist artisans, merchants, officials, priests, and rulers; an effective concentration of economic and political power; the use of conventional symbols for recording and transmitting information (writing), and equally conventional standards of weights and measures of time and space leading to some mathematical and calendrical science. The starting point, too, in each series was, rather less abstractly, similar—at least in the economic sphere—inasmuch as all the first barbarian cultures examined were based on the cultivation of the same cereals and the breeding of the same species of animals. But the intervening steps in development do not exhibit even abstract parallelism."

Thus the emergence of the first ciivilizations, the first cities, in the Tigris-Euphrates basin of Mesopotamia, in the Nile Valley of Egypt, in the Indus Valley, and on the Huang-Ho in China. From these beginnings, either by diffusion or renewed innovation, grew the first preindustrial cities of the world, some eventually to decline and disappear, for cities may die as well as be born, and some to become in turn industrial, and later, kinds of cities. Urbanization in this context is thus a process of a long time-span in general, though sometimes short in particular places, or sometimes recurring in others.

The reasons for the differing appearances and time-scales of this urbanization are, of course, due to the differing appearances of the preconditions mentioned above: the ecological base was inadequate perhaps, or technology backward, or social organization unsuitable—or all three difficulties may have prevented the emergence of cities. Certainly, as Childe implies, the actual form of civilization, or the path which it took, differed from place to place. There is a rather nice academic argument arising at this point as to whether there were any true cities in Africa south of the Sahara which were indigenous and did not arise from the implantation of other civilizations, particularly that of Islam, an argument mainly hingeing upon the criterion of writing, which Childe, probably correctly, considered as "essential to the categorization of the city, implying as it does the existence of a highly-specialized non-agricultural group that has the necessary leisure to develop such a complex skill."

The point also applies to early cultures of Meso-America, as does a certain degree of technological backwardness in the absence of wheeled transport. But these cultures did have the advantage of maize as a staple food, a less-demanding agriculture being involved, and so implying both a different ecological base and a less-developed technology from that of the areas of different grain-cropping. Thus Childe and Sjöberg would call the culture of the Yoruba of the Western Sudan "quasi-urban." As late as 1931, the towns of Yorubaland could be characterized as *rus in urbe* cities. Some 28% of the Yoruba population then lived in nine cities of 45,000 inhabitants, while 34% lived in sixteen cities of over 20,000 inhabitants. "These towns consist mainly of agriculturists whose farms are made on a belt of land surrounding the city to a depth of 15 or more miles. Since farming is based largely upon family and kinship, these institutions set the pattern of life in the town which reflects in turn the personal character of relationships in the countryside. There is also a specialized group of weavers, dyers, iron workers, diviners, medicine men, who supply all other members with their particular goods and services" (Little, 1965).

This description as quasi-urban might be applied too, to the early Maya of

Central America, despite the highly developed social organization of the Yoruba and the complex and unique architectural accomplishments of the Maya. But the point *is* academic, as has been said, given that one understands the different manifestations possible at different times and in different environments of the forces of urbanization: the splendid ruins of Great Zimbabwe in Rhodesia must represent an urbanizing process of some kind, even if they are more aptly described (as some also claim for the Maya sites) as a "ceremonial centre", just as the terraced valley slopes of the Inyanga area, also in Rhodesia, presumably represent some agricultural technological adaptation which could be seen, broadly, as being part of a long process which eventually might lead to town building, rather than being a specific materialization of "civilization". The word "might" here stresses the probability that, as in biological evolution, the evolution of cities probably requires many attempts, many "false starts". For example, Robert F. Gray (Bohannon and Dalton, 1962) noted that specialization of production does exist in the Sonjo villages of Tanganyika, but the modest surplus is used for land acquisition, bride payments, and water rights purchase, and does not become part of a market economy which might eventually become an urbanizing force.

It may be as well to recapitulate the main essentials of the urbanization process, here concentrating on the founding of cities, very briefly, as an aid to further discussion and conceptualization:

(1) the setting up of towns requires an agricultural surplus, originally close at hand, thus an ecological base (which will include supplies of water);

(2) the agricultural surplus frees some people from dependence upon their own labour for their own food: they, or some of them, representing a rural population surplus, move to the town and to other activities, i.e. urbanization involves migration;

(3) the town, as it grows, will demand more agricultural surplus, thus technically more advanced or more productive agriculture, or command of a wider agricultural area;

(4) urban growth is by natural increase and/or more inward migration;

(5) the new urban dwellers become specialists in various trades and occupations, though early towns inevitably include food producers, fishermen, and primary producers such as miners and foresters;

(6) new economic processes are set up, of barter and exchange, with first travelling then permanent markets, etc.; the surplus is stored in the city;

(7) organization structures arise, including processes for the administration of the food and water supply, the storage, counting and recording and defence of the surplus, and of the organization itself; this implies a power structure of some kind;

(8) technological processes are advanced in the city, of transport and storage, of hand manufacture: these use energy on a greater scale, though still largely animate energy;

(9) growth of the town requires growth of its parts and processes as well as of its command of external resources.

However, one must note the objection raised by Oliver Cox (1969) to a too-hasty acceptance of a temporal sequence: first surplus, then city? As Cox says: "The neo-Malthusian idea that food-producing technology had to develop first before cities could arise and grow seems to be a popular illusion taken as axiomatic . . . There are certain crucial objections to this notion. A surplus may arise in response to increasing demand during a constant level of agricultural technology; the growth of cities may increase agricultural specialization and thus enhance efficiency; and improvement in distribution, which may involve quantity not quality of transport and communication technology, can maximize the amount of food available. Indeed, it is possible for development of agricultural technology to run ahead of need; and this points to the possibility that the urban aggregation may be the cause of improved technology rather than vice versa. In other words, an agricultural surplus for urban consumption may be derived indirectly from production in cities . . . correlation may not indicate causation."

A further view in opposition to that of Childe, but dwelling more on the institutional framework, is put by Keyfitz (1965): ". . . we oppose the assertion that the 'surplus' created the institutions, including the cities, and say instead that the institutions created the surplus. More precisely, the building of cities is part of a process that includes instituting a surplus." Pointing to the slow rate of urbanization of India (only 11.4% of the population was urban in 1921, and only 21% in 1975), Keyfitz postulates: "The reason why performance in respect of city growth was so far below potential can only be that existing agricultural technology was not effectively used; the surplus is not 'there' the moment it is technically possible but only after it has been institutionalized through taxes, trade, or other means. Before this the peasant does not grow all he can; what he grows he uses lavishly since he has no reason to save it." Keyfitz goes on: "The modern state is as much as anything the institutional means by which the primate city wraps around itself, so to speak, a territory in which its food will be produced."

The self-generating, i.e. positive-feedback growth of cities is obviously due to a combination of net natural increase plus net migration, located in some, possibly large, but nonetheless fairly specific geographic area. This phenomenon of growth plus concentration, is urbanization, of course. The reasons for continuing urbanization in a particular context may be complex, but, as Artle (1972) has reminded us, the basic situation, in economic terms, is easily discerned: increase in family income through moving from a rural to an urban location may be a sufficient motivation.

The degree of income elasticity of demand varies between food and other agricultural products, and other consumer goods, including urban goods and urban services. As income grows over time, proportionately, less of it will be allocated to food, and more to other goods and services: the demand for food has a low income elasticity, in comparison with the demand for other consumer goods, as depicted in the graph (Fig. 2.1).

In this sense, therefore, a city is a system which delivers to consumers agricultural goods of increasingly lower income elasticities, and "urban" goods of increasingly greater income elasticities. It should be no surprise, therefore, to find that urban systems concentrate on providing non-agricultural products and services of increasing numbers and diversity, i.e. specialization of both products and labour. Markets will increase in size both with population growth and with rising incomes: bigger markets will give rise to greater specialization: the biggest cities offer the largest range of more specialized services. Learning: the improvement of performance, and through it, the goods and services offered, is a further outcome. The increasing division of labour, i.e. specialization, and learning as a general process, are interrelated. Increasing returns to scale are implied by the increasing disparity between the food and non-food income elasticities, so far as the latter is concerned; such increasing returns are associated with indivisibilities which occur in many aspects of urban systems.

The list of aspects of the urbanization process might also be paralleled by a kind of converse list of changes to the rural milieu which urbanization brings: the agricultural surplus, the implied rural population surplus, the bringing of rural affairs under the aegis of the town so as to ensure the control of the food supply, the looking towards the town for services, for education, for markets, and so on. Stent (1948) makes well the point that what is implied in urbanization is, in fact, a situation of disequilibrium, of change in the relative productivity of urban and rural activities. Such a disequilibrium changes from time to time, presumably tending to create a new state of equilibrium between urban and rural. Curiously, the exodus from rural life can owe its economic

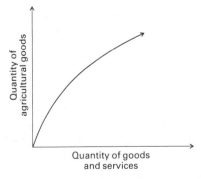

Fig. 2.1. Income elasticities of demand for foods and non-food goods (Artle, 1972).

origins to widely diverse reasons: an impoverished agriculture incapable of supporting the many may lead to rural unemployment just as a highly organized and productive agriculture using up-to-date technology may also be incapable of providing direct employment for many, though producing more food for the population generally. It is also not unknown for the unthinking application of modern western agricultural techniques to produce erosion, soil loss, and eventual impoverishment, especially in Africa. Where rural population increases through natural causes, rather than movement, the carrying capacity of the land may be exceeded: a circumstance that might have led to migration to unsettled lands in former times. But where there is a general and widespread pressure of population upon land resources, such rural to rural migration may not be possible, and rural to urban migration, or continuing urbanization, becomes the only alternative. Also, where there is no saleable surplus of agricultural produce, the only marketable commodity to offset poverty and starvation is labour: hence the widespread African migrations to often distant urban labour markets.

Considerations of the interlinkage between urbanization and rural change have led some commentators to use the terms 'generative' and 'parasitic' when referring to the growth of cities in developing countries (Hoselitz, 1955), though these terms may be regarded as rather too pejorative. The emergence of cities, according to Childe's statement of civilization, requires an agriculture which is so advanced as to be able to feed a relatively large non-rural population. Transactions between rural and urban areas would follow, with the cities supplying non-agricultural goods and services. Hence the course of evolution of such an economy would entail the shift of labour away from primary occupations in agriculture and extraction to secondary occupations in manufacture and processing and to tertiary occupations in servicing activities. Urbanization was part and parcel of this process, providing labour for gradually-developing agglomerations of industry and services, with expected falls in costs of production through external economies associated with the urban environment. In turn, renewed calls for rural and urban labour would be set up, to supply further food and raw materials for further manufacture and servicing, so that economic growth would occur, propelled by, and also propelling the urbanization process. Such was the "generative" hypothesis.

The "parasitic" city, on the other hand, tends to retard the growth of the national economy, due to various causes. One such is the import-based city which makes use of food and raw materials from outside its own country, sending back its earnings to pay for the imports. Another cause might be the citywards migration of those without urban jobs, or the hope of them, impelled by starvation in the rural areas or by political upheaval or warfare. The city is literally swollen, swollen beyond its "natural" level in terms of the economy within which it exists.

What seems likely, however, is not that a city is necessarily of one or the other of these kinds, but that the forces acting upon the urbanization process alter in strength and direction from time to time, as in many systems: the upward spiral due to positive feedback being replaced by negative feedback producing stability, or downward positive feedback, from time to time (cf. Hardin's (1963) succession of "homeostatic plateaux"); (see Fig. 5.3).

As Janet Abu-Lughod (1965) has pointed out, Egypt has often been cited as an "over-urbanized" country, both from the point of view of international and of internal comparisons. Thus, in 1950, when only 13% of the world's population and only 9% of the population in under-industrialized regions lived in cities having 100,000 or more inhabitants it was claimed that almost one-fifth of Egypt's population was in cities of this size; by 1960, the proportion in Egypt was nearer to one fourth. In 1947, when 40% of Egyptian occupied males were engaged in non-farming occupations, some 26% of the population resided in "urban" communities, according to data revised by Mrs Abu-Lughod. Such figures have been suggested as showing a high degree of "over-urbanization", but in fact, are based upon a number of statistical or definitional aberrations. Furthermore, the particular and peculiar geographical and ecological characteristics of Egypt, with the narrow alluvial Nile valley and the wide, but finite, Nile Delta, mean that many rural settlements have perforce to absorb increased rural population, thus becoming unusually large as yet-still-rural communities miscalled "urban centres". But, of course, the primary cause for the statistical picture of urbanization presented by Egypt is the existence of Cairo, a city of over 2 million people in 1947 and 3.3 million in 1960, and more than 10 million now. As Mrs Abu-Lughod points out, Cairo's role is very much more than that of a national capital, and so it cannot be regarded simply as a case of "parasitism".

More recent information (UNDP, 1976) suggests that the "urban" population of Egypt has been increasing at 3.6% per annum in comparison with a 1.5% increase in rural areas. By the year 2000, it is forecast that total urban population may have grown from 16 million in 1975 to 45 million: a 29 million increase in 25 years, compared with 11 million from 1945 to 1975: even if economic growth rates are lower than anticipated, a 23 million increase is likely in this period, to 39 million in total. The total urban population then might be 30 million, even without any further rural-urban migration. The population of Cairo could then be in the range of 15 to 20 million by the year 2000 solely through natural increase, even if migration ceased altogether; Alexandria might have 6.6 million. In 'rural' areas, the Nile Delta would then contain nearly 24 million people, and Upper Egypt nearly 16 million: the problem of accommodating the 14 million "rural" population of the Delta without destroying its rich agriculture is obviously a very considerable one.

In his *Analysis of Over-urbanization* (1964), N. V. Sovani demolishes much of the myth of "over-urbanization"; much misconception seems to have arisen in comparing urbanization indices for very unlike groups of countries. There is no logical reason why urbanization indices for developing countries in the twentieth century should be like those for now-developed countries at their earlier stages of growth, perhaps a century or more ago. One of the major lessons to be learnt in respect to "development" as Felipe Herrera (1971) amongst others has convincingly argued is that it does not occur in precisely the same way in different countries at different times: it is not even clear, in some cases, that "development" will occur at all; many false starts may be involved, as in many biological systems.

Then, much of the criticism of "over-urbanization" stems from misconceptions as to the nature of economic development: is it really possible to devote resources, even scarce ones, only to economic growth? Does not economic growth, in fact, require the development of *all* or most other social and economic systems, and especially urban ones? Felipe Herrera, former President of the Inter-American Bank, suggests that large cities are a very necessary part of the economic development process. Other criticism of "over-urbanization" may stem from a concern with the size and nature of the social problems of swollen Third World cities—a very real concern indeed; but attacking a mythical dragon called "over-urbanization" is not helpful to the real problems, which, at root, are problems of population change and poverty, not the mere size of cities.

Two main themes are therefore essential at this juncture, they are:

(1) The process of population change by natural increase, and how this is apparently affected by other factors, of which urbanization (and its often accompaniment by industrialization) is one;
(2) The process of population movement, i.e. migration, which both swells and diminishes naturally changing population levels, especially where urbanization is also present.

Consideration must be given also to the major economic and social aspects of urbanization.

Population Change

It is obvious that population change is composed of the difference between births and deaths over time in the group considered, to which must be added or subtracted the number emigrating from or immigrating to that group in the same time. So, with a basic knowledge of the initial population and of birth and death rates, one can arrive at natural change in the population, to which some hypothesis about migration can be applied. It must be remembered, though, that as in all such projections, one is using data from the past to produce projections into the future; in this case, the assumption is that current (i.e. past) birth and death rates will apply for some future period, either unmodified or modified in accordance with some hypothesis, e.g. about health care, medical knowledge, change in standard of living, etc. It is thus possible to produce *alternative* projections of population at future times, based upon alternative fertility and mortality hypotheses.

Likewise, alternative views on migration can be included in the projections, and whilst those concerning emigration are based upon the population group for which the projection is being performed, those relating to immigration are based upon quite other (and may be very diverse) population groups, knowledge of whom, by definition, is likely to be less easy to come by, especially if in other countries or remoter territories of the same country. Of course, it is the *net* effect of migration, the difference between in-and-out-flows, which is the crucial effect.

Obviously, then, we have the following:

Future population = Base population at start of period
+ Surviving births in period
− Deaths in period
+ Net migration in period

—and it is now usual to perform such a calculation in a disaggregated fashion by incorporating age and sex cohorts. This, on the one hand, enables closer identification of the cohorts of women of child-bearing age to which the appropriate cohort fertility rates can be applied, and at the output end gives the possibility of a useful disaggregation, e.g. including children of pre-school age, children of school age (disaggregated into primary and secondary education groups), men (and women) of working age, people of retirement age. This implies, naturally, that cohort data is available to start with, including mortality by cohort.

A cohort-survival population model is the outcome normally programmed for the computer, though also being feasible for hand calculation, if somewhat laboriously so. Such a model is, in fact, a small simulation model, where the growth (or decline) of the given population is simulated over time in accordance with the fertility/mortality/migration hypotheses involved. Once such a simulation has been performed, it is relatively simple to re-run it at future times, provided the input data is kept up to date in appropriate form and provided the relevant hypotheses are reviewed at such times.

Over long periods of time, it may be that a general population change is observed—indeed, it is usually claimed that population growth is exponential in character when seen in large aggregations, e.g. at the world scale, and such estimates of world population as are available tend to bear this out. Thus curves of the general form $y = e^x$ might be expected to illustrate population growth over long periods of time, though it could equally well be—and for the future of world survival *must* be—that such curves, in fact, are of the logistic form, i.e. have an upper stabilizing limit, so that the shape may be of S-form instead of the normal exponential, i.e. the curve may be described instead by an equation of the form:

$$x = L/1 + be^{-ct}$$

where L is the assumed saturation level of the variable x and b and c are constants. Other curves with upper limits, e.g. as in Gompertz's Law which produces a non-symmetrical S-curve, might also be an appropriate representation of population change:

$$x = L \ exp(-b \ exp(-k \ exp \ t))$$

Over shorter periods of time, and for smaller populations, the form of curves of growth is much more conjectural: "explosions", "surges", and "ripples" are likely, and such disturbances over short periods may obscure a longer-term trend: if, indeed, there is such a trend. This is especially true of developing countries, and a case-study of Mauritius may illuminate the point. Mauritius is an island* so that migration in and out of the country is well-defined; it is also a former British Colony, and has the advantage of having had 14 Censuses of Population since 1846, so that a long series of data is available. The 1972 *Population Census of Mauritius*, Volume 1, Preliminary Report, 1974, shows the considerable change which has taken place over 126 years, from 158,462 people in 1846 to 826,199 in 1972 (Table 2.2). The average annual rates of increase are most revealing, ranging from a net loss in the decade 1901–1911 of 0.06% per annum to a huge increase at 5.87% between 1851 and 1861. This latter was due to the importing of indentured labour from southern India by the Colonial Government, as also in Natal and East Africa, to work the sugar plantations in the absence of ready supplies of indigenous (Mauritian Creole) labour: an event in all three areas which was to have unforeseen results a

TABLE 2.2. *Population of Mauritius as Enumerated at Each Census (1846–1972)*

Census Year	Population enumerated at Census			Intercensal increase	Average annual rate of increase %
	Both Sexes	Male	Female		
1846	158,462	104,598	53,864	—	—
1851	180,823	119,341	61,482	22,361	2.55
1861	310,050	202,961	107,089	129,227	5.87
1871	316,042	193,575	122,467	5,992	0.19
1881	359,874	208,655	151,219	43,832	1.31
1891	370,588	206,038	164,556	10,714	0.29
1901	371,023	199,552	171,471	435	0.01
1911	368,791	194,095	174,696	−2,232	−0.06
1921	376,485	194,108	182,377	7,694	0.21
1931	393,238	200,609	192,629	16,753	0.44
1944	419,185	210,326	208,859	25,947	0.49
1952	501,415	252,032	249,383	82,230	2.26
1962*	681,619	342,306	339,313	180,204	3.12
1972*	826,199	413,648	412,351	144,580	1.94

* *De facto* population—including European members of the Armed Forces but excluding the passengers and crews of ships lying in the harbour. (1972 Population Census of Mauritius.)

* Actually *two* major islands: Mauritius and Rodrigues, 300 miles apart; this discussion is about the former.

century later. A second traumatic event is also concealed behind the large intercensal increases for the periods 1944–1952 (2.26% per annum) and 1952–1962 (3.12% per annum)—here the occasion was the advent in 1948 of the World Health Organization malaria eradication programme, which had extraordinary results on the mortality rate, especially of infants, which dropped from142.8 per 1000 in 1949 to 76.3 in 1950, thus increasing effective fertility and producing a surge of population which is still of concern; although the latest intercensal increase recorded, 1962–1972, is down to 1.94% per annum. This latter figure is still a high one, in view of the very real spatial constraints of Mauritius: an island of 720 square miles which has as a main, indeed almost only, source of income, the extensive growing of sugar cane which demands that every possible piece of land must be put to agricultural use. But it is to be noted that a projection for 1972 prepared in 1967 on the basis of the 1962 census and assuming fertility constant at 1967 level, with declining mortality and no migration, has been proved to be in excess of the actual 1972 census figure by some 53,000 (Adams 1966, also CSO Mauritius). In fact, detailed figures of fertility trends in Mauritius (Director of Statistics, Mauritius) for the period 1958–1971 (Table 2.3) show a very real decline in fertility over this crucial period, the reasons for which are not yet fully known, though the Mauritius Government has been urging a birth control programme for some time.

Mauritius has a mixed population, each with presumed differences in social and cultural customs, including marriage and fertility, family structure, and so on (see Benedict, 1961), and the reproduction of the different groups seem to have been at differing rates over time. From being a minority group in 1851, the Indian population, then very largely male, has become the majority group and now represents two-thirds of the total population, with a more normal male/female ratio. Even so, at least some ten languages are commonly spoken in Mauritius, and 52 different religions are distinguished by the 1972 Census.

A very youthful population structure characterizes many developing countries, and Mauritius is no exception, although the fall in the rate of reproduction has had some effect since 1962. The ratio of dependents, i.e. children below 15 and people older than 65, was still high at 1972, but not as alarmingly so as in 1962 (Table 2.4).

The short discussion of Mauritius has shown how essential is the need for detailed statistical information as a basis for considering population change in any country, but especially in a developing situation—but, unfortunately, many of the latter countries lack all but recent disaggregated data, which frequently means that population prediction must be a rather more unreliable activity than even normally.

Demographic-Economic Models

Even a superficial look at the population forecasts and the resources available in many developing countries leads to the view that a growing

TABLE 2.3. *Fertility Trends in Mauritius 1958–1971*

	1958	1959	1960	1961	1962	1963	1964	1965	1966	1967	1968	1969	1970	1971
Crude birth rate	40.4	38.1	39.3	39.4	38.5	39.9	38.1	35.5	35.3	30.4	31.0	27.2	26.7	25.3
General fertility rate[a]	187.0	177.4	183.2	184.4	181.4	187.2	177.9	163.8	160.3	136.3	136.6	117.8	113.9	106.9
Gross reproduction rate[b]	2.92	2.80	2.87	2.95	2.90	3.04	2.94	2.72	2.70	2.24	2.27	1.92	1.86	1.71
Age Specific Birth Rates[c]														
Age of Women														
15–19	140.0	121.5	122.5	117.9	107.3	108.5	91.8	85.1	84.3	73.8	72.9	65.3	58.7	54.3
20–24	303.8	287.3	297.3	301.9	298.3	318.9	311.1	290.0	283.7	242.3	239.4	203.6	191.5	182.4
25–29	282.8	277.7	288.4	299.1	301.4	304.2	302.9	272.1	279.4	235.4	245.7	214.3	210.1	188.6
30–34	237.5	229.6	238.8	246.4	233.3	257.4	249.0	231.9	221.8	185.8	179.3	150.8	147.4	139.6
35–39	156.8	156.8	171.8	167.8	163.1	172.6	166.3	154.0	154.9	132.4	129.8	113.8	113.5	93.5
40–44	54.2	51.8	54.2	56.6	60.1	68.8	62.8	57.8	58.5	45.8	46.5	37.1	38.0	35.2
45–49	6.0	9.3	6.4	7.6	9.0	7.9	8.1	7.3	7.6	6.6	7.8	4.8	5.4	4.2

Note: The age specific general fertility and gross reproduction rates for 1958 to 1961 were computed on estimates of female population by age groups derived by "reverse-survival" of 1962 Census data.

[a] Births per 1000 women aged 15–49 years.
[b] The average number of daughters born to a hypothetical cohort of women subjected to current age-specific fertility rates throughout their child-bearing years.
[c] Births per 1000 women in each age group.
Source: Director of Statistics, Mauritius.

TABLE 2.4. *Age Structure of the Population of Mauritius as Enumerated at Each Census 1952–1972, and of the United Kingdom (1971)*

Age group (in years)	Mauritius 1952	Mauritius 1962	Mauritius 1972	UK 1971†
Under 15	40.2	45.3	40.1	23.4
15–64	56.6	51.5	56.1	64.3
65 and over	3.2	3.2	3.8	12.3
All ages	100.0	100.0	100.0	100.0
Dependency ratio*	767	943	781	555

* Number of persons below age 15 and those aged 65 or above per 1000 persons in the economically active age group 15–64.
† *Source: United Nations Demographic Year Book 1971.*
Source: Census of Mauritius, 1972.

population is likely to consume more resources than it is capable of producing, i.e. the rate of growth of a given national economy is likely to be less than the rate of growth of resources needed to support the increasing population, even allowing for the (later) productivity of the enhanced population. Of course, any programme to reduce fertility will absorb some of the scarce resources available, and the question arises: what level of expenditure on birth control is necessary in order to achieve a situation where available resources from a more slowly-increasing population will more than justify such expenditure?

The problem has been studied for some time by Stephen Enke (Enke, 1957, 1963; Enke and Zind, 1969). The results of the study by Enke and Zind suggest that a modest birth control programme, costing perhaps 30 US cents a year per head of population out of economic development expenditures of circa US$10 per head, can raise average income over 15 years by twice the percentage that it would rise without birth control. A programme of this kind, involving more people each year until half of them are practising contraception, is said to yield an undiscounted return on cost of 13 times in 5 years, and 80 times in 30 years. The value of permanently preventing the birth of a marginal infant is about twice that of the annual income per head in a developing country, and without birth control, to achieve similar rises in income per head, the rate of productive innovation would have to be about 1.5 times the typical rate assumed by Enke and Zind. Saving propensities would have to be from 2 to 3 times as great as are assumed to be typical if similar income increases per head are to be realized without birth control.

The Enke-Zind model uses age-specific death and fertility rates such as are normally involved in cohort-survival projection, and also consumption rates. It uses also a national production function that takes into account the changing stocks and productivities of labour and capital, saving propensities which vary with disposable income, and the rate of productive innovation. It can thus trace the effect in detail of whatever reductions in fertility might result from birth control programmes. Early considerations, using a static model, showed very large returns from the resources used to reduce birth, but this model was unsatisfactory in not tracing the full effects over time. The revised dynamic model (1969) uses a modified Cobb-Douglas function to relate innovations and increases in capital and labour to increased output.

The latest version of the Enke-Zind model, known as TEMPO, has been used by CERED in Morocco (1976), utilizing the material on population gathered there since 1974, together with the economic information available in the other departments of the Secretariat d'Etat au Plan et au Développement Régional, in Rabat. The model makes two sorts of projections: demographic projections based on alternative hypotheses concerning fertility and mortality, and then economic projections adapted to each of the demographic projections.

The TEMPO model is of broader interest than a limitation to forecasting the effect of population policies, of course. As a demographic-economic simulation model, it presumably has other economic planning possibilities, though these would lead one into fields quite outside the scope of this work.

Urbanization and the Demographic Transition

Implicit in urbanization—and, of course, migration—are differences in the demographic structure of urban and rural areas. But knowledge of such differences in mature, or long-urbanized (and long-developed) countries is apt to be very misleading when an attempt is made to fit such knowledge to the cases of developing countries. Taking Egypt (a long-urbanized, but nonetheless "developing" country) as a case-study, Janet Abu-Lughod (1964) has shown how very misleading experience of developed countries can be.

The first proposition that Mrs Abu-Lughod examined was that urban fertility is lower than rural fertility, and the typical urban family is smaller than the rural; thus the larger the city, the lower the fertility. But, in fact, there appeared to be no difference between urban and rural fertility patterns in Egypt, and the only evidence of higher fertility rates at that time was in the fast-growing Suez Canal towns, where this phenomenon was a function of a youthful population structure resulting from high in-migration, rather than being a function of size.

The second relationship proposed was that general death rates are lower in rural areas than in urban ones, though cities would have rather lower rates of infant mortality. In Egypt, though, urban mortality rates are substantially below those in rural areas, both for crude death rates and infant mortality.

Resulting from the two preceding propositions is a third: that the excess of births over deaths is higher in rural areas than in towns, with the rate of natural increase declining steeply with increasing size of city: urban growth, as a result should come principally from in-migration. The Egyptian evidence, as shown, is of virtually equal rural and urban birth rates, and of markedly lower urban mortality: it follows that the rate of natural increase in Egyptian towns and cities is considerably higher than the rural rate. Thus natural increase, rather than migration, becomes the most significant factor in city growth; Abu-Lughod quotes rates of natural increase of 32 per 1000 for Cairo and from 23 to 25 per 1000 population in rural areas. This finding is quite fundamental to any theory of urban growth in developing countries, if there is evidence of its wider applicability: ". . . one cannot believe that Egypt is simply a unique case. We would hypothesize that the largest Indian cities, for example, now have higher natural increase rates than prevail in their rural hinterlands, despite arguments to the contrary" (Abu-Lughod, 1964).

A fourth proposition is that urban and rural areas differ significantly in the age compositions of their populations. The percentage of population in the "productive years" is highest in the largest cities and declines smoothly with size of place; rural areas, on the other hand, contain concentrations of the very young and the very old. Differential fertility and mortality as well as selective migration create this situation. In fact, at 1947, the situation in Egypt was very little marked by this kind of a "gradient": the whole country had 39.3% of the population under 15 years and 45% between 15 and 50 years, whereas for cities over half a million population the comparative percentages were 37.1 and 52.1, and for cities of less than 30,000 people they were 39.5 and 48.7. Thus only in the very largest cities were deviations at all significant, a fact attributed to a pattern of migration in Egypt which tended to be directed towards Cairo and Alexandria rather than to include smaller cities and towns.

The fifth proposal was that different sex ratios are encountered in urban and rural populations: more females in cities, more males than females in rural areas. But in Egypt, the reverse is true, due to selective migration.

These phases may be illustrated more succinctly by a graph (Fig. 5.5) (Chung, 1966), which shows well the divergence between death rate decline and birth rate decline: the perception of the former event takes place only after a considerable time-lag, during which the population level soars. However, evidence, for example from Nigeria, the most populous African state (Caldwell and Igun, 1970), shows that, as in Mauritius and many other countries situations now in the Stage 2 phase are turning towards Stage 3 of the Transition. The question is: how long will it take for the full Demographic Transition to occur—and what increased population will these countries then be supporting? Chung has produced an interesting series of maps demonstrating the spread of this transition across the world from 1905 to 1960.

Paradoxically, a growth of the rural population, once urbanization has begun, is likely to mean more urban growth: more and larger urban centres, with the incidence of such centres reflecting differences in rural productivity and differences in the possibility of, and demand for, urban services. The more recent incidence of industrialism—defined by Sjöberg as: "that system of production in which inanimate sources of power are used to multiply human effort"—tends to obscure the original, and continuing role of the city as a provider of services for both urban and rural populations. For example,

Manama, the chief city of Bahrain in the Arabian Gulf, has 47% of its employment provided by services, 22% by trade, 21% by construction, and only 2% by manufacturing—though nowadays one may expect "inanimate power" to figure in services as well as manufacture.

Some caution must be exercised, of course, in equating the "service sector" of many developing country cities with those of developed economies, for there are distinct differences between those services necessary to support the more advanced primary and secondary sectors in the latter and the often-marginal activities of the former economies. One characteristic of the Third World city is the high incidence of very marginal employment: flower sellers at traffic lights, shoe-shine boys, food-vendors, soft-drinks vendors, newspaper sellers—all kinds of trading and service occupations which demand little stock, no fixed premises, minimum skills, and speedy returns. Such occupations conceal an unemployment situation by substituting under-employment to a large degree: it is not that the chosen occupations are not essential ones, for they fulfil a need in the urban spectrum, but rather that part-time, spasmodic, spontaneous employment has to evolve through "interstitial" occupations in the absence both of welfare-state handouts and of more formal employment opportunities. Thus official statistics of unemployment often do not take account of concealed unemployment and under-employment; for example, in 1971 Morocco had a stated male workforce unemployment rate of 8% whereas it was estimated that the total real male unemployed amounted to over 30%. In Nador province, in the north east of the country away from the more industrialized Atlantic seaboard and the phosphate mines, the real unemployment was estimated at 50% of the potential workforce, though in fact migration overseas was one response to lack of opportunities in this province. But, in general, in rural areas unpaid help on family farms and small holdings, and in urban areas unpaid domestic help, provide employment and at least subsistence, so that formal definitions of unemployment and potential workforce, etc., may be very misleading in relation to the "real" situation, urban or rural.

Urbanization and Economic Development

A general relationship between urbanization and economic development often has been assumed, i.e. that the most highly urbanized countries are, ipso facto, the most "developed", and that the most economically "advanced" countries must be also the most urbanized ones. Looking back to Gordon Childe's model of the emergence of cities, of course, one can see that there is an implication that cities spell "development" or economic and technological advancement. But although the relationship between "development" and industrialization, agricultural employment and capital formation has been studied by a number of eminent economists, the relationship between urbanization and "development" has received comparatively little attention.

However, Berry (1962) does attempt to fill this void. Berry lists 143 proposed indices of economic development and 95 countries for which the data may exist. Using principal components analysis, Berry concluded that the possible 95×43 matrix of rankings could be collapsed into four fundamental patterns of association of the indices, and accounting for over 90% of the variance of the data matrix. The first pattern, called by Berry a "technological scale", included indices relating to transport and communications, trade, energy production and consumption, national product, and public services. The second pattern, the "demographic scale", included demographic indices and those relating to population per unit area, per unit of cultivated land, and percentage of land area cultivated. The third group was of poor trading countries with low national products, high birth and population growth rates, but with large amounts of trade and international communications. The fourth dimension of the analysis differentiated between extremely large and extremely small countries. However, from the point of view of the association of levels of economic development and degrees of urbanization, only the first two patterns or dimensions need be considered.

It was found that the index expressed as percentage of population in the country in cities of over 20,000 inhabitants associated with those other indices collapsed into the technological scale, and thus, in Berry's view, there was a high positive correlation between economic development and urbanization, as this index clusters closely with many other "technological" indices representing facets of "development".

It should be stressed, perhaps, that this is a *general* finding, and that Berry was using c. 1960 data, i.e. data now 20 years old. It may be suspected that there may be many exceptions to these findings—for example, in the sort of "rural" cities mentioned by Janet Abu-Lughod in Egypt, or the Yoruba cities also previously mentioned: this kind of "urbanization" does not equate with advanced economic "development". In fact, in a later (1973) essay, Berry does acknowledge that very rapid urbanization is taking place in the "Third World" countries in Latin America, Africa, and Asia: countries with, as he says, the lowest levels of economic development, the lowest levels of life expectancy at birth, the poorest nutritional levels, the lowest consumptions of energy, the lowest educational levels. A new model of the urbanization process seems called for, therefore—or possibly a revision or qualification of the Gordon Childe version.

The essential basis of urbanization, in Childe's or any other model, is an ecological one: the presence of an adequate food supply to permit divorce, spatially or temporally, from peasant agriculture. The possibilities are several: part-time farming and part-time urban pursuits, pursued either in an urban or in a nearby rural location, the food surplus being achieved which buys time for urban trade, manufacture, or service; or the import of food from spatially remote sources, paid for by urban work, where the urban location is at some transport focus permitting a more economical distribution than at an extra-urban location; or a division of labour within families or tribal groups, this social organization permitting both food production and manufacturing.

Much is dependent upon the techniques, potentialities, and present organization of agriculture, paradoxically, therefore, in the quest for insight into urbanization. If there is potential additional labour in the agricultural areas, by reason of natural population increase, beyond that which agricultural production can usefully absorb, even on an unpaid basis (as is much agricultural labour throughout the world)—for even at subsistence levels, such unused labour removes a large part of the surplus of production—then clearly there is pressure for that labour to go elsewhere.

In general, the process of "economic development" can be seen as one in which the production of the cities, expressed in food-equivalent terms, overtakes population growth expressed in food-requirement terms (Keyfitz, 1965)—a purely physiological and ecological happening, in basis. For the cities to increase production requires capital, and this has been gathered by the city creating institutional means whereby it can levy payments of various sorts from the countryside around it: thus agricultural products may both feed the cities and add to city capital for industrialization.

Active Population

The active population of a country or region is, quite simply, that number or proportion of working age who are economically active, i.e. actually in the labour force. The proportion is expressed either as a participation rate or an activity rate:

Participation rate = Economically active population/Total population

and:

Activity rate = Number actually in employment/Total number potentially available for employment

whilst the inverse of the participation rate is termed a population multiplier:

Population multiplier = Total population/Economically active population

But the statistics of active population are often less than satisfactory in developing countries; to a large extent this is due to difficulties in defining and measuring employment—or unemployment. For example, one way of estimating the active population is to take various groups of people as being potentially available for employment, e.g. young and middle-aged men, plus a smaller proportion of women in the same age-groups, and to discount certain groups of children and older people, and women of child-bearing age. The percentage of economically active females among the urban population aged 10–64 years at 1978, in the few cases quoted by the World Bank (*World Development Report 1984*, Table 5: Status of Women), ranged from 8 or 9 in the cases of Iraq, Mali, and Iran, to 45 or 46 for the Philippines and Thailand. The lowest male rates quoted were 61 in Mali and 62 in Iraq, and the highest 83 in Niger. But it is known that certain proportions, and different ones at that, in each population group potentially active, are unemployed, or only partially employed, and thus are possibly available for further, full-time employment. For example, employment within a family group, especially in agriculture, may be unpaid or rewarded in non-monetary terms, e.g. by board and lodging, or may be only partial in time, or seasonal. There are also many "interstitial" kinds of employment; as has been remarked earlier: occupations which are not full-time but require little capital and can be carried out in public places; such people are not employed, though they are likely to figure in calculations as such.

Madeleine Trébous (1968) gives details of the then situation in Algeria, which is typical, still, of this kind of situation. For example, Algerian participation rates in the mid-1960s were:

Aged 15–19 years: 60% for men; 5% for women
„   20–24 „   90% „   „ 5% „   „
„   25–54 „   90% „   „ 10% „   „
„   55–64 „   70% „   „ 10% „   „
„ over 65 „   10% „   „ — „   „

The overall picture of active and inactive population in Algeria in 1966 is given in the following tables (2.5 and 2.6) (Trébous, 1968, p. 19).

However, the real active population of Algeria in 1966 was estimated as 2,335,200, which is a smaller total than that which is obtained from the

TABLE 2.5. *Distribution of the Population aged 6 and above present in Algeria according to Individual Situation in 1966*

Individual situation	Total	Men	Women
Employed	1,724,900	1,634,400	90,500
Unemployed having already worked	610,300	606,500	3,800
Unemployed looking for their first job	262,900	257,000	5,900
Children of 6 to 14 *not* attending school	1,396,500	593,300	803,200
Schoolchildren and students	1,636,000	1,048,200	587,800
Housewives	2,877,300		2,877,300
Retired and assimilated	72,200	39,200	33,000
Invalids	183,400	116,200	67,200
Other inactive persons 15 to 64 years of age	28,600	18,000	10,600
Other inactive persons 65 and over	295,300	120,800	174,500
Total	9,087,400	4,433,600	4,653,800

Source: General Population and Housing Census—Abridged data—Results of the Survey—Ministry of Finance and the Plan, 1966 (Trebóus, 1968).

TABLE 2.6. *Algeria: Real Active Population according to Branch of Economic Activity, 1966. (The classification used is that recommended by the United Nations)*

Agriculture and animal husbandry	1,277,700
Forestry, hunting and fishing	22,300
Total agriculture and assimilated	1,300,000
Mining and quarrying—Total	23,600
Food industries and assimilated	36,000
Textiles and clothing industries (including footwear)	37,800
Engineering industries and assimilated	37,700
Other manufacturing industry	49,000
Total manufacturing industry	159,900
Building and public works—Total	121,100
Electricity, gas, water and sanitary services—Total	11,700
Commerce, banking, insurance and assimilated—Total	149,500
Transport, warehousing and communications—Total	87,900
Government services	133,200
Community services	96,500
Business services	65,700
Entertainments and personal services	77,000
Total services	372,400
Miscellaneous or ill-defined activities—Total	109,100
Grand total	2,335,200

Source: Taken from the results of the 1966 General Census provided by the National Population Census Commission (Trébous, 1968).

seemingly relevant parts of the above table; the make-up of this real active population is as above, again from Trébous (p. 20).

Information as to actual employment, by sector, in Algeria in 1966, though, shows 1,927,820 people in employment (Trébous, p. 21). It is known that during 1962–1966 one-seventh of the wage earners and one-fifth of the non-wage earners worked less than 30 hours a week and one-sixth of the latter worked less than six months of the year. In the case of agriculture, the rate of under-employment was estimated to be 68.5% in 1966, regarding men as fully employed when they worked for 250 days, and women when they worked for 100 days, per annum. For the country as a whole, Trébous quotes under-employment in 1963 as 49%, and for the active urban population 64%; and in 1968 it was estimated that the number of permanent jobs at that time concerned only 900,000 people for all sectors of employment, i.e. hardly a half of the active population who were in employment, and representing only about 35% of the total labour supply; it was estimated that the activity rate for total active population was 23.4% in 1966. Data for Morocco shows a very similar position.

A further multiplier is obtained by disaggregating the employment situation into "basic" or export-oriented employment, i.e. producing goods (and services) not consumed locally, and "non-basic" or "service" employment, i.e. producing goods and services which are consumed locally. This disaggregation underlies the export base study, which divides the appropriate urban or regional system under study into sectors which serve markets outside the system, in return for which goods, services, or money flow into the system from outside; and sectors which serve markets within the system. The inference is that "export" activities are considered to be the prime movers of the system of concern—and also that the basic/service relationship is a relatively stable one, and is thus predictable.

Difficulties arise in the application of the export-base theory due to problems of data availability or interpretation; and multipliers of this sort are often used in situations where some future population or employment component is to be predicted and no really parallel situation is available for analysis: witness the wrangles over the Third London Airport employment forecasts (Third London Airport Commission, Final Report 1971, pp. 202–3). It is obvious that, even in a relatively stable situation, there is apt to be a wide variation in levels of employment, dependent upon population and employment structure, age and types of industrial plant, social habits, and so on; for example, in the United Kingdom in 1967 the ratio of manufacturing employment to total population was 1:2.6 overall, but 1:3.1 in South-East England, whereas in the New Towns it was 1:1.7. In developing countries, where there is often no experience of industrialization, or no available statistical information or both, the device of falling back upon experience elsewhere has its own dangers. In the case of a Nigerian steelworks project, the multiplier for "indirect" industrial jobs from basic employment was estimated to rise in stages from a range of 1.5 to 3.0, to an eventual ratio in the range of 5.0 to 10.0.* In North African examples (Morocco and Algeria), rather similar projects have used a figure of only 1 service job to every 2 jobs in basic employment sectors, eventually rising to parity with basic employment under certain policy alternatives. But, as one of the growing distinguishing features of "Third World" cities is precisely their reliance for employment on services rather than manufacturing, *per se*, the utility of the export base concept as a forecasting or predictive device is bound to be limited.

As a case study of activity rates, etc., a simple model of a local economy, using activity or participation rates, and multipliers, was formulated in 1975 as part of the Ismailia town study in the Suez Canal region of Egypt (Clifford Culpin and Partners, 1975).

The model was as follows:

1. $P = PR + PU$

where: P = total population of the study area.

PU = population of Ismailia city and any other major urban cities in the study area.

PR = (rural) population of the rest of the study area.

2. $PR = \dfrac{n}{x} \cdot EA$

---

* But see Britton Harris's comment, p. 91.

where: EA = direct agricultural employment.
n = rural employment multiplier.
x = rural participation rate.

3. $$PU = \frac{m}{y} \cdot EU$$

where: EU = basic, i.e. non-population-related urban employment.
m = urban employment multiplier.
y = urban participation rate.

4. $$EA = fA + ea$$

where: f is a functional relationship depending upon the agricultural technology, land tenure, cropping patterns, etc.
A = area of reclaimed land.
ea = agricultural labour force on existing land.

5. $$EU = g + h + i + j + \ldots$$

where: g = employment by Suez Canal Authority.
h = employment in formal manufacturing industry.
i = employment in the hotel and tourist industry.
j = employment in non-local services such as a regional university.

Population and Employment

One of the striking features of some underdeveloped economics in the past—and this is certainly true of sub-Saharan Africa—has been the existence of a backward-sloping labour supply function: that is, that people in these economies work less at higher wage rates and more at lower ones. There is a great deal of historical evidence for this seemingly irrational phenomenon, which is reviewed by Berg (1961), who points out a number of important factors surrounding it. The first factor is that the phenomenon characterized, to a large extent, times which are passing or past. Africans have greater wants now, more definitely structured than in the days when they were limited and, once attained, served as a disincentive to work outside the home village. But the labour supply is composed not simply of a total labour force which is constant, but an always-changing aggregation of men who may spend a shorter or longer time in employment: thus it will require a shorter time to attain a given money target if wage rates rise, and if this is a fixed target, the tendency will be to discontinue employment after a shorter time at work—hence the backward sloping supply curve. But if there is a rising realization that savings targets can be increased with rising wages, then the tendency is to spend longer at work to take advantage of the possibility. As Berg puts it: "For while the 'men in employment' function (relating number of migrants to rates of wages) was positively sloped, the 'average time in employment' function (relating average time spend in paid employment to wage rates) was sharply backward-bending, and the effect of the latter probably outweighed the effect of the former." But now the positive first aspect swamps the second negative aspect; also at each wage rate much more labour is now available due to transport and communication changes as well as rising material want and needs for income: the territory from which labour is drawn is now much larger.

The Lewis model (Lewis, 1955) is one of several which have been applied to so-called "economic growth". It assumes disguised unemployment in subsistence agriculture, and a higher wage rate in industry, sufficient to overcome the immobility of labour; also the industrial wage, and thus the differential between it and the agricultural wage, is assumed to remain constant so long as there is disguised underemployment in agriculture. Provided that profits are re-invested, with the industrial wage held constant, the share of profits in national income will increase: more profits mean more investment, so capital formation will grow with national income. The development of industry will draw more and more labour from agriculture, and so economic growth and labour absorption are achieved at the same time.

Robert Mabro (1967) has tested the Lewis model in relation to Egypt between 1937 and 1965, finding that its hypothesis of disguised unemployment seems to be true when properly interpreted. But the reallocation of labour to industry over 28 years has been extremely slow: "The Egyptian situation shows clearly that the expansion of an industrial sector cannot absorb over a relatively long period of time more than a small share of the natural increase in the labour force, even if all Lewis' assumptions with regard to wages, terms of trade and capital intensity are met. . . . But, by far the most important challenge is population growth. Lewis . . . underestimates its signifiance. In fact, it dominates the labour reallocation process, adding to the pools of underemployed at a rate that may exceed for a long time the rate of absorption into industry." Mabro goes on to make the point that new investment is required in agriculture as well as industry, to ensure that the growing population is fed, that there is a continuing surplus to facilitate the transfer of labour, and also to form a larger market for industrial products: a model which covers the multiple relationships between population, agriculture, and industry, is needed.

One of Mabro's findings relative to Egypt is reinforced by Harris and Todaro (1969) in relation to Kenya: more investment in industry commonly means better productivity, and thus less opportunity for increased labour participation: output grows but employment lags. Thus urban employment is added to rural unemployment or underemployment, in contrast to the rather simplistic view of industrial growth mopping up employment generally. The same conclusion is reached by Reynolds (quoted by Harris and Todaro, 1969) in relation to Puerto Rico, where between 1950 and 1962 output tripled in real terms, but employment only rose by 65%. Thus there are two alternative policies for developing countries as postulated by Harris and Todaro: high output, capital intensive industry with high wages and a smaller labour force and thus increasing unemployment as the population continues to grow; or low output, labour-intensive, less "modern" industry with lower wages, (but still a differential over agriculture), a larger labour force and thus some attempt effectively to contain unemployment. The trap of the latter approach is that implied by the Lewis model: low output means lower profits to plough back into development, thus slower "growth". This seems to be relevant to the point made by Kuznets (1959), that levels of living in the now economically advanced areas were higher at their point of "take-off" in economic development than is prevalent in many undeveloped countries today: in other word perhaps "development" in such countries is premature as yet, and progress must be at a slower pace for some time—until, perhaps, *all* the subsystems of "development" reach appropriate thresholds?

A refreshing view of the economic development field which subsumes all such models is that given by Irving Kristol (1978); it is worth quoting him at length:

"There have been, in fact, two great economists who offered explanations of economic growth that are perfectly congruent with our historic and personal experience. They are Adam Smith in the eighteenth century and Joseph Schumpeter in the twentieth. Moreover, their explanations are almost identical and can be summed up in the following propositions:

Where people are given the freedom to engage in economic activities for the purpose of bettering their condition, and, most important, where the entrepreneur is given the freedom to innovate, then you get economic growth. Where such freedoms are restricted by government, you get relatively slow or no economic growth.

The truth of these propositions is confirmed by the most casual historical survey, as well as by simple observation of the economic conditions of various nations in the world today. But it is an uncomfortable—for many an unacceptable—truth because of all the things it does not say.

It does not say, for instance, that even in the most favourable circumstances all nations will grow at equal rates. Varying traditions, cultures, religions, and customs will result in varying rates of growth. This is no problem: People have a perfect right to choose among various rates of economic growth, since such growth will always incur social or cultural "costs" (i.e. changes to their accustomed way of life). It will become a problem, however, if equality—including equality among nations—is an important ideal to be realized. Most "growth economists" are very much attached to the ideal of greater equality among nations and are distressed when economic growth does not seem to achieve it.

They are also attached to the ideal of greater income equality within nations, and find the Smith–Schumpeter prescription deficient in its silence on this topic. And, in truth, it only predicts that everyone will better his condition—not that everyone will do so equally. In actuality, because the human race is much more homogeneous than heterogeneous, with talents and abilities widely diffused, a capitalist economy does not increase inequalities of income, and over time appears to lessen them somewhat. But to those who think equality to be as important or more important than growth, these results will be of no comfort . . ."

At which point, one ought to confirm what "equality" means: if we were all truly "equal", we would all be precisely alike, of the same sex, born at the same time . . . . The idea of "equality" is clearly ludicrous and untenable—but *equity*, which means the attainment of some minimum norm or standard, beyond which the individual may have as much or as little as he or she wishes to or can attain—is a sensible and realistic ideal: attainable by the Smith–Schumpeter model of an economy. As we have seen already, hierarchy is a characteristic of systems—including human ones.

Migration and Potential

Migration is a phenomenon of *flow* or movement, whether permanent or temporary. In the latter event there will be at least two flows appertaining to any point at which migration is being considered: an inflow and an outflow, though these may have a first origin or destination which is not locationally the same as a subsequent origin or destination, i.e. temporary migration may be of the "flow and return" kind as with some seasonal agricultural occupations or attendance at some market place, or it may be of the "stepping stone" kind where movement is from one place to another and then to a third, and so on—again as in some seasonal agricultural practices. Permanent migration must also be seen as the net difference between an inflow and an outflow in relation to a particular place, not as a single-flow process (see Fig. 2.7).

At first sight, it is only the time-scale which appears to distinguish temporary migration from daily, weekly, or seasonally-affected flow, perhaps: but the definition of migration as *involving a change of abode or habitat* (OED) suggests that, for urban or regional purposes, migration as a flow process must be linked to a process of land and housing occupancy which may take place at both ends of the flow, i.e. both vacation and occupation. (This is no surprise in system terms: stocks give rise to flows which give rise to stocks: Figs 2.8 and 2.9). So: movement which involves land or house occupancy change may be characterized as migration; that which does not involve such change is a normal flow process, related to a temporal change in stock (of people, houses, urban land, etc.) which is below some threshold beyond which the stock change acquires a further degree of significance.

It is to be noted that migration implies the crossing of some system boundary, implied by the level of resolution at which the system (and its

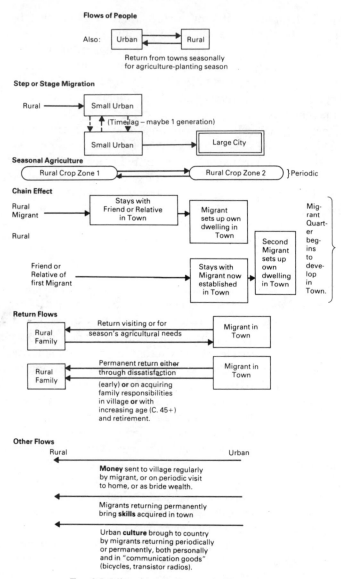

Fig. 2.7. Migration: diagrammatic illustration.

subsystems, etc.) is defined: inter-regional migration implies the definition of regional systems, intra-regional migration implies the definition of regional subsystems, and so on. The recording of migration is thus in terms of flows crossing system boundaries at which recording takes place, at least in principle, but it must be noted that much, perhaps most, migration studies are based on birthplace information and thus *implied* migration, i.e. where people

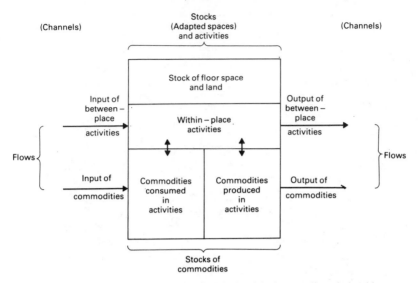

(Channels)   Stocks   (Channels)
                        (Adapted spaces)
                         and activities

FIG. 2.8. Stocks and Flows. A simple model of activity/commodity relationships.

are recorded in a census as living in one place but having been born in another. This is not the most satisfactory way of measuring migration, of course, one major difficulty being that the time-dimension of that migration is lacking, whilst information as to the motivation behind the migration is also absent; step-by-step migration, i.e. from one place to another, and then to another, etc. is obscured also in such birthplace-only recording. J. C. Mitchell (1958) has suggested that migration in Africa—and no doubt elsewhere—operates along three "axes" simultaneously: a "normative axis", an "economic axis", and an "individual axis". Of these, perhaps the economic is the most significant: poverty and potential starvation* are potent motivators; but the aspiration to have cash to use in purchases of various kinds regarded as necessary to well-being, and the perception of opportunities elsewhere, has come to be important also.

Theories to account for migration are not new, and in a general way the gravity or potential formulation seems very plausible, if only as a beginning: if we postulate "attraction" as being directly dependent upon some factor

* Cf. Little (1965): "One of the reasons [for West African urbanization] is increased pressure of population upon land resources because, while technological developments in terms of improved health facilities and child-care have led to a general growth in population, there has not always been an accompanying rise in food production. On the contrary, quite often indigenous methods of cultivation continue to be practised with a shorter and shorter period of fallow. This, by reducing the fertility of the soil, brings about an overall decrease in the margin of substance and the density of population which the land can support. Hunger, therefore, may supply one of the reasons for men and their families seeking a living elsewhere. It probably accounts for a good deal of the seasonal migration."

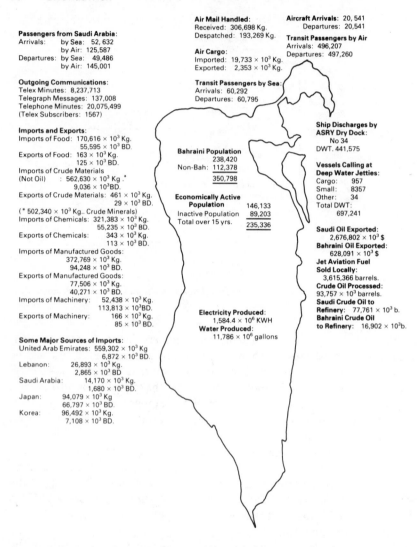

Passengers from Saudi Arabia:
Arrivals: by Sea: 52, 632
             by Air: 125,587
Departures: by Sea: 49,486
             by Air: 145,001

Outgoing Communications:
Telex Minutes: 8,237,713
Telegraph Messages: 137,008
Telephone Minutes: 20,075,499
(Telex Subscribers: 1567)

Imports and Exports:
Imports of Food: 170,616 × 10³ Kg.
                 55,595 × 10³ BD.
Exports of Food: 163 × 10³ Kg.
                 125 × 10³ BD.
Imports of Crude Materials
(Not Oil)   : 562,630 × 10³ Kg.*
                9,036 × 10³BD.
Exports of Crude Materials: 461 × 10³ Kg.
                 29 × 10³ BD.
(* 502,340 × 10³ Kg.. Crude Minerals)
Imports of Chemicals: 321,383 × 10³ Kg.
                 55,235 × 10³ BD.
Exports of Chemicals: 343 × 10³ Kg.
                 113 × 10³ BD.
Imports of Manufactured Goods:
                 372,769 × 10³ Kg.
                 94,248 × 10³ BD.
Exports of Manufactured Goods:
                 77,506 × 10³ Kg.
                 40,271 × 10³ BD.
Imports of Machinery: 52,438 × 10³ Kg.
                 113,813 × 10³BD.
Exports of Machinery: 166 × 10³ Kg.
                 85 × 10³ BD.

Some Major Sources of Imports:
United Arab Emirates: 559,302 × 10³ Kg
                 6,872 × 10³ BD.
Lebanon: 26,893 × 10³ Kg.
                 2,865 × 10³ BD
Saudi Arabia: 14,170 × 10³ Kg.
                 1,680 × 10³ BD.
Japan: 94,079 × 10³ Kg
                 66,797 × 10³ BD.
Korea: 96,492 × 10³ Kg.
                 7,108 × 10³ BD.

Air Mail Handled:
Received: 306,698 Kg.
Despatched: 193,269 Kg.

Air Cargo:
Imported: 19,733 × 10³ Kg.
Exported: 2,353 × 10³ Kg.

Transit Passengers by Sea:
Arrivals: 60,292
Departures: 60,795

Aircraft Arrivals: 20, 541
Departures: 20,541

Transit Passengers by Air
Arrivals: 496,207
Departures: 497,260

Bahraini Population
238,420
Non-Bah: 112,378
350,798

Economically Active
Population   146,133
Inactive Population 89,203
Total over 15 yrs. 235,336

Electricity Produced:
1,584.4 × 10⁶ KWH
Water Produced:
11,786 × 10⁶ gallons

Ship Discharges by
ASRY Dry Dock:
No 34
DWT. 441,575

Vessels Calling at
Deep Water Jetties:
Cargo: 957
Small: 8357
Other: 34
Total DWT:
         697,241

Saudi Oil Exported:
2,676,802 × 10³ $
Bahraini Oil Exported:
628,091 × 10³ $
Jet Aviation Fuel
Sold Locally:
3,615,366 barrels.
Crude Oil Processed:
93,757 × 10³ barrels.
Saudi Crude Oil to
Refinery: 77,761 × 10³ b.
Bahraini Crude Oil
to Refinery: 16,902 × 10³b.

FIG. 2.9. Bahrain 1981: a national system of commodity flows.
Source: State of Bahrain: Statistical Abstract 1981.
("BD" = Bahraini Dinars).

("attractiveness of a place") and inversely proportional to distance from a place, we have the potential model in essence, and no doubt "attractiveness" can be explained in a number of ways. Two sorts of attractiveness seem important for their likely effect on urban growth and change: they are "temporary attractiveness" as in the holding of a market, and "permanent attractiveness' as in the offering of employment opportunities which lead to migration. It seems probable that the two may be related, and certainly the two attractions may exist at the same time in the same place.

However, one of the most frequent complaints about the gravity formulation is its lack of explanatory validity: it cannot answer the question: *why* do people move? Thus a theory which explains migratory movement and which can no doubt become a theory which predicts the same movement is needed, and an elementary basis for this is provided by the "push-pull" hypothesis. Attention in the early gravity models was focused upon "attraction" of a place, but even in a system of many "attractive places" there must be "loose" or potentially migratory "particles" able to respond to the attractive forces at work. In human terms, a pool of "potential movers" must exist before any movement is possible, and one reason for the existence of these potential movers must be—to continue the attraction metaphor—a "negative attraction" or repulsive factor at work. So the idea of a "push" as well as a "pull" force arises, and in the "push-pull" model can be seen the seeds of further explanatory variables at *both* ends of the migration process, which may be able to account to a greater degree than the simple gravity model for migratory flows. The number of modelling approaches has widened and a classification of migration models has been provided by Stillwell (1975), though it does focus upon "macro-analysis", i.e. the distribution of migrants once the decision to move has been taken, rather than "micro-analysis" which is concerned with the behavioural basis of the decision to migrate (cf. Wolpert, 1965). Stillwell is largely concerned with inter-regional migration; and Morrison (1973) very properly suggests an integration of micro and macro-models: first selecting a pool of potential movers (based on variables such as age, occupation, prior migration experience), and secondly distributing these movers on the basis of push and pull variables.

Migration Studies in Developing Countries

Direct study of migration in developing countries—as distinct from the use of census material only—is still relatively rare, but nonetheless direct surveys of migrants are the only reliable guide to the motivation behind migration, as well as the only means of accurately showing its time—and place—related dimensions. Even so, such study has, of necessity, to be on a sample basis, and its results must be generalized with some risk of misinterpretation or over-emphasis.

Two studies of actual migrants, one in Chile, and one in Ghana, have been reported by Herrick (1965), and by Caldwell (1969) respectively. Chile, as Herrick points out, is not one of the least developed countries, nor is it one of the more developed, with a per capita income (1965) of c. US$300–400.

Herrick's study was based upon a number of sources, including labour force surveys carried out in greater Santiago between 1956 and 1963, and a series of surveys in other cities and in rural areas since 1960; however, the main source was a direct interview survey of 310 economically active recent migrants in Santiago, carried out in January 1964. The main findings regarding recent migration in Chile, from both sources, are summarized below.

There was an observed decrease in the relative number of migrants as distance increased; Santiago was seen as having more "pull" than the rural areas having "push". Sixty-five per cent of the sample of migrants surveyed had lived in towns of more than 5,000 people immediately before coming to Santiago. Urban migration did not seem to respond to changes in the observed magnitude of the unemployment rate, though this could be partly due to a shift towards service employment in the economy: a sector in which underemployment or disguised unemployment was more prevalent than in manufacturing. The stereotyped view of the migrants as a majority of a large subsistence sector within the urban society was not true: the relative number of migrants living within the *callampas* ("mushroom" squatter settlements) of Santiago approximated to their proportion in the population as a whole, i.e. one-third of the total population. (And also 50% of migrants living in the *callampas* had been there for more than 10 years, according to the UNECLA in 1963.) Rural-urban migration was only a small fraction of the total movement toward Santiago—in fact, the majority of migrants to the capital city were of urban origin, and it was suggested that emigrants from rural areas were settling mainly in the cities of fewer than 50,000 people. (This latter evidence coming mainly from an examination of rural-urban birth rate differentials and the growth rates of cities of varying sizes.) In general, a two-stage or two-generation model of migration emerged: a first-generation migration from the rural areas to the smaller towns, and a second-generation movement from the towns to the capital city. This was found to echo the pattern of stage by stage migratory movement found in nineteenth-century England and commented upon by Ravenstein.

The Ghana survey was more comprehensive, both in size and scope: some 16,943 persons in total, representing 2367 households, were surveyed: 13,776 persons (1782 households) being in rural areas, and 3167 persons (585 households) being in urban areas, in March/April 1963. The larger size and rural emphasis of the Ghanaian survey enabled a fuller picture to be painted, especially when added to the 1960 Census indications (Caldwell, 1969, p. 54):

"The new ways of life and the new ideas do not remain isolated within the towns, for their populations are so new as to retain strong links with the countryside. The 1960 Census showed that those born in the town numbered less than half in Accra, less than two-fifths in Kumasi, and less than one-third in Sekondi-Takoradi. Furthermore, many of the town-born were the young children of immigrants from the rural areas. The townspeople born outside of the town of enumeration, but in Ghana, made up about one-third of the population in Accra and around half in Kumasi and Sekondi-Takoradi. Many of them certainly came from large cities, defined as towns by the census, but their move was usually to somewhere more urban than the place they left. This urban population of rural or semi-rural origin visits the villages for social reasons, for family or clan conclaves, for the ceremonies that surround births, deaths and marriages, for celebrations and for affairs connected with the traditional or fetish shrines. In 1960 this incessant movement between village and town was catered for by 60,000 persons providing transport, almost two-thirds of them working on the lorries, and being supplemented by a further 11,500 who spent their lives maintaining these vehicles. Those returning to the village take with them industrial products bought in the town as well as ideas and behaviour patterns foreign to traditional rural life. Almost half of the population of rural Ghana have some first-hand experience of the towns.

Thus, in Ghana at least, the isolation of the rural fastnesses has largely become a thing of the past. Admittedly, over two-thirds of those born in the villages have never been to the town to live, but half of these are children. Many of these children will certainly make the journey; indeed, at the time of the survey, more 10–19 years olds were planning to do so than was the case in any other age group. Nor are those who go for long periods to the town lost sight of; half were permanently or temporarily back in the villlage at the time of the survey.

Not all those who crowded into the towns came from rural, or even urban Ghana. In Accra and Sekondi-Takoradi one-sixth of the population were of foreign birth, and in Kumasi one-eighth. A high proportion of these people were true rural-urban migrants, for until recently national borders have not been forbidding barriers in West Africa. For many villages in Togo and Upper Volta, Ghana's three largest towns are the nearest centres with over a hundred thousand inhabitants.

No single feature of a rural area determines the volume of migrants travelling to the towns. Socially and economically advanced areas can produce a high proportion of young people who would prefer to work in the town. In point of fact their agriculture, such as the cocoa farms of southern Ghana, may not be very labour intensive. But backward areas, such as Ghana's north, may have an agricultural system too primitive to cope fully with the harsh wet-dry cycle of the climate and expanding too slowly to provide extra employment rapidly enough. In these circumstances, a considerable proportion of the migrants may be seasonal ones, a form of existence most fitting in with the lives of young males.

Longer-term migration may produce permanent urban residence, but there are also return flows of two main types. The first arises from the failure to become established in the town or to adjust to its way of life. Many permanent returnees to the village are young and were in the towns for a comparatively short period. The second arises from the completion of what may be regarded as a town working life and the acquisition of enough capital to be able to return 'home'. This does not necessarily occur only for people of 60 or over; the return flow is quite strong at all ages after about 45 years."

Among the factors appearing to influence migration in Ghana, distance, as always, was important in that the number of long-term absentees fell steeply as distance from the nearest large town rose. The proportion of those who had never migrated rose with distance from the large towns except for distances over 250 miles, where the special problems of the North, and at least seasonal pressure to migrate from it, became important. But, added to distance *per se*, higher education levels nearer larger centres, and greater general affluence also, may be both cause and effect of migration. The young, i.e. those in the 15–29 age group, were most mobile, with males most in evidence, though this may be a result of the male-oriented education in the rural areas; but educated girls also want to go to the towns. Education of itself turns people towards urban life, and was thought of as preparing young people for urban occupations—thus increasing the danger of adding to urban employment. Position in the family was also significant, the eldest sons and daughters being less likely to migrate, and more likely to return to family responsibilities if they did migrate earlier. Chain migration was a prevalent theme: once migration from a certain family or village began it tended to gain momentum; visits often preceded permanent migration, and a new migrant would join a relative or a fellow villager who had already migrated to the town. However, step-by-step, or staged migration from town to larger town over time by different members of a family or village group is not discussed by Caldwell, though the role of towns, as distinct from rural areas, in migration to the larger cities of Ghana is noticeable from his account.

Other evidence, some of it from direct investigation, which reinforces the two case studies already mentioned, comes from Egypt (Abu-Lughod, 1961). The *1947 Census of the Governorate of Cairo* gave the population of Cairo then as a little over 2 million, of which only about 1.3 million people had been born within the city: some 630,000 Cairo residents in fact came from the rural areas of Egypt. These rural migrants tended to move in chain fashion, coming first to a friend or relative from his own village, and afterwards settling in the same neighbourhood, so that the ecology of parts of the city became characterized by groupings of immigrants from the same or nearby rural areas (see Fig. 2.10). However, information which might support the step-by-step pattern of migration via smaller towns is either obscured or has not been sought, though it is quite clear (Abu-Lughod, 1965) that the 1960 *Census of Egypt* shows growth rates of Cairo, Alexandria, and some of the towns of over 100,000 population (mainly on the Suez Canal or in the Nile Delta), which are much greater than those of smaller towns in general and may be partly the result of direct migration from the rural areas.

Migration in Central and Southern Africa—that is, to the Copper Belt of what is now Zambia, to the larger towns of Rhodesia, and, above all, to the mines and major urban areas of the Republic of South Africa—is a phenomenon that is often regarded as unique; but it is clear from studies in many parts of Africa, and indeed throughout the world, that the same forces

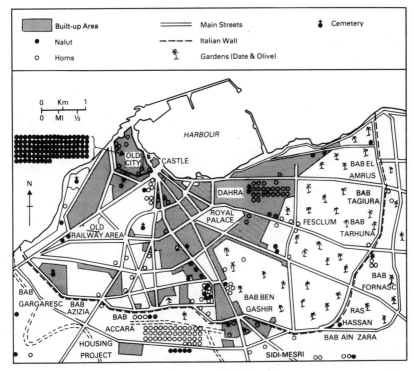

FIG. 2.10. Grouping of migrants in Tripoli, Libya. Each symbol equals one migrant on a sample
survey basis, 1963–1964 (Harrison, 1967).

are at work here as elsewhere. What is different, in a world context, are the
particular aspects of this migration which are essentially African: related, that
is, to the particular structure of African tribal life and custom, and also to
African agriculture.

The size of this migration, and its concentration especially upon the
Witwatersrand and certain other industrial areas in the Republic of South
Africa, is large in total, though, as always, composed of aggregations of
individual decisions to move—and to return. Wilson (1972) quotes the
following overall figures for the sources of foreign black migrants at work in
the economies of Rhodesia and South Africa in 1972, totalling about 840,000
in all, about 600,000 of whom were in South Africa, and about 296,000 of them
in employment in the mining industry:

Workers from Malawi:	33% or about	277,200
,, ,, Mozambique:	26% or ,,	218,400
,, ,, Lesotho:	25% or ,,	210,000
,, ,, Botswana:	7% or ,,	58,800
,, ,, Zambia:	5% or ,,	42,000
,, ,, Swaziland:	4% or ,,	33,600

TABLE 2.11. *Geographical Sources of Black Labour Employed by the Chamber of Mines on the Witwatersrand and in the Transvaal only*

Proportion of total labour force coming from:	1896–98	1936	1972
Transvaal	23.4%	7.0%	1.8%
Natal and Zululand	1.0%	4.9%	1.2%
Swaziland	—	2.2%	1.4%
Cape	—	39.2%	17.7%
Lesotho	11.1%	14.5%	18.5%
Orange Free State	—	1.1%	1.6%
Botswana	3.9%	2.3%	5.2%
Mozambique	60.2%	27.8%	21.4%
North of latitude 22°S	0.5%	1.1%	32.2%
(i.e. Malawi, Angola, Rhodesia, North of South West Africa, etc.)			
Total	54,000	318,000	381,000

Source: Wilson, 1972.

The particular distribution of these male migrants has varied over time, as has also the total volume migrating, shown by the above (Wilson, 1972); both internal and external movements are included in these figures, i.e. within South Africa as well as from neighbouring territories.

Such migrations are the result, as the push-pull hypothesis suggests, of factors operating at both ends of the migration process: of rural agriculture inadequate to supply both traditional wants, e.g. bride-price, and also those now regarded as essential, e.g. bicycles and transistor radios, and of an urban life seen as exciting (the "bright lights" syndrome), the benefits of a money economy (to be found in urban areas), the contrasting of the dull known with the stimulating unknown—many studies all over Africa, and elsewhere, have testified to these factors. The particular African slant to such migration is that it has been rarely seen as a permanent change of abode; it is largely a migration which is fitted into a traditional life, with alteration between rural and urban: an African head waiter in a Salisbury restaurant will return seasonally to his tribal home in Rusape at the appropriate time to plant his mealies, or a worker from Malawi will return there permanently on a family bereavement when he has to assume new family responsibilities. Clyde Mitchell (1969) has used the term "Labour Circulation" to distinguish this kind of ebb and flow, which may go on for half a lifetime, from migration of a permanent kind. His paradigm of a labour migrant career shows well the background to such successive movements between rural and urban milieus. Whether such circulation will diminish as time goes on in favour of more permanent migration is a question which can only be answered by a long investigation into change in both African agriculture and in African tribal life. In the meantime, one supposes that circulatory flows could also be modelled on the basis of some push-pull hypothesis, were appropriate data to be available—though such flows and return flows may be more amenable to simulation modelling, perhaps, using Monte Carlo techniques.

The presence of "capital-surplus oil exporting" countries (as the World Bank classifies them) next to non-oil exporting nations in the Arab world of North Africa and the Middle East has led to quite complex international migration movements. Firstly, there have been movements of Arabs from one country to another, as the economies of the oil-rich countries have received unanticipated stimuli; secondly, as the demand for labour has grown, Moslems from other countries have been added to the flow; thirdly, other non-Moslems have brought additional labour and skills to the capital-surplus countries; and, fourthly, those Arab countries exporting labour to their richer neighbours have had to bring in replacement labour from elsewhere, in turn, to fill the vacancies created (Figs 2.12–2.14). Thus Kuwait, in 1975, had a migrant community of approximately 502,000 persons, or more than half of the total population of the country. In Saudi Arabia in 1975, migrants formed 43% of the total workforce, although: "nationals significantly outnumber migrants in the workforce as a whole, but their contribution to the modern sector workforce, or even to the productive sectors, is so limited that in some areas of the labour market migrants comprise an overwhelming majority" (Birks and Sinclair, 1980). In fact, in 1975, about 52% of all active Saudi Arabian nationals worked in the traditional sector as farmers or fishermen. This process, of increasing needs for migrant labour, has reached such a level that Kuwait has restricted its own industrialization, pointing out that "every additional job provided by a project will have to go to a non-national, and this, in turn, will entail considerable added investment in services and infrastructure" (Kuwaiti Government official, quoted by Birks and Sinclair, op. cit.). Likewise, the division of service organizational labour into many hand-tasks performed by individuals, as is the case in many Middle Eastern countries, does not necessarily give jobs to local citizens, but is likely to lead to the employment of additional numbers of migrants from elsewhere. Replacement migration is typified by Jordan, where Jordanians have gone to work in the Arabian peninsula, where rewards are higher; the resulting vacancies are not all filled by other Jordanians, especially those in less attractive jobs; as a result, Egyptians and Pakistanis have replaced some of the original migrants.

Most information concerning migration in developing countries comes from official statistical sources, especially the conclusions which may be drawn from a comparison of two or more censuses of population. Such a case is that of Indonesia, especially concerning the city of Jakarta; here (Sethuraman, 1976) it was possible to draw a comparison between the 1961 population census, population projections for 1971 made on the basis of the 1961 census assuming zero migration, and the actual population recorded by the census of 1971. The city had a population of 2.91 million at 1961 and the no-migration projection from 1961 to 1971 was about 3.68 million; in fact, the 1971 actual

TABLE 2.12. *Migrant Workers in the Arab Region by Country of Employment and Region of Origin, 1975*

Country of employment	Arab		Asian						Europe and America		Africa and other		Turkey		Iran		Total	
			Pakistan		India		Other Asian		All Asian											
	No.	%	No.	%	No.	%	No.	%	No.	%	No.	%	No.	%	No.	%	No.	%	No.	%
Saudi Arabia	699,900	90.5	15,000	1.9	15,000	1.9	8,000	1.0	38,000	4.9	15,000	1.9	10,000	1.3	500	0.6	10,000	1.3	773,400	100.0
Libyan Arab Jamahiriya	310,350	93.4	4,500	1.4	500	0.2	500	0.2	5,500	1.7	7,000	2.1	500	0.2	9,000	2.7	—		332,350	100.0
United Arab Emirates	62,000	24.7	100,000	39.8	61,500	24.5	2,000	0.8	163,500	65.0	5,000	2.0	—		37	0.0	21,000	8.3	251,500	100.0
Kuwait	143,280	68.9	11,038	5.3	21,475	10.3	1,103	0.5	33,616	16.2	2,028	1.0	107	0.1	—		28,933	14.0	208,001	100.0
Qatar	14,870	27.7	16,000	29.8	16,000	29.8	2,000	3.7	34,000	63.3	846	1.6	—		—		4,000	7.4	53,716	100.0
Bahrain	6,200	21.2	6,680	22.8	8,943	30.5	981	3.3	16,604	56.7	4,442	15.2	57	0.2	—		1,982	6.8	29,285	100.0
Jordan (East Bank)	32,800	99.7	—		—		—		—		100	0.3	—		—		—		32,900	100.0
Oman	8,800	12.4	32,500	46.0	26,000	36.8	200	0.3	58,700	83.0	2,800	4.0	—		—		400	0.6	70,700	100.0
Yemen	1,350	95.9	—		—		—		—		100	4.1	—		—		—		2,450	100.0
Iraq	15,200	23.1	5,000	7.6	5,000	7.6	—		10,000	15.2	500	0.8	—		—		40,000	60.9	65,700	100.0
Total	1,295,750	71.2	190,718	10.5	154,418	8.5	14,784	0.8	359,920	19.8	37,816	2.1	10,664	0.6	9,537	0.5	106,315	5.8	1,820,002	100.0

— = no migrants recorded for this country or region.
Sources: Birks and Sinclair, 1977, 1978a, 1978b, 1978c, 1979c; plus authors' estimates using a wide variety of primary sources (Birks and Sinclair, 1980).

TABLE 2.13. *Capital-poor States: National Populations and Workforces ranked by size, 1975*

State	Population (thousands)	Workforce (thousands)	Crude participation rate (%)
Egypt	37,364.9	12,522.2	33.5
Sudan	15,031.3	3,700.0	24.6
Syrian Arab Republic	7,335.0	1,838.9	25.1
Yemen	5,037.0	1,425.8	28.3
Jordan (East Bank)	2,616.7	532.8	20.4
Democratic Yemen	1,660.0	430.5	25.9
Total	69,044.9	20,450.2	29.6

Source: Birks and Sinclair, 1980.

TABLE 2.14. *Capital-rich States: Employment by Nationality, 1973*

State	Nationals No.	%	Non-nationals No.	%	Total employment
Saudi Arabia	1,026,500	57.0	773,400	43.0	1,799,900
Libyan Arab Jamahiriya	449,200	57.5	332,400	42.5	781,600
Kuwait	91,800	30.6	208,000	69.4	299,800
United Arab Emirates	45,000	15.2	251,500	84.8	296,500
Oman	137,000	66.0	70,700	34.0	207,700
Bahrain	45,800	60.4	30,000	39.6	75,800
Qatar	12,500	18.9	53,700	81.1	66,200
Total	1,807,800	51.3	1,719,700	48.7	3,527,600

Sources: Birks and Sinclair, 1977, 178b, 1978c; Saudi Arabia, 1978 (Birks and Sinclair, 1980).

population was 4.55 million, a difference of 862,000 people. The distribution of the estimated number of migrants by age-group showed that nearly all migrants were under 29 years old, and about 53% of them were in the 15–29 age bracket: the remainder were either younger children brought by this group, or their offsprings after coming to Jakarta (Nathan Keyfitz, quoted in Sethuraman). Both sexes were under 29 years old, and about 53% of them were in the 15–19 age bracket: the remainder were either younger children brought by this group, or their offsprings after coming to Jakarta; (Nathan Keyfitz, quoted in Sethuraman). Both sexes were equally represented in the migrant population, and a large proportion (54% of men, 39% of women) were unmarried.

Nearly 75% of the Jakarta migrants had less than 6 years of education, and about 25% had no education at all. The characteristics of migrants to Jakarta did not appear to be very different from those of migrants to other urban areas in Java, but a rather larger proportion of the migrants in Java's urban areas were found to be young, single, and better educated than the migrants to

Java's rural areas. Two-thirds of the migrants to Jakarta came from West and Central Java at 1971, i.e. neighbouring provinces, whereas a large part of the remainder came from the other islands of Indonesia. About 60% of all household head migrants to Jakarta went there in search of employment opportunities; and it appears that few migrants were unemployed for long periods. From an actual survey in 1973, a larger proportion of these migrants who had no education reported that they were better off after moving to Jakarta, than did those with some schooling. Forty-three per cent of the 1973 migrants had worked in agriculture or fishing before moving, and 15% were described as traders or vendors; after moving, about 33% were traders and vendors, 16% were in government service, 14% were labourers, and the rest in a variety of occupations. It appears that many of these migrants join the lower circuit economy, and: "that migration is beneficial, socially and economically, for those involved. Migrants to the city seem to take on whatever jobs are open at the time of their arrival, instead of remaining unemployed, and move on to more preferred jobs as time passes by. Presumably they pick up in the process whatever skills they can in order to facilitate the change of job" (Sethuraman, op. cit.).

Unemployment in Jakarta cannot be attributed, Sethuraman avers, either wholly, or even mostly, to the flow of migrants; however it does seem that migration contributes to underemployment, as seen in terms of lower productivity of labour and earnings. Over most of Indonesia—except for West Java and Jogjakarta in 1974-1975—the rural-urban wage differential was quite small, and, if anything, in real terms the advantage may lie with the rural area where the cost of living might be lower. Thus the reason for rural-urban migration in Indonesia circa 1971 was thought to lie in unusually high rates of unemployment in rural areas, although such unemployment was probably seasonal in nature. Earnings averaged over the year, i.e. full-time rather than seasonal wages, might be much more attractive as a reason for migration, therefore, than simple weekly or other short-term wage differentials.

Models of Migration in Developing Countries

The last decade has been notable for a number of attempts to model migration flows in developing countries, using almost exclusively census data relating to birthplace, and thus implied migration. One of the most popular formulations for these models has been a combination of the basic gravity model with measures of the comparative advantage or origin and destination areas: an approach due to Lowry (1966).

A logarithmic form of the expression is usual, allowing parameter fitting by regression analysis, e.g.:

$$\log M_{ij} = a_0 + a_1 \log P_i + a_2 \log P_j + a_3 \log D_{ij} +$$
$$a_4 \log X_1 + a_5 \log X_2 + \cdots + a_n \log X_n + U$$

where M_{ij} is the number of migrants from region i to region j during the period under examination;

P_i, P_j are the populations (or some proxy of population) of regions i and j, respectively;

D_{ij} is some measure of the distance between region i and region j;

$X_1, X_2, \ldots X_m$, are indices of the comparative attractiveness of the regions i and j. These can be expressed either separately as X_i, X_j, etc., or in terms such as $(X_j - X_i)$, or (X_j/X_i).

U is a stochastic disturbance term;

and:

a_0, a_1, a_2, a_3, etc., are coefficients.

The earliest study under consideration is that by Beals, Levy and Moses (1967) of migration in Ghana, using data from the *1960 Population Census of Ghana* which lists the distribution of population, by age and sex, by region of birth, and by region of residence at 1960. Thus the number of 1960 residents born in each region is known, though multiple movements by a person are not detectable (e.g. from birth in region i to moving to region k, and then moving to region j where he is enumerated); also the timing of movements cannot be discerned, as has been said before. The measure of migration between region i and region j is the number of adult males (i.e. aged between 15 and 55 at 1960) born in i and residing in j in 1960. The analysis was based on seven statistical regions of Ghana, average income per adult male being estimated for each region, whilst measures of urbanization and education were derived from Census data.

The formulation used by Beals *et al.* was:

$$\frac{M_{ij}}{P_i} = f(d_{ij}, Y_i, Y_j, P_i, P_j, E_i, E_j, U_i, U_j, \text{random errors});$$

where
M_{ij} = number of males, aged 15–54, born in region i and enumerated in region j;

d_{ij} = road distance in miles between major cities of region i and region j;

Y_i = average labour income in origin region;

Y_j = average labour income in destination region;

P_i = number of males, age 15–54, born in origin region;

P_j = number of males, age 15–54, born in destination region;

E_i = percentage of males, age 15 +, enumerated in origin region, who have attended school.

E_j = percentage of males, age 15 + enumerated in destination region, who have attended school;

U_i = percentage of population of origin region residing in cities of 5000 or more;

U_j = percentage of population of destination region residing in cities of 5000 or more.

The parameters of the expression were estimated by least-squares regression, and both linear and log-linear functions were considered, log-linear functions giving the best fit. It was assumed that the explanatory variables were independent of the rate of migration, which is the dependent variable, though in fact wage rates might well be affected by the rate of migration, as might educational levels and the degree of urbanization of a region. The regression showed a high degree of explanation of inter-regional migration for the seven regions of Ghana ($R^2 = 0.91$) and alternative runs with regional population density, instead of degree of regional urbanization showed little difference in this respect. It was concluded that distance was a strong deterrent to migration, though distance was regarded only as a proxy for variables of other socio-economic kinds (e.g. culture, language, social organization in addition to transport costs). Migrants clearly tended to move to regions with high wage levels, and to regions of large populations, though not proportionately. (The results do not directly imply the attractive power of large *cities*, for the variable in use is *degree of urbanization of a whole region*, or its population density). Education appeared to be negatively related to migration—a finding which is in conflict with Caldwell's study, mentioned previously.

The next study is that by Adams (1969) for Jamaica, using the *Census of Jamaica, 1960* which includes distribution data by region of birth and by region of residence in a similar way to the 1960 Ghana information. The formulation and method of this study were also similar to the Ghana exercise, though some of the variables differed:

$$\frac{M_{ij}}{P_i} = f(D_{ij},\ Y_i,\ Y_j,\ U_i,\ U_j,\ E_i,\ E_j,\ W_i,\ W_j,\ J_i,\ J_j)$$

where M_{ij}, P_i, P_j as before

Y_{mi}, Y_{mj} are average income of male wage earners in regions i, j, respectively;

Y_{fi}, Y_{fj} are as Y_m but for female wage earners;

U_i, U_j are proportions of regions i, j, respectively living in towns of 2000 and over;

F_i, F_j are proportions of total land acreage in regions i, j, accounted for by farms of 100 acres and over;

$E_{mi}, E_{mj}, E_{fi}, E_{fj}$ are proportions of male and female populations respectively of regions i, j, who have completed 6 or more years of schooling;

W_{mi}, W_{mj} are proportions of male labour force unemployed in region i, region j, in 1960;

W_{fi}, W_{fi} are as W_m but for female labour;

J_i, J_j are proportions of labour force employed in agriculture in i, j.

It was found that distance and wage-income differentials explained the majorpart of the rate of migration, i.e. 86% of the variance. As in Ghana, it was deduced that distance *per se* was in fact proxy to a number of socio-economic "costs" of movement, though, as would be expected, the shorter distances in Jamaica were somewhat less of a deterrent to movement than those of Ghana. The income variables were significant, though the destination region appeared to have a stronger "pull" in this respect than that of the origin region. The unemployment variable seemed significant only in respect of a "push" effect from the origin region, but the urbanization variable proved to be quite insignificant. For males, the regression gave a best R^2 of 0.868, whereas the fit for females was less good, the best combination of variables giving $R^2 = 0.818$. A further analysis, differentiating between younger and older males, gave very similar results so far as income differentials were concerned to the previous all-age male regressions, but it was found that distance was slightly more of a deterrent to the older male group than the younger group.

A third study, by Greenwood (1969), of Egypt, was also based on 1960 census material and, whilst of the same general approach as the two previous studies, used total migration as the dependent variable. Independent variables other than those of distance and population size included: average annual money wage rates paid, percentage of population living in urban areas, and estimated number of years of education per male. The regression gave $R^2 = 0.75$, and distance was highly significant. Migration was away from low-wage and towards high-wage regions, also towards regions of large population and high urbanization. The inference concerning education level variables was not conclusive.

Greenwood (1971) also carried out an analysis of migration in India, using the *Census of India 1961* data. This data shows clearly that very large flows occur between urban areas (see Fig. 2.15), and that urban-to-urban migration as well as rural-to-urban migration must be taken into account; furthermore, "stepping stone" migration involving rural-urban, etc., flows may well be occurring on a considerable scale. Migration flows to urban areas of India are specifically examined by Greenwood, who comments that in many ways the migration data in the 1961 Census is the best available for less-developed countries, interstate flows being identified by rural or urban residence in a state of origin and by rural or urban residence in a state of destination. This enables the study of both rural-urban and urban-urban migration.

The relationships used were of the form:

$$M(r_i u_j) = f(D_{ij},\ Y_{ri},\ Y_{uj},\ U_i^*,\ U_j^*,\ e)$$

and

$$M(u_i u_j) = g(D_{ij},\ Y_{ui},\ Y_{uj},\ U_j^*,\ e)$$

where: $M(r_i u_j)$ = number of males born in rural areas of state i and
enumerated in urban areas of state j in 1961 divided by the

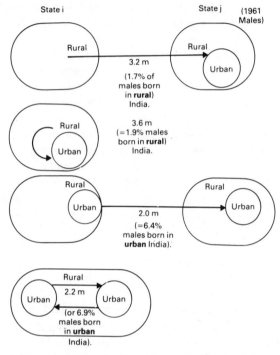

FIG. 2.15. Migration flows in India, 1961 (Greenwood, 1971).

product of the 1961 rural male population of i and the urban male population of j;

$M(u_i u_j) =$ number of males born in urban areas of state i and enumerated in urban areas of state j in 1961 divided by the product of the 1961 urban male population of i and the 1961 urban male population of j;

$D_{ij} =$ rail distance in kilometres between representative cities in states i and j;

$Y_{ri} =$ an estimate of the average annual income in rural areas of state i, 1961;

$Y_{ui}, (Y_{uj}) =$ an estimate of the average annual income of workers in urban areas of state i (j), 1961;

$U_i^*, (U_j^*) =$ percentage change in the degree of urbanization of state i (j) between 1957 and 1961;

$e =$ random errors.

Stepwise multiple-regression analysis was used to fit log-linear relationships as before, giving a best R^2 of 0.54 for rural-to-urban migration, and 0.63 for urban to urban. The distance variable-proxy, as in other cases, for all "costs" of movement, is highly significant. To test the significance of the differences in the two regression equations, a third analysis was made combining both kinds of migration; the results suggested that rural people who migrate to urban areas find distance to be a more serious deterrent to migration than do urban dwellers who migrate to other urban areas. It is also suggested that migrants to urban areas tend to come from relatively high income rural areas.

A study which contrasted the utility of the combined "comparative-advantage" as against the simple gravity model was carried out by Goddard and Masser (1972), using data for Uganda from the Census of 1969. The "advantage" variables included: average per capita income from wage and cash crops together with the inputed value of subsistence production; proportion of males of working age employed in the urban wage sector; and proportion of males recorded as having some education. The combined gravity/comparative advantage model showed greater explanatory value over the simple gravity formulation ($R^2 = 0.73$ as against 0.54). A general pattern of short distance movements between rural areas emerges, with flows from the poorer rural areas to the wealthier urban areas superimposed.

A more complex approach was adopted by Sahota (1968) in respect of migration in Brazil, using data from the Census of 1950 which was less satisfactory than the Indian data used by Greenwood (1971). The study was confined to adult males, disaggregated into two age groups, and using explanatory variables of wage rate, education, urbanization, density of population, distance, and level, rate of growth, and dispersion of income, for both origin and destination regions.

A single-equation model was tried first:

$$M_{ij} = M(R_{ij}, C_{ij}) = M(w_j, w_i, E_j, E_i, g_j, g_i, D_{ij} \ldots)$$

where M_{ij} = number of migrants from region i to region j;
M_i = total migration from region i;
$m_{ij} = M_{ij}/M_i$;
R_{ij} = potential returns to a migrant from origin region i to destination region j ($= R(w_j, E_j, g_i \ldots)$);
C_{ij} = costs of migration from i to j ($= C(w_i, E_i, g_i, D_{ij} \ldots)$);
w_i, w_j = wage rate per production worker per year in region i, region j;
y_i, y_j = per capita income in region i, j;
Y_{mi}, Y_{mj} = income originating in manufacturing in region i, j;
δ_i, δ_j = a measure of the dispersion of income in region i, j;
g_i, g_j = two-year rate of growth of the state's per capita income, 1949–1951, in i, j;
E_{1i}, E_{1j} = percentage of educated people in age group 15–29 in region i, j; E_{2i}, E_{2j}, likewise for the age group 30–59;
E_{3i}, E_{3j} = percentage of educated people in the agricultural sector in region i, j;

E_{4i}, E_{4j}, likewise for the non-agricultural sector in region i, j;

U_i, $U_j =$ index of urbanization measured by the percentage of population in cities of 5000 or over in region i, j;

d_i, $d_j =$ density of population per km^2 in region i, region j;

$D_{ij} =$ distance in kilometres from capital city of region i to capital region j.

The actual function decided upon was:

$$M_{ij} = W_j^{\alpha 1} \cdot W_i^{\alpha 2} \cdot E_j^{\alpha 3} \cdot E_i^{\alpha 4} \cdot g_j^{\alpha 5} \cdot g_i^{\alpha 6} \cdot U_j^{\alpha 7} \cdot U_i^{\alpha 8} \cdot$$

$$\exp(\alpha_9 \sqrt{D_{ij}} + \alpha_{00} + \sum_{i=2}^{I} \alpha_{0i} \theta_i + v_{ij})$$

where v_{ij} is a disturbance term assumed to have zero mean and constant variance and is uncorrelated with the explanatory variables; the θ_i are the region dummy variables that take a value of 1 for the region concerned and zero for the others. Least-squares estimation was used, resulting in a "best" fit R^2 of 0.52 for the younger age group and of 0.57 for the "middle-aged" group. Once again, distance is highly significant as a deterrent, whilst density of destination region is a strong "pull" factor, as is education in the destination region. However urbanization of origin region appears to encourage migration away from it whilst destination urbanization discourages it, but urban people are more mobile than rural people: urban to urban migration is more significant than rural to urban movement.

In order to take account of a possible simultaneity among the variables of the previous equation, Sahota formulated a two equation model using the previous key variables, as follows:

$$m_{ij} = \tilde{W}^{\alpha 1} \cdot \tilde{d}^{\alpha 2} \cdot \tilde{U}^{\alpha 3} \cdot \tilde{g}^{\alpha 4} \cdot \tilde{E}^{\alpha 5} \cdot \exp(\alpha_6 \sqrt{D_{ij}} + \alpha_{00} + \sum_{i=2}^{I} \alpha_{0i} \theta_i + \eta_1).$$

This is the equation for migration supply.

The migration demand equation was written as:

$$\tilde{W} = m_{ij}^{b1} \cdot \tilde{d}^{b2} \cdot \tilde{U}^{b3} \cdot \tilde{g}^{b4} \cdot E_j^{b5} \cdot \exp(\sum_{j=2}^{I} b_{0j} \cdot \theta_j + b_{00} + \eta_2)$$

and, of course, supply may equal demand for migrants.

However, although the model, with two endogenous variables and two equations, is logically complete, statistically it is overidentified due to coefficient restrictions: two-stage least-squares regression was used to estimate the coefficients, resulting in a best value of R^2 for log $m_{i/j}$ as dependent variable of 0.478, and for $\log_e \tilde{w}$ of 0.786. Amongst the major outcomes of the Sahota analysis is the finding that internal migration in Brazil in 1950 was highly responsive to earning differentials. Distance was a strong deterrent to migration, and there seemed to be some evidence that education attracted migrants both in origin regions and destination regions. Economic issues (costs and returns) appeared to be dominant, however, with industrialization and urbanization playing some role in this. Population density appeared to exercise a "pull" also.

An alternative approach to the modelling of migration has been pioneered by M. P. Todaro of the Institute of Development Studies in Nairobi (Todaro, 1969; Harris and Todaro, 1970). However, this approach, based on urban-rural real income differentials and the probability of a potential migrant obtaining an urban job becomes "An Analytical Model of the Structure and Mechanism of Urban Labour Markets", i.e. a model of an urban economy, and as such is rather beyond the terms of reference of this work. Moreover, the model has not yet been applied to a particular case study.

The model assumed that the percentage change in the urban labour force as a result of migration in any period is governed by the differential between the discounted streams of expected urban and rural income expressed as a percentage of the discounted stream of expected rural real income:

$$\frac{S^0}{S}(t) = F\left[\frac{V_u(t) - V_R(t)}{V_R(t)}\right], F' > 0$$

where: S^0 = net rural/urban migration;
          S = existing size of urban labour force;
          $V_u(t)$ = discounted present value of expected urban real income stream over unskilled workers planning horizon;
          $V_R(t)$ = discounted present value of expected rural real income stream over same planning horizon.

One of the flaws in the Harris–Todaro hypothesis has been pointed out by Mazumdar (1979), utilizing material from an empirical survey of workers in Bombay. Contrary to earlier assumption, migrant labour coming to a city for work is not of homogeneous quality in respect to a range of significant variables, e.g. age, health, education, experience, and particularly in relation to family status. Some male migrant workers live as single men in the city, often lodging with kin or with other migrants of similar status; others may have families to support in the city, rather than in the rural areas from which they came:

"The importance of this distinction between the two types of migrants is that they differ in their supply prices as well as in their desirability for urban employers. The difference in supply prices means that migrants with families are willing to accept employment only at a higher urban wage than individual migrants. The major reasons for the difference in supply prices are: (a) the substantially higher housing costs for the family migrant in town; (b) the lower earning strength of the family in town, because women and children are less easily part of the urban labour force than they are of the rural; and (c) the existence of disguised unemployment on family farms, which could make the marginal contribution of an individual worker low relative to the average income per earner of the family."

"The (rural) family gains an amount equal to the average income because the departing migrant no longer shares in the family pot, and it loses a smaller amount equal to the latter's marginal product. Thus an individual wanting to help his family would be willing to migrate at a very low supply price, perhaps one that will merely cover his subsistence cost in town. This is especially relevant for people who migrate for only part of the year (seasonal migration) or part of their working life."

Thus the workers having urban families to support are likely to be more permanent or stable residents in urban areas, requiring higher wages and offering in return a stable, and, in time, experienced labour force to employers: thus such workers are likely to be found more in the higher-wage formal sectors of the urban economy, whilst the shorter-stay single migrants are likely to work in the lower-wage sectors.

It was found that the lower-income jobs had a higher proportion of migrants who had been resident in the city for a short time, and this, together with the distribution of workers by length of stay in their current job and the degree of mobility in the labour market generally, suggests a high amount of return migration in low wage activities. It was also observed that unemployment for migrants before obtaining the first urban job was uncommon in Bombay. Graduation to higher-paid jobs in upper-circuit employment was of a significant level, but with the low rate of mobility prevailing, the process is slow and was unlikely to make a difference to the calculations of migrants.

Migration, Urbanization, and Economic Development

The relationship between the economic development of a country and its rate of urbanization, in quantitative terms, can be seen as reasonably well-defined. B. Renaud (1977) has examined this relationship between short-run changes in the dynamics of the national economy and the movement of people from the agricultural to the non-agricultural sector, in the case of Korea.

The rate of migration out of the agricultural sector is regarded as the annual rate of urbanization, and a simple model based on the annual growth rate of output in the non-farm sector can explain over 80% of the variance in agricultural out-migration over the period studied, 1955–1975. It was found that a delay or lag of 2 years occurred between growth in non-farm output and current migration, and that fluctuations in agricultural output have little impact on the rate of urbanization, i.e. there was more "pull" than "push".

It is known that the trend of urbanization for a country can, in general, be described by a logistic curve showing percentage of urban population against time. The period of most rapid change occurs at the point of inflexion of the curve, i.e. around the 50% level of urbanization; this region was crossed by Korea round about 1970, and so the inference may be drawn that, in Korea, urbanization in the period covered by Renaud's study had reached levels that

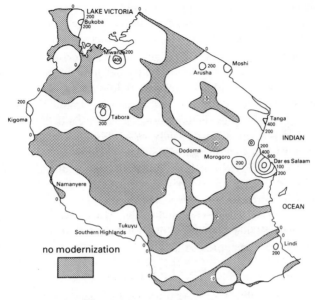

Tanzania: The modernization surface in the early twenties

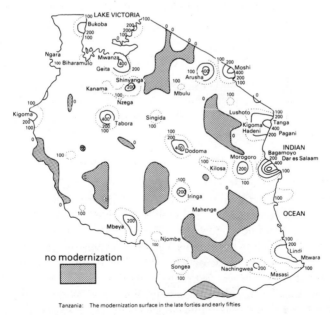

Tanzania: The modernization surface in the late forties and early fifties

Fig. 2.16. "Development" and accompanying urbanization in process: the "modernization surface" resulting from the synthesis of "scores" relating to communications, administrative services, health care, education, utilities and facilities, for Tanzania (previously Tanganyika) c. 1920–1950 (Gould, 1970).

are unlikely to be observed again. Future migrational transfers, whilst still significant, are likely to be at increasingly lower levels. One factor in this process, obviously, is that mobility in Korea—and no doubt elsewhere—is greatest between the ages of 14 and 35, so that migration causes a significant ageing of the farm population structure, with smaller proportions of people on farms coming within the mobile cohorts as time goes on.

Decisions to migrate in Korea are consistently found to be based on expectations of better employment opportunities, especially for the children of migrants: "for an individual, and equally for a household, migration between two different jobs and two different locations (the most common combined move) should, in theory, be a function of the net expected value of the investment made in the move. In other words, the decision-maker will compare the discounted stream of expected earnings for the household unit in its present situation with the discounted stream of anticipated earnings in the new location, net of the cost of relocating" (Renaud, ibid.).

Such a pattern can be expressed as:

$$Y_t = \alpha + \beta X_t^* + U_t$$

where Y_t is the probability of migration, X_t^* is a certain expected level of economic opportunities in year t, and U_t is a random variable with zero mean . X_t^* is not observable directly, but one can suggest that the change in expectation in year t may be proportional to the difference between expected level of opportunity in the previous year, and its actual value, i.e. X_{t-1}^* and X_{t-1}; so that:

$$X_t^* - X_{t-1}^* = (1 - \lambda)(X_t - X_{t-1}^*)$$

or: $$X_t^* = (1 - \lambda)X_t + \lambda X_{t-1}^*$$

where $$0 \leq \lambda \leq 1.$$

Following substitution, we may write:

$$Y_t = \alpha + \beta(1 - \lambda)(X_t + \lambda X_{t-1} + \lambda^2 X_{t-2} + \ldots) + U_t.$$

Such a model has a lag structure which gives a continuously declining influence of economic conditions as one moves away from those current; it can be estimated in a number of ways. In the case of Korea it was found that the effect of past economic conditions did not decline smoothly with time. Distributed-lag models of this type using relative urban-rural earnings and the terms-of-trade in the farm sector gave mediocre results for Korea; models utilizing growth rates of the farm and the non-farm sectors, though, gave significant results. The lag structure involved 2, or possibly more than 2 years.

The interesting conclusion of this model, therefore, is that the handsomely-realized growth targets of the Korean non-farm economy, during the period concerned, were the major determinants of the speed of urbanization, becoming effective after a 2 to 3 year lag: fluctuations in the growth rate of the farm sector itself were not at all significant.

It is clear, therefore, that there may be a direct relationship, in cities of developing countries, between rural-to-urban migration and urban employment—and thus, also, to unemployment, both urban and rural. The major reason for the high degree of unemployment is said to be that urban wages are much higher than rural wages, and this has the effect of attracting more migrants to the urban areas than there are jobs to be filled by them. Many migrants will take the chance of unemployment in the hope that, soon, a well paid urban job may become available for them. In the meantime, they may be supported by kinsfolk already in the city, or even by direct remittances from their rural family. Thus urbanization and unemployment exist together, and new jobs are created at a lesser rate than that of the migrant inflow: indeed, the more jobs that become available the greater the rate of urbanization tends to be, and the larger the pool of urban unemployed becomes. An additional factor is the increasing tendency for the productivity of the modern sector of the urban economy to increase at a faster rate than its employment requirements: more output with few jobs. Thus, again, even with rising urban output, unemployment will tend to overtake the creation of new jobs. Therefore, as Todaro (1969) pointed out, it is not the simple urban-rural real income differential which motivates rural-urban migration, but this differential must be adjusted to allow for the probability of finding an urban job in the modern sector: "this probability variable acts as an equilibrating force on urban unemployment rates". An important result of this situation is that the new migrant is very likely to spend some time in the urban traditional sector before, hopefully, moving into the more modern, formal sector of employment —and thus obviously reinforcing that aspect of a dual economy (see Fig. 2.17).

Once established in urban employment, urban wage-earners often send back some of their income to relatives or friends in the rural areas, thus modifying the distribution of incomes as between urban and rural areas. In a 1971 sample survey in Nairobi (Johnson and Whitelaw, 1974), of 1140 African households, it was found that 89% of them regularly sent money out of the city to rural areas. The average amount sent was 20.7% of the sample urban wage bill (including those who sent nothing); most of the money sent was intended to support the extended family of the urban employee. The proportion of the urban income remitted to rural areas was observed to decline as income increased. In this way, urban incomes may support the rural economy, at least up to a certain level.

The view that urban unemployment in many developing countries results from an excess of population, and thus labour force, growth in the cities above the potential rate of growth of urban employment may require some degree of modification, though. The rural-urban migration which causes, in some cases, say 50% of this population/labour force growth, persists even in spite of the

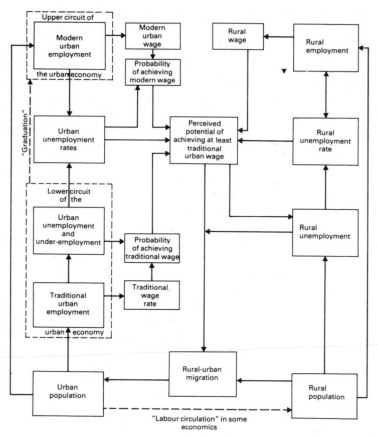

Fig. 2.17. A modified model of rural-urban migration in a developing country.

acknowledged urban unemployment. A probable explanation for this continuing migration in the face of apparently disadvantageous reception circumstances lies in the existence of the lower circuit of the urban economy*, which may have a great capacity for the absorption of labour, although at relatively lower wage rates than the upper circuit activities.

This explanation appears to be supported in the case of Jakarta, capital city of Indonesia (Sethuraman, 1976). For many years, Jakarta had a sustained rate of population growth close to 4.5% per annum, although the natural rate of increase was only about 2%. Yet a large formal manufacturing sector was absent from the city's economy, but it had a very large tertiary sector, and an estimated 41% of all employment in registered and unregistered enterprises was provided by "the informal sector" at 1967 (see Table 4.11).

* See Chapter 4.

The Future of Urbanization

There is reason to suppose that the immediate future—i.e. the next 20 or 25 years—will see a crucial change in the urbanization rate and extent in most developing countries, and thus of the whole world, amounting in all probability to a once-for-all change, not only of most urban systems, but also of many rural systems. This is the view—and it is a well-supported one—of an important World Bank Staff Working Paper (Beier *et al.*, 1975), though its supporting statistical data is now a little dated. The following pages paraphrase the arguments of this paper with due acknowledgement and with added comment on appropriate aspects.

Taking the developing countries as being represented by Asia, Africa, and Latin America, at the beginning of the century, less than 5% of the population of these continents lived in cities; but by 1950 this figure had increased to 15%, and by 1975 to 36%. By the year 2000 it will be at least 42%, and still increasing: at least 70% of the total increase in population to year 2000 of the developing countries will be absorbed by their cities—a staggering 1.3 billion people (Table 2.18). This pressure of urbanization seems likely to be the most severe in India and China, due to their already large populations, but in very many countries severe problems are probable as already large cities become even larger.

Beier and his colleagues point out that the urbanization experience of the now-developed countries is not a guide to that now in process in developing countries: European urbanization happened against a background of much lower population growth, higher incomes, and slower technological change. Thus there was an adequate time in which the relevant institutions able to regulate urban changes could emerge, whilst the supply of economic resources

TABLE 2.18. *Rural and Urban Populations, 1950–2000 (in millions)*[a]

	1950		1975		2000
Less Developed Countries					
Urban	273	+546	819	+1,334	2,153
Rural	1,382	+693	2,075	+864	2,939
Total	1,655		2,894		5,092
More Developed Countries[b]					
Urban	429	+302	731	+317	1,048
Rural	402	−40	362	−95	267
Total	831		1,093		1,315
World Total					
Urban	701	+850	1,551	+1,649	3,200
Rural	1,784	+653	2,437	+770	3,207
Total	2,485		3,988		6,407

[a] UN Population Projections, medium tempo, medium variant.
[b] Europe, N. America, Soviet Union, Japan, Australia, and New Zealand.
Source: Beier, G. *et al.*: World Bank Staff Working Paper No. 209, 1975.

available to support urbanization was more adequate. In contrast, developing countries are now faced with very rapid population growth; often low levels of rural income and (in some cases) a decline of the available agricultural land per capita; a decline in the costs of transport and communication; and frequently fixed national boundaries which deter or reduce international migration possibilities.

Of these factors, the sheer increase in population growth rates is of overriding concern: European urbanization was at its most rapid when national population growth rates were of the order of 0.5% per annum, whereas rates today for most developing countries average 2.5% to 3.0%. Thus natural population increases already within cities are much larger, and population movements to the cities are also larger. The greater agricultural production required to support these populations is unlikely, in many cases, to be practical from a more extensive cultivation, whereas more intensive production does not necessarily require more labour; the pressure to migrate from the rural areas is not lessened by the need for more food, in such a situation.

Of course, such generalizations must be tempered in individual country situations, though Beier *et al.* suggest a typology of four categories as an aid to a closer appreciation of the situation:

Type I. Those countries in which the process of urbanization is well underway. The population is already more than half urban, incomes relatively high and there is little pressure of population on arable land and natural resources. The end of the urbanization process will occur before the turn of the century when most of the population will be in urban areas and rural areas will begin to experience absolute declines. (Includes most of Latin America.)

Type II. In these countries the urbanization experience is more recent. Over half the population is still in rural areas. Population pressures exist on the land and incomes are at relatively low levels. If population pressures can be eased and resource constraints overcome, this group of countries by the turn of the century should obtain levels of urbanization similar to those found in the Type I countries today. (Includes such semi-industrialized countries of Asia and North Africa as Egypt, Korea, Malaysia, the Philippines.)

Type III. This group of countries is predominantly rural but urbanizing rapidly. Even so, by the year 2000 they will still be predominantly rural with high rates of growth of the rural population. The outcome of the race between population growth and resources (and the resulting growth of per capita income) is uncertain. (Includes most of Africa south of the Sahara.)

Type IV. These countries are dominated by severe pressures on the land in largely rural, subsistence-level-income societies. If the projected population growth rates are sustainable they will still be characterized in the year 2000 by large and growing rural populations living in absolute poverty. (Includes most of the large countries of Asia.)

Using this categorization, Table 2.19 shows the anticipated urbanization situation in a representative selection of developing countries. The high compound urban growth rates of the Type III countries are noteworthy, though, except for Nigeria, the forecast urban population totals are small relative to those in other groups.

Nigeria is the most populous country in Africa, with an estimated 1963 population of about 80 million according to Nigerian sources (Fourth National Plan, 1981–1985), but quoted in the World Bank Atlas of 1976 as 73,044,000. The population growth rate is put at between 2.5 and 2.8% per annum, i.e. a doubling every 28 years. The birth rate is high: about 50 births per 1000 population, and the death rate is declining and in the region of 20 deaths per 1000, though infant mortality is still high at about 187 per 1000 live births.

Urbanization was reported as proceeding rapidly in Nigeria, but even quite recently the proportion of urban dwellers was said to be only 20% of the total population, spread over 183 towns with populations over 10,000. Lagos, however, was estimated to be growing at from 9 to 12% per year, though still modest in size compared with other Third World capital cities.

The enormous tasks of urbanization confronting India and China are readily apparent from these figures, especially if a comparison is drawn also from Table 2.20 which shows the potential rural incomes in these countries.

The projections of urbanization in the preceding tables were carried out on a basis of cohort-survival-derived total population projections for each country concerned. The urbanization effect is seen in terms of a constant growth rate differential between the urban and rural sectors, with the percentage share of the urban population forming a logistic curve over time.

The model used is as follows. Taking T_0, U_0 and R_0 as the total, urban, and rural populations respectively at time $t = 0$, and with u and r as the exponential rates of growth of the urban and rural populations, the difference, d, between the rates is:

$$d = u - r.$$

And at time t:

$$U_t = U_0 \cdot e^{ut}$$

and

$$R_t = R_0 \cdot e^{rt}.$$

The urban/rural differential is then:

$$(U/R)_t = (U/R)_0 \cdot e^{(u-r)t} = (U/R)_0 \cdot e^{dt}.$$

TABLE 2.19. *Urbanization Prospects in Some Less-Developed Countries*

Country	Per capita GNP level in 1972 US$	Size of population (in 000's)				Percentage of urban population		Compound urban growth rate		Compound rural growth rate	
		1975		2000		1975	2000	1970–75	1995–2000	1970–75	1995–20
		Urban	Rural	Urban	Rural						
Type I											
Argentina	1.290	20,293	5,091	29,288	3,573	79.9	89.1	2.19	1.11	-2.46	-1.66
Mexico	750	37,349	21,855	103,287	28,957	63.1	78.1	4.86	3.60	1.19	0.82
Colombia	400	15,938	9,952	40,115	11,349	61.6	78.0	5.24	2.96	2.58	0.13
Brazil	530	65,128	44,602	161,604	50,903	59.4	76.1	4.72	3.13	1.67	0.31
Type II											
Algeria	430	8,432	8,455	27,205	11,199	49.9	70.8	6.78	3.85	1.52	0.94
Egypt	240	17,822	19,546	42,716	23,726	47.7	64.3	4.20	3.24	1.15	0.49
Korea	310	16,074	17,875	36,019	15,979	47.4	69.3	6.66	2.26	-1.36	-0.68
Philippines	220	15,837	29,468	46,068	47,956	35.0	49.0	4.25	3.66	3.02	0.99
Malaysia	430	3,641	8,666	9,888	12,589	29.6	44.0	3.34	3.28	2.09	0.58
Type III											
Senegal	260	1,262	3,190	3,740	5,013	28.4	42.7	3.89	4.18	1.83	1.47
Ivory Coast	340	994	3,891	3,718	5,899	20.4	38.7	7.02	4.46	1.51	1.54
Nigeria	130	11,419	51,511	40,953	94,008	18.2	30.3	4.67	5.10	2.07	2.36
Sudan	120	2,400	15,782	9,438	31,704	13.2	22.9	6.10	5.43	2.57	2.69
Kenya	170	1,483	11,625	6,458	24,743	11.3	20.7	6.48	5.61	3.38	2.83
Upper Volta	70	502	5,556	1,827	9,828	8.3	15.7	5.01	4.87	1.84	2.10
Type IV											
Pakistan	130	18,939	53,418	65,357	93,170	26.2	41.2	4.45	4.28	2.42	1.53
India	110	132,367	488,742	354,872	748,834	21.3	32.2	3.62	3.92	2.09	1.27
Indonesia	90	26,232	110,284	78,433	171,519	19.2	31.4	4.54	4.01	2.32	1.29
China (Mainland)	170	207,510	630,406	478,404	673,555	24.8	41.5	4.31	2.75	0.84	-0.07

Sources: UN, Urban-Rural Projections from 1950–2000, October 1974 (medium tempo with medium variant). World Bank *Atlas*, 1974 (Beier *et al.*, World Bank Staff Working Paper No. 209, 1975).

TABLE 2.20. *Potential Rural Incomes (US$1970 prices)*

Country	Rural per capita incomes in early 1970s (US$) (1)	Rural per capita incomes in 2000 if total rural income grows (US$) @ 2.6% (2)	@ 4.0% (3)
Type I			
Mexico (1970)[a]	219	334	437
Argentina (1971)	463	1,260	1,867
Brazil (1970)	141	260	340
Type II			
Egypt (1973)	101	163	204
Algeria (1970)	48	106	141
Korea (1972)	171	393	499
Malaysia (1970)	122	162	212
Philippines (1970)	68	79	119
Type III			
Nigeria (1970)	82	87	113
Ivory Coast (1972)	143	184	234
Senegal (1970)	92	115	150
Kenya (1971)	58	52	67
Type IV			
India (1971)	62	78	100
Pakistan (1972)	43	47	60
Indonesia (1971)	47	60	77

Source: Income data, World Bank, adjusted to 1970 prices and estimated as follows: total agricultural value added, plus 15% to take rough account of non-agricultural rural incomes, divided by rural population. Population data, UN, 1974 estimates, medium tempo, medium variant.
[a] Year of observation.
(Beier *et al.*, World Bank Staff Working Paper No. 209, 1975).

The level of urbanization, U/T, is then expressed as:

$$(U/T)_t = (U/(U+R))_t = \frac{k \cdot e^{dt}}{1 + ke^{dt}}$$

where $$(U/R)_0 = k.$$

This, of course, is the equation of a logistic curve.

Despite differences in growth rates and levels of urbanization, it has been found that urban-rural growth rate differentials are of the same order: between 2.0 and 4.0—in both more developed and less developed countries. The lowest rate for the period 1950–1970 was found to be 1.11 in India, and the highest 5.71 in Korea. Countries with current high rates will tend to move towards lower ones, and those with lower rates may change towards higher ones, in accordance with the logistic relationship.

TABLE 2.21. *Populations of Selected Urban Areas 1950–2000, in millions*

Country	1950	Average annual rate of growth	1975	Average annual rate of growth	2000
Type I					
Mexico City	2.9	5.4%	10.9	4.4%	31.5
Buenos Aires	4.5	2.9%	9.3	1.5%	13.7
São Paulo	2.5	5.7%	9.9	3.9%	26.0
Rio de Janeiro	2.9	4.4%	8.3	3.4%	19.3
Bogota	0.7	6.5%	3.4	4.2%	9.5
Type II					
Cairo	2.4	4.3%	6.9	3.6%	16.9
Seoul	1.0	8.3%	7.3	3.8%	18.7
Manila	1.5	4.4%	4.4	4.3%	12.8
Type III					
Kinshasa	0.2	9.7%	2.0	5.6%	7.8
Lagos	0.3	8.1%	2.1	6.2%	9.4
Type IV					
Shanghai	5.8	2.8%	11.5	2.6%	22.1
Peking	2.2	5.8%	8.9	3.7%	22.0
Jakarta	1.6	5.1%	5.6	4.7%	17.8
Calcutta	4.5	2.4%	8.1	3.7%	20.4
Bombay	2.9	3.7%	7.1	4.2%	19.8
Karachi	1.0	6.2%	4.5	5.4%	16.6
Developed Countries					
New York	12.3	1.3%	17.0	1.3%	22.2
London	10.2	0.2%	10.7	0.7%	12.7
Paris	5.4	2.1%	9.2	1.2%	12.4
Tokyo	6.7	3.9%	17.5	2.0%	28.7

Source: UN, City Projections, medium tempo, medium variant (December 1974) (Beier *et al.*, World Bank Staff Working Paper No. 209, 1975).

The same technique has provided the basis for the projections of the populations of major cities, given in Table 2.21. These projections must provide very substantial food for thought as to the future of the cities concerned. Three cities, Mexico City, Tokyo, and São Paulo, will be within a 25–30+ million population bracket. Eight cities: New York, Shanghai, Peking, Calcutta, Bombay, Rio de Janeiro, Seoul, Jakarta, will be within a range from 17.5 to 22.5 million. And of the 20 cities shown, only three (two of them in Africa) are projected to have a little less than 10 million inhabitants at the year 2000. And, at the growth rates postulated, very many of these cities will continue to grow very, very fast, and to even more enormous sizes, for a substantial time beyond year 2000: even a lower growth rate on a large base population will produce very large annual increments of population just from natural increase, quite neglecting any migrational changes. Moreover, this growth is not confined simply to the larger cities, but will occur in all sizes of city; even smaller cities of 20,000 population upwards in many developing countries can expect a doubling of size in 20 years or so. The whole urbanized system of these countries will change in size and new urban centres may be expected to appear; functional as well as size changes, are implied also, as the system of cities both accommodates and provides the base for development of economic activities and social needs.

3. Urbanization, City Distributions, and City Locations: Systems of Cities

Urbanization

The World Bank commonly used index of urbanization is taken as the difference between the rate of growth of the urban population and that of the rural populations: however, this method of calculation allows of the possibility that urban and rural populations may grow at the same rates, through natural increase, thus keeping the index constant—and yet urbanization will be occurring, i.e. urban growth taking place. This index, therefore, is designed to show mainly migratory, i.e. net rural-urban changes but without calculating them directly. The index is capable, also, of interpretation of a high growth situation in widely differing circumstances, as Renaud (1981) points out:

"(1) a country at a low level of urbanization can have a high rate of urban growth because the absolute base is very small (the case of Papua New Guinea);

(2) a country may have a high rate of growth because of international migration combined with a declining rural population (the case of Singapore and Hong Kong);

(3) a country can have a high rate of urbanization combined with a rapidly declining rural population and a total population growth rate which is falling (the case of Korea); and

(4) a country may have a high total population growth rate and a high rate of farm out-migration with its rural population still growing (the case of Algeria)."

Other measures of urbanization commonly in use include the ratio of urban to total national (or regional) population at a given time: a *rate* of urbanization in this case would require this index to be calculated at various times. The rate of growth of urban population, per annum, is also much quoted, sometimes disaggregated into natural increase and migratory change within a city or set of cities.

The purposeful nature of urbanization has been well stated by Mills and Song (1979), in their review of urbanization in Korea:

". . . urbanization serves three basic functions in developing and developed countries. First, urbanization permits a wide range of specialized processing and service activities to be carried on at a scale at which scale economies can be realized. An important problem in developing countries is that markets are too small to permit production at efficient scales. This is obvious and widely appreciated in manufacturing, but it is true also in service industries. Although the absolute scale needed to attain efficent production is not large in service production, firms tend to be highly specialized. A substantial market is required to be able to support enough firms to ensure competition in many service sectors. Evidence for this is the much greater variety of services found in large urban areas than elsewhere in developing countries. Especially in countries where incomes are low, large urban areas are necessary to provide a large enough market to support a wide range of activities."

"Second, and closely related, transport over long distances is expensive, especially in less-developed countries, where transport systems are poorly developed. Urban areas enable consumers and businesses to find a wide range of products and services close at hand, thus avoiding expensive shipments over long distances. Because facilities can be used intensively the costs (can be) spread over many users."

"Thirdly, many cities serve the physical and service requirements of international trade in less-developed countries. Most developing countries have large international sectors and many have only a few good natural harbours. Thus international trade tends to be concentrated in one or two ports in many less-developed countries. It is frequently advantageous to locate processing activities close to ports from which processed goods will be exported. It is then advantageous for related enterprises, employees, and activities providing goods and services to employees also to locate near ports. The same considerations induce users of imports, processors of imports, and related activities to locate near ports. Consequently, it is often advantageous to have large urban areas at ports."

It has been noted increasingly that developing countries have urbanized more rapidly in recent times than countries which are now developed did at their period of most rapid growth. In Western Europe, the maximum rate of urbanization in the nineteenth century was of the order of 1.5% per annum, and in more recent times about 1%; in contrast, most developing countries have experienced urbanization rates of between 2 and 3% per annum during the period 1950–1975: in Korea, the rate during this period was 4.1% (Mills and Song, 1979). This phenomenal average rate of urbanization was strongly related to the movement of workers out of agriculture to other activities: the percentage of the Korean labour force involved in manufacturing grew from less than 3 to more than 17. Some activities were even more concentrated in towns than manufacturing industry, however: 45.5% of total employment in Korea in 1970 was in cities of more than 20,000 population, and 79.7% of manufacturing employment was in the same set of cities. The most urbanized activities, though, were services: 92.2% of construction employment; 89.1% of retailing and wholesaling employment; and 92.8% of real estate and banking employment were in the same towns, and the growth of the services sector was a fundamental aspect of urbanization (Mills and Song, op. cit.).

Average rates of increase conceal the performance of individual cases, of course, and possibly some of the highest city increase rates have been recorded in Mexico. Here, between 1940 and 1970, four cities grew at annual average rates over 7%; these were: Tijuana, Acapulco, Mexicali, and Ciudad Juarez, all probably influenced by their proximity to the USA. But five other cities in Mexico had annual average rates of growth of more than 6%, and a further five had annual rates of more than 5% (Scott, 1982).

Mexico's period of most rapid urbanization occurred in the decade 1940–1950 and was due mainly to migration from rural areas; but in the 1950s and 1960s the continuing growth of Mexican cities was primarily due to natural increase. Migratory flows, though, were very selective in direction: even during the 1940s, 76% of all growth due to migration in cities of over 15,000 population occurred in only ten cities; and even in the 1950s this selectivity continued, with 82% of all migratory growth occurring also in ten cities. The three largest cities: Mexico City, Guadalajara, and Monterrey, had the largest share in the total growth due to migration, with Mexico City accounting for 49%, and the three largest cities together for 60% of all growth due to migration in the 1940s. In the 1950s the respective figures were 42% and 64% (Scott, op. cit.).

Fast urban growth in some cases has been stimulated by political, as well as economic changes. Although it was estimated that the level of urbanization in North Africa was then only of the order of 30 to 40% of total population, evidence quoted by Blake (1975) suggested that the annual percentage rate of increase of the urban population in these countries had increased from 3.3% in the period 1900–1936, to over 5% since 1960. This was despite the exodus from such countries—and probably mainly from their cities—of large numbers of Europeans and Jews, with the coming of independence and the "Moslemization" of urban life. This out-migration from the cities of non-Moslems has been accompanied by in-migration of Moslems from rural areas, with an increasing incidence of the underemployment and unemployment already in evidence in these towns, and a still greater emphasis on the service sectors of their economies (Figs. 3.1, 3.2) (Abu-Lughod, 1971, 1976).

In Algeria, massive in-migration was the cause of urban growth during and after independence, but in other North African countries the better sanitation and health services of the cities over the rural areas allowed high rates of natural increase—3 to 4% per annum perhaps—and in-migration was proportionately of less importance.

In Blake's view, step-migration via smaller towns appeared to be an important factor in Morocco and Algeria, as well as direct migration to the largest cities such as Casablanca, (which increased at an average rate of 5.2% per annum between 1952 and 1960). Most migration was regarded as

TABLE 3.1. *Population and Percentage in Large Cities (100,000 plus), North African Countries, 1950–1975*

PART I. TOTAL POPULATION

Datum and year	Algeria	Egypt	Libya	Morocco	Tunisia
1950 est.	8,920,000	20,000,000	999,000	8,959,000	3,555,000
1951				8,004,000	
1954	9,529,726				
1956					3,441,696
1958				11,095,000	
1960 est.	10,784,000		1,349,000	11,640,000	4,157,000
Census		26,062,000		11,626,470	
1962				11,870,000	
1963	10,670,000				
1964				12,629,000	
Census			1,564,000		
1966	11,833,000				
Census	12,101,994	30,000,000			4,533,351
Estimate	12,096,347		1,728,059		
1968			1,808,000		
1970 est.	13,663,000		1,850,000	15,519,000	4,882,000
Off. est.	13,547,000	33,000,000			
1971 census	14,643,700			15,379,259	
1972 est.			2,084,000		
1973			2,257,035		
1975	16,500,000	37,000,000	2,500,000	17,388,633	5,700,000

PART II. PERCENTAGE OF POPULATION IN CITIES 100,000 OR MORE, 1950–75

	Algeria	Egypt	Libya	Morocco	Tunisia
1951 est.	11.9	19.0 (1947)	11.4	15.8	17.3
1951				17.1	
1956					25.8
					19.6
1960 est.	16.4		21.3		
Census		27.0	25.5 (1964)	18.9	
1966 est.			17.0		
Census	15.0				24.0
1970 est.	13.6	31.0	26.1	23.4	22.2
1971 census				24.1	
1973			36.2		
1975					23.0
	20.0	36.0	38.0	28.0	27.0

Source: Abu-Lughod, 1976

permanent by families, and with weak home ties. Migration appears to have taken place without prospect of employment or accommodation, and thus, it is said, the growth of *bidonvilles* on the periphery of the cities. (The existence and growth of such squatter areas, though, seems likely to be due to more complex population movements, according to many observers.)

In view of the spectacular growth of some very large cities in developing countries, e.g. Mexico City, São Paulo, Calcutta, Cairo, Seoul—it should be stressed that the results of the urbanization process are systems of cities, not individual metropoli. Migration takes place to (and from) all human

TABLE 3.2. *Major Cities of North Africa: Current Population Estimates and Growth Trends Between 1950 and 1975*

Cities by current descending rank-size (approx.)	Population c. 1950	Population c. 1960	Population c. 1970–75	Recent annual growth rate
Over 500,000:				
Cairo, Egypt	2,000,000 (1947)	3,500,000 (1960)	6,500,000 (1970), 8,300,000 (1975)	
Alexandria, Egypt	919,000 (1947)	1,500,000 (1960), 1,800,000 (1966)	2,032,000 (1970)	
Casablanca, Morocco	680,000 (1952)	965,000 (1960), 885,000 (1966)	1,506,000 (1971)	
Algiers, Algeria		943,000 (1966)	1,100,000 (1970)	
Tunis, Tunisia	558,000 (1956)	721,000 (1966)	1,000,000 (1975)	
Tripoli, Libya	114,000 (1950)	210,000 (1964), 330,000 (1966)	551,000 (1973), 650,000 (1975)	9.0
Rabat-Salé, Morocco	200,000 (1952)	303,000 (1960)	523,000 (1971)	5.0
250,000 to 500,000:				
Oran, Algeria		327,000 (1966)	368,000 (1970), 332,700 (1971)	3.0
Marrakesh, Morocco		243,000 (1960)	374,500 (1975)	3.0
Fez, Morocco		216,000 (1960)	325,300 (1971), 374,400 (1975)	3.6
Benghazi, Libya		160,000 (1966)	264,500 (1973), 310,000 (1975)	8.0
Constantine, Algeria	116,000 (1947)	255,000 (1966)	280,000 (1970)	2.7
Mahalla el-Kubra, Egypt	140,000 (1947)	172,000 (1960)	255,800 (1970)	4.8
Tanta, Egypt		184,000 (1960)	253,000 (1970)	3.0
Meknes, Morocco		176,000 (1960)	248,300 (1971)	
Sfax, Tunisia		70,000 (1966)	279,000 (1975), 250,999 (1975)*	
Egyptian Canal Cities:				
Ismailiya	68,000	276,000* (1960)	345,000 (1966)	
Suez	107,000	203,000 (1960)	315,000 (1966)	
Port Said	178,000	244,000	313,000 (1966)	

* Boundary change. (J. L. Abu-Lughod, 1976.)

Tables 3.1 and 3.2 are reproduced from J. L. Abu-Lughod "Developments in North African Urbanism: The Process of Decolonization", pages 196 and 299 in: *Urbanization and Counter-Urbanization*, edited by B. J. L. Berry. Copyright c. 1976 B. J. L. Berry and Sage settlements to some degree, and all human settlements will change by natural increase or decrease: settlement systems are not stationary entities, but are continually changing, and the spectacular rates of growth and large numerical and physical size of the great conurbations should not detract attention from change in whole urban systems. For example, there is now quite a lot of evidence—from Egypt, from Mexico, for example—that some smaller cities in certain countries have faster growth rates than have the largest cities in those countries, although numerically flows to the biggest cities are still greatest; the Suez Canal towns in Egypt (Port Said, Ismailia, Suez) are cases in point. In Costa Rica, which is a small country (2.1 million population estimated, mid-1977), the maximum population concentration in the Central Valley and around San José occurred early in the country's history, and regions outside the Central Valley have been steadily increasing their share of population, from 22.7% in 1864 to 43.2% in 1973, or from 27,000 to 808,000 persons. The Central Valley, with 1,064,000 population at 1973, though growing still, is only maintaining its relative proportion of the national total population, despite the dominance of San José as the major urban focus. Costa Rica, though, is atypical of both Central and Latin America, with its birth rate of 29 per 1000 as against 37 per 1000 for Latin America; its natural rate of increase of 2.4% per annum against 2.7%; and its infant mortality rate of 38 per 1000 live births against 78 per 1000, at 1977; (Herrick and Hudson, 1981). Also, the rural towns of Costs Rica appear to be unusually urban, with only 14% of their economically active population employed in agriculture: in Mexico and Nicaragua, the range is from 30 to 70%.

Systems of cities exhibit the rank-size distribution, and also often the phenomenon of primacy; however, primate cities do not appear to have figured in the rank-size hierarchy of North African population systems to the extent that might have been anticipated (Fig. 3.3, after Blake, 1974).

Interestingly, though, a kind of regional primacy exists. The predominant feature here is the concentration of cities over 2500 kilometres of coastline, from the Atlantic coast west of Casablanca to the Mediterranean coast east of Tripoli. This belt is less than 250 kilometres deep, and is most densely occupied within 100 kilometres of the sea; its existence, of course, is related to climatic and water-availability considerations (see Fig. 3.4, from Blake, 1974).

The dynamic nature of relative change in size of cities within urban systems, even with primate cities, is well shown by Scott (1982), in his analysis of urban development in Mexico:

"With respect to primacy (that is, the proportion of the total population of the various combinations of the twenty-five largest cities [twenty-five being an arbitrary number] compared with that of Mexico City), the record is somewhat ambiguous. Up to 1950 urbanization was associated with increasing primacy whatever the measure used. After 1950, however, only the measure relating the population of Mexico City to the largest base (the second to twenty-fifth ranked cities) showed a continuous increase. There was a clear

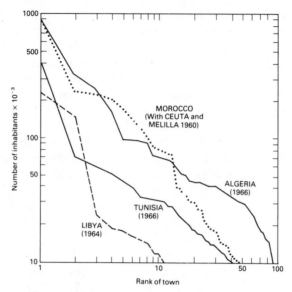

FIG. 3.3. North Africa: Rank-size of urban populations (Blake, 1974).

decline in the ratio between the size of Mexico City and the size of the second-ranked city (Guadalajara), whereas the ratios between the size of Mexico City and the cities occupying the second to tenth ranks gradually stabilized. These changes imply that a maximum degree of primacy in the urban system had been reached in the late 1940s; that the dynamism of other large centres had by then begun to rival that of Mexico City; and that the growth in the expanded group of large cities continued to out-pace that of most of the relatively smaller cities, as well as the smaller cities as a group. The urban system thus became somewhat more balanced after 1950 as its base expanded. (That is, the number of smaller cities performing real urban functions and within the sphere of influence of the large cities increased.) The urban hierarchy also became increasingly stable during this period."

Such dynamics are difficult to capture in modelling, easier to trace in time-series data over several decades—but their existence must not be overlooked. The full description of such a system via what must be necessarily a family of models, is an incredibly difficult task. Perhaps it is the difficulty of this task which has made the distribution of models essayed rather like that of certain of the phenomena considered: a considerable skewness in that much effort has gone into certain aspects and parts of the field, and little into others, especially into seeing such systems as wholes rather than an assembly of (a few kinds of) parts.

Thus the patterns of settlements as service centres: "central places" in the jargon, has been much studied, and such patterns may have relevance still in some developing countries (cf. Abiodun, 1967). But, increasingly with

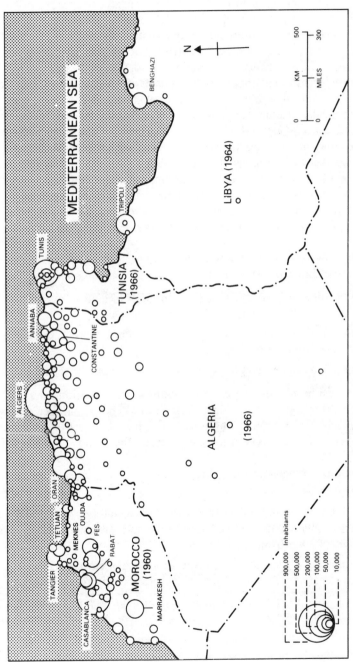

FIG. 3.4. North Africa: Towns with over 10,000 inhabitants at latest census (Blake, 1974).

"development", service centre relationships may be overlain with other patterns which cannot be explained by reference to the same phenomena: regularity and seeming randomness may be cotenants of settlement patterns, perhaps, or rather explanations involving both regularities and random occurrence seem very likely in describing the totality of effects.

A view of urban and regional systems as fields of forces may demonstrate the complexity involved. Firstly, taking primary economic activities, some are fairly specifically located, e.g. mining; and others may be undertaken on an extensive basis, e.g. agriculture. The site-specific activities seem likely to be explained only in a very particular way, whereas more general rules may be derived for the broader areas of location. Such locations and/or allocations would seem to require consideration in terms not only of any location or site characteristics *per se*, but also in terms of their various input requirements and of their various output relationships—as they may vary over time, and not neglecting any relationships with other activities, whether of the same or other kinds.

The, by now, "classical" economic and geographic theory which attempts to explain these things has three main facets at the regional scale:

the location of agriculture or the allocation of land to agriculture, via considerations of rent (Ricardo, Von Thünen, etc.);

the location of market or service centres: "central places", market areas, and rank-size relationships (Christaller, Lösch, Zipf);

the location of industry via cost-minimization approaches (Weber).

To these must be added a more recent interest in urbanization *per se*, largely approached through "innovation" (Hägerstrand) and "multiplier" concepts (Pfouts, Tiebout), and also in migration, though a full theory of urbanization does not seem to have been attempted, outside the broad scope of Childe's work.

To complete the picture, intra-urban theory* may be said to have the following aspects:

the linkage of rental, land value, accessibility, building and land use and density phenomena, derived from economic argument (Haig, Clark, Turvey, Richardson, etc.);

attempts to suggest land use dispositions, e.g. sectors, rings and so on, from social as well as economic considerations (Burgess, Hoyt);

the explanation of social processes such as migration and filtering which lead to phenomena such as clustering and neighbourhood identification (Abu-Lughod).

Many of the geographical or "space-economy" theories mentioned seem to be founded on a number of basic precepts, which might be listed as:

* ". . . in many respects, urban land use theory is a logical extension of agricultural location theory." W. Isard: *Location and Space-Economy*, M.I.T. Press, 1956.

(a) the concept of "rational man";

(b) following from (a), the "principle of least effort";

(c) a concern with the minimization of the "friction of space", following from (b);

(d) an incorporation of the inverse-distance effect subsumed in the gravity model, thus linking with (c);

(e) a division of geographic space into fields consistent with the above and with a rigid hierarchy of service or market centres derived from a "rational" division of functions and areas served;

(f) the minimization of "cost" and the maximization of "profit", linking with the theory of the firm on the one hand, and welfare economics, cost-benefit analysis, etc. on the other.

Criticism of the conventional theories has been made by Allan Pred (1969) and others, and as in other fields (Simon, 1957) the concept of "rational man" and the general striving for rationality has come under considerable fire. It is necessary, therefore, to distinguish between normative theory which tries to explain how things "ought" to be, and theory which is more pragmatically oriented and thus attempts to explain how things are in reality. Normative theory is helpful in understanding situations and in analysis, but it is not a good guide to real-world decision-making, being in the nature of a Procrustean bed in this respect. Pragmatic theory aims at being a useful aid to real decision and action, but may lack verifiable or justifiable foundations in some cases and thus be open to suspicion. The distinction between the two is pointed up by the well-known "ice-cream salesman on the beach" analogy, derived from Hotelling (1929). In this example, the "rational" solution—the "planned" or "welfare" solution perhaps?—is to station each vendor along the strip of beach so that each has an equal and non-overlapping potential sales area which corresponds to $1/n$th of the beach, where n is the number of salesmen. However, in real life, clustering will occur, with each vendor trying to command the whole of the beach, i.e. competing with all other salesmen for the total trade, and thus attempting to maximize his profit, not accepting only $1/n$th of it. This illuminating example shows clearly why rational theory is unsatisfactory and why "planned solutions" are not to be desired. The ice-cream sales example is also of interest in reinforcing the view that competition and clustering, due both to fields of competition and to the existence of mutually-reinforcing needs or services, are usually important elements missing from the rational models—though they are included in some intra-urban theories (Fig. 3.5).

The City Size Distribution

It is perhaps logical to begin at the broader scale. Hope T. Eldridge (1956) has suggested that urbanization has two major elements: the "multiplication of points of concentration", and the "increase in size of individual

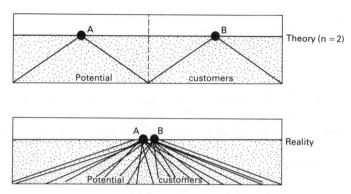

FIG. 3.5. The ice-cream salesmen on the beach: Hotelling's principle.

concentrations". The distribution of cities increases: not only larger cities, but more of them.

The distribution of city sizes exhibits a characteristic pattern in which few cities of larger size occur, but many cities of smaller sizes are found. Such a distribution, strongly skewed in statistical terms, can be described mathematically in three ways: by the so-called "rank-size" rule, by the log-normal distribution, or by the Pareto distribution. All three methods are so similar that discussion still continues as to which is the most appropriate, though for most practical purposes, the simplest description in a given instance may well be the most useful.

The log-normal distribution may be written:

$$N = \log x,$$

where N is the cumulative percentage of cities, and x is city size.

The Pareto distribution is:

$$y = A \cdot x^{-\alpha},$$

where x is the number of people in a city, y is the number of people inhabiting a community of size x or larger, and A and α are parameters estimated from the size distribution.

When $\alpha = 1$ and thus $x = A/y$, x being the number of people in a given city and A being the number of people in the largest city in the system, then y is the rank of a city of size x: this is the "rank-size" rule. It may be noted that the case where $\alpha > 1$ seems to represent the dominance of the largest city, i.e. a primate distribution; whereas if $\alpha < 1$ cities of intermediate sizes might predominate.

As Richardson (1973) has pointed out in his excellent review paper on the theory of the distribution of city sizes, many models have been put forward to account for the statistical patterns observed: these he classifies as hierarchy models, stochastic models, quasi-economic models, and Markov chain models. Martin Beckman (1957) also has provided an elegant demonstration of the hierarchical theory involved, in his paper: "City Hierarchies and the Distribution of City Size".

City-Distributions in Practice

Many studies have been made of national systems of cities to see whether the rank-size rule holds good for the particular country in question. Vapnarsky (1959) showed that the rank-size rule fitted the city-distribution of Argentina very well for data from five censuses from 1869 to 1960—with the exception that primacy was demonstrated at all times by Buenos Aires—"primacy" (Jefferson, 1939), being the situation where the largest city in a country is disproportionately greater than the second one, i.e. much greater in size than the rank-size rule would lead us to suppose to be the case. Interestingly, Vapnarsky showed that four regional city-size distributions in Argentina at 1947 also demonstrated both a primate city and the rank-size rule (Figs. 3.6, 3.7).

Janet Abu-Lughod (1965), as part of her continuing investigation of urbanization in Egypt in general, and of Cairo in particular, has shown that Egypt, often referred to as "over-urbanized", is indeed a special case: more than one out of every three Egyptians lives in an urban place. In fact, the

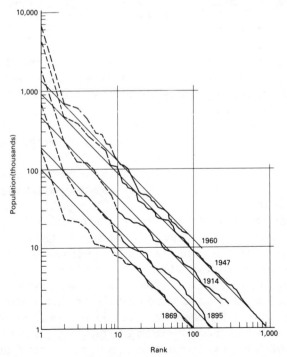

FIG. 3.6. Argentina: city size distribution at each census date (Vapnarsky, 1969).

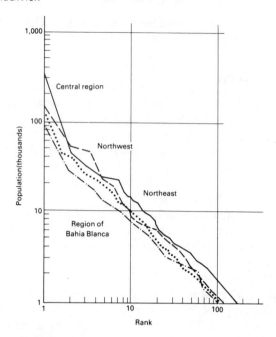

FIG. 3.7. Argentina: four regional city size distributions exhibiting a primate city and the rank-size rule fulfilled by the remaining cities 1947 (Vapnarsky, 1969).

picture of over-urbanization in Egypt is distorted by problems of definition of "urban": many "urban" places are simply swollen villages, crowding being induced by the peculiar agricultural circumstances of the Nile Delta. What is striking about the city distribution of Egypt, however, is the primacy of Cairo and also a kind of "dual primacy" where Cairo and Alexandria are far, far bigger than the rest of the distribution would lead one to believe, with a yawning gap between these two and Ismailia and the other Canal towns and Giza (which is really part of Cairo), which are in the next size band. More recently in Egypt, migration to the provincial towns has increased at the expense of migration to Cairo and Alexandria, though these former towns are still small compared to the metropolises of the Nile. But, as Mrs Abu-Lughod points out, Cairo is the capital of the whole Arab world as well as a regional capital and a national capital, and this fact must be taken into account in any attempt to assess "over-urbanization".

Large cities tend to grow faster than smaller cities, a fact which has been observed many times, and usually accounted for by pointing to the greater gravitational "pull" of larger masses. Such a situation is an aspect of the general biological principle of allometric growth, though, as seen earlier when discussing migration, the factors involved may be more complex than a simple gravity model would suggest. Abu-Lughod has shown (1965) that allometric growth occurred in Egypt, again if Cairo and Alexandria are excluded from the comparison. Here, the striking feature of recent times is that the middle-sized cities have been growing *faster* than the two metropoli: as if Cairo and Alexandria are so full of people that they do not now attract proportionately, i.e. the quality of life there may have become a disincentive to growth of an allometric kind. Of course, the actual *quantities* of growth, rather than the rates of growth, are still much larger in the cases of the two big cities than for the middle-size towns. (See Figs. 3.8–3.10.)

But the allometric principle explains only about one half of Egypt's urban growth patterns, as city size accounts for only this proportion of the observed differences in growth rates, according to Abu-Lughod's calculation of rank correlation coefficients. It is suggested that geographic location within Egypt is also a major influence, with proximity to the two major cities or proximity to the Suez Canal being an important factor.

History also plays a part in city-size distributions, fairly obviously—a point made by both Vapnarsky and Abu-Lughod in discussing the primate cities of their case studies. It appears very likely—especially in "undeveloped" countries—that external influences may have distorted the "natural" rank-size relationship by inducing more-than-allometric growth for certain cities. These cities may be "world" cities or regional capitals, or the seats of colonial governments, or in entrepôt situations to large, otherwise inaccessible hinterlands, or near to important mineral or other resources in world demand: examples are numerous. Which also means that, in these cases, if one investigates merely the national system of cities, one is possibly investigating the wrong system.

TABLE 3.8. *Distribution of Urban Population of Egypt by Size of Community, 1897–1960*

	% of urban population in size class by year						
Size class	1897	1907	1917	1927	1937	1947	1960
Cairo-Alex. primates	64.9	64.7	56.3	56.1	55.0	55.0	52.0–53.5
Other cities over 100,000	0.0	0.0	0.0	3.6	3.4	12.0	22.3
Cities 20,000 to 99,999	35.1	35.3	43.7	40.3	41.4	33.0	26.0
Total urban	100.0	100.0	100.0	100.0	100.0	100.0	100.3

[a] Data from the Censuses of 1897 to 1947 have been adapted from processed material appearing in the Appendix of a paper by Alphonse Said.
[b] Data for 1960 have been taken from the Preliminary Returns of the Census of 1960, op. cit. Computations J.A-L. Low estimate of 52% is based on present boundaries of Cairo; high estimate of 53.5 is based upon correction of boundary.
[c] If the high figure of 53.5% is accepted, the percentage of urban population in cities of over 100,000 must be reduced to 20.8.
[d] Not 100.0 because of rounded estimates.
(J. Abu-Lughod, 1965.)

TABLE 3.9. *Percentage of Total Population and of Urban Population in Egyptian Cities of Various Sizes, 1937, 1947, and 1960 (percentage rounded)*

Size class	Number of cities			% of total			% of urban		
	1937	1947	1960	1937	1947	1960	1937	1947	1960
Primates[a]	2	2	2	12.5	16.0	19.0	55.0	55.0	52.0
Large cities[b] (100,000–299,999)	1	5	12	1.0	3.0	8.0	3.0	12.0	22.0
Smaller cities (20,000–99,999)	43	50	72	9.5	9.5	9.3	41.0	33.0	26.0
Cities (50,000–99,999)	n.a.	9	9	n.a.	3.4	2.3	n.a.	12.0	6.2
Large towns (30,000–49,999)	n.a.	15	25	n.a.	2.8	3.5	n.a.	10.0	9.9
Small towns (20,000–29,999)	n.a.	26	38	n.a.	3.3	3.5	n.a.	11.0	9.7
Total	46	57	86	22.9	28.9	36.3	100.0	100.0	100.0

[a] Cairo and Alexandria throughout.
[b] In 1937, Port Said; in 1947, Tanta, Mehalla Kubra, Suez, Mansura, and Port Said; in 1960, Ismailiya, Giza, Port Said, Suez, Tanta, Mehalla Kubra, Mansura, Embabah, Damanhur, Zagazig, Asyut, and Fayoum.
(J. Abu-Lughod, 1965).

A seemingly useful hypothesis on the phenomenon of primary relative to a city rank-size distribution might be that primacy indicated an "immature" situation relative to economic development. As has been seen, B. J. L. Berry (1959) tested this theory by collecting indices which could be held to relate to the economic development of countries, and then by using principal components analysis to derive dimensions of economic development. A relationship between level of urbanization, (regarded as the percentage of population in cities of 20,000 people and greater), and economic development was established. But upon classifying frequency distributions on city sizes in 38 countries as to their lognormal, primate, or intermediate nature, it was found that there was no correlation between level of economic development and rank-size distribution. It was found, however, that the advanced countries with primate distributions were usually very small, and the less-developed countries with lognormal distributions were generally very large and having long histories of urbanization, as if the lognormal distribution might, after all, indicate a steady-state condition, arrived at only over a long time and based upon urban system interactions of some complexity.

H. W. Richardson (1977) has given figures (Fig. 3.11) which broadly support Berry's findings relative to urbanization and economic development. Figures quoted by Richardson for 1970 Four-City Primacy Indices also give support to

TABLE 3.10. *Average Percentage Increase in Population for Egyptian Cities in Different Size Classes, Intercensal Periods 1937–47 and 1947–60*

Size class	Average (mean) % of population increase 1937–47		1947–60	
Cairo metropolitan area and Alexandria[a]	47.0		67.8	(Includes M.S.)
Other cities of 100,000 or more (latest year of intercensal period)	67.5	(Canal cities 78.9) (Provincial capitals 59.2)	92.3	(Canal cities 144.2) (Provincial capitals 43.4)[b]
Cities of 50,000 to 99,999 (latest year of intercensal period)	44.0	(Canal and M.S. 81.3) (Others 33.4)	38.5	(No canal or M.S. in size class in 1960)
Cities of 30,000 to 49,999 (latest year) of intercensal period)	27.4		29.5	(Includes high-growth Aswan)
Cities of 20,000 to 29,999 (latest year of intercensal period)	25.9	(Excludes Helwan) (see note a)	18.2	

[a]The Cairo Metropolitan Area has been "invented" for statistical purposes and has no administrative significance. In order to keep the area constant throughout the several redistrictings that have taken place between 1937 and 1960, we have combined the following units: Cairo, Helwan (included with Cairo in 1937, separated in 1947, included again in 1960), Embabah (included with Cairo in 1947, separated in 1960), and Giza (part of 1947 Cairo ceded to Giza in 1960).
[b] Excludes Embabah and Giza.
(J. Abu-Lughod, 1965.)

Berry's contention that a general correlation between level of economic development and the rank-size distribution cannot be identified (Fig. 3.12).

The relationship between urbanization and economic development is by no means a simple one, as Britton Harris (1959) has pointed out: "India . . . has a well-balanced structure of urban places, while many smaller underdeveloped areas have a single large capital, (usually a port and administrative centre), and no other significant metropolis. Considering the extreme limitations of the market upon specialization, I cannot in these countries regard the size of those primate cities in itself as evidence of parasitism or unbalanced development. Throughout the developing areas, in fact, a special conditioning factor which should be recognized is the fact that these countries are combining several states of development in one era. In particular, they are using primitive, intermediate, and modern techniques together. Their range of specializations is greatly extended by comparison with the early stages of Western economic growth. It follows, therefore, that in order to provide the economies of scale appropriate to the most modern sectors of the economy and culture, the size of efficent cities is much larger than was the case in our own historical development."

"Another factor contributing to the large size of cities in developing areas is the degree of urban unemployment, under-employment, and employment in

MURS – D*

TABLE 3.11. *Urbanization Levels in a Sample of Less-Developed Countries*

Country	Per capita GNP level in 1972 US$	Percentage of urban population 1975
Argentina	1290	79.9
Mexico	750	63.1
Brazil	530	59.4
Algeria	430	49.9
Malaysia	430	29.6
Colombia	400	61.6
Zambia	380	36.1
Ivory Coast	340	20.4
Korea	310	47.4
Senegal	260	28.4
Egypt	240	47.7
Philippines	220	35.0
China (mainland)	170	24.8
Kenya	170	11.3
Pakistan	130	26.2
Nigeria	130	18.2
India	110	21.3
Indonesia	90	19.2
Upper Volta	70	8.3

Source: Richardson, H. W.: *City Size and National Spatial Strategies in Developing Countries*, World Bank Staff Working Paper No. 252, 1977.

TABLE 3.12. *Extremes of Primacy, 1970 (Four-City Index)*

Developing countries			
Primate		Non-Primate	
Peru	5.32	Saudi Arabia	0.50
Philippines	4.56	Nigeria	0.57
Argentina	4.03	Syria	0.52
Chile	3.97	India	0.68
Cuba	2.48	Brazil	0.77
Iran	2.21	Pakistan	0.88
Egypt	2.08		
Burma	2.07		

Developed countries			
Primate		Non-Primate	
Denmark	3.50	The Netherlands	0.50
France	3.10	South Africa	0.50
Austria	2.70	Canada	0.63
United Kingdom	1.53	Italy	0.69
Norway	1.48	Australia	0.70
		Switzerland	0.71
		United States	0.77
		Belgium	0.77

Source: K. Davis (1969). (Reproduced by Richardson, World Bank Staff W.P. 252, 1977.)
Note: Sample restricted to countries with at least four cities greater than 100,000. Eastern Europe is excluded because of difficulties of classification.

low-productivity service industries. These make the "multiplier effect" of the base or externally-oriented activities very high in terms of population, since the base activities tend to be higher-income industries and less labour-intensive than the local service activities. In some views, these phenomena are taken as indications of 'over-urbanization'."

Returning to Richardson's typology of city size-distribution models, J. Tinbergen's model is noted; we follow Richardson's outline of this "more general urban hierarchy" model. The model is couched in terms of income, assumes initially that each city only exports its highest order goods, and is applicable to manufacturing industry since it does not depend on central place functions. Tinbergen assumes a closed economy, with H industries, such that $(h=0, 1, \ldots, H)$, where h is the rank of an industry, with $h=0$ for agriculture. Each industry consists of firms of optimal size from the point of view of their scale economies. Taking a product h, demand is satisfied by n_h firms and total demand is $a_h \cdot Y$, where Y is the national income and a_h the demand ratio for h. It is assumed that the number of firms in each industry varies with its rank, i.e. $n_1 > n_2 > n_3 \ldots > n_h$. All income is spent, thus $\Sigma_h a_h = 1$.

There are M orders of centre $(m = 1, 2, \ldots, M)$. In any centre of rank m there will only be industries for which $h \leq m$. The number of firms in each industry in each centre is assumed to be just enough to meet local demand for those industries of a rank lower than the centre's own rank, that is, the industry of rank h in centre of rank m satisfies both the local demand and the demand for that product from centres of lower rank. Exports all down the hierarchy of centres are equally distributed among all of the m centres.

The total income at any stage of the hierarchy can now be calulated, e.g.:

$$Y_0 + Y_1 + Y_2 = \frac{a_0 Y}{1 - (a_1 + a_2)}.$$

Thus total income earned in all centres, Y_m, can be seen as:

$$Y = \Sigma_m Y_m = Y_0 + \Sigma_m \Sigma_h Y_{mh} = \frac{a_0 Y}{1 - \Sigma_h a_h}.$$

The number of centres of each rank, n^m, can be derived on the assumption that there will be only one firm of the highest rank in each centre:

$$n^m = n_h \cdot \frac{a_0}{1 - \Sigma_h a_h}.$$

These two last equations will determine the size of distribution of cities.

Richardson's next category, of stochastic city-size-distribution models, are suggested as incorporating two possible approaches: those which treat the factors influencing urban growth as being proportional to size of city, and those where the city size distribution is seen as a probabilistically arrived-at steady state situation.

The Pareto distribution can be seen as describing the steady-state outcome of a stochastic process, as H. A. Simon (1955) has pointed out in discussing the rank-size rule and similar phenomena in other fields:

"A number of related stochastic processes that lead to a class of highly skewed distributions (the Yule distribution) possessing characteristic properties that distinguish them from such well-known functions as the negative binomial and Fisher's logarithmic series. . . . The probability assumptions we need for the derivations are relatively weak, and of the same order of generality as those commonly employed in deriving other distribution functions—the normal, Poisson, geometric and negative binomial. Hence, the frequency with which the Yule distribution occurs in nature—particularly in social phenomena—should occasion no great surprise."

The Yule distribution is J-shaped, or highly skewed, with a very long upper tail, where the tail can generally be approximated by a function of the form:

$$f(i) = (a/i^k)b^i$$

where a, b, and k are constants, and b is very close to unity. The exponent, k, is greater than 1, and in many cases, including urban populations, is very close to 2, as demonstrated by Zipf (1949). Simon points out that this distribution could be expected "if the growth of population were due solely to the net excess of births over deaths, and if this net growth were proportional to present population. . . . Moreover, it need not hold for each city, but only for the aggregate of cities in each population band. Finally, the (situation) would still be satisfied if there were net migration to or from cities of particular regions, provided the net addition or loss of population of individual cities *within any region* was proportional to city size." The characteristic of allometric growth—growth proportional to size—is stressed here by Simon.

This approach is seen by Richardson as an application of the "law of proportionate effect". Applying the principle to cities, of course, each city need not grow proportionately to its size, so long as, over the whole system of cities, city growth is proportionate to size. Ward (1963) has used the principle in his market opportunities model where the major assumption is that all changes in city size are due to migration and that the main stimulus to migration is that of employment opportunities. The probability of there being employment opportunity in a given city is proportionate to city size.

Richardson next refers to entropy maximization models, but we pass instead to a group of "quasi-economic" models discussed by him. The first of these is by Davis and Swanson, 1972.

This approach combines economic growth theory with a stochastic process so as to generate a lognormal distribution of city sizes. Each city is constrained as to its investment by local savings which are assumed to be a constant proportion of output; Cobb–Douglas production functions are assumed.

The Cobb–Douglas Production Law states that, for large economic aggregations such as a national system, the wage share in the value of the total production tends to remain constant over long time periods and to have a very small variance. Thus the value of output (q_t), in constant prices after having subtracted the value of intermediate purchases, is related to aggregated labour input (L_t), and the value of the aggregate stock of capital (K_t) as follows:

$$q = A(t)L_t^{\alpha} \cdot K_t^{1-\alpha} \cdot \ln \eta_t$$

where t is a time index; $\ln n_t$ is a random error; $A(t)$ is an unspecified function of time, reflecting productivity changes. Generally, $0 < \alpha < 1$, and $dA(t)/dt > 0$. Often, $A(t) = Ae^{\lambda t}$.

Douglas and Cobb noted that if competitive forces in an economy are sufficiently strong, it is reasonable to expect the value of the marginal product of labour to equal its observed nominal wage, or:

$$P_t \cdot \frac{\partial q_t}{\partial L_t} = W_t$$

where P_t = output price at t,
and W_t = wage rate.

Thus:
$$\alpha \cdot P_t \cdot \frac{q_t}{L_t} = W_t$$

or:　　　　　　$\alpha = W_t \cdot L_t / p_t \cdot q_t$ = labour's share at time t.

Least squares regression of q_t on L_t and K_t gave estimates for the USA that were close to historical observations of this parameter.

Taking the Cobb–Douglas relationship as a basis, equilibrium in product markets is obtained through the equality of savings and investment. The differential growth of city labour forces, assuming constant participation rates, changes the distribution of city sizes over time. The supply of labour is perfectly elastic as workers from a hinterland can be drawn in by higher urban wages. Income is distributed according to marginal factor products.

An efficiency progress function, $\varepsilon(t)$, a random variable is specified, and its distribution over all cities can be described in lognormal form. The distribution of city labour force growth rates, $l(t)$, can be expressed as a function of the efficiency progress function:

$$l(t) \approx p\beta + sc^{1-\beta}[\varepsilon(t)]^{\beta}$$

where s is the propensity to save in each city; $\beta = \alpha^{-1}$, where α is capital's share in output; and $c = W(1-\alpha)^{-1}$, where w is the constant real wage. The variable $l(t)$ is a lognormal variable with the threshold parameter equal to $p\beta$.

Other models discussed by Richardson are subject to the disadvantage of being only partial and not producing the kind of distribution of city sizes observed empirically.

In conclusion, in his review of city size distribution models, Richardson himself develops two models which are worthy of a fuller exposition. One is a Markov chain model, and the second utilizes the multiplicative form of the Central Limit Theorem.

En passant, it is also possible to utilize Markov formulation in relation to city growth generally. Multiple regression analysis can be utilized as a means of representation of urban growth as a Markov chain, i.e. a series of linear probabilities. This may be done by setting up an appropriate multiple regression equation for each time period of concern, with urban growth as the dependent variable and various independent variables discovered by relevant analysis. A series of equations can be written, of the form:

$$Yt_0 = at_0 + bt_0\,x_1 + bt_0\,x_2 + bt_0\,x_3 + \cdots + bt_0\,x_n + \beta$$
$$Yt_1 = at_1 + bt_1\,x_1 + bt_1\,x_2 + bt_1\,x_3 + \ldots + bt_1\,x_n + \gamma$$
$$\vdots \qquad\qquad\qquad\qquad\qquad\qquad\qquad\qquad \vdots$$
$$Yt_n = at_n + bt_n\,x_1 + bt_n\,x_2 + bt_n\,x_3 + \ldots + bt_n\,x_n + \phi$$

where N equations represent the N terms of the Markov chain; the first equation representing urban growth at time t_0, the second at t_1, and so on. The Markov chain is thus of the form:

$$Y_n = f(Y_{n-1})t_0; f(Y_{n-2})t_1; f(Y_{n-3})t_2; f(Y_{n-4})t_3 \ldots (N);$$

or, growth at each time (t_i) is a function of growth at the time (t_{i-1}) immediately preceding, back to time (t_0).

Mathieson (1972) reports the initiation of a study of city growth in India, based on this Markov chain approach, and utilizing principal component analysis, as a substitute for multiple regression, in the formulation of a Markov model.

Richardson (1972), advances a number of reasons why the national hierarchy of leading cities: "fulfils other purposes that give justification to the view that it is an instrument for achieving national growth". Firstly, the urban hierarchy is seen as: "an efficient vehicle for transmitting new technology, managerial expertise and general economic functions from the centre of the economy to the periphery". Evidence in support of this contention is given by Herrera (1971), in the case of Brazil: ". . . the instruments for resource transfer may have been able to function efficiently in Brazil because of the existence, in its most important economic centres, of firms with the capability to export technology and know-how to other centres within the country. As a rule, such capacity is found only in firms that have reached a certain size and have evolved to a point where they can initiate new activities, frequently in new lines of production and in new places. The experience of the developed world seems to indicate that such firms can be found only in the largest metropolitan centres . . . if countries seek dynamic national development, they must have urban centres large enough to permit the generation of new activities, and therefore capable of creating and stimulating new development centres."

Herrera goes on to advocate a "new urbanization model", perhaps characterized by: "The still more intensive growth of national centres until they reach a scale sufficient to produce the conditions required for the creation of secondary centres, (possibly 5–6 million inhabitants). Since the smaller countries do not enjoy the conditions required to reach this scale, they will have to associate in subregional compacts or accept the domination of another regional centre."

A further point is that such a distribution of what is also a structural hierarchy of functions involved in industries and commerce is easier to arrange over an urban hierarchy, though obviously without necessarily a one-to-one correspondence between the two hierarchies.

Secondly, Richardson suggests that an urban hierarchy "permits specialisation, division of labour and differentiation in economic function. Market size requirements, infrastructure needs and agglomeration economies differ between firms in the same industry, (many industries have a size distribution of firms similar in form to the distribution of city sizes), and between industries."

Thirdly: "the hierarchical structure of cities dominant within their own regions enables each city to function in a manner appropriate to the size and character of its interland region".

Agricultural Allocation

The allocation of land to agriculture, given certain simplifying assumptions, was regarded by von Thünen, in *Der Isolierte Staat*, 1826, as the outcome of a relationship between the rent per unit of land at a given location and various factors related to the costs and yields from production on that land. Thus rent, L, per unit:

$$L = E(p-a) - E \cdot f \cdot k.$$

where E is the yield per unit of land, p the market price per unit of commodity, a is the production cost per unit of commodity, k is the distance from the land to the market, and f is the transport rate per unit of distance for each commodity.

Martin Katzman (1977) has applied a version of this model to the case of São Paulo State in Brazil (Fig. 3.13). As crops with a higher value per unit of weight and lesser direct production costs per unit areas, both relative to marketing costs, have more distant commercial limits of cultivation, so crops fetching low prices, having high yields, and which are costly to market, will be produced closer to the market. Rents will be highest closest to the market and lowest further out, i.e. at the agricultural frontier, as demonstrated by the rent bid curves. In the case of São Paulo—the biggest food market in Latin America—perishable food, perhaps including bulky crops like sugar, will be grown closest to the city, with coffee further out, and high value crops like cattle, rice, and beans furthest away; beyond will be subsistence peasant

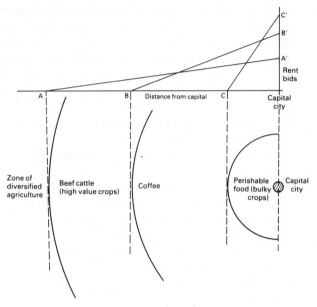

Fɪɢ. 3.13. The spatial structure of São Paulo agriculture as determined by rent-bid gradients (Katzman, 1977).

farming. Similar cases of the applicability still of von Thünen's theory to developing countries are said to be known in India, Ghana, and Nigeria (Henshall, 1967).

Urban land rent theory might be derived from similar argument, no doubt, as will be seen later.

City Locations: The Spatial Distribution of Cities

City size distribution theory, or the theory of the urban hierarchy, is non-spatial in nature. There is also a spatial hierarchy, an arrangement of cities and settlements in physical spatial relationship to one another, and there is no necessary symmetry between the two aspects of the urban hierarchy. It is the intention of central place theory to attempt an explanation of both aspects of the hierarchic structure of settlement patterns, but this attempt is limited by its deliberate exclusion of certain important urban functions.

Central place theory is now so well known that a complete exposition of it is by no means necessary (Baskin, 1966; Berry and Pred, 1961, 1965).

Christaller's aim was to "explain the size, number and distribution of towns", in the belief that some underlying principle could be demonstrated. The main aspects of his thesis are:

(1) That the basic function of a city is to be a central place providing goods and services for an area around it. Christaller used the term: "central place" because, in his view, such a service place will locate at the centre of the minimum aggregate travel of the area served: such a position should optimize its maximum profit area.

(2) A place may be central to a greater or smaller service area, introducing a concept of "order" of place.

(3) A place of higher "order" will offer more services and will require a larger tributary area and population in order to be able to do so: such higher order centres will then be more widely spaced than places of lower order.

(4) Lower order services will be those for which consumers will not wish to travel very far. Higher order centres will also tend to supply lower order goods to smaller areas around them, whilst still exercising their higher order functions.

(5) Thus a hierarchy of service centres ensues, with a nesting of lower order trade areas within higher order trade areas, also with a hierarchy of routes joining the centres.

(6) Christaller showed specific instances based on certain assumptions limiting population distributions, with hexagonal-shaped market areas organized in nesting by threes, fours, and sevens.

It is possible to organize a hierarchy of settlements in a number of different ways, i.e. with different locational patterns of the central places and their trade area boundaries. In Christaller's exposition, these patterns are made up of triangular spatial elements composing into hexagonal trade areas. The basic Christaller model is that which gives the maximum number of central places, so as to minimize movement by the consumers of goods and services from these central places. The number of places at a given level in the hierarchy served at the next higher level by a central place is frequently termed the K-value, and it can be shown that this basic movement-minimization model is where $K = 3$, i.e. a nesting pattern by a rule of threes. Other K-values are possible, of course, as shown by Lösch (1954), e.g. $K = 3, 4, 7, 9, 12, 13, 16, 19, 21$ etc.; these patterns are obtained by varying the orientation of the hexagonal trade areas in relation to the pattern of settlements, and also the size of the hexagons. If the various trade area networks feasible, from $K = 3$ to $K = 25$, are superimposed on one another so that they all have the same central point, this central point, so Lösch argued, will be the site of a metropolis, the highest order of central place. By a rotation of these networks about this central place, a pattern can be derived having sectors with many, and sectors with few, settlements; this pattern was termed an "economic landscape" by Lösch, a pattern in which the aggregate distance between all places is minimized and the maximum number of supplies can be had locally, i.e. at the nearest central place.

Various empirical studies have been carried out to try to determine whether the Christaller/Lösch theory is valid in reality, and it seems true to say that some regularities of this kind are detectable, but the divergences from the regular model are many. One important finding is that population density declines logarithmically with distance from a central metropolis, thus service areas should be smaller closer to the metropolis and increase in size as distance from it increases: Isard (1956) has suggested graphically a pattern of this kind. The metropolis itself, of course, is a major service area of (relatively) small extent but very high density. Indeed, in highly urbanized regions the overwhelming fact is that the metropolis serves itself, and although retaining its central place functions for a wider area, the number of interactions and their density renders the simplicity of central place theory somewhat inadequate as a basis for explanation: the problem becomes one of intra-urban theory. However, central place theory is open to the objection that it does not, and cannot, account for all the functional activities and interrelationships, of a system of cities (cf. Pred, 1969).

As Parr (1978) points out, though, central-place theory is one of the few macrotheories of the location of economic activity, and: "provides a framework for examining the simultaneous or sequential location of a particular set of economic activities, and the patterns of urbanization to which this gives rise", though having certain serious weaknesses. The chief weakness, of course, is that the theory relates only to spatially-dispersed activity, e.g. the provision of sales services from a central point or points to a market area or areas. Any spatially concentrated activities, such as secondary sector manufacture, must be explained by some other theory.

Berry and Garrison (1958), using only the concepts of threshold and range of a good, or dimensions of a trade area under competition, have showed how a hierarchy can result without limiting restrictions on the distribution of population and purchasing power. However, the concepts of threshold and range in themselves are hierarchical and a degree of tautology cannot be avoided.

Hoover (1955), in discussing a paper by Vining (1955), made several trenchant criticisms of Christaller's theory. He asserts that this theory "automatically yields a series of city tributary areas arranged according to the rank-size rule". The Christaller system can also be built up on a square, not hexagonal plan, with each class of city four times as numerous as the preceding one—and also with the rank-size rule applying. Also, as Hoover points out, the rank-size relationship implicit in the Christaller model is a relationship between the rank and size of the *city's tributary area*, and hence tributary population, and *not* the population of the central city. Hoover suggested the proposition that the population of cities tends to be directly proportional to their maximum hinterlands, bearing in mind the "overlap" of hinterlands at the different service order levels mentioned, and cites Rutledge Vining's findings that population density tapers off logarithmically with distance from urban centres. A logarithmic curve also appears to cover the frequency distribution of the lengths of haul of goods to and from given centres.

Central place models assume generally that all centres within the physical space considered supply different functions to market areas of different sizes: a centre of level m provides functions 1 to m to market areas 1 to m, respectively, with a successively inclusive hierarchy, i.e. a centre of level 5 supplies functions at level 5 to the largest area available at that level; it will also supply level 4 functions to an area of lesser extent; level 3 functions to a lesser area and so on. (These lesser level service areas are also served in part by lesser level centres, of course.) A functional hierarchy thus exists as in the exposition by Christaller. However, Christaller's model entails a hierarchy invariant value for K: K being the "nesting factor", which demonstrates the equivalent number of service areas of level $(m-1)$ which are contained within a market area of level m $(m>1)$. As Parr (1978) has shown, the K-value need not be invariant hierarchically, i.e. K may vary over the whole system, and thus Parr's model is a general one, whereas Christaller's is not. Parr's model also may produce square service areas as Hoover had suggested. What Parr terms the "span of control", i.e. the number of centres of a lesser order dominated by the centre of the next higher order, is equal to Christaller's "nesting" factor, K, minus one, i.e. $K = S + 1$. This span of control, S, is constant at all levels in the hierarchy, as noted, in Christaller's model, but is variable in the Parr model, thus the Parr model qualifies as more general: this appears to be borne out by an application to Lower Austria made by Parr, whereas the Christaller alternatives produce widely disparate fits to that data.

Service Centres in Developing Countries

It seems probable that present day service centres, or "central places" originated as temporal and mobile arrangements, provided by itinerant tradesmen or pedlars and periodic markets or fairs. Indeed, in many countries, e.g. in Africa, this is still the case (Bohannon and Dalton, 1962), whilst in countries where fixed provision is widespread, weekly or twice-weekly markets are still to be found, not only for the supply of perishable goods but for non-perishable goods also.

J. H. Stine (1962) has developed an interesting explanation of the periodic market system of Korea, where there is a general system of markets meeting every five days, on a rotational basis, with the market traders moving round a well-defined circuit. He uses two concepts, of maximum and minimum range of commodities. The maximum range is the distance at which the marginal consumer for a particular commodity is located from the centre of service for that commodity. In the circumstances of no competition and a countryside of homogeneous population, income and access, the maximum range would be characterized as the radius of a circle within which all consumers of some of the commodity will lie. The minimum range relates to the profit level of the firm supplying the commodity: the radius of a circle enclosing a total demand just large enough to secure the profitable operation of the firm. When the maximum range is greater than or equal to the minimum range, the firm can survive and may be fixed in position relative to a continuing demand. When the maximum range is less than the minimum range, either the firm will not survive, or the firm will move from place to place. In the latter case the firm will be seeking to extend the maximum range by moving from place to place, until the marginal cost of operating is at least offset by the marginal revenue.* A greater difference between the maximum and the minimum range, with the maximum being less than the minimum, will result in more locational moves.

Income density in Korea has been low, although population density is not: this tends to produce a larger minimum range. A short maximum range is also evident as foot travel is slow and means a high opportunity cost in lost time on farms. These factors appear to support a mobile system of provision of facilities through markets, rather than the establishment of fixed service centres, such as might occur if transport costs fell and income levels rose. Competition will also tend to occur on a temporal, as well as a spatial basis: an agglomeration of competing firms on market days, rather than a series of temporally-independent single mobile traders, i.e. Hotelling's principle at work in time as well as space.

As Boesch (1952) has pointed out, it is the quality, i.e. the variety and level, of services available in a given area which defines the degree of "centrality" of the place serving it, whilst the quantity of services is generally only a function of the number of people served. In a developing country it is likely that both the quality and quantity of services offered by the service centre function of towns or cities will vary widely: the system of service centre functions, like the system of cities which houses them, is likely to be incomplete in terms of the provision offered by more mature city-systems. Just as the rank-size structure of cities in a developing country may display primacy in terms of city population sizes, i.e. an "over-large" principal city or metropolis and a lack of certain sizes of city at other levels in the hierarchy, so the services provided by those cities are unlikely to approximate to the hierarchy of service centres postulated by central place theory. The connection is obvious, especially in a slowly-industrializing country where the size of cities as yet owes little to the needs of manufacturing industry.

Two studies of service centres in West Africa are relevant to the discussion: the first by Grove and Huszar (1964), the second by Josephine Abiodun (1967). The former study, of Ghana, has been open to some methodological objections, but its authors claim to distinguish five levels of a national service centre hierarchy from its results. They suggest that "it is uneven development rather than underdevelopment that causes deviations from a clearer pattern of

---

* This appears to be a similar explanation to that of the application of Charnov's Marginal Value Theorem, at p. 298.

hierarchy." Mrs Abiodun's study, of south western Nigeria, is more comprehensive and uses component analysis, though still requiring a degree of subjective judgement of the relative importance of the various service functions at an early stage. A clear hierarchy of service centres in Ijebu Province is demonstrated to exist, closely following the Christaller hierarchy for $K = 3$, but only so far as the upper four levels of the hierarchy is concerned. It appears that the lower levels of the hierarchy are absent: the villages or hamlets which might have been the locus of the appropriate services, in fact not providing any of these functions (see Table 3.14 and Fig. 3.15).

TABLE 3.14. *Number of Settlements in Regional System when K = 3*

Size-class of place	Theoretical number of places	Actual number of places Nuremberg (Christaller)*	Actual number of places Ijebu Province, Nigeria
0	486	462	—
1	162	105	—
2	54	60	36
3	18	23	25
4	6	10	10
5	2	2	2
6	1	1	1

* W. Christaller, op. cit., p. 199; also in Lösch, op. cit. (Abiodun, 1967).

Berry and Barnum's Model

This model (1962) was an attempt to put central place theory on a firmer footing theoretically, rather than to begin with empirical evidence. The model stated that the population of a centre showed a log-linear pattern of association with the number of different central functions provided by that centre; the number of functions having been shown in previous work to be an accurate index of the "centrality" of that place. For each new function added, the population would increase by a constant percentage of its previous size, the relationship being log-linear. The model also held that the number of units providing functions would increase by a constant percentage of the previous total for each central function added. A further aspect implied a maximum distance which consumers would travel to a centre of any particular size, i.e. the "range of a good". The trade area population was a function of densities, and the size of centre, so that the trade area would increase as the population of centres increases exponentially; and increases in the total population served will depend upon densities and the exponential increase in urban population. Three empirically-derived inequalities included were held to identify discontinuities arising from the existence of an urban hierarchy; the parameter values were determined by a principal components analysis of data relating to southwest Iowa, in the United States of America.

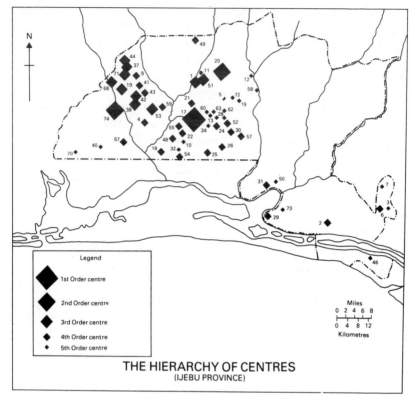

FIG. 3.15. The hierarchy of centres, Ijebu (Abiodun, 1967).

The Distribution of Economic Activity

Theories of urban growth or change have been approached in a number of ways, dependent firstly upon how "growth" is defined or measured. Thus if growth is defined demographically, i.e. simply as a measure of population change, then a judicious addition of cohort-survival population modelling plus some kind of a migration model would provide a basis. However, such an approach does not deal with the *causes* of change, but involves a number of implicit assumptions as to the continuation of present forces. Such forces may be social, but inevitably also are economic, and it might be argued that urban change is primarily the result of economic activity.

Attempts to explain the functioning and growth of urban areas have largely and traditionally proceeded either by way of central place theory or via economic or export base theory, though neither is satisfactory by itself.

Central place theory sees an urban area as essentially a supplier of goods and services to a surrounding region, so that the population and spending power of the area served determine the size and rate of change of the central place. Export base theory, in contrast, sees the size of economic activity in a town which supplies goods anywhere outside itself as being the major determinant; it recognizes urban services industries which cater solely for its own residents, but sees them as entirely related to the base or export sector of the urban economy. So, in practice, the application of economic base theory requires each industrial sector, and perhaps even the output of each firm within a sector, to be allocated a "basic" or "non-basic" (i.e. "service") label accordingly as its markets are "export" (i.e. outside the community in which the industry is located), or "local" (i.e. inside the community)—and economic change is regarded as being dependent upon the former, not the latter, a "multiplier effect"* taking place and creating service jobs from the addition of new basic jobs, or "local" output from "export" output.

It is obvious that in reality things are more complicated than either of these two theories suggest, though each contains some particles of an explanation of urban existence. An improvement on the base theory approach is provided by Czamanski (1964), though his model is simplistic still. There are three sectors in his economy instead of two: geographically-oriented or mobile industries, complementary industries which serve other industries in the same city, and urban-oriented industries which serve the city in which they are located.

Total population is thus expressible as a function of employment in geographically-oriented industry. But this is still a static view of urban relationships.

This kind of simultaneous-equation approach is valuable, however, and has been foreshadowed in the treatment elsewhere of migration models. In fact, the logical advance in theoretical approach—assuming a dynamic approach to dynamic phenomena—would be towards systems of equations which are not only simultaneous but also of difference or differential form. In theory, at least, it would be possible to set up a comprehensive model in this way, which would deal with "everything".

Paelinck (1972) has taken the simple basic/non-basic employment relationships and developed a dynamic model as follows:

If P is total population;
  A is total active population;
  E_i are the basic urban activities;
  E_s are the service activities;
  E is the total employment;

then the following can be defined:

$$\Delta' E_{i,t+1} = \alpha(A_t - E_t) + \alpha^* E_{i,t}$$
$$\Delta' E_{s,t+1} = \beta(\beta^* P_t - E_{s,t}) + \beta^{**} E_{s,t}$$
$$\Delta' A_{t+1} = \gamma \Delta' P_{t+1} + \gamma^*(E_t - A_t)$$
$$\Delta' P_{t+1} = \delta(E_t - A_t) + \delta^* P_t$$
$$E = E_i + E_s.$$

---

* Oscar Lange: "A multiplier is the marginal effect of a change in one (economic) variable upon another variable of which the first one is a component."

According to Paelinck, these equations describe, respectively, how basic activities are attracted by the available manpower; how employment in service industries tends progressively to an equilibrium level $(\beta^* P_t)$; how active population is generated as a function of total population and of the pressure resulting from excess demand for manpower; how population is attracted towards the city; and finally an accounting identity for total employment. A solution of this equation system is demonstrated using matrix notation; however for larger systems of equations a simulation approach becomes more suitable. [N.B. In general linear systems of equations are to be preferred in such models, being capable of solution whereas non-linear systems are not; but simulation avoids a number of problems that may arise even with linear systems.]

The Location of Industry

Industrial location theories have been of several kinds: those which see the issues as one of finding the place of least cost, those which are concerned with finding the location which commands the largest market, and those which seek the point of maximum profitability. An example is Alfred Weber's model of 1909, which states that industries will locate at points of least cost in relation to transport, the provision of labour, and factors of agglomeration. However, as in all such situations, the present location of industry, or future industrial locations, can be explained only against a background of what is there already, and in terms of factors operating at the present or future relevant time. As with the theories of von Thünen, Christaller, or Lösch, the assumptions necessary as a basis for these models are much at odds with real world cases: their explanatory power is much modified by history, topography, economics, and cultural phenomena.

The inadequacy of central place theory as a complete explanation of city systems has been mentioned, but it does provide, of course, a framework within which the location of essentially local market-oriented industries could be explained. The construction, printing and publishing, and food-processing industries—all local market-related—can be regarded as generally located in terms of the Christaller/Lösch hierarchy or urban sizes. However, as different industries have different market size thresholds, and thus require different numbers of plants of differing sizes to cover regional and national markets, some kind of a hierarchy of manufacturing industry plants exists which may be compatible with—though not explained by—the city rank-size concept. Larger industrial plants with larger market requirements may tend to occur in—or near to—larger centres of population due to market accessibility, but also owing to advantages of agglomeration; linkage patterns, and historical factors. Lösch's "city rich" sectors, in fact, provide a welcome milieu for industrial enterprise, by reason of the combined larger market that is provided, the high accessibility of such zones, and the presence of other, complementary, industries and services.

In a developing country, the location of manufacturing industry may depend to a large degree on the existence of the principle inputs of labour and energy, and on the state of the transport system. Labour, as has been seen, may have to migrate to areas of economic opportunity: and that labour may be also the main market; food availability is important, too, in the industrial locality.

Agglomeration Effects

Isard (1956), along with other commentators on "Location and Space Economy", classifies location factors as belonging to three, possibly overlapping, groups. The first group includes transport costs and certain transfer costs which tend to vary regularly with distance from given reference points. The second group of factors includes "the several costs associated with labour, power, water, taxes, insurance, interest (as payment for the services of capital), climate, topography, social and political milieu, and a number of other items." The costs of these factors may be seen as varying independently of both distance and direction. The third group comprises those factors giving rise to agglomeration and deglomeration economies. In the former economies might be included those of scale, localization and urbanization; in the latter diseconomies, those within a firm going beyond its natural scale of operating rises in rents and service costs associated with congestion, and food supply costs as urban size makes adverse location changes in contributory agricultural areas.

Agglomeration effects, though having a place in the economic theory of industrial location, have tended to lack a more specific crystallization in quantitative form. Richardson (1974), however, has provided an interesting, if still theoretical, model in the form of agglomeration potential, intended to be a generalization of the concept of income potential:

The familiar expression for population potential may be written:

$$iV_j = I_{ij}/P_i = K \cdot P_j \cdot d_{ij}^{-\beta}$$

where iV_j is the potential of j on i; I_{ij} is the interaction between i and j; P_i, P_j are the populations respectively at i and j (or maybe some other mass variable); d_{ij} is the distance between i and j; K and β are parameters. Normally, the potential at any i of all js is measured by aggregation, and if income, Y, is substituted for population, then income potential may be written as:

$$iV = K \cdot \Sigma_j(Y_j \cdot d_{ij}^{-\beta}).$$

Such potentials may be mapped as lines of equal income potential. Figure 3.19 shows an example of the technique applied to the State of Saõ Paulo, Brazil, but using value added, rather than income, as a measure of potential; the high potentials near the metropolis of São Paulo are noteworthy. As Richardson

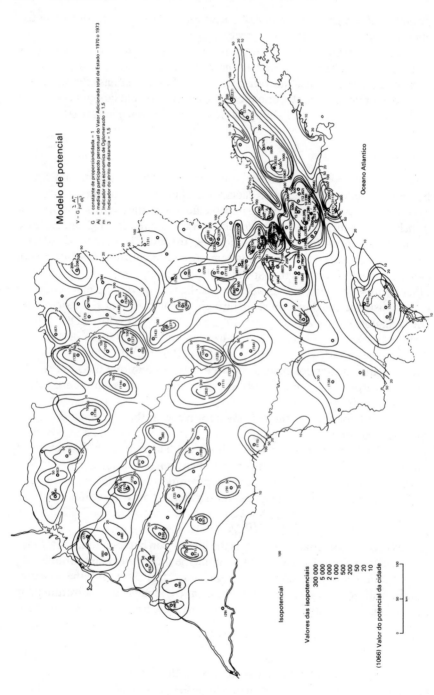

Modelo de potencial

$$V = G \sum_{j=1}^{n} \frac{A_j^m}{d_{ij}^\lambda}$$

G = constante de proporcionalidade = 1
A_j = média da participação percentual do Valor Adicionada total da Estado − 1970 o 1973
m = indicador das economias de Oglomeração = 1,5
λ = indicador do atrito da distância = 1,5

Isopotencial ⌐100

Valores das isopotenciais
300 000
5 000
2 000
1 000
500
200
50
20
10

(1066) Valor do potencial da cidade

Oceano Atlantico

Fig. 3.16. Modelo de potencial, São Paulo State, Brazil (Estado do São Paulo).

points out, the formation of a potential surface of this kind tends to obscure the effect of any particular place, and, instead, he introduces a new term, agglomeration potential of a city or place (Z), where the numerator in the agglomeration potential of a city may be represented not solely by its population but also by other variables, each of which implies one particular economy or diseconomy. He regards agglomeration pull as essentially multidimensional and should include more than income or population. Other formulations of the gravity model have implied that physical distance is only a surrogate for other possible "distance" measures, e.g. travel costs, time, and frequency, modal alternatives, or intervening opportunities, or "social distance" variables; a parallel approach might be used to specify a disaggregation of the spatial aspects of agglomeration potential.

However, unless all the economies or diseconomies are measurable in monetary units, the resulting agglomeration potential will not be measurable in money units per mile, as with income potential.

Richardson presents both a multiplicative agglomeration potential function and an additive function; the former is

$$iZ_j = f(\Pi_n A_n^j / \Pi_x d_{ijx})$$

and the latter:

$$iZ_j = f(\Sigma_n A_n^j / \Sigma_x d_{ijx}).$$

There are advantages, and problems, involved in using either form of the model, which are set out by Richardson. One point in favour of the multiplicative version is that it will tend to be compatible with a lognormal city size distribution; but, on balance, the additive form may be preferred.

Intra-Urban Theory

Von Thünen's argument as to the allocation of land to various kinds of agricultural activity can be applied equally well to other uses of land within urban areas. Urban site rentals, like farm land rentals, can be seen as being related to market accessibility: the land most accessible to the market for the "production" of a given use will have the highest rental. The underlying assumption here is that higher rents will be offered for savings in transport costs, thus those uses which can command a bigger market by having a highly accessible location will come to be located at those most accessible points by reason of their ability to pay the higher rentals which those locations can command. In theory, cities are circular in plan form, and the centre of a circle is a point, which by definition has no area. Thus, the normally most accessible point in a theoretical city, its geometrical centre, is of very limited area and yet commands the highest rental. This results in the highest capitalized value of land rental at the centre, and also in attempts to enlarge the area of floor space at this most central location so as to reduce the unit area cost of location by the tenant on the one hand, and to increase the overall floor area for which higher rental can be asked by the landlord, on the other hand. Hence central locations will tend to be more densely built up: taller buildings of more site coverage.

Thus, as Haig (1926), Turvey (1957), and many others have expounded, site rental patterns, land value patterns, land use patterns, building bulk and height in cities all can be explained by a simple economic relationship between location, rental, and accessibility—not forgetting that "special accessibility" in which proximity to complementary or like uses (cf. Hotelling) must be added to general "market" accessibility. However, accessibility patterns have changed, and cities are not always, or necessarily, circular in plan, and so the flattened cone shape of a city skyline, especially in its innermost parts, is often modified, though still being demonstrated in principle. Twentieth-century cities often exhibit a kind of "saw-tooth" pattern of contrasting high and lower building blocks, even in their central areas, and such a pattern can be seen as a very direct expression of urban land values: of values actually realized with lags in the development/redevelopment process, that is, rather than poten-tially-realizable values. Cities in developing countries often exhibit consider-able contrasts in this respect, with older, smaller, even domestic buildings often cheek by jowl with very tall and most modern structures, due to time-lags in potential new rents and site values being realized, in some cases also to over-anticipation of market increases.

Change in accessibility patterns will modify the patterns of use, building, market value, and so on, though with lags due to the nature of building investment and construction. The historical centres of many older, now-large cities, may be no longer highly accessible, due to congestion, or to investment in transport facilities elsewhere. An example in a relatively modern city is in Sydney, Australia, where the Central Railway Station originally provided the focus for the commercial city centre some way inland from Sydney Cove: the streets north of the station towards the water front being culs-de-sac. However, the opening of the Harbour Bridge, carrying both rail and road, as well as the general growth of road and cross-harbour transport, made the areas and streets nearer to Sydney Cove more generally accessible to the growing city on both sides of Sydney Harbour, resulting in a commercial migration northwards, away from Central Station. The main retail and office areas of the city are now rather nearer to Sydney Cove than to Central Station, and, indeed, office uses now also have leaped the Harbour and are well established in North Sydney. The shifts of location of retail shopping areas to suburban or ex-urban areas in North America, and to some extent in Western Europe, are well known: that is to areas more accessible, with widespread car ownership, to appropriate sectors of the population, than their previous traditional and now congested city centre locations. Similar shifts within cities are also known, and the rise of the Avenida Paulista in São Paulo as a very good address for new offices and banks may be due to the increasing congestion of the old city centre. Likewise, in Hong Kong there is a gradual overtaking of Victoria, on Hong Kong Island, by Tsimshatsui and Nathan Road generally, in Kowloon across the Harbour, as more people now live in Kowloon and the New Territories; and this despite the construction of the cross-harbour tunnel.

However, in those very many cities in developing countries of moderate size, such effects will be less marked as people rely more on foot, bicycle, and bus transport, and private car ownership is severely limited. In the city of Jeddah, in Saudi Arabia (current population 1 + million), walking is still an important means of communication in the old city (Al Balad): the *hara* of Hal Yamen and Ascham, (close to the city centre), in 1978, produced 81,643 daily person trips, 22,379 of them, or 27% being on foot. However, Jeddah is atypical also in now having very high rates of car ownership and use. The data appended (Table 3.17) for Jeonju, a Korean city of c. 350,000 population is probably representative, not only of many Korean towns, but also of many other moderate-income developing country situations.

TABLE 3.17. *Travel Characteristics in Jeonju City, Korea, 1978*

Modal split: daily journeys by:		%
Foot*	252,900	44.5
Bicycle	40,851	7.2
Motor cycle	3,102	0.5
City bus	220,595	38.8
Taxi	11,726	2.1
Private car	6,809	1.2
Company and school bus	18,686	3.3
Train	3,102	0.5
Other	10,818	1.9
Total journeys	568,589	100

(* average walk was 770 metres in length.)

Travel purpose: daily journeys for:		%
School	166,371	30.8
Commuting*	55,173	10.3
Shopping	22,319	4.1
Business*	20,676	3.8
Social	12,173	2.3
Return home (work?)*	233,506	43.1
Others	30,144	5.6
	540,362	

* The exact descriptions of these purposes is not clear.
Journeys per day by mode: 1.34 per person.
Journeys per day by purpose: 1.41 per person.
Source: City of Jeonju Plan, 1980, (in Korean), Korea Research Institute for Human Settlements, Seoul.

Intra-Urban Theory and Models

Intra-urban growth

It has been known for a long time (e.g. since Levasseur, 1889), that population within a large urban area tends to be distributed according to a decaying exponential function. More recently, Clark (1951) has done empirical work to support this contention by using data for major cities of the world—many of them old, long-founded cities in Western countries, though, for example, Rangoon in 1931 was included amongst his examples, as well as the major Australian cities, including Brisbane in both 1901 and 1947. The relationship involved is normally expressed as:

$$D_d = D_0 \cdot e^{-bd}$$

where d is distance from the centre of the city (0) and D is the density of resident population. Normally, the function is plotted as a log-linear relationship:

$$\log_e D_d = \log_e D_0 - bd.$$

Later work by Stewart and Warntz (1958, 1968) supports Clark's thesis. More recently, Newling (1969) has offered a quadratic exponential equation as giving a better fit with observed data, as it allows for the "density crater"* at the centre of the city:

$$D_d = D_0 \cdot e^{bd - cd^2}$$

where D_d and D_0 are as before (D_0 extrapolated to centre), b is the instantaneous rate of change in density with distance, and e is the instantaneous negative rate of change in density with the square of the distance. Thus:

$$\log_e D_d = \log_e D_0 + bd - cd^2$$

Niedercorn (1971) formulates an equation for deriving urban land rent as:

$$r(x) = r(0) \cdot e^{-(b/y)x}$$

where $r(0)$, $r(x)$ are rents at the city centre and x miles out; b is the rent curve gradient; y is a Cobb–Douglas type exponent of the variable quantity of land used at a distance x, equal to the percentage of change in rent when the quantity of land is increased by 1%. As $(-b/y)$ is a constant, this, in effect, is the negative exponential equation again.

Richardson's version is:

$$d_0 = A^* \cdot b_t^c$$

where d_0 is the density at the centre of the city; (A^*) and b stand for initial

---

* Fewer people live in city centres, as commerce can more usually afford to pay the higher rents required for the most accessible position.

conditions of population size and gradient slope; and c represents the relative growth rates of population and income:

$$A^* = N_0 \cdot b_0/2$$

$$c = e^{(N-y)t}$$

where N is the population growth rate; y is the income growth rate, t is the time period. The model involves the assumption that income increases at a constant rate, y, and that it is related to a constant decline of the gradient, b—assumptions which, as Galbinski (1978) points out, limit the potential use of the model in developing countries, where it is often held that the average household income increases at a lesser rate than the growth of urban population (Sovani, 1975; Fishlow, 1972).

In an interesting analysis of two Brazilian cities, Galbinski (1978) draws samples from Recife and São Paulo, using a random sampling procedure for the 1970 Census tracts used, rather than taking the whole of a given annulus and averaging its population over its whole area. Seven different functions were tested, and it was found that the negative quadratic exponential function gave the best fit for Recife-Olinda and also for São Paulo. The curves for the two cities, however, are different: in Recife a density crater is shown and the density approaches zero at 16 kilometres from the city centre; in São Paulo there was no "crater" and the curve does not approach zero: Recife is a traditional, single-centred city, whereas São Paulo is now a very large (c. 12 million), sprawling industrial conurbation. Both cities had a smaller density gradient at 1970 than any of the cities analysed by Clark, and with higher densities at the centre of the city; but particular differences in the density profiles, after factor analysis, were held to be due largely to employment distribution differences: concentrated in the city centre in Recife, and occurring in several major sectors of the city in São Paulo. Income distribution differences were also thought to affect the profiles.

Studies of the tendency of cities in developed countries to decentralize or suburbanize have received mention, but similar studies of cities in developing countries are rarer, as has been noted in relation to Galbinski's work. However, data on changes in Korean cities have been provided by Mills and Song (1979), in their comprehensive study on urbanization in the Republic of Korea. The type of relationship utilized by Mills and Song is log-linear:

$$g_i^* = a_0^* + a_1^* \log P_i + a_2^* \log Y_i$$

where g_i^* is the density gradient of the ith city when it has adjusted to the values of the independent variables; $\log P_i$ is the natural logarithm of population of the urban area; and $\log Y_i$ is the natural log of the per capita income; a_i^* are parameters to be estimated. a_1^*, for example, represents the effect of a given percentage change in population on the density gradient.

The hypothesis involved here is that the population density gradient will flatten as the urban population grows and as income per capita increases. This change in gradient will occur only after a time lag which may be considerable: thus change is likely to be towards a new equilibrium situation, but not reaching that equilibrium before it has shifted to another sought-for value. Thus g^* is not detectable from observed data, although g (actual density gradient) is measurable. However, the assumption that g will adjust each year by an amount that covers a certain fraction of the difference between g and g^* is defensible:

$$g_i = g_{i-1} + \lambda(g_i^* - g_{i-1}) = \lambda g_i^* + (1 - \lambda)g_{i-1}$$

where g_i, g_i^* are as previously, and g_{i-1} is the density gradient at some earlier time; λ is the fraction of difference between g_i^* and g_{i-1} by which g_i is assumed to adjust between observations.

We can therefore write, from the above:

$$g_i = a_0 + a_i \log P_i + a_2 \log Y_i + (1 - \lambda)g_{i-1}$$

thus eliminating the variable g_i^* which cannot be observed. Also $a_j = \lambda a_j^*$.

For the period 1970–1973 for 12 Korean cities, the estimated equation was:

$$g_i = 0.1075 - 0.0223 \log P_i + 0.00097 \log Y_i + 0.9194 \, g_{i-1i} \quad (R^2 = 0.994).$$

Surprisingly, the coefficient of $\log Y_i$ is positive, indicating that the density function becomes steeper as income increases; this is contrary to experience elsewhere. However, a component of such a situation is a low income elasticity of demand for housing, which is certainly a characteristic of the Korean housing situation.

From this estimation, $\lambda = 0.0806$, i.e. an adjustment of about 8% between successive (3 year) observations, or about 2.7% adjustment in g_i annually. The equation for g_i^* can now be written as:

$$g_i^* = 1.334 - 0.277 \log P_i + 0.120 \log Y_i.$$

Both population and income have grown rapidly in Korean cities as economic growth has occurred rapidly and brought increasing urbanization; thus Korean cities are more centralized and are likely to decentralize over a longish period of time. For example, Suwon in Kyonggi province, south of Seoul, was calculated by Mills and Song to have an equilibrium gradient only about half of its 1973 actual density gradient.

Mills and Song found also that land value gradients in four Korean cities (Seoul, Pusan, Daegu and Suwon) were very close to the corresponding density gradients, or slightly less than them. Land value gradients also showed the same propensity to decline over time as was found with population density gradients. Land values near the centres of Korean cities have risen less than values on the outskirts, and land values near the centre of Seoul seem to have risen less than values near the centres of smaller cities; in fact, as elsewhere, cities decentralize as they grow larger, with accessibility improving: this involves suburban densities and land values also rising, relative to those near city centres.

Insofar as actual densities were concerned, 35 cities of Korea had an average density at 1974 of 3700 person/km^2, or more than ten times the country's average population density of 350 persons/km^2. Mills and Song (op. cit.) quote the following overall data for the density configuration of Seoul (1970):

TABLE 3.18.

	Distance from centre			
	0–20 km	20–40 km	40–70 km	Total
Population (1000s)	6,053	1,571	1,270	8,894
Area (km^2)	1,422	3,501	6,648	11,571
Density (persons/km^2)	4,256	449	191	769

The population density of three of the central *Ku* (districts) of Seoul in 1973 was nearly 24,000 persons/km^2, or almost as high as Manhattan, New York, in 1963, and higher than Tokyo.

Systems of Cities

The review of the various part theories and specific models which have been considered in this chapter is necessarily superficial when compared to the literature already available and the intellectual effort which it represents. Much of that effort, though, has been expanded on attempts to explain phenomena which, in terms of the overall dynamics of cities, must be seen as only partial behaviour. Much of the effort, too, is directed at explaining European-style cities, and does not deal with the distinctive cases of cities in developing countries. In outline, the process by which cities evolve, as systems, and by which systems of several cities develop, can be stated quite simply: the difficulties lie in the more exact expression of the relationships involved.

Thus: population change is a primary force.

Economic activity: primary, secondary, tertiary, becomes fundamental in channelling and locating enterprises, thus influencing population location.

The particular location and clustering of population is influenced by socio-cultural considerations, as well as economics.

The secondary processes of land development give physical form and subsequently induce inertia in urban change.

The ecological backcloth of the rural areas must remain to underpin the city systems with support by way of food, water, and basic resources.

The number of systems, or subsystems involved is large, and thus analytical attempts to replicate, by way of models, all such subsystems, represent a big task. Approaches via simulation may well be more fruitful, certainly more expeditious, and for this reason systems dynamics simulation models of urban and regional systems figure in later discussion.

4. The Plural Society, the Dual Economy, and the Two Circuits

J. S. Furnival (1942) seems to have been the first to use the term "plural society", though then mainly in regard to activities in the economic sphere. More recently, Benedict (1961) has defined the term more closely in a social context:

"When we use the term 'plural society', we presuppose not only a number of different sections or communities, but also some way in which they fit together to make a society. We look both for criteria and activities which separate one section of society from another, and for activities in which there is contact between communities."

The idea of duality of the economies of developing countries, as distinguished from their societies *per se*, seems to have begun with Boeke's work in 1953, and was subsequently the basis for the well-known papers by W. A. Lewis on "Development with Unlimited Supplies of Labour" (1954 and 1958). In introducing his study of dualistic economic theory, derived from a first-hand study of Indonesia, Boeke says:

"It is possible to characterize a society, in the economic sense, by the social spirit, the organizational forms, and the technique dominating it. These three aspects are interdependent and in this connection typify a society. . . . It is not necessary that a society be exclusively dominated by one social system. Where, on the contrary, simultaneously two or more social systems appear, clearly distinct the one from the other, and each dominate a part of the society, there we have to do with a dual or plural society. It is however, advisable to qualify the term dual society by reserving it for societies showing a distinct cleavage of two synchronic and full grown social styles which in the normal, historical evolution of homogeneous societies are separated from each other by transitional forms . . . and which there do not coincide as contemporary dominating features."

Boeke continues to make the point that, in a dual society, one of the two prevailing systems, in fact always the most advanced, he maintains, will have been imported from abroad, and will have been able to exist in the new environment, but without being able to oust or assimilate the indigenous system. A frequent form of dualism is where western capitalism has been imported and has penetrated, but been unable to supplant a pre-capitalistic agrarian society. Other forms include the attempts to introduce soviet-style communism in similar agrarian societies, for example in parts of Africa.

In many developing countries which are said to exhibit a dual economy, the two sectors concerned are found to comprise a subsistence or peasant economy normally identified with agriculture, and a sector relying on the input of capital normally identified with industry. However, this agriculture/industry dichotomy can be very misleading, as can be the attempted traditional/modern division of the economy, and it seems more helpful to view such a situation in other terms. The basic distinction between the two sectors of a dual economy may be more meaningful if regarded as one of resources, perhaps: the "peasant" sector is based upon the provision of the labour of individuals and families for their own enterprises; the "modern" sector is based upon the use of capital as a means of purchasing labour, as well as other required inputs. Seen in this way, "development" has been regarded as the process of the reallocation of labour from the peasant sector, where, for example, it may be surplus to food production requirements, to the capital sector, i.e. from a largely subsistence/barter economy to a money economy.

The terms "plural" and "dual" have been used interchangeably, or rather loosely, and it may be well to be reminded of cases of countries which may exhibit both a plural society and a dual economy, as the two are not necessarily synonymous. Mauritius, for example, though now virtually entirely a money economy according to Benedict (1961), still has a dual economy; it is very obviously also a plural society, composed of many individual communities and cultures. As Mauritius's major, almost only, resource is an agricultural one, i.e. sugar-cane growing and milling, it also provides a reminder that agriculture can be a highly-capitalized activity, just as much as manufacturing industry, with estates owned by large firms existing alongside canefields owned by villagers having just a few *arpents* of land each, often located in dispersed strips and patches as a result of inheritance via the Code Napolèon.

It should be noted, also, that some writers, mainly approaching the topic from a geographical standpoint, use the term "dual economy" in a much looser way, as covering what is mainly a core-and-periphery situation in a developing country. Now, the core-and-periphery idea is simply an abstraction from a potential model; moreover, all countries, developed and less-developed, exhibit cores and peripheries in terms of areas of differing population or economic potential. The term, used in this way, does not seem very helpful, though referring to an inevitable and natural phenomenon, particularly when a rather pejorative note is struck: "Here then we find an early example of a "dual economy", one in which large cities have leeched the countryside of energetic and talented young people and instead of rewarding their daring and ambition had exploited their productive power with shameless avarice. In this Belgian example is a prototype of what is occurring today in all too many developing countries" (Johnson, 1970).

In a sense, of course, this interpretation of the term "dual economy" does recognize, albeit dimly, two kinds, or two major sectors of the economy, but in a wholly spatial—and, it must be said, thus highly inaccurate—way. A more useful terminology requires a more exact usage: one which also recognizes the spatial intermingling of the two aspects of the economy.

More recently, a number of attempts have been made to rephrase and amplify the original idea of the dual economy, in referring to the two "circuits"—"upper" and "lower"—of the economy. Geertz (1963), in fact, referred to a "firm-centred economy" and a "bazaar economy", from his work in Indonesia; however, in referring especially to the urban economy, Santos (1971) used the terminology of the "upper" and "lower" circuits, and this nomenclature seems to be preferable to the others.

However, before considering in detail "the coexistence of wealth and poverty, modernity and traditionalism", (Roberts, 1978), it is as well to take note of two *caveats* also stressed by Roberts. The first of these is that a strong, centralized state most often exists in a developing country before it begins to concentrate on "development" and modernization. Perhaps there is an echo here of the issue raised by Childe's conception of the advent of a civilization: organization *before* surplus? Secondly, and again unlike the earlier experiences of industrialization, especially in Britain, the industries nowadays with which developing countries can begin their "growth" can be of large-scale and high technology, as technological transfer is much more feasible today.

Roberts utilizes Geertz's analysis based on the bazaar economy and the firm-centred economy, as noted. The characteristic features of the bazaar economy are: a high number of separate enterprises, small in size, relying on the intensive use of mainly family labour, highly competitive with each other, but seeking rather to minimize risks than to maximize profits. In the cases studied by Geertz (in Indonesia) this kind of economy was found mainly in the tertiary sector, i.e. in personal and commercial services; however, in other places it also includes small-scale manufacturing. The bazaar economy, with its seemingly less-than rational approach and its emphasis on the most effective use of household labour, represents, as Roberts rightly puts it: "a basic strategy of social and economic survival". This rural, family-based organization is transferred to the cities on migration, in anticipation of its similar relevance in urban conditions: "a dynamic form of economic activity, with a considerable capacity for absorbing labour and representing the transfer of the peasant mode of survival to the cities of underdeveloped countries." (Roberts, op. cit.)

The bazaar economy, in its urban setting, becomes linked not only with the peasant, agricultural economy, but also with the firm economy, for the firm-centred economy also has to deal with small markets, seasonal demands, limited profitability and increased risks; it does this by invoking the assistance of the bazaar economy. In these circumstances as Roberts insists, "it is premature to view the small-scale economy as simply an expedient and transitional form."

It is important to discern the bazaar economy as a social, as well as an economic kind of organization. Personal relationships, kinship ties, are necessary to the securance of flexible commitments by which to combat the risks of existence: trust and understanding are essential as the basis for economic relationships. Highly competitive and low-cost services can only be provided by, firstly, using household or family labour, and, secondly, by being able to extend not only labour but credit and other commitments, via a network of personal relationships of a trustworthy nature. The household should be seen as the unit of commitment and labour, rather than individuals: large households of small income-earners can collectively produce a household income which, though small, can be lived on. Poverty must be judged on a household, rather than an individual-earnings basis. Small enterprises, also, can escape the net of government regulations, taxes, or the payment of recognized minimum wages for helpers.

The Two Circuits of the Urban Economy

Returning to Santos's elaboration of this kind of "dual economy" theory, the crucial point of differentiation between the two circuits is still, at basis, the way in which personal labour, on the one hand, and capital, on the other hand, are both involved in those enterprises which collectively make up the economy, or a sector of the economy. In a lower circuit enterprise, the individual family can command only the labour of its members, though co-operation with others is not ruled out; but—unless capital can be found to buy more labour—the limit of its enterprise and its production is determined by its own resources of labour. In the upper circuit, labour becomes a commodity with a monetary value, to be hired, as also may be mechanical aids to production. In a socialist or communist economy, the ultimate sanction is that of force to constrain personal labour towards particular ends. Ignoring this latter aberration, an example of the two circuits in a developing country city might include that of a lower circuit consisting of non-capital-intensive industry and personally-supplied services and trading. The upper circuit would include banking, export trade, modern industry and services, wholesaling, and organized forms of transport like railways, shipping, or airlines. Characteristics of the two circuits are compared in Table 4.1 (Santos, 1979).

It is important to note two things in relation to these circuits of the urban economy: they are parts of the whole economy: subsystems of the urban economic system, and not separate systems; and this interrelationship is because both circuits are based on technological modernization of the urban economy—the lower circuit is not just "traditional". There may be at least three subsystems of the economy, therefore: two urban circuits and a peasant, possibly subsistence, rural economy—although two rural subsystems, analogous to the two urban circuits, are very likely, (cf. Mauritius, previously quoted). Santos (1979), taking this technological perspective, makes it clear

TABLE 4.1. *Characteristics of the Two Circuits of the Urban Economy in Underdeveloped Countries*

	Upper circuit	Lower circuit
Technology	Capital-intensive	Labour-intensive
Organization	Bureaucratic	Primitive
Capital	Abundant	Limited
Labour	Limited	Abundant
Regular wages	Prevalent	Exceptionally
Inventories	Large quantities and/or high quality	Small quantities poor quality
Prices	Generally fixed	Negotiable between buyer and seller (haggling)
Credit	From banks, institutional	Personal, non-institutional
Profit margin	Small per unit; but with large turnover considerable in aggregate (exception = luxuries)	Large per unit; but small turnover
Relations with customers	Impersonal and/or on paper	Direct, personalized
Fixed costs	Substantial	Negligible
Advertisement	Necessary	None
Re-use of goods	None (waste)	Frequent
Overhead capital	Essential	Not essential
Government aid	Extensive	None or almost none
Direct dependence on foreign countries	Great; externally oriented	Small or none

(Santos, 1979)

that modernization in developing countries has a limited effect on the creation of jobs as many such industries are capital-intensive; also at least a proportion of the indirect employment which such industries give rise to is located in other countries supplying the technology or is for expatriate workers. Both manufacturing industry and modernizing agriculture cannot meet the demand for more jobs from an increasing population: hence the growing pressure for urbanization already discussed. As Santos emphasizes, many people living in the cities of developing countries have no stable employment or stable income.

Santos goes on to point out that both of the two circuits result from modernization: the upper circuit due to direct pressure, the lower circuit due to indirect influences. Each circuit will distribute and also consume goods and services which it produces, resulting in differences both of kind and of quantity which are apparent in the society as a whole.

Santos's explanation seems convincing, though he seems to overstress a self-sufficiency of each circuit which does not exist. As he notes elsewhere, the dependencies of both circuits upon the other are marked, and goods produced in one circuit are not exclusively consumed within that same circuit. This interdependence is illustrated by Santos's diagram (Fig. 4.2).

It will be observed that many of the activities in each circuit are mixed in the sense that they operate or cater for more than one circuit, or indeed have

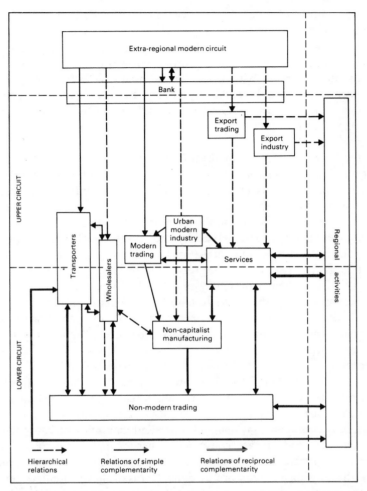

Fig. 4.2. Santos's diagram of the relationships between the Two Circuits (Santos, 1979).

relationships outside the urban area altogether. The pivotal role of wholesaling, transport, and services, is crucial to the entire urban economy.

Santos proceeds to explain what he regards as the fundamental differences, technological and organizational, between the activities of the two circuits. He claims that the upper circuit makes use of an imported, and capital-intensive technology; but although in the lower circuit the technology is labour-intensive and often either indigenous or locally adapted, it also may have considerable innovative potential. Activities in the upper circuit can rely on getting credit from banks, but the activities of the lower circuit are based both on credit and on cash, the credit here, though, being of a direct and personal kind; repayments are piecemeal, and actual cash is always short.

Small quantities of goods characterize the lower circuit, both in production and distribution, whereas most upper circuit activities are concerned with large quantities. This situation is due to the respective amounts of capital available, to its organization, and also the demands which it is to meet.

In the upper circuit, with wages as the dominant labour relationship, progressively fewer people are directly employed in relation to the volume and the value of the production. Government and service employment increase over time, where the lower circuit can manage without bureaucratic organization.

In the lower circuit, employment is rarely permanent and the average number of persons per enterprise is small; but the number of enterprises is large, and thus the lower circuit can provide employment for many people. Also, due to its nature, the lower circuit can breed new enterprises more easily, and thus absorb more labour in the form of new migrants.

The upper circuit is characterized by fixed prices, but in the lower circuit bargaining is the custom and fluctuations in price may be large. In the lower circuit, short-term issues are of the greatest importance, and the major issue is the day-to-day survival of the family and of the business: capital accumulation is not so important as the ability to have some modern consumption goods, once survival is ensured. The upper circuit, on the other hand, must accumulate capital in order to be able to continue to reproduce its own economic activity.

The lower circuit is very much concerned with the re-utilization of consumer durable goods, for example, second-hand refrigerators or air-conditioners or television sets—or bicycles and cars. Small-scale repair shops and used clothing or household equipment shops are a feature of the lower circuit. This kind of activity is created by demand, a demand that is fairly localized, in the sense that its products are consumed either in the city itself, or in its neighbouring rural areas—not in some other city or even overseas, as is the case with many upper circuit productions. Nor is the lower circuit dependent upon the provision of social overhead capital by governments, as is the case for upper circuit activities.

Santos's exposition of the two circuits in action in "the shared space" of the cities of developing countries is very convincing as an explanation of the particular characteristics which are observable in them. His theory—especially his insistence on the essential relationships between the two circuits, stressed also by Roberts (1978), offers a fundamental basis, not only of the economic, but also of the social relationships involved: Roberts is worth quoting again, here:

"The poor in cities of Latin America are not socially or politically isolated. The activities in which they must engage to make a living mean that they develop complex patterns of social interaction that are not confined to neighbourhood. The urban poor also find ways of interpreting the uncertainties of their economic and social position which are compatible with an active

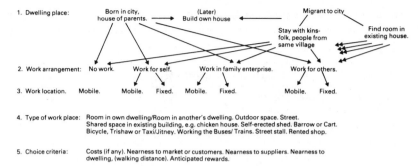

FIG. 4.3. Lower Circuit Activities.

TABLE 4.4. *Suggested Criteria for Identifying Informal Sector Enterprises*

1. *Manufacturing.* A manufacturing enterprise may be included in the informal sector if it satisfies one or more of the following conditions:
   (a) It employs 10 persons or less (including part-time and casual workers).
   (b) It operates on an illegal basis, contrary to government regulations.
   (c) Members of the household of the head of the enterprise work in it.
   (d) It does not observe fixed hours/days of operation.
   (e) It operates in semi-permanent or temporary premises, or in a shifting location.
   (f) It does not use any electricity in the manufacturing process.
   (g) It does not depend on formal financial institutions for its credit needs.
   (h) Its output is normally distributed direct to the final consumer.
   (i) Almost all those working in it have fewer than 6 years of formal schooling.

2. *Construction.* A construction enterprise may be included in the informal sector if it satisfies one or more of the following conditions:
   (a) Any of 1(a)–(c) or (i) above.
   (b) It does not own power-operated construction machinery and equipment.
   (c) It is engaged in the construction of semi-permanent or temporary buildings only.

3. *Transport.* An enterprise providing services related to transport, storage and communications may be included in the informal sector if it satisfies one or more of the following conditions:
   (a) Any of 1(a)–(e), (g) or (i) above. Condition 1(e) does not apply to transport activity *per se*.
   (b) It does not use any mechanical power.

4. *Trade.* A trading enterprise may be included in the informal sector if it satisfies one or more of the following conditions:
   (a) Any of 1(a)–(e) above.
   (b) It deals in second-hand goods, or sells prepared food.

5. *Services.* A service enterprise may be included in the informal sector if it satisfies one or more of the following conditions:
   Any of 1(a)–(e) above.

Source: Sethuraman, ILO, 1976.

(These criteria are probably too restrictive, for example in the use of power and mechanical equipment.)

Hart (1973), from studies in Ghana, has defined the "informal" sector *en passant*, via income opportunities (Table 4.5); his tabulation embraces both circuits.

TABLE 4.5. *Income Opportunities in a Third World City*

Formal income opportunities
  (a) Public sector wages.
  (b) Private sector wages.
  (c) Transfer payments—pensions, unemployment benefits.

Informal income opportunities: legitimate
  (a) Primary and secondary activities—farming, market gardening, building contractors and associated activities, self-employed artisans, shoemakers, tailors, manufacturers of beers and spirits.
  (b) Tertiary enterprises with relatively large capital inputs—housing, transport, utilities, commodity speculation, rentier activities.
  (c) Small-scale distribution—market operatives, petty traders, street hawkers, caterers in food and drink, bar attendants, carriers (*kayakaya*), commission agents, and dealers.
  (d) Other services—musicians, launderers, shoeshiners, barbers, night-soil removers, photographers, vehicle repair and other maintenance workers; brokerage and middle-manship (the *maigida* system in markets, law courts, etc); ritual services, magic, and medicine.
  (e) Private transfer payments—gifts and similar flows of money and goods between persons; borrowing; begging.

Informal income opportunities: illegitimate
  (a) Services—hustlers and spivs in general; receivers of stolen goods; usery and pawnbroking (at illegal interest rates); drug-pushing, prostitution, poncing ("pilot boy"), smuggling, bribery, political corruption Tammany Hall-style protection rackets.
  (b) Transfers—petty theft (e.g. pickpockets), larceny (e.g. burglary and armed robbery), speculation and embezzlement, confidence tricksters (e.g. money doublers), gambling.

Source: Keith Hart, "Informal Income Opportunities and Urban Employment in Ghana". *The Journal of Modern African Studies* II, no. I (1973): 69, Cambridge University Press.

attempt to cope with the day-to-day problems of urban living. Thus, the religious practices of the urban poor can be viewed in this way and also demonstrate the cultural heterogeneity that accompanies uneven economic development.

Social relationships are crucial to survival in these cities. Obtaining housing as well as jobs is a question of developing an effective social network. Indeed, the striking feature about the urban poor is their activism in the face of seemingly appalling conditions."

Other discussions, though valuable, have tended to treat what Santos terms as the lower circuit as a separate phenomenon, to some degree. The "informal sector", though appreciated by the International Labour Office in their study of Kenya (ILO, 1972) and in later work, and rightly emphasized in importance by them, is not part of a full-developed theory of the social and economic operation of developing countries in the same way as it is with Santos, and Roberts. However, the support of an international body in firstly studying, and then, secondly, suggesting policies for the "informal sector," cannot be overemphasized:

"The informal sector provides income-earning opportunities for a large number of people. Though it is often regarded as unproductive and stagnant, we see it as providing a wide range of low-cost, labour-intensive, competitive goods and services. Not only does it provide them without the benefit of the government subsidies and support that are received by many firms in the formal sector, but operators in the informal sector are often harassed and hampered by restrictions imposed from outside."

Suggested criteria for identifying informal sector enterprises, used by ILO in a number of studies, are shown in Table 4.4 (Sethuraman, 1976).

Two "Informal Sector" Models

Some support for the view of the lower and upper circuits being integrated, rather than the "informal sector" being: "a reservoir of unemployment and marginally productive activity into which those who cannot obtain paid jobs in the formal sector sink, barely making ends meet by begging, hawking or embarking on petty crime", comes from the ILO report on Kenya (ILO, 1972). Linkage effects and product substitution were regarded as quite significant in Kenya at the time, and should be strengthened in the future. A four-sector model to show these interlinkages was proposed (ILO, 1972, pp. 506–508), comprising small-holder agriculture, the "informal" (non-agricultural) sector, the private "formal" sector, and the government sector. With the outputs of these sectors as X_1, X_2, X_3, X_4 respectively, the following input–output row can be constructed:

$$X_2 = a_{21}X_1 + a_{22}X_2 + a_{23}X_3 + a_{24}X_4 + X_{2F}$$

where the 'a's are coefficients and X_{2F} is the final demand for the "informal" sector output. The ILO group listed the most important goods and services supplied by the "informal" sector to itself and the other three sectors as:

Using sector	Goods and services supplied
1. Agriculture	Grain-grinding, building materials, transport, marketing, repair and maintenance.
2. "Informal"	Furniture for commercial use, tools, transport, repair and maintenance.
3. Private "formal"	Marketing and distribution, transport, furniture, repair and maintenance.
4. Government	Construction, furniture, transport.
5. Final demand	Clothing, prepared food, furniture, repair and maintenance.

"Informal"-sector output, from the above, can be written as:

$$X_2 = \frac{1}{1 - a_{22}}(a_{21}X_1 + a_{22}X_3 + a_{24}X_4 + X_{2F}).$$

Assuming the capital stock of the informal sector to be constant, then a change in X_2 production is $\Delta L_2 \cdot \Delta X_2/\Delta L_2$ where $\Delta X_2/\Delta L_2$, at the limit, is the marginal product of labour in the informal sector. The relationship can thus be written in terms of employment:

$$\Delta L_2 = \frac{1}{1-a_{22}} \cdot \frac{\Delta L_2}{\Delta X_2} [\Delta(a_{21}X_1 + a_{23}X_3 + a_{24}X_2 + X_{2F})].$$

An increase in any X sector will therefore increase employment in the informal sector if none of the input coefficients is zero. A given increase in total output will have an effect on employment in the informal sector determined by the values of the coefficients and the sectoral composition of the increase in output. The model can thus be used to analyse the effects of changes in product choices throughout the various sectors, e.g. quantity and quality of labour and technology involved. The recommendation on employment made by the ILO group—that there was considerable scope for further employment in the "informal" sector in Kenya at 1972—was reached through the use of this model, utilizing "arbitrary but moderate" data assumptions.

The structure of a dual economy is reflected also in the specific intensities of both capital and labour in the national economy of a country like Zambia, (Gesellschaft für Regionale Strukturentwicklung e.V., 1971), as the following formalism demonstrates:

If C^T = capital assets in the traditional sector.
   C^C = capital assets in the cash economy.
   L^T = number of persons employed in the traditional sector.
   L^{*T} = imputed total of wages in the traditional sector of the national economy, i.e. number of persons employed in the traditional sector x average income in kind and in cash of hired labourers on commercial farms.
   L^C = labour force, i.e. persons employed in the cash economy.
   L^{*C} = total of wages and salaries in the cash economy, i.e. labour force in cash economy x average per capita earnings in the cash economy.

It is assumed that capital assets in the traditional sector are comparatively low, thus:

$$L^T/C^T > L^C/C^C$$

and although: $$L^{*T}/L^T < L^{*C}/L^C$$

still: $$L^{*T}/C^T > L^{*C}/C^C.$$

Thus, the rate of fall of the gradient of labour intensity between the traditional sector and the cash sector is a steep one; each decrease in labour intensity in the cash economy widens the gap between the two sectors. In a developing country at Zambia's stage of development, it was held that as many jobs as possible should be created with the funds available for investment.

There is often a real dilemma between the need for specialized skills not locally available but essential to promotion of development and the cost of their importing: both the absence of these skills and their presence, in terms of costs of bringing them in, may be limiting factors on development in different ways.

The tendency of the economic development process may be hypothesized as the occurrence of:

$$L^{*C}/C^C > L^{*T}/C^T$$

but, even so, in a newly-industrialized country like Korea, large increases in C^C must be kept pace with by appropriate increases in L^{*C}—*and* increases in L^C as L^T declines.

Rural Activity and the Two Circuits

The profusion of labels is generally misleading and may confuse: it is proposed to use the "upper" and "lower" circuit terminology in this work.

An interesting question is whether, in fact, the two circuits model, evolved as an explanation of urban economies, can be applied to the rural situation, and thus encompass a whole economy, urban and rural. Objections to previous attempts to apply a crude "dual economy" model to Latin American situations—and thus, perhaps, giving support for identifying an upper and a lower circuit in the rural-urban economy relationship?—have been raised by Barraclough, (in Field, 1970):

". . . identification of the subsistence economy with agriculture and the modern capitalist economy with industry makes little sense. In Latin America, unlike what happened historically in much of Europe, the colonists and *conquistadores* established their cities and towns before they subdued the countryside. Almost immediately, however, they organized capitalist enterprises to exploit mines and the land (and the Indians and slaves who worked them), long before they began to organize urban manufacturing and other industries. Large-scale capitalist production in Latin America virtually began with the colonial plantations and *haciendas*.

Urban industry, on the other hand, has seldom been distinguished in Latin America for its dynamic capitalist traits. Fostered originally by a protective merchantilist imperial system, only permitted in restricted fields where it would not compete with the home country, usually controlled by foreign investors and protected from competition by elaborate monopolies, tariffs, quotas, and franchises, its outstanding characteristics have been its high cost structure and its dependence upon paternalistic government. Profits, far from being relentlessly accumulated and reinvested, have frequently been repatriated, dissipated in consumption, or securely invested in agricultural land and other real estate. . . . In short, to identify urban industry as the principal dynamic and capital-accumulating sector in the developing Latin American nations stretches both facts and credulity.

To suggest that Latin American "agriculture" in some manner approximates to the sluggish, non-capitalist "subsistence sector" of the dual economy models also requires both imagination and a disregard for reality. Capitalist farm organization is the rule in contemporary Latin America. Subsistence-type peasant farming, even if broadly defined, is limited mostly to marginal areas and is dominant in terms of production only in a few regions such as parts of the Andean highlands.

There are, to be sure, many traditional large estates or *haciendas*. These are technically backward, and their owners depend heavily upon quasi-feudal labour services, rents, and tributes for their incomes. They often market a sizeable surplus, and profits are almost always an important management objective. The traditional *haciendos* are more akin to Malthus's and Ricardo's landlords whose primary function is to consume than to the prototype capitalists with their passion to produce, accumulate, and invest.

We must conclude that the dual economy models purporting to analyse the terms of trade between agriculture and industry during development are in many respects irrelevant for understanding Latin American agrarian problems. The theoretical insights derived from the models concerning the some of the possible consequences of a surplus of labour in rural areas, however, are much more pertinent. To ignore these, or to deny the existence of rural unemployment and underemployment . . . leads to a very unrealistic appraisal of the rural development problem."

It would appear feasible to derive a modified version of the two circuits models for the situation described by Barraclough, no doubt, as also for the Mauritian situation mentioned previously, with some agricultural enterprises being of an upper circuit nature, and some being regarded as lower circuit phenomena. Another aspect of the "urban vs. rural" application of the two circuits theory could have important conclusions.

Commenting on the increasing proportions of the population of many cities now living in squatter housing, Mountjoy (1976) expresses the view that, in Africa, South-east Asia, and some parts of Latin America: "we are no longer seeing the urbanization of rural migrants but rather the growing ruralization of the towns." The physical forms of these squatter settlements, he says, is becoming like those of rural villages—which may well be true—and he avers that the socio-cultural organization of such settlements is also rural, rather than urban.* Consequently, he fears that the function of the city in the Third World as a focus for modernization and growth will decline and atrophy as it becomes increasingly ruralized.

Whether this argument is valid, or not, seems to depend on the relative status of the upper and lower circuits: squatter settlements represent the housing solution to lower circuit problems, and many of those who live in such housing may live and work exclusively in the lower circuit; in which event they are unlikely to influence the development process except as consumers of

---

* This is confirmed also by some of Abu-Lughod's 13 "Sub-Cities" of Cairo, (1971).

goods and services coming from the successful growth of the upper circuit either through the market or via government policies. However, some of those employed in the upper circuit undoubtedly will come from squatter settlements, but this proportion seems unlikely to influence the fate of growth and development to any considerable degree. The "ruralization leading decline in development" thesis seems to require reconsideration in the light of actual cases where the two circuits of the economy are readily identifiable.

The Question of Numbers

One of the principal problems in evaluating the contribution, scope and importance of the lower circuit of an economy—urban or rural—is a simple lack of knowledge: of relationships, of numbers. Mostly, this may be attributable to either a lack of concern for, or indeed a sheer prejudice against, what is seen as tarnishing the image of the new, shiny "developed" future that politicians are anxious to present and promote. Also, few governments collect any data that is relevant to any analysis of the lower circuits of their economies. However, an examination has been made of a number of statistical and other sources in developing countries, with a view to the discernment of some of the dimensions of the situation.

Three examples may be culled from Southern Africa, though the special circumstances of these countries, neighbouring the employment magnets of the Zambian Copper Belts and the Witwatersrand of South Africa should be borne in mind.

The Republic of Botswana Population Census of 1971 showed a total population of 620,000, made up of 563,000 *de facto* Batswana; 11,000 aliens living in the country; and 46,000 Batswana temporarily absent elsewhere. The labour force of the country was reckoned to be 385,000 persons aged 10 or more; of that:

> 7% were active in the cash sector only;
> 6% were active in both the cash sector and subsistence agriculture;
> 60% were active in subsistence agriculture only

—leaving 27% of the total not accounted for. (Note that 68% of the population at that time had no education).

The *paid* employment in Botswana, from a 1974 survey, covered:

9,201 persons in agriculture, mining and quarrying,	(21.5%)
2,491 persons in manufacturing	(5.8%)
23,556 persons in services	(55.1%)
7,517 persons in government employment	(17.6%)
42,765 total paid employment*	(100%)

(* *Excludes* an estimated 10,000 domestic servants.)

In Swaziland, the 1966 Population Census enumerated a total *de facto* population of 374,697; there were 20,567 absentees. The population of working age (15–64) was estimated in 1974 at 227,329 persons, but the economically active labour force (African resident population only) was estimated as 116,288. This latter total was made up of 53,737 in paid employment; 8,678 unemployed; and 53,873 in the subsistence sector. "Considerable and frequent, as yet unmeasured, movement between the two sectors" was said to be typical of the Swazi economy.

Jobs in *paid* employment, in 1972, were:

27,100 in agriculture, forestry and mining	(49.2%)
7,700 in manufacturing	(14.0%)
10,100 in services	(18.4%)
10,100 in the public sector	(18.4%)
55,000 total employment	(100%)

In Lesotho, the 1966 Population Census, quoted by Monyake (1971), showed that:

(a) of the *de facto* population over 14 years of age, 39% were self-employed, (95% of them in subsistence agriculture); 8% were employed for wages (mainly in teaching and the civil service); 39% were family workers (more than 90% in subsistence agriculture); and 14% others, (housewives, unemployed seeking work, etc., excluding school children).

(b) Eighty seven per cent of the *de facto* population were dependent on agriculture.

(c) Twelve per cent of the *de jure* population were outside the country, (90% of whom are employed in the Republic of South Africa)."

Lesotho is a land-locked country, almost all of which is over 5000 feet above sea-level. It suffers from much soil erosion, and agriculture is difficult. There is not sufficient agricultural land to give employment to all the population. According to the Lesotho 1960 Census of Agriculture, (again quoted by Monyake, 1971), the average size of agricultural holding had dropped from 5.8 acres in 1950 to 5.1 acres in 1960; the average size of holdings per head was 1 acre. About 50% of heads of households without land were outside the country, and about 80% of all absentee heads of households had holdings less than 6 acres.

Despite the variations in these figures—the three countries are vastly different in extent and natural resources—some similarities appear. Paid employment in each country is only a small proportion of the total labour force, however reckoned; little of this paid employment is in manufacturing; and in addition to the paid internal employees, a substantial proportion of the total paid labour force appears to be working outside the country of its origin.

Paid employment requires the pricing of labour: a commodity which is unpriced in subsistence agriculture. Attempts to assess the value of the output of such agriculture in African economies also involve the pricing, in market terms, of non-marketed commodities: to assign such prices involves the assumption that market prices would be unchanged if the subsistence agricultural output, of large volume, was to be placed on sale. In spite of this, the following Table 4.6 shows an attempt to include both the monetary and non-monetary-valued outputs as components in the Gross Domestic Product of Malawi in 1964. Malawi's population in 1963 was 3.75 million, of whom about 170,000 were out of the country working in Rhodesia (about 120,000), South Africa (30,000), and Zambia (20,000). If these GDP figures are representative, in 1964 60% of Malawi's total GDP came from the rural sector, and the largest single contribution—nearly 50%—came from African agriculture.

Mauritius is another country exhibiting at least two circuits of the economy. The 1971 *Four Year Plan* states that: "As much of the economic activity on the island can be considered sub-marginal, the concept of employment in the present Mauritian context is somewhat indeterminate. . . . The concept of the economically active population cannot, in the current pattern of employment

TABLE 4.6. *Malawi: Gross Domestic Product by Industrial Origin 1964*

	£ million
1. Rural sector	
(i) African agriculture-own consumption	20.0
(ii) African agriculture-sale	3.4
(iii) African rural household services	4.9
(iv) Non-African agriculture (incl. tea)	3.6
	31.9
2. Commerce and industry	
(i) Manufacture (excl. tea)	2.0
(ii) Building and Construction	1.9
(iii) Electricity and Water	0.5
(iv) Distribution	5.7
(v) Real Estate and ownership of dwellings	0.8
(vi) Transport and Communications	2.4
(vii) Domestic services	0.6
(viii) Services, other	1.3
	15.2
3. Public sector	
(i) Public Administration	2.9
(ii) Education	1.4
(iii) Health	4.9
GROSS DOMESTIC PRODUCT	52.0
Monetary	27.1
Non-Monetary	24.9

Source: Malawi Budget 1966, Government Printer, Zomba 1965 (Pike, 1968).

in Mauritius, be given a precise definition; with so much part-time and barely remunerative employment, any estimate of the degree of unemployment and underemployment of the economically active population would hardly be meaningful. That there is a great deal of unemployment and sub-marginal employment is a matter of observation." Total employment, including self-employment, at the peak time of year, was estimated at about 195,000 persons out of a total (1970) population of 815,000. Later, in 1973, unemployment was estimated at 16% of the population of working age.

The details of employment and productivity in Mauritius at 1969 are given below; (Table 4.7). The very large employment in agriculture is notable, as is the high productivity value of agricultural processing, mainly of sugar cane. As the *Four Year Plan* (1971) says: "The structure of land holding in Mauritius is polarized, with, at one end, a little over half the area under cultivation farmed by twenty-one estates cultivating between 1000 and 11,000 arpents each, (1 arpent = 1.04 acres); and, at the other end, over 25,000 smallholders cultivating 20% of the acreage under crops in holdings of around 1.5 arpents and for the most part even less; 40 cane growers and 23 tea growers with holdings of some hundreds of arpents farm 10% of the cultivated acreage, and 2500 small and medium-sized farmers, with holdings ranging from five arpents upwards, farm 20% of the land under cultivation." More than 42% of

TABLE 4.7. *Employment and Productivity in Mauritius, 1969*

	Employment numbers	Productivity per person	GDP at factor cost 1967–69 average R million
Agriculture, Forestry and Livestock	72,300	2,800	203
Lagoon and Offshore Fisheries	3,500	500	2
Marine Fisheries	300	3,600	1
Mining and Quarrying	400	2,500	1
Processing Agricultural Export Crops	6,600	11,820	78
Manufacturing:			
Establishments employing 10 or more persons	9,000	5,000	54
Artisanat*	9,400	1,200	
Construction and Public Works	13,000	3,920	51
Electricity, Water and Public Utilities	1,300	23,080	30
Transport and Communications	13,400	7,610	102
Import and Export, Wholesale and Retail Trade	19,800	4,540	90
Services	32,100	6,040	194
Public Administration	13,900	3,160	44
Total	195,000	4,360 (Average)	850

Source: Government of Mauritius: 4-Year Plan, 1971–1975.
(* Artisanat: small-scale hand or craft industries.)

employment was in the primary sector, and less than 10% in manufacturing, at 1969.

Some idea of the size of the lower circuit in Mauritius was given by earlier statistics of 1967–1968. At that time "small industrial establishments", i.e. of less than 13 persons engaged, accounted for a total of 7597 persons; of these 4070 were "working proprietors and unpaid family workers", whilst 3527 were employees, mainly in the footwear and clothing industries. The total engaged in "large establishments" at that time was only 16,379 persons, so it would appear that the "informal" sector at that time, in industry only, covered about 32% of total industrial employment.

On Egypt, Mabro (1967), using data from the 1960 Census, notes that:

"The bulk of the natural increase in the labour force (1.1 out of 1.9 million) [1937–1960] found employment in the services and in 'activities not adequately described', ... only 169,000 were absorbed in construction and transport; the expansion of employment in government, commerce, personal and other services is strikingly high. The service sector was already important in 1937 (1.4 million, 24% of the labour force). Its relative importance increased to 31% with 2.43 million persons in 1960. For each new person engaged in manufacture we have three new entrants in the services. The analysis suggests that the service sector hides considerable disguised unemployment."

TABLE 4.8. *Egypt: Population and Employment*

	1937	1960
Population	15,920,696	25,984,101
Labour Force	5,809,272	7,726,651
Agriculture, Forestry and Fishing	4,020,431	4,406,379
Mining and Quarrying	10,828	21,109
Manufacturing	352,706	713,100
Electricity, Gas and Water	20,966	36,808
Construction	120,702	158,885
Transport	138,911	260,210
Commerce	439,542	641,408
Other Services	701,749	1,369,432
Activities not adequately described	3,437	119,320
Not stated	—	7,647

Source: Mabro (1967), from 1960 Census.

Later, comparative figures for Egypt, Sudan, and Yemen Arab Republic are given by Birks and Sinclair (1980), Tables 4.9, 4.10.

In Morocco in 1971, "independent workers" numbered 1,244,500, and family help, mainly in agriculture, was 744,000 persons: a total of 1,988,500 or nearly 55% of the 3,631,600 total in all employment. At that time, 348,900 were unemployed, of whom 158,200 were active, i.e. had been in employment at some time.

In Kenya: "Small African businesses come in a wide variety of forms. There

TABLE 4.9. *Employment Distribution: Three Red Sea Countries*

Category	Egypt (1976) %	Sudan (1973) %	Yemen A.R. (1975) %
Agricultural workers	50.7	55.2	57.9
Informal sector	11.5	14.5	14.5
Modern sector	33.1	28.6	6.6
Modern (Government)	(25.7)	(8.6)	(2.8)
Modern (Private)	(7.4)	(20.0)	(3.9)
Workers abroad	4.7	1.7	20.9
Total number	12,811,500	513,236	355,085

TABLE 4.10. *Employment in the Urban "Formal" and "Informal" Sectors: Three Red Sea Countries*

Country	Year	Urban formal sector Number of workers	% of total workforce	Urban informal sector Number of workers	% of total workforce
Egypt	1976	3,900,000	33.3	1,500,000	12.8
Sudan	1973	120,000	2.6	713,000	15.3
Yemen A.R.	1975	90,180	6.6	196,727	14.3

Source: J. S. Birks and C. A. Sinclair, Chapter 4 of Blake and Lawless (eds., 1980).

are small-scale manufacturers who utilize salvaged materials and who operate in extremely primitive quarters. There are the vehicle mechanics who, with several helpers, operate from vacant lots with very little by way of tools. There are the petty traders who dominate almost all traditional markets. . . . Total employment provided by all small-scale African business appears to be of the order of 480,000 or over 60% of the total non-agricultural employment. To put these numbers into perspective, it should be pointed out that these estimates of employment in small business largely do not find their way into official employment statistics; most of the enterprises are unregistered and, indeed, many are illegal. . . ." (Report of the Working Party on Small Business Development, Nairobi, 1972, quoted by Friedman and Sullivan.)

A series of case studies of employment was developed by the International Labour Office c. 1974–1976, covering Calcutta, Abidjan, São Paulo and Jakarta; it was followed by a further group of studies focused to a greater extent on what the ILO defined as the "informal sector", in: Jakarta, Manila, Colombo, Cordoba (Argentina), Campinas (Brazil), Lagos, Kano and Onitsha (Nigeria), Kumasi (Ghana), and Freetown (Sierra Leone). It would be tedious to cover all these cities here, but the Jakarta situation, (Sethuraman, 1976), is worth reviewing.

The Jakarta study utilized the same identifying characteristics of the "informal sector" as had been used in 1972 by the ILO report on Kenya, i.e.:

ease of entry to the sector; reliance on indigenous resources; family ownership of enterprises; small scale of operation; labour-intensive and adapted technology; skills acquired outside the formal school system; and unregulated and competitive markets. Data available was old and via registration of enterprises; at 1967, two-thirds of all registered enterprises in Jakarta had four, or less, workers per establishment, whilst about 83% of the enterprises had a sales turnover of only US$4000 equivalent at that time. In 1971, only about 38% of total employment in Jakarta was given by registered enterprises, and by a residual calculation (in the absence of direct statistics) it appeared that 505,000 persons out of the 1,179,000 employed at 1971 depended on the informal sector. The 1967 situation, from the residual calculation, is shown in Table 4.11 (from Sethuraman, 1976a); of interest are the 70,000 persons shown as employed in the construction aspect of the informal sector, and 37,000 persons in its agricultural sector. From other evidence, including direct surveys of underemployment, it appears that hours worked by most of those in the low-income group were long, and wages low, although surprisingly 54% of the (small) sample interviewed owned their own houses.

Other, more direct evidence of the two circuits, comes from Bombay, from statistics collected by H. and V. Joshi and quoted by Mazumdar (1979). The term "organized" sector covers all public sector establishments and privately owned establishments employing 25 or more workers, and relates to data collected by the Indian Directorate of Employment and Training; the "unorganized" sector is the difference between the former figures and the Census returns for the same year. The "Others" column refers to single workers on daily contracts, family workers, and workers in household industries (Table 4.12). The large proportions of "unorganized" workers in the trade and commerce, and service sectors are noteworthy.

Similar information for manufacturing employment only regarding seven African countries is given in Table 4.13, from Page (1979), although here couched largely in terms of size of firms. Unregistered employment, again, is calculated as a residual, as indeed must be the case in these situations: the "unorganized" or "informal" sector, by definition, is difficult to identify fully and to number directly. Deduced in this way, unregistered employment varies from 49% of the total manufacturing labour force in Kenya in 1969 to nearly 78% in Ghana in 1970, whilst Nigeria (1972) showed 59% and Tanzania (1967) nearly 56% in this category. Where this figure was not available, the range in artisanal (i.e. small) firms shows a very wide variation, from only 6.6% of total employment in Ghana in 1970 via 26% in Egypt (1966–1967) to as much as 83% in Ethiopia in 1971. The high proportion of employment in larger firms in Egypt is not unexpected, in terms of relative stages of economic growth of the various countries shown.

A second table (Table 4.14) from Page shows the distribution of employment in the smaller industries in a different sample of African countries. Clearly, the clothing industry in all these countries is responsible for a major

TABLE 4.11. *Employment in Registered and Unregistered Enterprises by Sector, Jakarta 1967, (Sethuraman, 1976a)*

Sector	Total	Registered commercial enterprises	Unregistered enterprises	Government and formal non-commercial enterprises	Informal sector	Informal sector as % of total $(5) \div (1)$	Distribution within informal sector (%)
	(1)	(2)	(3)	(4)	(5)	(6)	(7)
Agriculture and related industries	42,940	5,899	37,041	—	37,041	86	8.5
Manufacturing	124,132	96,723	27,409	—	27,409	22	6.3
Construction	83,247	12,782	70,465	—	70,465	85	16.2
Public utilities	6,053	2,155	3,898	—	3,898	64	0.9
Transport, storage, communication	121,910	38,660	83,250	—	83,250	68	19.1
Trade	254,560	164,179	90,381	—	90,381	36	20.8
Banking and financial institutions	29,039	23,731	5,308	—	5,308	18	1.2
Services	369,670	32,305	337,365	220,000	117,365	32	27.0
Others (including mining, quarrying and unknown)	25,931						
Total	1,057,482	376,434	655,117	220,000	435,117	41	100.0

Source: col. (1): interpolated from 1961 and 1971 population census data: col. (3): derived from cols. (1) and (2) as a residual: col. (5) derived from cols. (3) and (4): col. (6): derived from cols. (5) and (1): col. (7): percentage distribution of col (5).

TABLE 4.12. *Structure of Employment, Greater Bombay, 1961*
(Percentages of the Total Workforce)

Industry	Organized employees	Unorganized sector Total Employees	Others	Employers	Total
Manufacturing (including) Primary Production)	28	12	7	5	2	43
Construction and Utilities	3	1	*	1	*	4
Trade and Commerce	3	12	5	7	3	18
Transport and Communications	6	5	3	2	*	11
Services	9	14	10	4	*	24
Total	50	45	26	19	5	100

Note: The total workforce of Bombay in 1961 was 1.687 million. An asterisk means less than 1%. Some totals do not add up exactly due to rounding.
Source: Joshi and Joshi (1976). (Table III.2, pp. 54–55). Quoted by Mazumdar (1979).

proportion of employment in smaller-scale enterprises, followed by the woodworking/furniture industry, although vehicle repair becomes locally of some importance in one or two countries.

A case study of "petty commodity production" in Ujung Pandang, Indonesia was made by Forbes (1981). Indonesia's economy was growing at between 7 and 8% all through the 1970s, but South Sulawesi, including the city of Ujung Pandang, apparently played little part in this expansion, compared with parts of Java, Sumatra, and Kalimantan. Capitalist, i.e. upper circuit forms of production have made uneven advances, and petty production in areas like Ujung Pandang seems to be expanding faster than upper circuit activities, at least so far as employment growth rates are concerned. As Forbes puts it: "the transition to capitalism is not a straightforward one of invasion and succession—it is a more complex process of interdependence and qualitative change which simultaneously creates both development and underdevelopment."

Forbes estimated that petty commodity producers were about 30 to 44% of the total work force of Ujung Pandang in 1976: a somewhat smaller proportion, perhaps, than has been identified in other cities, where 50% or more seems common—but, obviously, cities may be expected to show some degree of variation in this respect.

Surveys of street food vendors in the Philippines and Indonesia have shown that most of them make wages at least equivalent to the minimum wage (in Manila), or the regional urban household income (in Iloilo City, Southern Philippines), or low-level civil servant's wages (Bogor, Indonesia). Such street vendors are not only an employment source, but also an important aspect of food supply in such cities. In many cases, all these street vendors had second jobs, whilst 25% of vendors in one sample employed one other, non-family worker. (Data from proceedings of a Conference at De La Salle University,

TABLE 4.13. *Distribution of Employment in Small and Artisanal Industries for Selected African Countries*
(Percentage of Total Sector Employment)

	Nigeria Western State 1972	Ghana Accra 1972	Sierra Leone 1974–75	Tanzania 1961–67	Senegal 1972	Cameroon 1978	Zaire Kinshasa 1973
Clothing	51.7	33.0	31.3	26.2	45.3	41.3	33.2
Shoes	4.2	3.8	1.4	9.4	10.0	2.9	—
Carpentry/Furniture mfg.	10.7	8.2	16.4	19.2	10.8	13.5	14.7
Vehicle repair	9.3	16.5	1.6	16.9	6.9	5.5	13.4
Metal products	4.1	11.2	15.3	5.4	3.8	4.1	9.9
Printing	1.6	7.0	—	—	—	—	6.0

Notes: — indicates data unavailable. Nigeria: Firms employing less than 50 workers. Ghana: Firms employing less than 50 workers. Sierra Leone: Firms employing less than 30 workers. Tanzania: Firms employing less than 50 workers. Senegal: Registered Artisans in Production and Service employing less than 5 workers. Cameroon: Firms employing less than 5 workers. Zaire: Firms employing less than 50 workers. (Page, 1979.)

TABLE 4.14. *Employment of Small Scale, Artisanal and Unregistered Firms in the Manufacturing Sector of Selected African Countries*
(*Thousands of Employees*)

	Tanzania 1967	Egypt 1966-67	Kenya 1969	Ghana 1970	Ethiopia 1971	Nigeria 1972	Sierra Leone 1974
Total manufacturing sector labour force	92.3	766.0	204.1	380.1	281.7	1100.0	92.7
Large and medium firms	34.5	490.0	83.9	56.9	48.7	160.0	4.1
Small scale firms[a]	6.2	76.8	20.2	1.2	—	290.0	88.6
Artisanal firms[b]	1.3	199.6	—	25.1	233.1	—	—
Unregistered employment[c]	52.2	—	100.2	296.2	—	650.0	—

Note: [a] Employing 10–49 workers.
[b] Employing 1–9 workers.
[c] Residual estimate. — Not available.

Sources: Tanzania: Republic of Tanzania, Population Census 1967. Republic of Tanzania, Survey of Employment and Earnings, 1967. Egypt: World Bank (1977a). Kenya: Child (1977). Ghana: Republic of Ghana, Population Census, 1970. Republic of Ghana, Employment Statistics, 1970. Checci (1976). Ethiopia: World Bank (1973). Nigeria: G. Shepherd, "The Structure of Small Scale Industry: Nigeria" Washington D.C.: World Bank, West African Projects Department, 1978, Mimeographed. Sierra Leone: Liedholm and Chuta (1976). (Page, 1979.)

TABLE 4.15. *The Relative Position of Small-Scale Enterprises in Manufacturing Employment, in Korea and Taiwan*

| | Korea | | | | Taiwan[g] | | | |
| | 1975A | | 1975B | | 1966[g] | | 1971 | |
	Thousand workers	% of total	Thousand workers	% of total	Thousand workers	% of total	Thousand workers	% of total
1. Total employment	2,211,181[a]	100	1,699,922[b]	100	589,660	100	1,201,539	100
2. Factory employment (size of establishment)	1,420,144[c]	64	1,420,144[c]	84	566,213	96	1,170,179	97
3. 5–49	247,133	11	247,133	15	177,256[h]	30	285,843[h]	24
4. 50–99	124,126	6	124,126	7	51,176	9	110,785	9
5. 100+	1,048,885	47	1,048,885	62	337,781	57	773,551	64
6. Non-factory employment	791,037[d]	36	279,848[d]	16	—	—	—	—
7. Very small establishment	156,783[e]	7	156,783[e]	9	23,447[i]	4	31,360[i]	3
8. Household production	634,254[f]	29	123,065[f]	7	—	—	—	—

[a] Include all workers age 14 and above who worked more than 1 hour during the survey period. The figure is from the 1975 Population and Housing Census Report Vol. 2 Five Percent Sample Survey 3–1 Economic Activity (Seoul: Economic Planning Board, 1978), Table 7.

[b] Include all workers (employers, unpaid family workers, self employed, and regular employees) age 14 and above. Excluded are temporary and daily employees. The figure is from the 1975 Population and Housing Census Report Vol. 2 Five Percent Sample Survey 3–1 Economic Activity (Seoul: Economic Planning Board, 1978), Table 7.

[c] 1975 Report on Mining and Manufacturing Survey (Seoul: Economic Planning Board, 1976), Table 1–4.

[d] Row 1 minus row 2.

[e] Report on Mining and Manufacturing Census 1973, IV Minor Establishment (Seoul: Economic Planning Board, 1974), IV–1. This is the average number of workers employed by manufacturing establishments with 1–4 workers in 1973.

[f] Row 6 minus row 7.

[g] The 1966 data are from General Report on The Third Industrial and Commercial Census of Taiwan The Republic of China (Taipei: Commission on Industrial and Commercial Censuses of Taiwan, 1968), Vol. III, Table 37, The 1971 data are from the 1971 Industrial and Commercial Census of Taiwan and Fukien Area Republic of China (Taipei: The Committee on Industrial and Commercial Censuses of Taiwan and Fukien Area, 1973), Vol. III, Table 38.

[h] Enterprises with 4–49 workers.

[i] Enterprises with 1–3 workers.

(Ho, 1980.)

Manila, on "Problems of Rapid Urbanization: Provision of Food and Basic Services", 1983.)

Two rather differently-placed economies, those of Korea and Taiwan, are enumerated in Table 4.15 (Ho, 1980); again, the data here relates to manufacturing employment only. The Korean data for 1975 (A) includes temporary and daily employees, who appear to be a large proportion of the non-factory and household production employment totals: the percentages for these two categories, 36 and 29, are very significant, and even in the "B" statistics the proportion of non-factory employment is still equal to that in the smallest group of manufacturing establishments. Unfortunately, the Taiwanese figures are not as complete as the Korean ones in this respect.

Data regarding location in relation to size of establishment is available also for Korea and Taiwan (Tables 4.16 and 4.17 respectively), for 2 years in both cases. Significantly, in Korea, at 1975 74% of all manufacturing employment was located in the two largest cities, Seoul and Busan, and their neighbouring provinces, Gyeonggi Do and Gyeong Sangnam Do: a concentration increasing since 1958 when it was 58%. The smallest size of establishment, employing 5 to 9 workers, however, was still to be found in the rest of the country, rather than in the two big cities, although the next size bracket, 10 to 19 workers, had also become more concentrated in the biggest cities between 1958 and 1975. Interestingly, although the largest establishments were still overwhelmingly in Seoul and Busan and their immediate regions at both 1958 and 1975, nonetheless the rest of Korea had gained a little in the proportion of establishments in the 200 to 499 size bracket by 1975—possibly indicating some limited success with policies of industrial decentralization to the more backward regions.

In contrast, although the data for Taiwan is more disaggregated, by sectors, and includes construction, trade, and some services, there appears to be much less concentration of all sectors, not only in the Taipei region, but also in all cities of the country, both at 1966 and 1971. Very small scale manufacturing is still largely located in the rest of Taiwan, rather than the cities, as are the smallest enterprises in all sectors. The Taiwan data generally suggests a different, possibly earlier situation so far as relative location of economic activity is concerned, than is the case in Korea. Data also quoted by Ho shows that annual growth of manufacturing employment in both Korea (1958–1975) and Taiwan (1954–1971) is strongly correlated with size of plant (i.e. number of workers): the largest enterprises grew at nine or ten times the annual rate of the smallest ones.

Many of the examples quoted above are from rural economies, without —except in the case of Egypt and Korea—large cities. It is appropriate, therefore, to consider the cases of one or two very large cities in relation to the two circuits model: São Paulo and Hong Kong have been chosen on the basis of personal knowledge, as well as their other characteristics.

The two circuits have been detected in many cities in developing economies,

TABLE 4.16. *Number of Establishments by Location and by Size of Establishment. Korea, 1958 and 1975*

	Total	Size and establishment (workers)						
		5–9	10–19	20–49	50–99	100–199	200–499	500+
Establishments, 1958	12,971	7,019	3,192	1,917	518	210	89	26
Distributed by location %								
Seoul and Busan areas	46	43	44	50	62	66	78	66
Seoul	18	16	18	21	26	25	38	35
Busan	8	5	7	13	19	22	19	23
Gyeonggi Do	10	11	9	7	10	8	13	8
Gyeongsangnam Do	10	11	10	9	7	11	8	0
Rest of Korea	54	57	55	50	37	34	21	35
Establishments, 1975	22,787	9,641	5,146	3,739	1,764	1,148	872	477
Distributed by location %								
Seoul and Busan areas	54	41	56	62	71	74	73	80
Seoul	24	17	27	28	35	33	31	34
Busan	11	8	12	14	11	13	15	17
Gyeonggi Do	12	8	11	15	19	20	21	20
Gyeongsangnam Do	7	8	6	5	6	8	6	9
Rest of Korea	46	58	44	37	28	26	27	19

Employment, 1958	260,427	44,064	40,969	54,871	33,880	28,555	27,002	31,086
Distribution by location %								
Seoul and Busan areas	58	42	45	52	63	66	78	79
Seoul	25	15	19	22	26	25	36	40
Busan	16	5	8	14	20	23	19	29
Gyeonggi Do	9	11	9	7	9	8	14	10
Gyeongsangnam Do	8	11	9	9	8	10	9	0
Rest of Korea	42	58	55	48	37	34	21	21
Employment, 1975	1,420,144	62,621	69,242	115,270	124,126	163,078	266,472	619,335
Distributed by location %								
Seoul and Busan areas	74	41	57	63	73	74	74	82
Seoul	30	18	27	28	36	33	30	31
Busan	18	8	13	14	11	13	15	23
Gyeonggi Do	18	8	11	16	20	20	22	17
Gyeongsangnam Do	8	7	6	5	6	8	6	11
Rest of Korea	26	57	44	37	27	26	26	17

Sources: Final Report—Census of Mining and Manufacturing 1958 and Report on the Mining and Manufacturing Survey 1975. (Ho, 1980.)

TABLE 4.17. *Number of Establishments by Location and by Size of Establishment, Taiwan, 1966 and 1971*

	Total	Size of establishment (workers)						
		1–3	4–9	10–19	20–49	50–99	100–499	500+
Manufacturing, 1966								
Distributed by location	28,771	11,271	9,323	3,919	2,605	782	719	149
Taipei area	22	11	22	33	40	40	42	36
Taipei and Keelung cities	10	4	10	17	18	18	13	12
Taipei Hsien	12	7	12	16	22	28	29	24
Other major cities[a]	16	10	20	20	18	18	15	18
Rest of Taiwan	62	79	58	47	41	36	43	46
Manufacturing, 1971								
Distributed by location	44,092	15,495	14,560	5,951	4,335	1,676	1,707	368
Taipei area	22	10	22	33	39	37	34	34
Taipei and Keelung cities	10	4	10	17	19	15	12	12
Taipei Hsien	12	6	12	16	20	22	21	22
Other major cities	17	13	23	18	14	14	17	20
Rest of Taiwan	61	77	55	48	47	49	49	46
Construction, 1966								
Distributed by location	4,752	1,402	1,079	742	804	369	314	42
Taipei area	26	10	30	28	32	30	28	31
Taipei and Keelung cities	19	3	21	22	24	25	26	29
Taipei Hsien	7	7	9	6	8	5	3	2
Other major cities	14	11	16	14	18	15	17	5
Rest of Taiwan	59	79	54	57	50	55	55	64
Construction, 1971								
Distributed by location	5,848	1,349	1,397	1,060	1,180	540	291	31
Taipei area	26	18	36	38	28	29	33	42
Taipei and Keelung cities	20	12	29	31	22	20	28	35
Taipei Hsien	6	6	7	7	6	9	5	7
Other major cities	15	11	15	13	16	18	26	16
Rest of Taiwan	59	71	49	49	56	53	42	42

Trade, 1966							
Distributed by location	124,532	109,213	13,256	1,562	373	79	38	2
Taipei area	25	22	44	63	68	52	53	100
Taipei and Keelung cities	17	13	39	60	66	52	47	100
Taipei Hsien	8	9	5	3	2	0	5	0
Other major cities	13	12	14	11	8	6	24	0
Rest of Taiwan	62	66	42	26	24	42	24	0
Trade, 1971							
Distribution by location	160,797	136,651	20,330	2,824	761	151	75	5
Taipei area	30	25	57	73	75	67	67	60
Taipei and Keelung cities	23	17	52	71	71	64	63	40
Taipei Hsien	7	8	5	3	4	3	4	20
Other major cities	14	14	17	14	15	16	16	0
Rest of Taiwan	46	61	26	13	10	17	17	40
Other Industries, 1966							
Distributed by location	61,234	44,572	11,611	2,570	1,799	495	203	34
Taipei area	22	21	37	37	37	41	49	62
Taipei and Keelung cities	13	12	28	30	31	38	47	62
Taipei Hsien	9	9	9	7	6	3	2	0
Other major cities	14	13	19	20	18	18	15	18
Rest of Taiwan	63	66	44	43	45	41	35	20
Other Industries, 1971							
Distributed by location	67,920	46,483	13,633	3,710	2,855	833	344	62
Taipei area	27	20	40	41	38	45	54	42
Taipei and Keelung cities	20	13	33	37	33	40	49	39
Taipei Hsien	7	7	7	4	5	4	4	3
Other major cities	15	13	18	20	25	23	20	13
Rest of Taiwan	58	67	42	39	37	32	26	45

a The cities of Taichung, Tainan, and Kaohsiung. Includes hotels, restaurants, transport and storage, financial and commercial services, recreation services, personal services and unclassified industries.

Sources: General Report on the Third Industrial and Commercial Census of Taiwan, the Republic of China and the Report of the 1971 Industrial and Commercial Censuses of Taiwan and Fukien Area, Republic of China. In both censuses, repair establishments and tailor shops are included in other industries. (Ho, 1980.)

even in São Paulo, a metropolis of now over 12 million people (or 2.5 times as big as the whole of Hong Kong), and internationally characterized as a still-rapidly growing "modern" industrial complex: "the locomotive of Brazil". Thus Bryan Roberts (Wirth and Jones, eds., 1978):

"The existence of alternative flexible economic arrangements has resulted in the co-existence of two distinct trends in São Paulo: a modern, capital-intensive sector of the urban economy and an "informal" labour-intensive sector. This situation explains the persistence of apparently marginal forms of employment as well as underemployment. Complex patterns of stratification are created among the urban workforce by these economic arrangements; such patterns often become associated with differences of ethnicity, race, or rural-urban origin. These differentiations weaken the solidarity of the working class, thereby reducing both pressure on wages and the force of demands for improvements in urban infrastructures and social services."

What seems significant here is not size of city or community, but age or period of development: both Hong Kong and São Paulo are of very recent growth to great size, as the following figures demonstrate, (Table 4.18):

These post-World War II metropolises are thus unlike older cities of the same, or lesser size, as the interesting Stanford comparison and contrast of Manchester and São Paulo demonstrates, (Wirth and Jones, op. cit.); both have been cities of very rapid growth but separated by a century in time and by very different supportive agrarian backgrounds, as Roberts has shown:

"The Manchester experience is unique in many respects. São Paulo is neither repeating the sequence of Manchester's growth nor is it simply a developing country version of that growth. Both cities were produced by the same underlying force: the development of industrial capitalism. Yet, each city experienced this change at different stages of economic development and within a different international context. Both cities have had similar importance in the consolidation and expansion of capitalism within their respective countries. Through the factory system and the massing together of a workforce totally dependent on wage labour, both cities contributed directly and indirectly to radical economic, social and political changes. The purpose of comparing Manchester and São Paulo is thus not to produce any single model of urban industrial development. The interest of the comparison is that it shows that there are various paths to economic development under capitalism, and that political and social factors are as important in determining that development as are purely economic factors."

"In striking contrast to Manchester, São Paulo's urban industrialization began at a time when the transformation of its agrarian structure was still in progress. The agrarian changes commenced in the region of São Paulo and subsequently spread throughout Brazil. Not even in the region of São Paulo has this transformation ceased. The colono system has only recently been replaced by casual labour forces from nearby towns and villages. Livestock ranching and small-scale commercial farming oriented to the urban market

TABLE 4.18(a). *Population of the City of São Paulo and its Metropolitan Area*

Year	1872	1890	1900	1920	1940	1950	1960	1970	1980
City (000s)	31	65	240	579	1,318	2,198	3,709	5,979	8,589
Average annual growth (%)	—	4.12	13.96	4.51	4.20	5.25	5.37	4.89	3.68
Metropolitan area	—	—	—	—	1,318	2,367	4,791	7,883	12,709
Average annual growth	—	—	—	—	—	6.02	7.31	5.11	4.89

Source: Instituto Brasilero de Geografia e Estatistica.

TABLE 4.18(b). *Population of the Colony of Hong Kong*

Year	1941–45*	1947	1957	1961	1967	1971	1977	1979	1980
Population (000s)	600	1,800	2,797	3,130	3,761	3,937	4,567	5,017	5,100
Average annual growth	—	20	5.54	2.9	3.36	1.17	2.67	4.95	—

* 1941–1945: estimated: the Colony lost population during the Japanese occupation.
Source: Annual Reports of the Hong Kong Government. (N.B. the Colony includes some quite remote rural areas.)

are becoming predominant in the region, but sharecroppers and pockets of peasant cultivation still remain. In other parts of Brazil which constitute both a market and a labour reserve for São Paulo industry, there are indications that peasant production is in fact expanding. This is notably true in the northeastern portions of the country."

"The patterns of development in Manchester and São Paulo stand in sharp contrast to each other. Manchester first grew on the prior commercialization of its agrarian structure and the increasing prosperity of the English domestic market. Its subsequent growth in the nineteenth century was affected by the role of external markets. Ireland, the Americas, Africa and Asia sustain Manchester by providing a market for its manufacturers, and Ireland also supplied the city with a migrant workforce. São Paulo grew as a service centre for an agricultural economy which not only exported its product, but also recruited its labour from abroad. Its agrarian structure was still in the process of change when urbanization began. The city's subsequent growth was sustained by the creation and gradual extension of an internal market for its manufactures and by the increase of internal migration."

In fact, it was Manchester's case that was exceptional, not São Paulo's for most of the non-developed world began to industrialize and to urbanize whilst their agricultures were still being transformed; the frontier—an *agricultural* frontier—was still available in many parts of the world in the nineteenth and early twentieth centuries, as an alternative to industrial work, and in Europe generally agriculture was still undergoing change.

However, it is worth following São Paulo's development a little further, as it exhibits characteristics typical both of a large city in a developing country, and those uniquely Paulista, especially in its upsetting of the primate city relationship in Brazil.

Firstly, São Paulo was a service centre for an agricultural economy recruiting labour from overseas, (predominantly Italy at this time), and selling its product, coffee, by export. Development was slow; the standard of living of the immigrants was low, and lack of purchasing power inhibited industry and urban growth. Then the improvement of internal communications via British investment in local railways which focused on São Paulo city and Santos, its port, stimulated movement, not only of coffee, but of people. Internal migrations followed, first from the State of São Paulo, then from Minas Gerais and other nearby States, and then from the remoter north-east of Brazil. Industry began to grow slowly; agriculture became more commercialized. Gradually, a new stage of development ensued, based on a localized labour supply, and thus a market close at hand. The population increased rapidly, by natural growth as well as migration: too fast for industry to take full advantage. But the absorption of labour into services rather than industry also facilitated the further growth of industry, both directly and indirectly. Services were cheap, due to low wages and excess of labour, and so more capital was available for the intensive capitalization of industrial development. This led, in turn, to growth in industrial employment. São Paulo's industry became oriented to export markets, although competing with more advanced economies; but the presence of a two-circuit economy means that work can be "put out" or sub-contracted profitably, leading to greater flexibility in management and less risk for capital—and more overall growth. São Paulo has also had the advantage of recent technology because of its recent growth, and its industrial plant can be relatively new; but it has severe problems requiring investment in infrastructure and social capital on a very large scale—just as Manchester did at its time of rapid growth, except that the São Paulo scale is enormous by comparison. The two circuits are expressed in the Avenida Paulista and the new Transit System on the one hand; the favelas and the lack, for the most part, of sewage disposal facilities on the other.

The overtaking by São Paulo of Rio de Janeiro as the largest city in Brazil is a most interesting, and highly unusual, phenomenon as has been commented.

(An earlier example of changing rank in a national hierarchy of settlement is afforded by South Africa before 1911, (Christopher, 1976, Fig. 51, p. 155); this hierarchy was quite unstable for more than half a century, with Johannesburg eventually supplanting Cape Town in the first rank.)

Martin Katzman, (Wirth and Jones, op. cit), attributes the former to the momentum produced by sheer size and to fortuitous local circumstances of timing: "In many ways, the ascendancy of São Paulo was an unlikely development. In the early 1900s, Rio appeared to have had all the inherent advantages—a port, an abundant supply of financial capital accumulated from the various staple booms, and, most important, a politically powerful elite whose favours could make or break an industrialist. While Rio indeed has been a growing industrial centre in this century, São Paulo appears to have offset Rio's initial advantage by the sheer force of its ever-increasing market size.

The historical stage at which this overtaking and surpassing occurred is of great significance. Since most important industries prior to the 1940s produced bulky consumer goods or processed natural resources, access to the market and raw materials supply area carried great weight *vis-à-vis* access to capital, political intelligence, or existing suppliers of machine tools and parts. Had the shift of the coffee frontier to São Paulo occurred after the metallurgical and mechanical industries had developed in Rio, São Paulo might have remained as rural and unindustrialized as Paraná, its successor as a coffee frontier*. This is because more complicated and roundabout industrial processes depend upon a greater division of labour among firms, and, given the backwardness of communications and transport, a high degree of proximity. This situation would have favoured the largest existing

---

* Paraná, in particular the city of Curitiba, is now rapidly industrializing, whilst the specialized coffee area in the north, around Maringa and Londrina, is about to move to a new agrarian structure.

industrial agglomeration, as suggested by the model of circular and cumulative causation."

The Brazilian economy, in terms of its real product, grew at an average annual rate of 5.4% during the period 1947–1966, largely due to the potential for import substitution which then existed, and which seemingly declined in the 1960s. During this period there was a growing spatial concentration of industry in São Paulo State, which accounted for 57.6% of the value of the country's industrial production in 1965. Within São Paulo State, the concentration of industry was largely in the metropolitan area of Greater São Paulo itself, which had 70% of the State's industrial labour in 1972; the number of industrial establishments in the metropolis grew at 2.4% per annum from 1967 to 1973, whilst employment grew at 3.2% p.a. Income per head in Greater São Paulo in 1970 was nearly twice the national average; (Schaefer and Spindel, 1976). The average annual growth rate of population in Greater São Paulo was: 5.25% from 1940 to 1950; 5.37% from 1950 to 1960; and 4.89% from 1960 to 1970. However, there has been a tendency for the proportion of employment in the secondary sector in the metropolis to grow at a slower rate than the total population, partly due to secondary sector growth outside São Paulo itself, and partly due to the increasing importance of the tertiary sector, (see Table 4.19).

TABLE 4.19. *Employment Structure, São Paulo State and Greater São Paulo, 1940–1970 (percentage)*

Year	Primary	Sector Secondary	Tertiary	Other activities
State of São Paulo				
1940	55.98	19.74	24.25	—
1950	43.21	29.12	27.64	—
1960	32.85	23.15	37.40	6.59
1970	20.57	35.71	43.72	—
Greater São Paulo				
1940	8.43	48.80	42.75	—
1950	5.44	53.22	41.31	—
1960	3.81	36.23	48.59	11.25
1970	2.02	46.79	51.19	—

Source: GEGRAN, op. cit., Vol. I, p. 158A; 1970 figures from IBGE: Censo demografico, 1970, special tabulations prepared for SERFHAU.
(Schaefer and Spindel, 1976).

The relative roles played by natural increase and net migration in São Paulo are shown in Table 4.20.

There is little doubt also that the large migrant flows experienced in Greater São Paulo led to increases in lower circuit employment generally. Schaefer and Spindel (1976) suggest that the "increasing activities of the tertiary sector" in São Paulo State created over 1.8 million new jobs between 1950 and 1970, of

TABLE 4.20. *Sources of Population Growth in Greater São Paulo, 1940–1970*

Item	Population	Greater São Paulo Natural increase	Net in-migration
Census estimates			
1940	1,568,035		
1950	2,662,653		
1960	4,747,001		
1970	8,106,250		
Increments			
1940–1950	1,094,608	230,483	864,125
1950–1960	2,084,348	727,366	1,356,982
1960–1970	3,359,249	1,250,498	2,108,751
Share of increments			
1940–1950	100.0	21.0	79.0
1950–1960	100.0	34.8	65.2
1960–1970	100.0	37.2	62.8
Annual rates of growth (percentage)			
1940–1950	5.5	1.4	4.5
1950–1960	6.0	2.5	4.2
1960–1970	5.5	2.4	3.8

Source: GEGRAN, op. cit. Vol. I, p. 63.
(Schaefer and Spindel, 1976.)

which over 1.1 million were in Greater São Paulo. Nearly 3 million jobs were provided in the metropolis by 1970, according to official Census figures, out of a total of 5 million urban jobs in the State; there were also 1.3 million rural jobs in São Paulo State at that time. Despite this achievement, the number of formal jobs was increasing at a lower rate than the total population: 5.4% between 1960 and 1970, as against 7%: consequently, unemployment and underemployment existed—as well as non-formal (but full time) employment, it is assumed.

Schaefer and Spindel (op. cit.) calculated open unemployment rates in Greater São Paulo at 1970, as a percentage of total economically active population, as being 64.3% for the 10–14 age group; 10.8% for the 15–65 age group; and 14.8% for the whole 10–65 group—or, alternatively: 50.3%; 6.3%; and 9.3% for the same age groups; (the two different sets of estimates are due to two alternative ways of defining the "economically active population"). Estimates of underemployment were also made using as a criterion those whose monthly income was less than the minimum wage set by the Brazilian Government. Using this yardstick, no less than 34.6% of the total employed population were regarded as underemployed at 1970. Underemployment was found to be especially high in the 10–19 age group, but was fairly equally located in the secondary and tertiary sectors of employment. Under-employment was also strongly related to poor education or only primary education. Although more migrants rather than non-migrants, in all age groups, qualified as being underemployed, this situation was by no means confined to migrant groups only, and seems to have been related more to age, education, and lack of skills or experience than to whether persons were migrants or established residents. The theory that migrants comprise a large pool of underemployed and unemployed persons on coming to large cities does not seem to be tenable, therefore, at least as far as São Paulo is concerned. However, migrant workers did tend to be concentrated in the lower income levels at 1970.

In the study of São Paulo reported by Schaefer and Spindel, two methods of estimating participation in the "informal sector" (as defined by the ILO) were attempted. The first method was to assume that all participants in "traditional" activities: commerce, construction, and personal and paid domestic services—were "informally" employed. Using this definition, 43.3% of the São Paulo active labour force were in the "informal" sector at 1970; 46% of these were recent migrants and 54% longer residents. The second method used the minimum wage criterion; using this, 34.6% of the total wage-earning population were regarded as "informally' employed; (44.4% migrants, 55.3% longer residents). (Tables 4.21 and 4.22.)

A 1974 survey of "informal" sector employment in Belo Horizonte, third largest city of Brazil, found that 19% of economically active males and 54% of the economically active females in that city were engaged in such activities. (Comparative figures, using the minimum wage criterion, for Greater São Paulo, were 24.8% of all working males and 54.1% of all working females.) The São Paulo "informal sector" was estimated to include 168,526 establishment, including self-employed persons, at 1970.

Hong Kong, like São Paulo, has a "modern" image: a very new city with old roots. And yet it is quite different from São Paulo. There are no motor car factories in Hong Kong, indeed no large-scale manufacturing industry: nearly 70% of its "manufacturing establishments" were in domestic premises at 1971. Despite its modernity and its economic growth record, Hong Kong is very definitely a Third World metropolis, not a European city cast up on the shores of the South China Sea.

Hong Kong is a unique city, set, within the Colony's boundaries, in a rural area, including many islands, which seem incredibly remote even only a short distance away from the dual city of Hong Kong–Kowloon. Much of the territory is mountainous, and virtually all accessible flat land has been built on, as have many steep (and sometimes unstable) slopes; in fact, flatter land is now made artificially by pulling down the smaller mountains and pushing them into the sea. Whilst Hong Kong is a colony of a western nation, and western administration is applied, including physical planning and building controls: "In Hong Kong (these policies) are relatively new, and on the local scale particularly they lead away from the style of land use and property use preferred by the people. The 'natural' human landscape in Hong Kong is

TABLE 4.21. *Differential Participation Rates of Employed Population in Informal Sector Activities and Informal Sector Employment by Sex and Migrant Status in Greater São Paulo, 1970 (Using Sector Criterion) (percentage)*

Migrant status	Participation rates of employed population in informal sector activities		Informal sector employment	
	Male	Female	Male	Female
Non-migrants	32.1	42.2	61.2	52.5
Migrants, residence 6–10 years	34.5	53.7	12.7	14.4
Migrants, residence 2–5 years	34.6	59.1	8.7	11.7
Migrants, residence less than 2 years	37.9	65.2	17.4	21.4
Total	33.1	48.9	100.0	100.0

Source: IBGE: Censo demo-grafico, 1970, special tabulations prepared for SERFHAU.

TABLE 4.22. *Differential Participation Rates of Employed Population in Informal Sector Activities and Informal Sector Employment by Migrant Status in Greater São Paulo, 1970, (Using Minimum Wage Criterion) (Percentage)*

Migrant status	Participation rates of employed population in informal sector activities	Informal sector employment
Non-migrants	28.6	55.3
Migrants, residence 6–10 years	36.7	13.6
Migrants, residence 2–5 years	41.9	10.4
Migrants, residence less than 2 years	51.0	20.5
Total	34.6	100.1

Persons earning less than Cr.$200.

Source: IBGE: Censo demografico, 1970, special tabulations prepared for SERFHAU. (Schaefer and Spindel, 1976.)

diverse, small in scale, mixed and varied in function and style; it seeks to unite diversity with specialization in one spot; it minimizes travelling and maximizes the versatility of the individual locality; it scorns no economic opportunity, whatever its shape, size, content and implications; multiplicity of uses is central to it; its hallways are shops or kitchens, its staircases stores, its alleys sculleries; its kitchens are passageways and its flats factories; its factories double as sleeping and eating places, its shops as dining rooms, and its pavements as shops or workshops. It is a landscape based fairly and squarely upon personal relationships, good and bad, among the people; a landscape of human symbiosis. All this has yet to be harmonized with the orderliness, hygiene and expense of the separation of uses." (Leeming, 1977, p. 19.)

Although no complete figures of the total number of people who work in the lower circuit are known in Hong Kong, yet some idea of the dimensions of the situation may be arrived at. In 1976 the estimated population of the colony was 4,402,990 persons, of whom 2,870,749 or 65.2% were of working age (15–65 years). Total employment at the time of the 1976 By-Census was only a little over 65% of the relevant age group, at 1,867, 480 persons; a proportion of the balance must have been women engaged in domestic activities, (women formed about 35% of those actually employed). Other data from the 1976 By-Census is given in Table 4.23. However, some older information is helpful.

In 1971 in Hong Kong, those classified as permanent workers for wages in factory units were some 77% of the labour force in manufacturing, leaving 23% of manufacturing labour presumably in the lower circuit. Only 59% of workers in commerce were then defined as permanent inworkers, so presumably the other 41% of commercial workers were in the lower circuit. In 1971 also, 29% of commercial labour was listed as self-employed. Factories in domestic premises were included in the 1971 Census of Manufacturing Establishments, and accounted for 69.7% of the total number of manufacturing establishments, 27.2% of manufacturing employment, and 20.4% of total

TABLE 4.23. *Population, Employment and Housing in Hong Kong, 1976*

Total population		4,402,990	
Working population	male	1,209,590	
	female	657,890	
	Total	1,867,480	
[Population of Working Age: (65.2%) of Total*)		2,870,749]	
(* Based on 1977 figures)			
Employment in:			
Agriculture, forestry and fishing		48,500	(=2.6%)
Mining and quarrying		1,020	(=0.05%)
Manufacturing		845,920**	(=45.3%)
Electricity, gas and water supply		9,710	
Construction		104,040	
Wholesale and retail trade, restaurants and hotels		361,680)	
Transport, storage and communication		136,180)	
Finance, insurance, real estate, and business services		62,090)	
Community, social and personal services		284,970)	
Unclassifiable		13,370)	

(** Employment in "all manufacturing establishments known to the Census and Statistics Dept." at December 1976 was: 773,746, i.e. 72,174 less.)

(March 1977): Persons accommodated (estimated):		
Housing Public	53,100	
	+1,859,400	(=42.6%)
Private	2,163,500	(=48.1%)
	+ 418,000	(Temporary = 9.3%)
		(+marine*)
Total	4,494,000	

* i.e. the original "boat people".

Source: Hong Kong: 1976 By-Census.

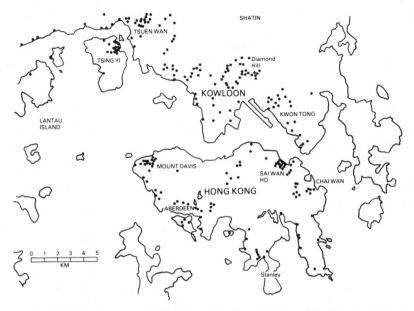

FIG. 4.24. The locations of 267 squatter settlements in existence as of March 1979.
(Hong Kong Government).

value of sales; (these figures do not include establishments in temporary structures). Total employment in factories in domestic premises at 1971 was 182,351 persons, in 17,962 establishments; there is reason to believe that this total employment, in fact, is somewhat greater, owing to non-returns of labour by family hands, (V. Sit, 1979).

These factories in domestic premises were engaged in a diversity of manufactures: 34.3% of establishments and 35% of employment were in wearing apparel; plastic products and fabricated metal products covered 22.4% of the establishments and 20% of employment. In general, the industrial structure of this group of enterprises closely resembled that of the overall manufacturing sector of Hong Kong. As regards size of establishment, 40.8% were household firms, employing less than five workers, and a quarter of this size group were one-man businesses; 48% employed between 5 and 19 workers; only about 10% of establishments employed over 20 workers; 28% of persons employed in these factories were members of the owner's family or out-workers, the balance being normal employees. The great majority of the firms had been set up using the owner's personal savings: none reported loans from commercial banks. A large proportion of enterprises also sold their output to other manufacturers or had links with other firms as sub-contractors, though these linkages changed frequently.

The location of these factories seemed to depend on rents and availability of premises, rather than on specific links or other requirements. Many of the

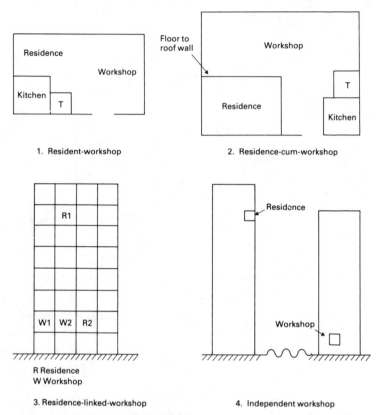

FIG. 4.25. Factories in Domestic Premises. Types of workshops (Sit, 1979).

premises were on upper floors of buildings, often associated closely with the dwelling of the proprietor. Dr Sit distinguishes four types of location characteristics (Fig. 4.25). The map (Fig. 4.26) also shows how widespread in Hong Kong this type of activity is, and how distinct, and often unrelated to, formal industrial location it is. A study by Dwyer *et al.* (1970) of small industrial units in Hong Kong also stresses the location of many small factories as being dependent on cheap accommodation on cheap land—a prescription which is realized in many suburban areas in the New Territories, where temporary structures, e.g. chicken houses may be available as well as local cheap labour. This is well illustrated by the survey of Hung Shui Kiu, 1969 (Fig. 4.27) showing the many factories set up in temporary structures.

It is one of the fascinations of Hong Kong that the two circuits of the urban economy are so well demonstrated there, with enterprises of both sorts cheek by jowl with each other, even on expensive central area locations: the illegal use of public, and even private space is a well-known Hong Kong characteristic. (Just as in Arab cities where the street is the most convenient

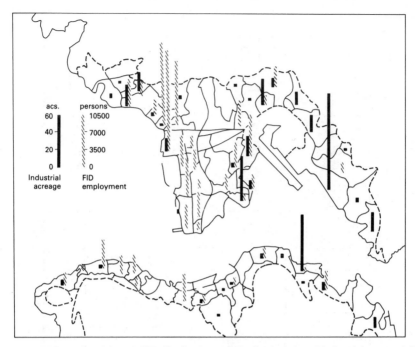

Fig. 4.26. Comparison between FID distribution and distribution of total industrial acreage (all industrial establishments). *Source:* 1971 CME (Sit, 1979).

space available on which to store building materials, for example). But Hong Kong—and also Singapore—also exhibit a third, or hybrid upper/lower phenomenon. The hawkers of Hong Kong (McGee, 1973), the street markets also, (Leeming, 1977), are only part of the service and retailing sector of this remarkable city: shopping in Hong Kong, appealing especially to the tourist market and located in the business areas of Hong Kong and Kowloon, is of an intermediate kind to a large degree. Here, the presence of a very large number of shops, (including many in hotels), though often small, selling high-value goods in not always the most favourable retail locations, can only be explained as family or extended family enterprises, in which the members are willing to provide their time and labour for possibly uncertain or infrequent reward. The bargaining situation prevailing here, rather than fixed prices, is also a lower-circuit characteristic.

Two Circuits One System

It is of the utmost importance to understand that the upper and lower circuits of an economy are subsystems of the same major socio-economic system.

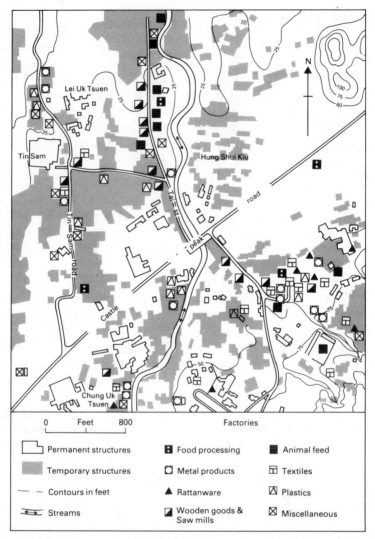

FIG. 4.27. Location of small industrial units in the Hung Shui Kiu area, August 1969 (Dwyer, 1971.) Note large proportion of industrial units in "temporary structures".

The title of Santos's book, *The Shared Space*, reminds us that the two circuits of an urban economy are subsystems in continual interaction, not isolated systems. The middle class has an interesting role here, as it tends to draw its consumption from, and to operate in, both circuits. But, of course, some activities are internal to each circuit; activities vary in strength and degree of integration; and a hierarchical relationship, i.e. domination of one activity by another, can be seen also as a supporting of the dominant by the dominated—Santos quotes the case of a wholesaler who acts as a "banker" for other lower circuit enterprises, and who could not survive himself without their support. Outside influences are also fundamental to the operation of either circuit: the existence of government help to the upper circuit by way of provision of infrastructure, for example, and the always-present tide of urban migration of the rural poor fuelling the lower circuit. However, whilst it is probably true that the external economies needed by the lower circuit can be self-created, (via its influence on rural-urban migration, or through the flexible nature of family groups and family income requirements, perhaps surprisingly), it seems unlikely that either the lower circuit will become more dependent upon the upper for its inputs, as Santos suggests, or that the upper circuit's requirements for lower circuit outputs will decrease substantially: the continuing pressure of migration to the cities in most developing countries seems likely to be the controlling factor in the long survival of the lower circuits.

The Future of the Two Circuits

In a developing country, the theory of the two circuits postulates that both upper and lower circuits of the economy will exist, side by side, and have interlocking relationships inasmuch as each is concerned with some sectors, possibly overlapping, of the same economy. Geertz, and McGee following him, held that as "development" advances, the lower circuit will give way to the upper, and that land use patterns in cities will evolve in ways which indicate that this happening. McGee (1973) has suggested a three-phase model of this change, (Fig. 4.28), based on his study of hawkers in Hong Kong. However, there seems to be no hard evidence that, in fact, the upper circuit will supplant the lower circuit entirely, if each continues to have a dependence on the other. Indeed, McGee's own "Dynamic Model of Structural Setting of Rural-Urban Mobility" for South and South East Asia, 1975–2025 (1977) does suggest a continuing "peasant" workforce, urban and rural, for a period of well over half a century. Much depends on the policies which are adopted to foster development, but the function and importance of the lower circuit as a provider of and seedbed for employment is likely to be the only way in which the many in-migrants to the cities can be accommodated: the lower circuit is at least likely to develop in this context as is the upper: the two circuit model will be with us for a long, long time. This seems to be borne out by Forbes's (1981) study of "petty production" in Ujung Padang, Indonesia, where it appears that this kind of activity, at least as measured by employment growth rates, is expanding faster than upper circuit production. It seems possible, too, that the recent growth of unemployment in developed economies could well be offset by the deliberate recreation of some aspects of lower circuit activity: encouragement of self-employment, small firms, service emphasis, the

158   G. Chadwick

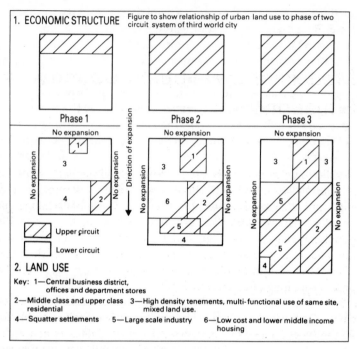

Fig. 4.28. Relationship of urban land use to phase of two-circuit system of third world city (McGee, 1973).

abandonment of too much control of location and land use, and self-help generally.

According to Forbes and others cited by him, four sectors of productive activity, urban and rural, are distinguished in Indonesia: petty commodity production and subsistence production, and capitalist production embracing both urban and rural activities; a similar situation has been suggested earlier in these pages, e.g. in Mauritius. Which suggests that the two-circuit model may really embrace two pairs of subsystems, urban and rural, or alternatively, that the upper and lower circuit might each be defined as a continuum embracing both urban and rural production: two activity spaces in socio-economic terms?

5. Models of Developing Country Situations

The earliest attempts to theorize about "development" were largely descriptive and historical in outline: Gordon Childe's definition of "civilization" might provide a ready paradigm. Then the system of exchange: barter-money-credit, could provide another basis, though only a broad one. But the most popular model of "the Stages of Economic Growth" is also largely historical, and largely descriptive: this is W. W. Rostow's model, concerned with "The Take-Off into Self-Sustained Growth" (1956); using the (hardly appropriate?) analogy of an aircraft flight.

The Rostow model begins with the state of a traditional society: a hierarchical structure socially and culturally, with a limited technological basis. As time goes on, external influences give rise to increases in investment, agriculture and extractive industries develop, and infrastructure is created: these are the necessary conditions before the take-off stage can be reached. During this take-off, occupying perhaps one or two decades, the society and its economy are transformed so that a steady growth becomes feasible thereafter. Some stimulus is necessary for this, and is shown in the rise in productive national investment, which Rostow sees as becoming over 10% of national income. Thus, substantial manufacturing sectors are created, having high growth rates, and an institutional and political framework is established which supports and encourages this growth. Then follows a drive towards maturity which involves the spread of growth to all sections of the economy. An age of high mass-consumption then develops, although in some variations a society may opt alternatively for a welfare state or the pursuit of power over others.

Opinion about Rostow's model has been divided, and unfortunately it cannot be supported historically as a series of well-defined, but related stages. Indeed, some countries, like Australia, appear to have reached the latter stages of growth contemporaneously with the earlier ones—though an explanation could be that there mass consumption was possible due to Australia's place in a Commonwealth, or even world economy, before "take-off" of home industry had begun, with Australia's traditional role of exporter of agricultural produce and raw materials providing the earlier basis. But it must be said that the historical evidence is tenuous, though a more serious criticism may be that the model does not show how, and why, the different stages are linked; possibly the Rostow model is useful in only a kind of normative way: directing attention to aspects of the situation, rather than necessarily explaining the relationships involved?

A more elaborate, and a more satisfactory, model is that presented by Gunnar Myrdal (Myrdal, 1956, 1957) described as a "Process of Cumulative Causation". In a free economy, it is held, economic changes do not give rise to opposing ones, but instead to supporting changes, which "move the system in the same direction as the first change, but much further". In other words: positive feedback occurs, rather than negative feedback in such circumstances. In the developing country situation, this means that, once a particular region has become the locus of new growth—due, in all probability, to some initial advantage of its location—then new or added growth will occur in that region or closely related to it, rather than in less-developed and thus less-advantaged regions of the country. Because of the higher potential of the developing area, flows of labour, goods and raw materials and capital, will develop from the less-developed areas to the developing region, thus decreasing the opportunities for growth in the contributory regions and increasing still further the competitive advantage of the growing region; goods and services flowing outwards from the growth region will further intensify this effect. But, in time, these "backwash" effects may be outweighed by the effects spreading outwards from the developing region: for example, the demand for raw materials may stimulate growth in contributory regions, and the improvement of transport links to stimulate one-way flows from these regions to the growth area has the effect of facilitating reverse flows also. Thus "spread" effects will also occur, and may lead to a diffusion of growth over time.

The Myrdal model has some obvious similarities to later theories of growth, for example the core–periphery concept (Friedmann, 1966; Fair, Murdoch and Jones, 1969); and the "growth-pole" idea (Perroux, 1955; Moseley, 1974). In spatial terms, these may be seen as elaborations from the gravity-potential model, and in a systems view they are clearly re-statements, in particular case and spatial/locational form, of the Principle of Competitive Exclusion (based on simple positive feedback considerations). And, in arguing for "Development as a Chain of Disequilibria", Hirschman (1958), though starting from different premises, reaches not dissimilar conclusions to those of Myrdal: "international and inter-regional inequality of growth is an inevitable concomitant and condition of growth itself". The diagram of a typical Myrdal "Cumulative Causation" model (Fig. 5.1) is almost cast in the form of a System Dynamics causal loop diagram, and might be so translated in a particular instance. All of which evidence appears suggestive of an underlying possibility of the interpretation of the "development" process in terms of General System Theory, through the agency of feedback movements—once there is some initial difference to exploit. The explanation of Competition and Exclusion depends upon the situation of competing species not occupying precisely the same ecological niche: it seems very likely that differences in geographic locations, in economic advantages and situations, likewise exist, even if small,

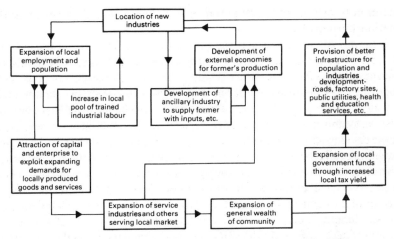

Fig. 5.1. Myrdal's Process of Cumulative Causation (Myrdal, 1957).

and growth rates of industrial enterprises and sectors are unlikely to be precisely the same?

At this point the concept of the multiplier seems relevant. The multiplier effect is the term given to the way in which growth in income or employment or output in one or a group of economic activities in a city or region appears to stimulate the growth or expansion of other groups or activities, commonly through an increased demand from the former activity or group, and those employed in it, for the goods or services produced by the latter. The multiplier effect has been much associated with the economic base concept, where the "basic" or exporting industries in a city or a region produce demands for "non-basic", or service, or locally-orientated industries, the multiplier depicting the relationship between basic and non-basic, or basic and total employment, income or output. It may be noted that, where two systems affect one another, chains of cycles in the one system may give rise to amplifying behaviour in the other: only where the two systems concerned have identical smoothing and delay behaviour will the cycles damp themselves away. The amplification in the second system of perturbation of behaviour of the first system is exactly what is described as the multiplier effect in an economic system. It is easy to see that an amplified, or multiplier income or output will fluctuate over time, and induced employment also will fluctuate, except that, in practice, other factors may make for relative inertia of employment with short term, even daily or weekly fluctuations of induced demand. Multiplier effects are time-related, though many calculations appear to assume them as being permanent.

It is significant that all three connected explanations, or attempted explanations, of "growth" infer a lack of stability in the given systems. There seems to be an exact analogy here between the transition to "growth" and the occurrence of those far-from-stability conditions in which, according to

Prigogine *et al.* (1971, 1977), self-organization of a system will occur, resulting in new forms and new behaviour.

Kaldor (1970) suggested that the principle of cumulative causation is, in fact, the existence of increasing returns to scale, including external and agglomeration economies, which favour the more developed regions and inhibit the less-developed. Kaldor used the export base concept, arguing that the way in which a region's production and exports move depends upon the rate of movement of "efficiency wages" in that region relative to others. (The movement in efficiency wages being the change in money wages relative to the change in productivity). Higher growth rates in productivity will occur in those regions with the fastest output growth rates, thus these faster growth regions will have the lower efficiency wages and growth in them will be reinforced, i.e. cumulative advantage to them will occur. This process can be represented as a "Cobweb Model" (cf. Richardson, 1970, 1974).

Allan Pred (1966, 1973, 1977) has found the circular and cumulative causation model to be helpful in explaining "the Spatial Dynamics of US Urban-Industrial Growth, 1800–1914" (Fig. 5.2). He found that the new manufacturing functions, whether for local markets or otherwise, had a first multiplier effect. Such functions, in fact, created two lines of demands: direct

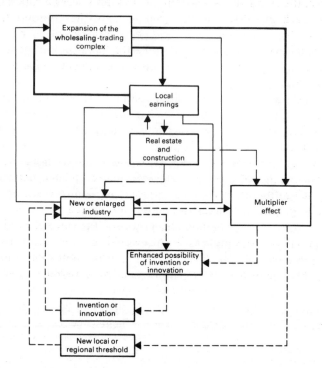

FIG. 5.2. The circular and cumulative process of urban-size growth for the American mercantile city, 1800–1840 (Pred, 1966).

ones from the factories themselves, and additional demands, created by the purchasing power of the new labour force, in all kinds of services, construction, professional, jobs, etc. Also, and especially due to large new firms or groups of single firms, linked industries might be expected to set up, associated with either "upstream" (input) or "downstream" (output) aspects of the first groups. Such new first and later arrivals might result in the surpassing of one or other new local or regional thresholds, i.e. larger markets, which might in turn support new manufacturing activities additional to the stimulation of added capacity or new factories in existing kinds of activity. Thus a circular and cumulative process is set up which continues until interrupted by diseconomies or growing competition from elsewhere. The economic base theory is clearly discernible as the major impelling force in the cumulative causation model, but, in fact, *any* economic activity may have its own multiplier effects, depending upon the qualitative and quantitative aspects of its linkages with other activities. It is here also that concepts of innovation and the circulation of information* may play their parts, though, in most attempts to identify the actual operation of the process of circular and cumulative causation; some reference to an initial advantage of the given situation, some triggering effect, is necessary to set the process in motion.

In essence, the cumulative-causation model simply seeks a rationale for a positive-feedback process at work, building upon the appropriate initial advantage, so that competition and eventual exclusion result as in biological processes. This is what Katzman (1977) terms the "polarization" paradigm, as distinct from the "equilibrium" or neo-classical paradigm, in his interesting essays on Brazil's development.

Katzman utilizes the centre–periphery concept as a basis for his review of the application of both paradigms to the Brazilian case: the centre, relatively, is industrialized, more prosperous, and growing, whereas the periphery, relatively, is rural, stagnating and poor.

The growth of the centre is regarded as being due to some initial advantage of a natural or induced kind. Initially, the centre and the periphery are sufficiently self-satisfying in their major needs of food, raw materials, and manufactured goods, with industrial production related very closely to the natural resources. Food, clothing, and processed agricultural products for export, e.g. coffee roasting in Brazil, would be the main industrial activities—for example, Brazil in 1919 reported industrial output as comprising: food 33%, textiles 27%, beverages 5%, tobacco 5%, wood 5%,

---

* Pred (1977) reminds us that, prior to the introduction of the electric telegraph in the USA, information transfer required personal contact, usually by business travellers, but also possibly by migrants. Similarly in developing countries, the transfer of information normally requires personal contact by migrants, attendance at markets, by pedlars, and itinerant craftsmen, and so on. However, in this century we have the situation of a duality of information transmission in most developing countries: by traditional means still, but also, especially in capital and post-colonial cities, of modern technological transfer alongside the older communications systems.

clothing 8%, furniture 1%. Even in 1980, the less-developed and predominantly agricultural regions of a rapidly-industrializing and urbanizing country
like the Republic of Korea show a marked reliance on food/textiles/timber
products in their industrial employment structure. Under such conditions, as
Katzman points out, industry will tend to be highly dispersed in a general
relationship to the location of the agricultural population.

Decreasing transport costs will tend to assist agglomeration tendencies at
the centre, with consequent economies, and both the average size of firms
located at the centre and the number of such firms will tend to increase. A
consequence of this is the eventual disappearance of cottage industry and
handicrafts, with consequent rural specialization in agricultural production.
The terms of trade will shift against the periphery, though the equilibrium
paradigm maintains that the periphery is still better off trading with the centre,
than not doing so. Migration is seen in this paradigm as a way of increasing the
wellbeing of both the migrant and those he leaves behind. The removal from
agriculture of surplus farm labour raises its marginal productivity. The
polarization paradigm, though, argues that the centre gains, and the periphery
loses, through the selectiveness of the migration process: the young, vigorous,
educated workers leave the periphery for the centre, whilst the periphery
retains the old and the very young and the least educated.

The chief claim of the polarization approach is that levels of industrialization, wages, and income per head between centre and periphery will continue
to diverge, whereas the equilibrium approach is more optimistic in seeing
wage differences as evening out in the long term, though the nature of the
forces leading to spatial agglomeration is recognized. In fact, Hirschman
(1958), sees both polarizing and equilibriating tendencies as continually in
operation, with the former dominating at the outset of the "development"
process, and the latter finally taking over and regional differences tending to
decline. The surfacing of agglomeration diseconomies might well be the reason
for this return to dominant negative feedback after periods of dominant
positive feedback operation—a process which might be represented in a very
similar way to the successive plateaux of stability paradigm (Fig. 5.3);
(Hardin, 1963; Prigogine et al., 1977).

The example of the growth of São Paulo is educative both in relation to the
centre–periphery paradigm, and also in its being a comparatively rare case of
one national metropolis being succeeded by another. Historically, São Paulo
has risen as a marketing centre for the coffee producing areas of São Paulo
State, and thus reciprocally as also a source from which agricultural
modernization has been diffused. Thus, for about 30 years, up to 1950, São
Paulo State had an economy very similar to the national one, with the reliance
on traditional industries outlined above.*

* Interestingly, a study by S. Czamanski and L. A. Ablas reported in 1977, found that in São
Paulo: "the older industries, such as those belonging to the textile complex, exhibited higher
multiplier effects than modern, capital intensive activities."

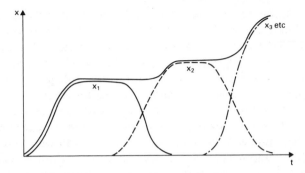

FIG. 5.3. A niche occupied successively by species of increasing effectiveness. This appears to be the equivalent of Hardin's "Plateaux of Stability". (Hardin 1963; Prigogine et al., 1977).

Katzman has carried out a shift-and-share analysis of the São Paulo situation over time. (Shift-and-share analysis is concerned with the relationship between total state or regional employment and total national employment, and with the growth rates of individual sectors of the economy, regional and national. The *share* effect is the difference between the two hypotheses: that total regional employment grows at the same rate as total national employment or that each sector of the regional economy grows at its own, sectoral, national rate. The regional *shift* effect is the difference between actual regional employment change and that projected on the assumption that each of the region's sectors will grow at its own national rate).

Katzman's results showed that, from 1920 to 1940, the industrial mix in São Paulo State was slightly more traditional even than the nation: a negative industrial mix effect. Nonetheless, the State increased its share of these and other industries, with nearly 30% of its growth in employment explained by this shift. For the period 1940 to 1959, about 83% of employment growth was attributable to the effect of national growth; only about 2% of the increase was due to a regional shift, but about 15% could be due to the state having a mix of fast-growing industry. From about 1950 to 1960, the State's gains in employment were considerably greater than those projected from national growth and its own mix of industry. More than 23% of the gain in employment represented a regional shift, i.e. regional growth rates in the particular industry exceeding the national average for that industry. The fast-growing industry mix accounted for about 13% of the employment gain; São Paulo was capturing a larger share of national employment in almost all industries, as well as having a mix of fast-growing industry. For the period 1960–1970, 90% of the State's employment gains were seen to reflect proportionate national growth, and only 8% its industrial mix.

Katzman found also that São Paulo, both State and capital, had a dualistic industrial structure relative to size of firms with higher proportions of both very small and very large firms.

São Paulo city's region in the pre-industrial coffee era, from 1870 to 1930, extended beyond São Paulo State into parts of Minas Gerais, northern Paraná, southern Goias and Mato Grosso, largely defined by the railway system centred on São Paulo. Rio de Janeiro's region, in contrast, included Rio State, Espirito Santo, and part of Minas Gerais. Taking the production of coffee, the major cash crop, as an indicator, the São Paulo-centred system overtook the Rio system just after 1890, becoming twice as large as the latter in 1900–1910 and 1910–1930. A redistribution of population and income in São Paulo's hinterland took place as the purchasing power of São Paulo suppressed that of Rio. Katzman has also calculated that São Paulo's market accessibility, regarded in terms of a national population potential model, has been a little superior to that of Rio since 1920. This superiority is considerably more marked if income potential, rather than population potential, is calculated.

Calculations by Katzman from the 30-sector Input-Output Matrix for Brazil for 1959 showed that there was no significant correlation between the consumer-orientation of an industrial sector, or its value-added ratio, and its tendency to concentrate in São Paulo State, in 1940, 1950, or 1960. This is not surprising, as national markets are not necessarily important to São Paulo industry: 65% of the output of metropolitan São Paulo is consumed in the State, and 41% is consumed in the metropolis itself. Of total São Paulo State manufactured exports, 31% goes to Guanabaro-Rio, 14% to Minas Gerais, 11% each to Paraná and Rio Grande do Sul, and only 33% to the rest of Brazil. This situation very forcibly points up the view that the metropolis, the very large city, to a considerable extent, serves itself with manufactures and services: the twentieth-century urban agglomeration is a long way from central place theory in this regard. The "Golden Triangle" of São Paulo-Belo Horizonte-Rio de Janeiro requires explanation in other terms, of which possibly a Hirschmanized positive-negative feedback version of the circular and cumulative-causation model may be the most persuasive.

So far as theoretical approaches go, for regional systems, H. W. Richardson, in his book on *Regional Growth Theory* (1979) examines and discusses a number of "popular" such theories, including:

Export Base
Neoclassical
Cumulative-Causation
Econometric models
Input–Output models
Multisector Development Planning Models

—although, as he points out, econometric and input–output models are hardly theories of growth, as such. Also—as Richardson rightly says—the multi-sectoral models are only applicable to a centrally planned economy, i.e. a totalitarian society, whereas the typical situation we are concerned with is that of a mixed economy, public and private enterprise together: "an interplay between several partially independent but hierarchically structured decision-making units". It may be, therefore that attention should be focused on the first three types of theory, noting *en passant* that econometric and input–output models, if not classifiable as theories, nonetheless have their valuable place in attempts to understand urban and regional systems.

The relationship of various national factors—national subsystems perhaps—to the process of "development" may be seen from the experience of the Republic of Korea up to 1980, though, of course, not every developing country is like South Korea. Wade and Kim (1977) open their penetrating study of public policy and economic development in the Republic of Korea with the following assertion:

"It is true, as discouraged observers have emphasized, that many countries are situated unfavourably by history and geography; some lack raw materials, suffered malign colonial experiences, have poor population to land ratios (all characteristics of Korea). But the Korean experience suggests that mismanagement and not original position is more often the cause of *continuing* underdevelopment, combined on occasion with social and cultural attitudes—and not necessarily those associated with traditional values—held by authorities hostile toward the entrepreneurial and pragmatic spirit required for development. That fashionable explanations of persistent underdevelopment are not at all apt is indicated by an examination of the growth leaders among the less developed countries: e.g. Hong Kong, Singapore, Taiwan, and South Korea. All of these are resource-poor and overcrowded, and South Korea and Taiwan suffered under exceedingly harsh and exploitive colonial regimes. All have combined an absence of self-pity with resolute decisions to expand and sustain development through public policies which encourage the mobilization of once latent cultural strengths and offer tangible inducements to individuals to act developmentally in their own interests".

Before the liberation from the Japanese in 1945, possibly 90% of the Korean population was illiterate: now the obverse is the case. The division by the United States of America and the Soviet Union dismembered a nation which had existed for 1300 years. The collapse of trade between the north (supplying the fertilizer) and the south (growing the rice) resulted in great hardship, near-starvation, and loss of manufacturing production; (electricity from the north was also cut off, in 1948, and most heavy industry was in the north, too). In the Korean War, 1950–1953, nearly a million South Korean civilians were casualties, and 40% of the South Korean military forces became casualties also. The physical losses were huge, too, rated as being equivalent to the whole 1953 GNP. The urban areas and the countryside of three-quarters of South Korea was devasted.

The two starting points of renewal in Korea were agrarian reform and education. The former, economically undesirable, was to reduce the average size of farms to less than 2.2 acres, in a countryside already the province of small-scale farming; but resulted in highly efficient production (by international standards) of rice, the staple food crop, and also in removing agrarian unrest as a political obstacle. Korean culture has always had a deep-seated impulse towards education, stifled for 40 years by the Japanese occupation, and after 1945 there was an explosion in school enrolments. Almost universal elementary education was achieved in 20 years.

At the same time, the population of the Republic of Korea was increasing at an annual average of 2.2%, so that the average annual growth rate in per capita income for the period 1960–1972 of 6.8% represented an annual average rate of increase of GNP of 9%. For the period 1965–1972, average annual population growth had fallen to 1.9%, and per capita income expanded at an annual average rate of 8.5%; GNP was thus growing at no less than 10.4% per annum for this latter period (Table 5.4). As Wade and Kim remark: "it is an intriguing and perhaps important fact that, with the exception of Greece, the Sinocultures of Korea, Japan, the Republic of China, Hong Kong, and Singapore have led the entire world in recent years in broadly-based rates of economic growth. (The People's Republic of China—the Empire at the Centre of the World which forms the culture core of East Asia—had unremarkable increases of 2.6% for both the 1960–1972 and 1965–1972 period)". As Wade and Kim also point out, this was at a time which, for the nearly one thousand million people living in the 35 countries included in the World Bank's category of lower-income developing countries, was "not one of impressive economic achievement": at this time, some 9 of these 35 countries had virtually zero growth, and 5 actually had a decline in per capita incomes.

The population density of Korea is one of the highest in the world,* and almost all of its feasibly cultivable land is already in use. Out-migration of population was not an option; indeed, during the Korean war probably as many as 1.5 million destitute refugees came into South Korea. Thus a predominantly agricultural economy, as South Korea was after partition, had to become an industrialized one if economic development was to occur. Natural resources were few and geographical location was not central to world supplies or markets.

There was also the matter of Korea's colonial history: disadvantage or opportunity? Again, Wade and Kim are worth quoting:

"The view that colonialism obviates development by having submerged talent and opportunities, destroyed previously productive cultures, and distorted the position of the colony in international trade, all in the interest of the metropolitan country, is an oftstated marxist and radical leftist claim which, however vaguely stated, has an initial persuasiveness. A colonial history, however, has not always been associated with the incapacity to sustain economic growth in the post-colonial period. Indeed, Singapore, Hong Kong, Taiwan and Korea, which have in recent years led the world in

---

* 325 people per Km^2 in 1979, or about ten times the world average density.

TABLE 5.4. *Korea: Comparison between National Plan Projections and Actual Performance (Average Growth rates, %)*

		First Plan 1962–1966	Second Plan 1967–1971	Third Plan 1972–1976	Fourth Plan 1977–1981	Fifth Plan 1982–1986
Gross National Product	(predicted)	7.1	7.0	8.6	9.2	7.5
	(actual)	7.7	10.5	10.9	5.7*	9.3†
Population	(predicted)	2.7	2.1	1.5	1.6	1.6
	(actual)	2.6	2.2	1.7	1.6**	—
Mining/Manufacturing	(predicted)	14.8	10.7	13.0	14.2	10.6
	(actual)	14.3	20.0	18.0	10.3*	10.8††
Agriculture	(predicted)	5.6	5.0	4.5	4.0	2.5
	(actual)	5.6	1.5	6.2	−5.0*	6.9†
Infrastructure/Services	(predicted)	4.5	6.6	8.5	7.6	8.8
	(actual)	8.4	12.6	8.4	6.7	—

* 1977–1980   ** 1975–1980   † 1983 only   †† 1983 (Manufacturing only).
Sources: Respective National Economic Plans, of Korea. Economic Planning Board, Seoul (1981).

broadly based economic development, are all former colonies, the first two of the British†, the second two of the Japanese. The colonial experience of Korea, as a matter of fact, may have been unprecedented in its degree of exploitation and the imported Japanese ruling class was among the largest imposed on any colonial country. When the Japanese departed in 1945, the status of the Korean population was as underdeveloped in terms of skills, education, land, leaders and future prospects as any newly emancipated colonial people anywhere." One might also add that in many countries, at least in Africa, colonialism has left a very useful legacy of organizations, capital cities (to be the locus of innovations from elsewhere), communication networks, and infrastructure: otherwise the new nations would have had to start from much further back.

A poor society apparently lacks capital and the ability to set aside from its current output any proportion for savings and investment. But it does appear that many countries do, in fact, have sources of capital for investment which can become available in conditions of political stability, as opposed to those conditions of political instability which have the effect of encouraging hoarding, present consumption, or export of capital. In Korea, with political stability came the realization that only Koreans themselves could create and encourage economic growth. Once sources of capital could be mobilized, initial conditions could be created for industrialization, which was to include borrowing of capital from foreign sources, the importing of needed raw materials, and the setting up of industries which would add value to these imports and return them as valuable exports. Importation of technology, added to the basically educated but low-wage labour force and cultural skills, further reinforced the pattern of growth. Supporting such growth requires an increasingly efficient agriculture, to feed the increasingly urbanized population: Korean agriculture has fully kept pace with this demand, and, for example, can demonstrate rice yields per hectare, in recent years, more than double those of most other rice-producing countries. This is due not only to the increased application of fertilizers and machinery, but especially also to increased human inputs in the fields and farms.

Industrialization must also require growth in services, both to supply and distribute for industry, and also to provide those things, e.g. education, health services, housing, security, etc. which make up what is regarded as the "quality of life". Increased productivity in services, e.g. banking, administration, transport, education, health, will also affect industrial productivity, directly as well as indirectly.

It is often asserted that defence expenditure in a developing country retards growth by removing resources from "productive" to "non-productive" activities. However, Benoit's (1973) examination of 44 countries for the period 1950–1965 showed that countries having high economic growth also had a

† Hong Kong, of course, is still a British colony.

high proportion of their total budgets spent on defence. Some countries exhibiting this correlation, including Korea, were recipients of foreign aid, in part for defence spending, and this factor points to part, but only part, of the reason. In Korea, as elsewhere, defence arrangements require and provide technical knowledge and managerial skills very similar to those generally needed in a growing industrialized economy. Improvements in transport and communications are essential for defence—as also for industrial and servicing purposes. National stability, required for confidence in investments and savings, is also enhanced by national security. Defence requirements themselves create industrial and service requirements in civilian sectors additional to normal needs, and have multiplier effects in these sectors.

Summarizing the Korean experience of economic development, Wade and Kim make an interesting and unfashionable deduction:

"The rapid growth in per capita income has thus been accompanied by striking transformations across a broad front of related dimensions. On every index of development effort examined, Korea ranks at or near the top in performance among less developed countries and often highly developed countries as well. The consistency of these patterns indicate that the Koreans have unlocked the secret (if that is what it is) of sustained economic progress by understanding development as involving complementary relationships in many sectors and not merely one of capital formation, or education, or agriculture, or exports, or taxation. The view that development requires the fixing of "priorities" according to some developmental theory which purports to isolate the factors deserving of greatest attention and commitment is, judging from the Korean case, inherently flawed. What seems to be required is a more balanced, *system-wide perspective* in which the contributions of one sector are seen as inextricably linked to contributions in other sectors. One is not more important nor less important than any other. The policy adjustments which will facilitate growth and linkages in the many spheres bearing on development need not, however, ensue from a grand and comprehensive national plan the construction of which requires immense data and calculations which most ordinary people are not competent to make. *The essential problem may be one of establishing systems of incentives by which individuals are encouraged to take self-interested decisions which, in their cumulative effect, construct a social setting conducive to growth*" (italics added).

The "Miracle on the Han River", then, is not so much a miracle as a considered view that policies would have to seek efficiency, promote exports, generate savings of foreign currency, allocate investment, not only through the national policy planning via macro-econometric, input–ouput, and mixed integer programming models; but also: "in erecting a generalized framework of rules within which the specific and self-interested decisions of individuals to work, save, invest, study, plan, and so forth—qualities always available in East Asian Society—have been aggregated into a social outcome which fits the requirements of development" (Wade and Kim). Such an incorporation of market mechanisms, as Charles Lindblom (1965) notes: "represents a revolution in practical economic thought and in the understanding of plan administration. The new view has not encompassed the world—and is either unnoticed or resisted in some nations—[a fact] in some part attributable to the influence of turn-of-the-century socialist thought on the intellectual and administrative traditions of some of the new or newly freed developing nations."

Wade and Kim attempt a summary synthesis of their view of the Korean experience of economic development in a hypothetical path analysis model. The central place occupied by Korean culture, with its traditional acceptance of a hierarchical structure of society and an acceptance of self-discipline within it is noteworthy. Its authors do not specify the place in this system of choices made by invoking market mechanisms: a policy choice or an outcome of the Korean culture? Whichever it has been, it has been significantly effective, so far.

A general enquiry into the relevance of various factors in the achievement of economic development in various low-income countries was carried out for the International Labour Office in 1964 (Galenson and Pyatt). This study considered 52 countries in six national income per head groups, ranging downwards from US$1000 in 1956/1958. The factors tested included education, health, housing, and social security.

Galenson and Pyatt's conclusions were as follows:

"(1) In attempting to determine the factors contributing to economic growth, a model which defines labour in terms of its quality provides a better explanation than one in which labour input is measured in numbers of persons.

(2) Of the labour quality indicators tested, the level of nutrition, as measured by daily calories available per head, seemed to yield the closest relationship with economic growth. Moreover, there are prima facie grounds for believing that a causal relationship runs from the provision of additional food to increased labour efficiency. However, the coefficients in the regression equations should not be taken too literally.

(3) The increase in higher educational enrolment showed some promise as an explanatory variable, particularly among the low income countries. However, the relationship was not sufficiently strong to warrant the flat assertion that an expansion of higher education was essential to growth.

(4) We do not feel that on the basis of our estimates one can conclude that other aspects of health, education, housing and social welfare do not contribute to labour efficiency and, through it, to development. To be in a position to reach such a conclusion, far more detailed work will have to be done. . . . it is likely that if the model

were applied to the non-agricultural sector of the economy and to manufacturing in particular, more significant results would be obtained. . . . whilst most of the labour quality indicators which were employed in the present study affect the non-agricultural labour force almost exclusively, . . . the growth, capital and labour force indicators cover the entire economy. Particularly in under-developed countries, where the agricultural sector is apt to be large, this discrepancy may have resulted in masking the effects of the labour quality inputs."

A more recent endeavour in this field is due to Wheeler (1980), who made particular efforts to cover the effects of simultaneity in this area: the difficulty of isolating and appreciating the effect of individual variables in a multi-variable system. As is often the case, simulation modelling appeared to be a promising method, essayed by Wheeler; his full dynamic model contained both recursive and simultaneous variables. The model was structured so that, within the growth periods simulated, income, population, and resource variables changed in response to the prevailing rates of birth, death, capital accumulation, and growth of the labour force; these rates, in turn, are affected by the whole set of induced changes.

The model will not be described in detail here, but the findings of the research are of interest:

(1) changes in per capita income had a significant effect on changes in literacy and life expectancy;
(2) a positive impact on output was due to calorie consumption as a measure of general nutrition;
(3) literacy change had a definite effect on economic output;
(4) when life expectancy change was used as a proxy for health improvement, no consistent results were obtained;

The utility of Wheeler's approach can be judged from his description of one of the simulation exercises undertaken:

". . . the predicted consequences of three different approaches to education are examined. The LOW results reflect the predicted evolution of the hypothetical African and South Asian societies under the assumption that the primary school enrolment ratio is frozen at 0.2 and no family planning activity is undertaken. The schooling assumption is quite pessimistic, of course, since both societies have enrolment considerably above 0.2 at the present time. The intent is to examine the sensitivity of the model to sharp shifts in important policy variables as well as to predict the implication of a specific policy alternative.

The MEDIUM simulation reflects the "normal" case which has been built into the model. Family planning is determined endogenously in this case. In each period, the primary school enrolment ratio is predicted using the results of a simple asymptotic regression fitted to cross-country data for 1977. In the HIGH simulation, the same model is employed, but the literacy rate is given an exogenous boost of 30% for the period 1977–1984.

In order for the impacts of these alternative assumptions to be demonstrated clearly, the three education simulations have been run through 84 hypothetical years."

"The dominant impression in both the African and South Asian cases is the persistent contrast between relative stagnation in the LOW cases and relatively rapid progress in the other two. The impact of the exogenous one-period boost in literacy is also quite striking. The model equations predict that this one shift will generate a time path which diverges substantially from that of the MEDIUM case for most of the crucial model variables."

"A sudden surge in literacy has three mutually-reinforcing effects. There are immediate responses predicted for the output growth rate and the investment rate. These reinforce one another in producing income gains, which in turn join with other variables in inducing gains in nutrition, health, and education. At the same time, the induced up-shift in the per capita income level produces a response in death rates and fertility rates. . . . The effect of all these forces is a simultaneous upshift in the growth rate of output and a downshift in the growth rate of population.

The relative stagnation in the LOW case . . . with primary schooling frozen at a very low level, successive age cohorts arrive at adulthood with very low literacy rates. At the same time, no outlet is provided for family planning activity as an additional instrument for lowering the fertility rate. The cumulative impact of these two lapses is seen in a birth rate which is so persistently high as to overwhelm the prevailing death rate. In addition, the absence of the self-reinforcing dynamic interaction between output and education growth leaves the economy dependent on the increment provided by changes in the capital stock and the physical quantity of labour, rather than the quality of labour.

The first result of this relative stagnation in per capita income and human resource indices is a country whose population is much larger and much poorer (in per capita terms) than that predicted by the MEDIUM and HIGH cases."

We come now to a basic hypothesis, which is foreshadowed in the work of Gordon Childe, and Braidwood and Willey, on the early development of civilization, and also underlies, in a non-explicit way, some of recent thinking about "development" in underdeveloped countries. The hypothesis is not revolutionary, therefore, but it does need stating. It is attempted as follows:

"Development" is not primarily an economic process, but rather a general cultural one. Economic development is not possible, and in any case would be a failure (as being only a "means-goal") without the corresponding development to appropriate levels of other systems, or subsystems of a given culture. That is, in systems terms, all human systems are interrelated, and related also to ecological and natural physical systems, by complex linkages, of which "multiplier effects" are a simple example. Change in one subsystem of a culture induces or inhibits change in another subsystem of that culture. This change (positive feedback) may reach far beyond some threshold within which stability has so far reigned, due to a prevalence of negative feedback loops; and some subsystems crossing such thresholds may carry others with them on to new trajectories. But, clearly, some relationships are directional, at least at certain times or stages: one subsystem furnishes inputs without which another subsystem cannot function; this is clearly the case with ecological systems which, both directly and indirectly (e.g. via farming, water gathering) supply fundamental inputs to human systems. It is believed that human economic systems likewise require supporting inputs—of people, for example, as trained producers or educated consumers—before "development" of such systems can be effective. "Development" has many dimensions, and the "software" of educated human beings is essential to the "hardware" of industrial plants, transport systems, power transmission lines, oil refineries, and so forth.

And so, one might search for the criteria for "development", not in the too obvious area of industrialization first of all, but in the forces leading to urbanization: the roots of civilization. An agrarian basis is essential, even if not close at hand; an increasing population, who can be divorced in part from the soil, is needed; an increasing literacy and numeracy must be found; and an organization, a social order or culture, with values and ideals from which can arise the direction (self-direction, or acceptance of some rule of law, market principle, or higher authority) must be there. All these are a necessary basis for the processes of specialization of task, manufacture and provision of service which lead to the elusive achievement of "development". The situation is thus complex: a multiplexed system of many components and not a few subsystems; the modelling of it cannot be easy in any real situation, for the relationships are sometimes hard to perceive, harder to quantify (and quantification must be attempted in modelling such phenomena). Stress may be laid, too, on the various subsystems giving rise to "development" being concerned very largely with endogenous relationships: the place of exogenous inputs, of "aid", capital, know-how, advice, may be much less relevant than that of "home-grown" inputs, arising from the nature of the cultural systems involved. Such systems are believed to be essentially "learning systems", in which a culture perceives and adjusts, and is adjusted by, its general environment, learning being a feedback process of trial and error; one's own mistakes are the best basis for learning, rather than those of a stranger. Perhaps all education is ultimately self-education?

Like all ecological systems, there will be lags and seemingly abortive starts or trial-and-error (i.e. learning) responses: a process occupying time, possibly a long time, even several generations (again, as in many ecological systems). The problem with much "development" effort is that virtually instantaneous response is often expected, and disappointment ensues if it does not occur. The correct analogy is not with any kind of mechanical or "hard" system, but with "soft" biological systems where many trials are involved in producing a small number of effective mutations or developments (see Ashby, 1950, pp. 82–3). A ready example is induced population change by changing social habit or increasing disposable income—which must take at least one (and commonly several) generations to produce an appreciable effect on total population. Such considerations appear to underlie, and be expressed in the Demographic Transition.

The Demographic Transition as a Basic Model

The spatial and temporal aspects of the Demographic Transition Model have been portrayed by Roy Chung (1966), using United Nations Demographic Yearbook source material. Chung's version of the demographic transition is a three-stage model (Fig. 5.5); with an alternative situation possible for Stage 2 of the model. Countries without a census or population registration were placed in Stage 1, as this is believed to be true of most such cases. The world maps presented by Chung, for 5 year intervals since 1905, show the progress of the demographic transition across the globe, though, as he points out, as of 1966, except for Japan and certain overseas neo-European countries, no area that had ever entered the explosive Phase 2 of the model had emerged from this stage of the transition: "The forerunners of the modern explosion which was initiated 30 to 35 years ago—Surinam, Honduras, Panama, Nicaragua, Dominican Republic—are still in the explosive stage in

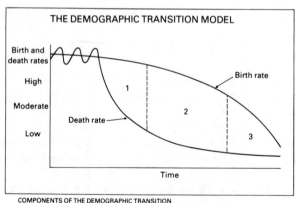

FIG. 5.5. The demographic transition model (Chung, 1966).

the 1960s with some of the highest birth rates in the world coexisting with low modern mortality rates."

The "Third World", i.e. Latin America, Africa, and Asia, started its transition in the 1930s, and is either predominantly in the explosive Stage 2, or even still in Stage 1; Chung sees some correlation between size of country and the timing of the beginning of the transition here. It is possible, perhaps, that this group of countries may not follow the transition model at all: as late as 1960, India had not entered the second stage, and China, Mexico, Brazil, Indonesia were then only recent entrants to it. Chung points out that "the population explosion" which started during the 1930–1934 period was for 20 or 30 years primarily an explosion of small countries"; for the relative ease of mortality control via DDT in a small country, a Mauritius or a Ceylon, cannot be repeated easily in an India, or a China, Brazil or Mexico, where the logistics of size are so different, and where regions may differ so much.

But there may well be a relationship to "modernization" or "development" also:

"In the Third World theory, death control often precedes modernization. It may very well be true that a minimum kind of modernization sufficient to affect the ideal family-size preference has to precede or accompany the acceptance of family planning for it to be optimally effective in the reduction of fertility." It may also be the case, when the transition to Stage 2 begins to take place in the very large countries, that "development" may have progressed to a point where fertility reduction becomes more rapid than earlier precedents might suggest, and thus the "explosion" may be less destructive. The mortality rate, historically, never declines before the birth rate: a decline in the crude death rate is accompanied, in very many countries, by a much sharper drop in the birth rate; death control, as it were, leads to fertility control."

A template for a Developing Country Model may already exist in the form of the various World Models which have been the outcome of some fundamental and distinguished efforts; unfortunately lack of space precludes a more detailed consideration of a number of these pioneering modelling attempts. A bare mention obviously must include Jay Forrester's World Dynamics model (World 2) of 1971, and the revised version (World 3) by Meadows et al. (1972) published under the title: The Limits to Growth for the Club of Rome, and also the subsequent controversy between "pessimists" (or Malthusians) and "optimists" as to the future of the world. The IIASA model directed by Mesarovic and Pestel (1974) was a larger and next-generation study of very considerable complexity using a more disaggregated approach. Less-extensive, but nonetheless interesting models which followed included the British SARUM 76 (Roberts et al., 1978), the Fundacion Bariloche of Argentina model (Bruckman, ed., 1974), and the agriculturally-oriented MOIRA by a Dutch team (Lindeman et al., 1972); all deserve investigation by the searcher for a world context for a national or (world) regional modelling endeavour.

The difference of aim in a World Model, and the data used, of course make such models only a general guide; moreover a World Model may generalize considerably, aggregating countries at several different stages of development, depending on the modelling approach chosen. A Developing Country Model cannot be, therefore, simply a scaled-down version of a World Model, helpful though the latter may be.

The point may be made in relation to an outline of a Systems Dynamics version of a model of the island of Mauritius (population c. 0.9 million), of which a causal loop diagram is shown later. This diagram is based on some aspects of the Meadows World 3 model, but incorporating various adjustments and additions thought to be necessary to replicate the behaviour of the Mauritian system. The model has not been validated by data, as much of the data needed would require a long period of on-site investigation which has not been possible; the model thus remains a hypothesis only.

An alternative, perhaps a better approach, would be to devise a series of submodels of various aspects of the cultural economy of a given developing country, and then to essay linking them together by a series of lags and delays, leading to thresholds of change, with appropriate feedback loops. For example, a demographic transition model might be linked with a food supply, agricultural growth model, and an education investment (or literacy development) model; an energy demand/supply model might link both with a capital investment model and the population model; and so on. The strategy of submodelling, or modelling of sectors has considerable merits in focusing attention not only on that particular sector, but also on its time-dependent relationships with other sectors It is also, it would seem, a very sound philosophy in cybernetic terms, drawing attention to the lags and gains between subsystems, for example.

Housing Stocks and Housing Demand in Developing Countries

Few developing countries have any systematic knowledge of the national housing stock. An exception is Mauritius, where both the main island and the island of Rodrigues (300 miles east of Mauritius) were covered by the 1972 Housing Census. The information available about the Mauritian housing stock is indeed comprehensive.

As the Census puts it: "Since as part of the housing census operation it was necessary to enquire about all buildings as defined (both residential and non-residential) in order to ascertain whether they were occupied as living quarters or not, it has been found convenient to enumerate:

(i) all buildings used at the time of the census for residential, commercial or industrial purposes or for the provision of services;
(ii) vacant buildings intended for the purposes in (i);
(iii) all structures not intended for the uses mentioned in (i) and (ii) but used as such at the time of the census;

(iv) improvized temporary structures inhabited at the time of the census;

(v) buildings under construction."

Thus only agricultural buildings, some improvized structures not used for habitation, etc., and unhabitable buildings and those awaiting demolition were excluded from enumeration. Two distinct sets of data were therefore forthcoming from the census: one set relating to buildings, and one relating to "living quarters" as defined. The number of households and certain of their characteristics were included also in the living quarters data.

The information as to age, condition, and structural type is very comprehensive, differentiating age, on or off foundations, and type of wall and type of roof. Wall materials covered: stone, concrete, concrete blocks and brick; asbestos cement; wood, iron or tin sheets; vegetable; and other. Roofing materials included: concrete slab, shingles, iron or tin sheets, vegetable, and other. Straw huts, of which there were then 7,337, were classified separately, with subdivisions of wall materials into wood, iron or tin sheets, vegetable, and other; the "straw" refers principally to the thatched roofs of these somewhat impermanent structures—though, 2,442 such huts were enumerated as being completed before 1960, although only 643 of these "cases en paille" were entirely vegetable* in origin. Straw huts of this type suffer badly in the tropical cyclones which visit Mauritius too frequently**; however, they also have the merit of easy and quick replacement, and cost literally nothing. Rodrigues had 983 straw huts out of 5,050 residential buildings of all sorts at 1972.

The total number of living quarters on the island of Mauritius was 156,446. Of the 149,131 such quarters which were then occupied, 145,097 were occupied by one household only, the remainder being each shared by two or more households. Only 40,522 of these quarters had piped water internally, though, but 104,765 were connected to the electricity supply. In general, the structural condition of Mauritian housing appeared to be good, but facilities were absent in many cases.

At the other end of the scale, the Municipio de São Paulo—which forms only a part of the enormous urban agglomeration of Greater São Paulo—in 1977 had 1,851,813 dwellings, of which: 45,304 were described as "Barracos e Favelas"; no less than 900,819 were described as "Precario"; 766,094 were listed as "Razoavel"; 117,247 were "Bom"; and only 22,349 were "Excellente". Clearly São Paulo has an enormous housing problem, seen especially when the dwelling type/condition information is correlated with the income level information, as in Table 5.6, below (referring to Greater São Paulo).

The problem of supplying housing in a developing country—as elsewhere —is not simply a matter of catering for net population increase. In Korea, between 1975 and 1980, the total population increased at an annual average

---

* Palm and Pandanus (Screw Pine) leaves were used, also no doubt sugar cane debris.

** Two cyclones struck Mauritius within one month in January/February 1960: 40,000 houses were destroyed or damaged: more than a quarter of the entire housing stock.

TABLE 5.6. *Greater São Paulo: Distribution of Dwellings by Income Groups and Building Types and Conditions, 1977*

Monthly family income	Shacks and favelas	%	Precario	%	Reasonable	%	Good	%	Excellent	%	Total	%
				Building types and conditions								
Without Income	1,353	(1.4)	2,545	(0.2)	922	(0.1)	165	(0.1)	74	(0.3)	5,059	(0.2)
0–1 Minimum Salaries	7,248	(7.5)	40,593	(3.1)	12,795	(1.4)	598	(0.4)	157	(0.6)	61,059	(2.5)
1–2 Minimum Salaries	29,202	(30.2)	145,409	(11.2)	38,153	(4.1)	2,068	(1.5)	139	(0.6)	214,971	(8.7)
2–3 Minimum Salaries	19,862	(20.6)	211,136	(16.3)	59,228	(6.4)	4,384	(3.2)	497	(2.0)	295,107	(11.9)
3–5 Minimum Salaries	24,342	(25.2)	357,061	(27.5)	144,097	(15.6)	7,371	(5.4)	700	(2.8)	533,571	(21.6)
5–7 Minimum Salaries	4,921	(5.1)	172,226	(13.3)	121,249	(13.2)	5,827	(4.3)	740	(2.9)	304,963	(12.3)
7–10 Minimum Salaries	3,167	(3.3)	144,522	(11.1)	152,814	(16.7)	13,613	(10.1)	1,351	(5.4)	315,467	(12.7)
10–15 Minimum Salaries	558	(0.6)	68,032	(5.2)	117,531	(12.8)	15,542	(11.5)	1,635	(6.5)	203,298	(8.2)
15–20 Minimum Salaries	666	(0.7)	24,439	(1.9)	78,413	(8.5)	17,161	(12.7)	2,311	(9.2)	122,990	(5.0)
Over 20 Minimum Salaries	417	(0.4)	17,986	(1.4)	81,389	(8.8)	38,429	(28.5)	9,825	(39.1)	148,056	(6.0)
Absent	3,137	(3.2)	54,631	(4.2)	57,807	(6.3)	18,197	(13.4)	4,911	(19.5)	138,683	(5.6)
Dwelling Vacant	1,724	(1.8)	59,251	(4.6)	56,515	(6.1)	12,069	(8.9)	2,794	(11.1)	132,353	(5.3)
Total	96,597	(100)	1,297,831	(100)	920,913	(100)	135,434	(100)	25,134	(100)	2,475,909	(100)
Percentage of Total Stock	3.9		52.4		37.2		5.5		1.0		100	

Source: Secretaria dos Negocios Metropolitanos, Estado de São Paulo, EMPLASA: Sumario de Dados da Grande São Paulo, 1978 (from O & D Survey, 1977).

rate of 1.53%, from 34.7 million to 37.4 million: a rate of increase perhaps only half of that of the fastest growing countries in Africa or Latin America. However, over the same period, the number of households in Korea increased from 6.6 million to 8.0 million, or an annual average increase of 3.8%, indicating a tendency away from the traditional extended family (and thus, it would seem, a loosening of traditional Korean cultural ties?) towards a preponderance of nuclear families.* Over the same period, housing units in Korea grew at 2.9% per annum, from 4.7 million to 5.4 million, this being slower than the growth in households: there were more households per housing unit in 1980 than there were in 1975, despite the construction over that period of 0.7 million new housing units.

The Korean housing problem, of course, is worst in the country's largest cities. Nationally, according to the 1980 Census, the total population of 37,448,836 persons formed 7,971,147 households and was accommodated in 5,463,185 housing units, giving an average of 4.698 persons per household, 6.855 persons per housing unit, and 1.459 households per housing unit. However, in the City of Seoul, the population of 8,366,756 formed 1,836,192 households and lived in only 993,661 housing units: averages of 4.47 persons per household, 8.42 persons per housing unit, and 1.848 households per housing unit. The second city, Pusan, had a 1980 population of 3,160,276, forming 687,370 households, accommodated in 352,857 housing units, producing average figures of 4.51 persons per household, 8.98 persons per housing unit, and 1.948 households per housing unit. Thus it is almost literally true that the largest Korean cities have only one dwelling to every two households, this being reflected in considerable sharing or multiple use of housing, even down to the letting of separate rooms in apartment blocks, with whole families of 7 or 8 persons occupying perhaps two rooms (though this frugal use of space is assisted by the traditional multiple use of rooms in Korean dwellings). Western, or European standards of housing space are inevitably seen as luxurious in the extreme against such statistics—the title of a Korean report on Housing Needs of the Homeless Households points up the moral without further discussion—but if one separate dwelling per household was taken as a policy target, it is very sobering to realize that both Seoul and Pusan, large cities by any standard, would require 100% more housing than they now have. Would this also mean largely doubling the physical size of these cities?

The problem is not limited to Seoul and Pusan, either, for, taking all cities of Korea, population increased at 5% per annum over the period 1975–1980, whilst households increased at 7% per annum. A housing forecast prepared by KRIHS (1981) suggests a cumulative need in the cities of Korea of 6.1 million housing units by 1991, if a standard of one dwelling per household is adopted. Such a programme would consume major national resources, for which

---

* One must not overlook the incidence of migration from rural to urban areas, which in many cases will have resulted in additional household formation.

competition exists for national economic development purposes: social versus economic needs? However, even now there is some difficulty in disposing of certain new housing units, due to the increase in the price of new housing outstripping the rise in household incomes, so that affordability, as well as physical need enters into the equation strongly. An important feature of Korean housing is the essential need for heating during the very cold winters—met, traditionally by the *ondol* system of underfloor heating, hence one sits on the floor, and sleeps on it also. The cost of providing central heating systems in new housing of course raises the overall cost per *pyong* of floor space, and thus becomes an important consideration in the affordability of housing for lower income householders.

An interesting aspect of Korean housing is that the bulk of the housing stock of all Korean cities—over 75% of the total—is in the form of detached houses, as against 15% in apartments. The traditional Korean house, rural or urban, is detached, on its own piece of ground, albeit a small one. Except in rural situations and higher income housing, house plots are small and densities fairly high for one or two-storey construction; space around the house is utilized mainly for drying and storage, including the ubiquitous rows of *kimchi* jars. Many Korean houses are approached only by narrow lanes, as vehicular access, except for carts, is not regarded as essential.

As an example of the sort of situation typical of Korean city housing, Table 5.7 gives details of two smaller cities in Jeonra Bug Do, one of the less-developed provinces of the country.

Housing conditions vary from country to country, of course, depending on many factors: climate, incomes, history, rate of population growth, social customs, and so forth. The incidence of climate is very important: in the tropics the requirements are different from those in a climate with cold winters: contrast the pleasant winter season of Mauritius with the severe cold of a Korean winter, necessitating heating as well as shelter. In a climate like that of Saudi Arabia shelter from the sun is essential, and air-conditioning or some other means of artificial temperature control is no longer a luxury in housing in many Middle Eastern countries.

The number of inadequate houses requiring some sort of improvement and the pressure of households still needing accommodation are two of the major factors needing action in housing policies in developing countries (see Table 5.8). The numbers are very daunting in some cities: Grimes (1976) quotes Calcutta as having more than 1,700,000 squatters and slum dwellers; Jakarta more than 1,125,000 and Karachi more than 810,000; all at 1974; the bustees of Calcutta house about one-third of the city's population. Location of housing, whether good or bad, is important in relation to employment opportunities: people who sleep in the streets of large Asian cities like Calcutta are not necessarily homeless—they may simply be unable to afford the time and money required to travel from their home on the outskirts of the city to their work, or their area of seeking for work. Areas which have grown

TABLE 5.7. *Housing Conditions in Two Smaller Korean Cities*, 1981

Household Income Groups	Average size of house (pyongs)		Average number of rooms/house		Average number of persons/house		Approximate average age of house	
City:	Jeonju	Iri	Jeonju	Iri	Jeonju	Iri	Jeonju	Iri
A	14.1	13.7	2.9	2.4	4.1	3.8	15.7	6.7
B	26.2	16.9	3.2	2.7	6.6	5.0	9.7	7.0
C	22.7	18.7	3.2	2.8	8.4	5.0	8.3	4.3
D	31.1	17.7	3.0	3.5	6.0	5.4	8.1	7.4
E	27.0	17.9	3.3	2.7	7.5	5.4	8.7	5.0
F	27.1	20.9	3.7	3.1	6.4	7.0	7.0	10.1
G	33.6	23.3	3.9	4.2	8.3	7.1	6.8	11.4
H	30.1	34.6	4.9	4.6	11.8	11.3	12.4	10.7

Source: Jeonju Regional Development Project Feasibility Studies, 1982, Ministry of Construction, Korea.

Notes:

(1) Household Income Groups: A: below 100,000 wons/month; B to E inclusive, in 100,000 won brackets from 100,000 to 200,000, to 400,000 to 500,000 wons/month; Group F: 500,000–750,000 w/month; Group G: 750,000–1,000,000 w/month; H: over 1,000,000 w/month. (US Dollars 1.00 were roughly equivalent to won 700 at this time).

(2) 1 pyong = 3.307 square metres.

(3) Most dwellings are shared, thus persons/house is not an indication of family (normally household) size. Average household size: Jeonju 5.05, Iri 4.95.

(4) Relative youth of housing stock is due to: (a) destruction during the Korean War and subsequent replacement; (b) urban growth in recent past.

(5) Population of Jeonju, (1980) = 367,000 in 72,862 households. Average households per dwelling unit = 1.74. Sample size: 469 households.
Population of Iri, (1980) = 145,358, in 29,582 households. Average households per dwelling unit = 1.62. Sample size: 324 households.

spontaneously for self-built, squatter housing may be highly unsuitable, not only because of their locations in relation to employment, but to the physical conditions there. Grimes quotes the case of Netzahualcoyotl, on the outskirts of Mexico City, with a population of more than 1 million: "It is located on a dry salt-lake bed, which permits no cultivation. Here the inhabitants face frequent flooding, typhoid in the wet season, and bronchial pneumonia in the dusty dry season. Infant mortality is four times higher in this area than in three low-income areas of Mexico City." Because of the propensity of squatters to utilize "unwanted" urban or peri-urban land, such problems as outright unsuitability for development (as at Netzahualcoyotl) are bypassed; the technical infrastructure for dealing with flooding or steep slopes or unstable ground, or pollution from adjoining uses, is absent, in addition to the general absence of utility services: roads, water, sewage disposal, electricity. Much "unsuitable" land may be developable in technical terms, but only at very high costs: such sites are by no means "low cost" solutions in any sense. Housing is seen by many economists as offering a bundle of services, of which shelter and space to live in represent only the most obvious: location in relation to employment, to local facilities, to transport. It is, of course, a fixed-location

TABLE 5.8. *Housing Conditions in Typical Cities of Developing Countries, c. 1970*

Country	City	Residential construction As % of country GDP	As % of country GDCF[f]	Gross population density of city (persons per square kilometre)	Urban housing condition in country[g]	Slums and squatter settlements as % of city population[h]
Relatively high-income countries						
Venezuela	Caracas	4.32	17.74	1,186	n.s.	40 (1969)
	Maracaibo	4.32	17.74	n.a.	n.a.	50 (1969)
	Barquisimeto	4.32	17.74	n.a.	n.a.	41 (1969)
	Ciudad Guayana	4.32	17.74	n.a.	n.a.	40 (1969)
Panama	Panama City	4.40	20.96	197	38.3 (1960)	17 (1970)
Chile	Santiago	2.82	18.79	n.a.	14.7 (1970)	25 (1964)
Hong Kong	Hong Kong	n.a.	n.a.	n.a.	n.a.	16 (1969)
Mexico	Mexico City	n.a.	n.a.	n.a.	47.4 (1960)	46 (1970)
Lebanon	Beirut	n.a.	n.a.	n.a.	n.a.	1.5 (1970)
Singapore	Singapore	n.a.	n.a.	n.a.	n.a.	15 (1970)
Middle-income countries						
Zambia	Lusaka	n.a.	n.a.	n.a.	n.a.	48 (1969)
Ivory Coast	Abidjan	n.a.	n.a.	n.a.	n.a.	60 (1964)
Korea	Seoul	2.71	10.93	9,031	58.9 (1960)	30 (1970)
	Busan	2.71	10.93	n.a.	58.9 (1960)	31 (1970)
Malaysia	Kuala Lumpur[c]	n.a.	n.a.	n.a.	n.a.	37 (1971)
Honduras	Tegucogapa	n.a.	n.a.	n.a.	n.a.	25 (1970)
Philippines	Manila[c]	n.a.	n.a.	5,116	30.1 (1967)	35 (1972)
Peru	Lima	n.a.	n.a.	4,380	33.7 (1961)	40 (1970)
	Arequipa	n.a.	n.a.	n.a.	33.7 (1961)	40 (1970)
	Chimbote	n.a.	n.a.	n.a.	n.a.	67 (1970)
Brazil	Rio de Janeiro	n.a.	n.a.	n.a.	2.8 (1969)	30 (1970)
	Belo Horizonte	n.a.	n.a.	n.a.	2.8 (1969)	14 (1970)
	Recife	n.a.	n.a.	n.a.	2.8 (1969)	50 (1970)
	Porto Alegre	n.a.	n.a.	n.a.	2.8 (1969)	13 (1970)
	Brasilia	n.a.	n.a.	n.a.	2.8 (1969)	41 (1970)
Colombia	Bogotá	3.76	20.01	n.a.	n.a.	60 (1969)
	Cali	3.76	20.01	n.a.	n.a.	30 (1969)
	Buenaventura	3.76	20.01	n.a.	n.a.	80 (1969)
Iraq	Bagdad[c]	n.a.	n.a.	n.a.	n.a.	29 (1965)
Ecuador	Guayaquil	n.a.	n.a.	n.a.	39.9 (1962)	49 (1969)
Senegal	Dakar	n.a.	n.a.	n.a.	n.a.	60 (1971)
Guatemala	City	n.a.	n.a.	n.a.	n.a.	30 (1971)
Turkey	Ankara	3.97	22.16	n.a.	29.2 (1965)	60 (1970)
	Istanbul	3.97	22.16	n.a.	29.2	40 (1970)
	Ismar	3.97	22.16	n.a.	29.2	65 (1970)
Ghana	Accra	4.76	40.95	n.a.	n.a.	53 (1968)
Jordan	Amman	n.a.	n.a.	n.a.	n.a.	14 (1971)
Liberia	Monrovia	n.a.	n.a.	n.a.	n.a.	50 (1970)
Morocco	Casablanca	n.a.	n.a.	n.a.	34.4 (1971)	70 (1971)
	Rabat	n.a.	n.a.	n.a.	34.4 (1971)	60 (1971)
Cameroon	Douala[c]	n.a.	n.a.	n.a.	n.a.	80 (1970)
	Yaoundé	n.a.	n.a.	n.a.	n.a.	90 (1970)
Poorest countries						
Sri Lanka	Colombo	n.a.	n.a.	n.a.	n.a.	43 (1968)

Table 5.8–continued

Country	City	Residential construction As % of country GDP	Residential construction As % of country GDCF[f]	Gross population density of city (persons per square kilometre)	Urban housing condition in country[g]	Slums and squatter settlements as % of city population[h]
India	Calcutta[c]	n.a.	n.a.	n.a.	n.a.	33 (1971)
	Bombay	n.a.	n.a.	n.a.	n.a.	25 (1971)
	Delhi[c]	n.a.	n.a.	n.a.	n.a.	30 (1971)
	Madras	n.a.	n.a.	n.a.	n.a.	25 (1971)
	Baroda	n.a.	n.a.	n.a.	n.a.	19 (1971)
Pakistan	Karachi	n.a.	n.a.	n.a.	59.0 (1960)	23 (1970)
Afghanistan	Kabul[c]	n.a.	n.a.	n.a.	n.a.	21 (1971)
Indonesia	Jakarta	n.a.	n.a.	n.a.	n.a.	26 (1972)
	Bandung	n.a.	n.a.	n.a.	n.a.	27 (1972)
	Makassar	n.a.	n.a.	n.a.	n.a.	33 (1972)
Kenya	Nairobi	2.92	15.88	n.a.	41.1 (1962)	33 (1970)
	Mombasa	2.92	15.88	n.a.	41.1 (1962)	66 (1970)
Togo	Lomé	n.a.	n.a.	n.a.	n.a.	75 (1970)
Malagasy	Tananarive[c]	n.a.	n.a.	n.a.	n.a.	33 (1969)
Nigeria	Ibadan	n.a.	n.a.	n.a.	n.a.	75 (1971)
Sudan	Port Sudan	n.a.	n.a.	n.a.	n.a.	55 (1971)
Tanzania	Der es Salaam	n.a.	n.a.	n.a.	n.a.	50 (1970)
Zaïre	Kinshasa	n.a.	n.a.	6,589	n.a.	60 (1969)
Ethiopia	Addis Ababa	n.a.	n.a.	n.a.	n.a.	90 (1968)
Malawi	Blantyre	n.a.	n.a.	n.a.	n.a.	56 (1966)
Nepal	Katmandu	n.a.	n.a.	n.a.	20.2	22 (1961)
Somalia	Mogadishu	n.a.	n.a.	n.a.	n.a.	77 (1967)
Upper Volta	Ouagadougou	n.a.	n.a.	n.a.	n.a.	70 (1966)

n.a. Not available.

[c] Metropolitan areas.

[f] Gross domestic capital formation.

[g] Percentage of occupied dwellings with three or more persons a room in urban areas.

[h] These figures are notional since definitions vary widely across countries; they are used to indicate rough orders of magnitude.

Sources: S. Jain and A. E. Tiemann, "Size Distribution of Income: Compilation of Data", Staff Working Paper No. 190 (Washington, D.C.: World Bank, 1973); L. Grebler, "The Role of Housing in Economic Development" (paper prepared for the Third World Conference of Engineers and Architects, Tel Aviv, December 1973); *World Bank Atlas* (Washington, D.C., 1973); and United Nations, *World Housing Survey* (New York, January 1974).
From: Grimes O. F.; 1976.

good, and is variously input and output for the many utility and other services commonly required. Only food normally takes precedence over housing in family expenditure, and from 15 to 25% of total expenditure may be on housing, on average—although these figures may vary widely with income levels.

In many developed countries, the construction of housing may represent 20 or 30% of gross fixed domestic capital formation (Grimes, 1976) or about 2 to

5% of GDP in many developing countries. In actual fact, due to unreported commercial building activity and self-help construction, these figures understate the situation in many countries. Investment in housing may rise faster than growth in GDP at lower income levels, and is believed to have substantial multiplier effects on income and jobs. Estimates for Colombia, quoted by Grimes (op. cit.) suggests a housing construction income multiplier of 2, and that about seven additional jobs may be created for every US$10,000 spent on dwelling construction. Korean data also suggests an income multiplier of two, and about 14 additional jobs per US$10,000 invested. Similar results have been suggested for Pakistan, India, and Mexico. The housing construction sector tradionally has been able to absorb significant numbers of low-skill labour in rapidly growing cities.

Grimes (op. cit.) reports a detailed study of housing affordability in a sample group of six cities: Ahmedabad, Bogotá, Hong Kong, Madras, Mexico City, and Nairobi. For each city, different locations were reviewed, mainly involving different land costs; (see Table 5.9A/B for urban land price variations for eleven major cities, including the selected six). Within each location group six combinations of housing type with individual shared or "basic" services, were costed. The results are set out in Table 5.10, and summarized as to affordability in Table 5.11 and Fig. 5.12.

In general, the results of the study show that a serious problem of housing affordability remains, even with ingenuity of provision and cutting of "minimum" standards:

"the cheapest new housing currently being built is still not affordable by the poor. Under reasonable repayment terms and at interest rates of 10%, one-third to two-thirds of urban families cannot afford the cheapest new housing in the cities studied. Existing housing policies thus exclude not only the poor but also many middle-income families. But under reasonable assumptions about reduced standards and livable space, housing could be brought within the range of all but the poorest families. In Bogotá, for example, a single-family dwelling of 20 square metres with individual water and sanitation, located at the periphery of the city, could be afforded by all but 17% of the population—and by all but 14% in Mexico City. In some cities rowhouses and other kinds of housing that economize on land could be afforded in intermediate locations of the city by about the same proportion of families as single-family houses at the periphery. Medium-rise dwellings—up to about five storeys—are a viable alternative in many settings. In low-income cities such as Ahmedabad and Madras, however, those measures would still leave about 40% of the population unable to afford the cheapest public housing. Other programmes, especially sites and services and upgrading of squatter areas, would be needed in these cities to reach the poorest groups."

Policies on land costs, especially in relation to location of low-income housing in relation to employment opportunities, and policies on land acquisition, emerge as being of exceptional importance in large cities in

TABLE 5.9A. *Land Price Variations, Selected Cities, Various Years (Current US dollars per square metre)*

City[a]	Year	Population (millions)	Periphery	Intermediate zone	Central business district, commercial	Centre/ periphery ratio
Seoul	1973	6.2	2.3	75.0	1,060.0[c]	460
Manila	1973	5.1	2.0	60.0–75.0	450.0–1,500.0[c]	225–750
Hong Kong	1973	4.2	84.5–126.8	127.4–255.0	1,275.0	15–10
Madras	1973	2.6	4.4–5.5	6.6	8.5–13.6	2–2.5
Bogotá	1970	2.5	3.6	32.0	130.0	36
Singapore	1973	2.3	45.0	140.0	3,275.0[c]	73
Ahmedabad	1973	1.7	3.0–4.0	24.0–29.0	22.0–44.0	7–11
Kinshasa	1971	1.5	0.5	9.0	150.0[c]	300
Abidjan	1972	0.6	0.4	9.0	139.0[c]	347.5
Gwangju	1973	0.6	0.75	28.0	114.0[c]	152
Nairobi	1972	0.6	6.9	3.1–14.9	210.9–361.6	30.5–52

D[a] In descending order of population.
[b] Actual or calculated market value.
[c] Maximum.
Sources: Korea, Korea Board of Appraisers and World Bank mission data; Philippines, Manila, Board of Real Estates Association; Hong Kong, New Territories Administration; Madras, Tamil Nadu Housing Board; Bogotá, estimate from sample information; Singapore, *Trade and Industry*, various issues; Ahmedabad, Gujarat Housing Board; Zaïre, Bureau d'Etudes d'Amenagements Urbains; Ivory Coast, Ministry of Finance; Nairobi, University of Nairobi, Department of Land Development.
From: Grimes, O. F., 1976.

TABLE 5.9B. *Cost of Basic Construction, Land Servicing, and Raw Land for Low- and Moderate-Income Housing, Selected Cities (US dollars, 1970 prices)*

City	Basic construction of housing unit per square metre of livable space	Cost of Land servicing per square metre of livable space[a]	Raw land per square metre
Ahmedabad	25.5–61.1	2.6–7.5	2.3–19.5
Bogotá	20.5–109.3	1.1–6.1	3.6–4.2
Hong Kong	41.5–133.5[b]		60.3–75.7
Madras	15.7–59.4	4.1–9.3	3.4–5.1
Mexico City	28.5–49.6	3.9–5.9	7.4–14.1
Nairobi	48.9–65.3	12.0–21.7	1.9–4.3
Seoul	55.7–69.2	5.4–5.8	6.7–8.1

[a] Includes utilities and land development.
[b] Includes share of cost for community facilities such as schools and community centres.
Source: Table A13.
From: Grimes, O. F., 1976.

TABLE 5.10. *Estimates of Cost of Housing Units of Various Standards and Locations and Percentage of Households Unable to Afford Them, Selected Cities (Cost in US dollars, 1970 prices)*

Type of housing[a]	Ahmedabad Cost	%	Bogotá Cost	%	Hong Kong[b] Cost	%	Madras Cost	%	Mexico City Cost	%	Nairobi Cost	%
1. Present cheapest housing unit	616	64	1,475	47	1,670	35	570	63	3,005	55	2,076	68
Periphery												
2. Single family, individual services[c]	531	58	754	17	d	d	747	77	1,243	14	1,860	66
3. Single family, shared services[e]	469	56	665	14	d	d	670	73	1,117	10	1,566	59
4. Single family, basic services[f]	408	51	576	11	d	d	592	68	991	6	1,272	52
5. Multifamily, individual services	605	64	1,086	36	1,734	38	651	70	1,181	12	1,836	65
6. Multifamily, shared services	491	58	884	23	1,568	32	541	65	975	7	1,496	58
7. Multifamily, basic services	377	41	681	15	1,402	25	430	38	768	4	1,156	47
Intermediate zone												
8. Single family, individual services[c]	1,888	91	2,884	73	d	d	837	81	18,786	95+	2,468	72
9. Single family, shared services[e]	1,826	91	2,795	72	d	d	760	78	18,660	95+	2,174	69
10. Single family, basic services[f]	1,765	91	2,706	71	d	d	682	73	18,534	95+	1,880	66
11. Multifamily, individual services	876	76	1,512	50	1,850	45	669	72	4,685	72	1,958	67
12. Multifamily, shared services	762	72	1,310	42	1,684	35	559	63	4,479	70	1,618	61
13. Multifamily, basic services	648	55	1,107	36	1,518	30	448	44	4,272	69	1,278	52
City centre												
14. Single family, individual services[c]	2,263	95+	10,234	95+	d	d	1,100	88	256,438	95+	18,930	95+
15. Single family, shared services[e]	2,201	95+	10,145	95+	d	d	1,023	87	256,312	95+	18,636	95+
16. Single family, basic services[f]	2,140	95+	10,056	95+	d	d	954	82	256,186	95+	18,342	95+
17. Multifamily, individual services	951	79	2,982	74	12,485	95+	722	75	52,220	95+	5,250	90
18. Multifamily, shared services	837	75	2,780	72	12,319	95+	612	68	52,014	95+	4,910	89
19. Multifamily, basic services	723	70	2,577	70	12,153	95+	501	63	51,807	95+	4,570	87

[a] Based on repayment period of 25 years, 10% interest, no down payments, and 15% of household income devoted to housing. Multifamily housing units have 20 square metres of livable space and 15 square metres share of land in a four-storey building.

[b] Peripheral and intermediate land prices are those prevailing at existing low-cost housing estates; city centres land prices are estimates for areas adjacent to the city centre.

[c] Single-family detached housing unit with 20 square metres of livable space and 75 square metres of land. Services include individual water, toilet, and kitchen.

[d] No single-family units built.

[e] Communal water supply, sewerage, and other services; site preparation and lighting.

[f] Single family: centrally located water and pit latrines plus minimal security lighting and site preparation; multifamily; greater sharing of facilities.

Source: Calculated from Table A17 through A21 in the statistical appendix.

TABLE 5.11. *Estimated Percentage of Population Unable to Afford Housing of Various Space Standards at Peripheral Locations, by Type of Housing, Selected Cities*

Type of housing[a]	Ahmedabad		Bogotá		Madras		Mexico City		Nairobi	
	20 square metres	10 square metres	20 square metres	10 square metres	20 square metres	10 square metres	20 square metres	10 square metres	20 square metres	10 square metres
Single family, individual services	58	30	17	9	77	61	14	5	66	39
Single family, basic services	51	22	11	6	68	39	6	3	52	24
Multifamily, individual services	64	31	36	10	70	29	12	2	65	33
Multifamily, basic services	41	14	15	3	38	10	4	1	47	18

[a] Based on repayment period of 25 years, 10% interest, no down payment, and 15% of household income devoted to housing. Single family = single-family detached housing unit with 20 square metres of livable space and 75 square metres of land. Individual services = individual water, toilet, and kitchen. Basic services = for single family, centrally located water and pit latrines plus minimal security lighting and site preparation, for multifamily, greater sharing of facilities. Multifamily = multifamily housing unit with 20 square metres of livable space and 15 square metres share of land in a four-storey building.
Source: Calculated from Tables A17 through A21 in the statistical appendix.
From: Grimes, O. F., 1976.

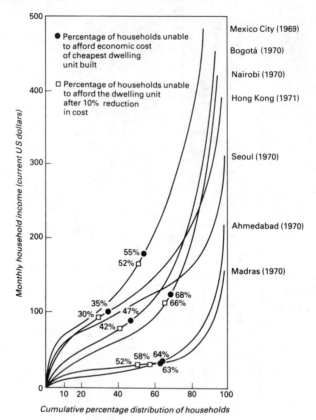

FIG. 5.12. Distribution of monthly household income and housing affordability in selected cities
(Grimes, 1976).

developing countries. It often appears possible to obtain land for major new road construction, but not for low-cost housing projects, and yet relatively few people own motor cars in such cities. Also of exceptional importance is low-cost finance for low-income housing, in relation to affordability.

Two Models of Urban Housing Supply and Demand for Korea

Mills and Song (1979) have presented a model of urban housing estimated from Korean data for the period 1962–1975. The model covers both supply and demand for the whole urban housing stock. Demand is seen as related to the incomes of urban households and prices of housing; supply is related to house construction costs and to the price of housing. The stock of housing at a given time is fixed, and demand for this stock determines its price: the stock will be increased by new construction if that price is higher than construction costs by an appropriate margin; this will have the effect, ultimately, of reducing the price and thus bringing about an equilibrium situation.

With a growing urban population, who also enjoy generally increasing incomes, demand for housing will rise; with continual growth, supply of housing will lag behind demand, as supply—due to the physical construction process—takes time to meet the demand.

The Mills/Song model is expressed as follows:

Housing demand per urban household is:

$$h_D = A p^{\alpha 1} y^{\alpha 2}.$$

Total urban housing demand is:

$$H_D = h_D \cdot N.$$

Total housing supply in equilibrium is:

$$H_s^* = B p^{\beta 1} \cdot W^{\beta 2}.$$

The actual stock of urban housing adjusts as:

$$H_s / H_{s-1} = (H_s^* / H_{s-1})^{\lambda}.$$

Each year, price clears the market:

$$Hs = H_D.$$

The complete notation is:

Endogenous variables:

h_D = housing demand per urban household
H_D = total demand for urban housing
P = price per dwelling of urban housing
H_s^* = equilibrium urban housing stock supply
H_s = actual urban housing stock.

Exogenous variables:

Y = real income per urban household
N = number of urban households
W = construction cost, a weighted average of real wage rates and real materials prices.

Predetermined variables:

H_{s-1} = lagged urban housing stock.

Parameters:

A = scale parameter in demand equation
α^1 = price elasticity of housing demand
α^2 = income elasticity of housing demand

B = scale parameter in supply equation

β^1 = price elasticity of supply

β^2 = supply elasticity with respect to construction cost

λ = percentage of housing stock disequilibrium adjusted in one year.

By making appropriate substitutions and taking natural logarithms, the result is:

$$\log H_D = \log A + \alpha^1 \log p + \alpha^2 \log y = \log N$$

and

$$\log H_s + \lambda \log B = \lambda \beta^1 \log p + \lambda \beta^2 \log w + (1 - \lambda) \log H_{s-1}$$

and:

$$H_s = H_D.$$

The equations were estimated by two-stage least squares from the data; the results are:

$$\log H_D = 5.375 - 0.134 \log p + 0.027 \log y + 1.157 \log N \qquad (R^2 = 0.969)$$

and:

$$\log H_s = 3.959 + 0.283 \log p - 0.377 \log w + 0.755 \log H_{s-1} \qquad (R^2 = 0.955).$$

λ is estimated at 0.245, so that $\beta^1 = 1.155$, and $\beta^2 = -1.539$ both elasticities indicating a responsiveness, to price and to construction costs, respectively. However, the demand price and income elasticities are very small. A similar result in relation to these elasticities was found by Renaud, Lim and Follain (1980), using a model based on that by Muth (1964, 1971).

The model reported by Renaud *et al.* is based on the hypothesis that one unit of housing stock produces one unit of housing services per period, given some minimum amount of operating inputs. (Housing services indicates the sum of all relevant services provided by a unit of housing, e.g. space, privacy, facilities and utilities). If the price per unit of housing services, p, is given, then the rent of a dwelling unit measures the number of units of housing services, q, produced by the dwelling, since rent = $p \times q$. Also, the value of a dwelling unit is equal to the price per unit of housing stock, P, times the Q units of housing stock provided by the dwelling.

The production function for the supply of housing services is:

$$q = q^*(Q, O) = q^*[Q(L, N), O]$$

where: q is a measure of the units of housing services per period;

Q is a measure of the units of housing stock;

L is a measure of the units of land inputs;

N is a measure of the units of structure inputs;

O is a measure of the units of operating inputs.

It is assumed that operating inputs are proportional to the units of housing stock, so that we can write: $q = q(L, N)$. Profit maximization will satisfy the conditions:

$$P_L/P = q_L$$
$$P_N/P = q_N$$
$$q = q(L, N)$$

where q_L, q_N are the marginal products of land and non-land services, respectively.

The logarithmic differentials (e.g. $q^* = d \log q$) of the above three relationships can be written as:

$$-k_N L^* + K_N N^* + \sigma p^* = \sigma p_L^*$$
$$K_L L^* - k_L N^* + \sigma p^* = \sigma p_N^*$$
$$q^* - K_L L^* - K_N N^* = 0$$

where σ is the elasticity of substitution of land for structures in the production of housing.

The utility maximization problem is:

$$\text{Max } U(q, X), \text{ subject to: } pq + X = Y$$

where $U(q, X)$ is the household utility function;
   X is the quantity of all goods other than housing;
   Y is the household income.

From this problem can be derived the following:

$$q^* = \varepsilon_p P^* + \varepsilon_y y^*$$

where ε_p and ε_y are elasticities of demand with respect to price, and income, respectively.

As the survey data provided expenditure on rents, or its equivalent, solving for $(pq)^*$ gives the following:

$$(pq)^* = (1 + \varepsilon_p)(K_L P_L^* + K_N p_N^*) + \varepsilon_y y^*$$

and:

$$p^* = K_L P_L^* + k_N p_N^*.$$

These two equations can be interpreted as follows: (1) changes in the demand for housing are a function of changes in the prices of land, and of non-land inputs, and changes in income; (2) that any percentage change in the price per unit of housing services, which results from changes in the price of land or non-land inputs, is a weighted average of the percentage changes in p_L and p_N. p^* is calculated first, as p_L and p_N are available from the data, there being excellent records of both land prices per dong (neighbourhood), and construction costs per pyong, in Korea (for details of the exact method of calculation, see Follain, Lim and Renaud (1980)); the value of p^* can then be substituted in the first of these two equations. Adjustments for short-run demand, and of income for transport expenditures, were also made.

Finally, an attempt was made to identify the principal socio-demographic determinants of the demand for housing, using the following:

$$\log R = \alpha_0 + \alpha_1 \log Y_i + \alpha_2 \log P + \alpha_3 S + \alpha_4 \log HS + \alpha_5 \log T \qquad (i = 1, 2)$$

where: R = imputed or explicit monthly rental expenditures;
$\quad Y_1$ = current disposable monthly income;
$\quad Y_2$ = total monthly consumption expenditure;
$\quad S$ = a housing shortage variable;
$\quad HS$ = number of persons in a household;
$\quad T$ = travel time to city centre.

An alternative formulation used averages of the variables by dong as the units. The authors of this paper (Follain, Lim and Renaud) conclude:

"Given the significant number of countries found within the income range between Korea's income at the time of the survey (US\$710 in 1976) and the US figure (\$7870), the finding that these two countries have strikingly comparable demand elasticities is of major importance. Lacking good local estimates of the price and income elasticities of the demand for housing policy analyses in other countries, one should rely on income elasticity estimates smaller than one and on price elasticity estimates also smaller than unity in absolute value. The best point estimate is 0.6 given that the estimates obtained with the two proxies for permanent income are the most precise. While further refinements of the findings presented in this paper are desirable, these first results give reason for optimism in that available econometric models developed for the analysis of cities in the United States could perform well in Korea and other countries."

This degree of optimism may be understandable, but does not such an analysis relate only to the upper circuit of the economy: the formal housing sector, where land is bought and construction paid for in money? The self-organized, "illegal" housing (which even Korea still has, for example in smaller cities like Jeonju and Gunsan), may cost nothing in money terms: self-erected, of waste materials, on "squatted" land—and no rents are paid. This is an important point in relation to lower-circuit life: household incomes may be small, but the absence of rent to pay, and the conversion of household energies and spare time into a capital asset worth perhaps one third as much as a legal housing unit (Yonsei University, 1970, quoted by Renaud, 1980), represents a helpful survival strategy in adverse conditions. Whilst Renaud (1980) deals with this point, to some extent, in relation to investment allocation to housing programme, this does not cover the whole issue; and the case studies of Korea, where illegal housing is less prevalent than in many other (especially tropical) countries, are not necessarily so representative of all developing countries. (Roughly only about 4% of households are recorded as living in illegal housing in Korea in 1972).

An example of an unusually far-sighted plan which considers the "informal sector" for housing and small-scale industry is the Egyptian/German Master Plan Study for the new desert city of El-Obour (1982). The contribution of informal housing to the national new housing stock of Egypt is said to be "very substantial"—about 3 out of every 4 units built; indeed, the same report says that no less than 84% of all housing units built in Cairo between 1970 and 1981 were "informal" housing (though the definition of "informal" here is not clear). Provisions for "informal" housing and "informal" economic activities are proposed in El-Obour, although more conventional new town approaches to housing and basic/service employment are included also. However, hard information about the presumed lower circuit activities, which might have added a more realistic line of argument for the provision of appropriate opportunities and facilities, appears to be lacking still.

Urban Systems in Developing Countries

A number of very fundamental differences exist between urban systems in developing countries—still in a highly formative state—and those in developed countries. These differences justify a detailed review.

Firstly, it is necessary to distinguish between the different types of cities in developing countries: there is a world of difference between, say, Cairo and a town like Faqus in the Nile Delta; this difference is not just one of size, though size is obviously a major factor. Nor is the difference to be accounted for by primacy alone, though again this appears a likely factor. In fact, it would seem that there are degrees of "developedness" *inside* developing countries, as well as between different countries: generalizations are often misleading, and clearly give rise to difficulty here.

It is, of course, the capital cities, or the upper bands of the rank-size pyramid, which tend to exhibit this difference most strongly; in many countries these are coincident with cities founded by colonial powers. It is customary nowadays to vilify colonialism (except where communist countries are concerned), but in fact without their colonial heritage many cities—and countries—would be much further back than they are on the ladder of "development". It is not accidental that it is these cities which have acted as the focii of communications, the locus of innovation, the seats of organization: "development" was transferred to them ahead of other, less accessible places, where the ground had yet to be broken for the seeds of economic change (and urbanization) to be planted.

Developing countries vary widely: a categorization that includes, for example, Lesotho, Mauritius, Egypt, Korea, Hong Kong, and Brazil must be an exceptionally broad one! Levels of economic activity vary widely also across the face of the World—as also within countries. We are apt to see national frontiers as system boundaries in general rather than simply administrative boundaries cutting across functional systems: these boundaries may contain some socio-cultural systems (though not always, by any means), but in general are incomplete containers of economic and communications systems. If cities are seen as nodes of economic activity in a continuous sheet of varying density of activity—or major aggregations of cells in a continuous cellular tissue again of varying density (and much conditioned by topography)—then we may have a better analogy to point up the distinction between the crude concept of "developing country" and the reality of meshing nets of activity systems which makes up the world space. The concept of "development", then, useful at times as an umbrella, can interpose conceptual difficulties if we take its application too far.

It follows, then, that there may be some explanations—and models, of course, usually attempt to explain (though not always, as in simulation)—of urban systems in developed countries which can be applied to those in developing countries. And equally there are some explanations which cannot be so applied. A gradation is implied, between, at one end, reasonable explanation of urban phenomena, and, at the other end, a lack of explanatory power. Thus, it may be no surprise to find that some (but not all) possibilities of understanding of urban systems in cities like, say, Seoul, São Paulo, or Hong Kong, may exist from a basis of similar understanding cultured in Western cities; it may well have no relevance at all in other cities in the same countries.

The size of cities may be cited as a second point. We have been accustomed to think of the largest cities as being associated with mature economies: the Londons, New Yorks, and so forth; more recently, we have found that Tokyo has joined and surpassed them. Now, we have the situation that quite immature (in the "development" sense) economies are productive of very large cities, much larger even than those of western economies; São Paulo is already half as big again as London; Mexico City is probably on the way to becoming the world's largest city. Such "developing" cities, by any reckoning, are going to become enormous conurbations in a relatively short timespan, with the "rank-size" rule on a world scale becoming heavily weighted towards developing, instead of developed, countries. In all probability, São Paulo, Mexico City, Calcutta, Cairo, and the like, will continue to grow exponentially for some time to come, presenting problems on a scale which, quite literally, has not been experienced at all before.

It is important to note that large size *per se* in developed countries came after the periods of fastest economic transition, whereas now, in developing countries large size may not result from a primary association with development, but may occur *before* it takes place, or at least at a different stage in the process. Thus a simple hypothesis, again drawn from western experience, that large urban systems result from economic growth seems to be inapplicable to "developing country" situations.

Associated with the question of city size, and indeed the reason for it, in quantitative terms, are the high rates of growth of cities in recently-developing economies. This is, of course, related to high rates of the natural increase of the populations, both of these countries in general and of their cities. It is also related to high rates of migration from countryside to city which are experienced there: a migration which obviously carries with it also the prospect of a further degree of natural increase. Again, the experience of non-developed-country cities at their stage of most rapid growth was different, though at the time the rates and numbers involved and the problems created were then quite novel, and no less pressing. In one sense, though, the experience of the Victorian cities of Britain *is* being repeated, a century and a half later: the scale and the rates of growth of "developing" cities, then as now, are unique, as are the problems created. As with our great-great-grandfathers, the need was, and is, to find newer solutions where needful and not to rely implicitly on standard western attitudes or solutions. (Though Edwin Chadwick would note a similarity between the Manchesters of the 1840s and developing cities still today in their need for municipal engineering: the provision of safe water supplies and sewage disposal remains a constant in city development).

In fact, this latter point is highly relevant, for better sanitation and health care are at the root of the changes in population dynamics which have taken place, especially in lowering death and child mortality rates. The demographic transition, the "overshoot" caused by the lag in perception of this situation and a positive effect on birth rates, takes perhaps a generation before family size is reduced. In the meantime, the divergence between natality and mortality results in an exponential population growth, later to be tempered. But subsequent growth rates, though later, are from a larger population base, and so actual numbers continue to be high.

Although the modern developing city tends to be more healthy than the countryside—due to better facilities there—which is the converse of the Victorian city situation—the countryside also experiences natural population increase, possibly at a fairly high rate. Such increase may be greater than is needed for replacement and for the needs of agriculture and rural life, even with increasing agricultural productivity. As in industry, increasing output in agriculture may not necessarily require proportionate additional employment, leading to a surplus rural population. Additionally, the availability of paid employment in the cities, as against possibly unpaid (except in kind) employment on farms, is also attractive, and so rural-to-urban migration occurs, fuelling city growth. Over a long period—perhaps the period of change from "undeveloped" to "developed"?—the rural-urban migration process may perhaps be representable by a logistic curve; in the fastest growth being at the inflexion point, of course, and presumably with a shifting upper limit.

The economy of the developing city is marked by its large dependency on services, including informal, part-time, or underemployment, due to the existence of a dual economy, even in very large cities. This is contrary to the developed city, where the "lower circuit" of the economy, though still existent, is quite minor.* The dual economy, of course, is associated with two factors already mentioned: the entry of migrants who may have neither skills nor formal jobs, but who have to earn a living, and the disparity between increasing output and employment as the formal sectors develop: economic growth and full employment are by no means synonymous.

A further aspect of the dual economy of the developing city, especially of the very large city, is that although much of its population may gain a livelihood from services, the traditional city—hinterland or central place relationship is not marked. Cities increasingly serve themselves as their own population increases relative to that of their hinterland, and in the informal sectors of the larger developing city this is likely to be increasingly the case, with a reliance on small-scale, localized services, mobile within the city but not outside it. Explanations of economic relationships of the central place or basic/non-basic kind, thus seem unlikely to be relevant where the dual economy prevails—or may be only partial explanations.

The dual economy of such cities suggests also that work place locations will be more widepsread, depending upon the extent of the dualism: formal "industrial areas" may be fewer, and localized services may disperse in broad and sporadic patterns. They may also be mobile within certain districts of the city, changing location with custom, supplies, or legal pressures. Again, views of urban systems which presume fixed locations, either of basic or service industry, will lack any explanatory value of such phenomena.

In developing cities, too, transport systems may differ especially in relation to journeys to work (Table 5.13). As urban incomes are low, much reliance will be placed on walking and on bicycles, on pushing or pulling carts. Car ownership will be low, and public transport, as buses and cheap taxis, will predominate over private modes except for trucks. The fare structure of public transport will be highly important as an articulator of urban form: flat fare rates for any distance will produce a more spread out pattern, as time spent in travel may not be highly valued; distance-based fares will have the opposite effect. Ubiquitous lorries or trucks may transport people, animals, food, manufactures, raw materials. Rail transport may play a part in industrial location in large countries or where government policy decrees it: rail may also provide transit systems in some very large cities.

If workplaces are dispersed, of course, journey to work patterns are not canalized and public transport becomes more difficult to organize and less economic. Working, shopping, and recreation habits may differ widely in various societies. The daily two peak hours experienced in most western city transport systems may be absent, or may be reinforced by others, as in many Middle East cities with their tidal patterns of virtually two work and two recreational/shopping (evening) peaks. A city with a traditional two-hour lunch break (as in Brazil), or one in a hot climate with mornings only being

---

* But may well be about to increase in view of unemployment in "formal" activities.

worked, and evening revival, will have quite different flow patterns to those of a "nine-to-five" economy.

Housing in developing cities has received a lot of attention, though focused mainly at the favela, the barriada, or the bidonville. However, in the broader picture, it is obvious that rapidly-growing urban populations involve considerable pressures on limited urban resources of all kinds, but particularly in housing accommodation. The stock of such cities can rarely keep pace with demand, which has two principal effects: multiple use of such accommodation as is available, and the spontaneous provision of additional accommodation (which may then also come into multiple use like any other dwellings available). Multiple use, i.e. the use by more than one household of a single dwelling unit, may take extreme forms, as in Hong Kong where quite small spaces may be rented out to individuals, or in the cities of Korea. In general, in such cities, floorspace standards will be small, facilities poor, and illegal structures numerous and varied.

The illegal structure, or illegal occupation of land, is common as a self-organized method of meeting the problem of accommodation in large cities in developing countries—or even in locally "big", but in world terms quite small cities such as Mbabane, the capital of Swaziland. Marginal urban land is usually taken—cases are known of very wet land being used, or steeply sloping land (as in several Latin American cities, and Hong Kong), or common land (as in the case of the Swazi Nation Land outside Mbabane), and considerable ingenuity is employed to develop land officially regarded as "undevelopable". Illegal housing structures on the roof-tops of conventional blocks of flats have been quite common in Hong Kong, for example. Such accommodation may be seen as representing the dual economy aspect of another urban function, being a spontaneous reaction which provides an extension of the formal housing and land market, and as such, the explanation of developed-country housing situations are unlikely to be relevant.

Closely associated with housing provision, of course, are urban utilities and infrastructure. Cities can, and do, develop without adequate provision in this regard: water seems to be the only service absolutely essential, and this can be carried, though not over very large distances on any scale without involving a formal technology. But very large cities must entail some kind of formal arrangements to this end—and thus some organizational requirements also. These formal arrangements may not reach full adequacy, or be inefficient (e.g.many cities in Korea register 30 or 40% water leakage rates; São Paulo has only a minor portion of its large population served by proper sewage disposal arrangements), but will be found to exist, in some localities, on some scale. Developed-country cities are accustomed to have quite luxurious standards, e.g. in paved roads, which are not necessary in cities which do not have to support large numbers of highly wasteful and costly motor cars. Thus standards of this sort should not be applied unthinkingly in situations where they are not at all necessary, and would be burdensome on the urban

TABLE 5.13. *Comparative Transport Data for Cities in Developing Countries*

City	Date	Population	Average trips per person per day	Transport mode (%)								Remarks
				Walking	Cycle	Bus	Taxi	Truck	Private	Rail	Other	
Greater Tokyo Region Japan	1975	24.1 million	2.5 (1968)	Data not available								
Greater São Paulo Brazil	1977	10.27 million	1.53	?	0.4	54.1	3.5	?	34.8	3.2 (R) 3.4(M)	0.5	Walking trips omitted from observations
Seoul Korea	1981	8.63 million	1.7	?	?	65	18	?	8	9 (s)	?	Walking trips omitted from observations
Greater Cairo Egypt	1972	6.5 million	1.92 (active persons 0.27 (not active)	37.6	1.8	54.1*	2.5	?	4.0	?	?	Home-Work trips
Delhi India	1974	3.7 million		44.7 35 25	0.9 42	45.9* 37*	4.6 ?	? ?	? ?	?	—	Other trips (Low income) (Middle income)
Caracas Venezuela	1966	1.72 million	1.73 work trips/employee 0.83 Service trips/person	Data not available								
Jeddah Saudi Arabia	1978	1 million +	1982 car ownership: c.288 per 1000 pers.	18	1	7	7	1	57	—	1	All trip purposes
Tripoli	1974	0.71 million	1.9	Data not available								

City	Year	Population											Notes
Libya													
Nairobi Kenya	1970	0.545 million	1.8	44.6	2.6	14	?	?	?	38	?	2	
Jeonju	1981	0.37 million	1.45	20.5	15.6	35.9+ 18.1**	0.7	—	5.1	—		5.7	Journey to work Mode data only
Korea	1975	0.25 million		44.3	1.5	10.6	1.5	2.4	16.8 +22.7	—		0.2	All trip purposes
Bahrain													
Iri	1978	0.15 million	(1.45)	35.3	29.5	17.6+ 4.8**	5.4	—	1.7	—		5.1	Journey to work mode data only

Sources: see below.

Notes: (R) = Suburban Rail; (M) = Metro; (S) = Subway.
  * = Defined as "Public Transport".
  ** = Company Transport, i.e. bus or utility van.

Sources of Transport Data:
Tokyo: Traffic in Tokyo, Tokyo Metropolitan Government, 1975.
São Paulo: Empresa Metropolitana de Planejamento da Grande São Paulo: O & D Survey.
Seoul: Professor No Chun-Li, Seoul City College, via Korea Herald.
Cairo: Traffic Survey for Greater Cairo Underground, 1972.
Delhi: Mohan, quoting A. C. Sarna, unpublished Ph.D. thesis, University of Waterloo, Canada, 1975.
Caracas: M. Echenique et al., 1973.
Jeddah: Jeddah Action Master Plans: Technical Report No. 5, Vol. 2: Transport Survey.
Tripoli: A. Shembesh, Proceedings of Town & Country Planning Summer School, 1979.
Nairobi: M. C. Mogridge, Traffic Engineering and Control, January 1975.
Bahrain: Hoff and Overgaard/Ministry of Works: Bahrain Road & Traffic Study, 1976.
Iri: Jeonju, op. cit.

population. These considerations apply also in other urban services, like education. Instead of the wasteful provision of education facilities which occurs in developed countries where classroom hours are low and space standards lavish, countries like Korea, Hong Kong and Singapore utilize a shift system where schools and colleges receive much more economic use, and urban education space requirements can consequently be halved.

6. Models of Specific Systems in Developing Countries: Some Case Studies

The previous chapter has discussed some more general considerations in the modelling of urban and regional systems of developing countries: the present chapter attempts a more detailed survey of a group of such models which, for the most part, have been built with the intention of their use in physical planning. Certain of the case studies of population change, migration, and urbanization which have been discussed in earlier chapters are also relevant, of course.

Models of specific urban or regional systems do need a context, an environment of policy or strategy. The various World Models which have been essayed by Forrester, Meadows *et al.*, Mesarovic and Pestel, and others, may be helpful here, though space unfortunately precludes any further discussion of them. However, one large-scale model effort at the national level should be mentioned as being directly relevant; this focused on long-term demographic and employment problems and was begun by the International Labour Office, Geneva, in 1972, supported by the United Nations Fund for Population Activities. The result was a prototype model, BACHUE-1, built in 1972, (Bachue being the Columbian goddess of love, fertility, and harmony between Nature and man). Over the following 4 years, 1973–1976, a BACHUE-type model of the Philippines was built, as a practical application of the theoretical approach of the earlier, generalized model; (Figs. 6.1, 6.2).

The conclusions of BACHUE-Philippines are regarded as controversial "in terms of the conventional wisdom" by the ILO: firstly, rapid fertility decline not being a panacea for the problems of the Philippines, and, they imply, for other countries also:

"Fertility decline has little impact on a broad range of economic, labour and distributional outcomes over a long planning horizon. It is only in a time horizon exceeding 30 years that important favourable effects start to cumulate from fertility decline—the economic gains sometimes alleged to flow from actual decline in fertility may emerge only in the very long term and fertility control cannot, therefore, be regarded as a substitute for development action."

Then: "the distribution of income is highly resistant to all but the most powerful packages of policies designed to restructure economic activity. Nevertheless, the model suggests that with structural shifts in development

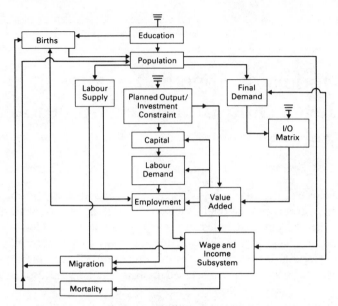

FIG. 6.1. Main relationships in BACHUE-Philippines (ILO).

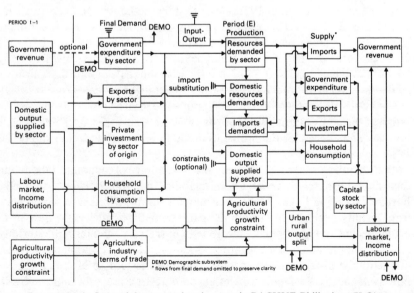

FIG. 6.2. Main flows of the economic subsystem in BACHUE-Philippines (ILO).

policy, strategies aimed at eliminating poverty can have significant impacts on inequalities and the satisfaction of these basic needs" over 25 years.

"An equilibrating force such as migration is an extremely important demographic mechanism by which income disparities can be ameliorated and 'trickle down' can occur."

The BACHUE model has three subsystems:

(1) Economic, in which final demand is generated and transformed into production via a Leontief input–output system. Certain components of final demand, and the internal terms of trade, are important endogenous variables here. However, the economic subsystem is not the main focus of the model, and a number of its other components are exogenous or largely exogenous, notably including the aggregate output level. Thus the model is not based on general equilibrium, and neo-classical mechanisms do not determine production;

(2) Labour market and income distribution, in which employment, self-employment, and unemployment are generated. Wages and income are derived from production, and distributed first to individuals who supply their labour, and then to households. The labour market attempts to portray the operation of long run institutional factors, as well as short run market clearing forces;

(3) Demographic, in which the population is tracked through time, and marriage, fertility, mortality and migration are all determined as functions of economic, demographic and educational variables. Underlying the demographic subsystem, (and to some extent the labour market subsystem), is a model of household decision-making, which interacts with the economy-level variables generated elsewhere in the model."

As a basis for comparison, one simulation run of BACHUE-Philippines was taken as a reference, based on a 7% aggregate growth rate for output, by which, (not surprisingly) the Philippines follows a "path of rapid economic development". The country enters the fertility decline phase of the demographic transition before the end of the century, though the net growth rate is then still over 2% per annum, with total population nearly doubling between 1975 and 2000. Urbanization is slow, though, rising from one-third urban in 1965 to almost one-half by 2000, rising rural incomes effectively restraining migration. In constant price terms, the agricultural sectors decline from over one quarter to less than one-fifth of total output, with manufacturing gaining substantially. Food prices rise though, because supply cannot keep pace with demand as incomes rise. But this growth does not eliminate poverty, the poorest 20% of both urban and rural households in 2000 having considerably below 1965 average incomes.

A number of "alternative futures" runs were then made of the model, assuming different output growth rates, followed by a series of "policy analysis" runs, each assuming a single policy: education, fertility, migration, labour force participation, labour mobility, wages control, self-employment encouragement, public works, technology choices, government sector changes. This type of analysis was regarded as incomplete: "Policies need to be financed, and usually packages of complementary policies are more effective than the independent application of specific instruments. A full analysis therefore requires that the impact of several policies, applied together, be assessed." Thus a number of more comprehensive "development strategies" were simulated, reflecting both the direct and the indirect effects of a set of policies, either aimed at a particular objective, or built around a set of policy instruments. Five such strategies were investigated, each consisting of 10 to 15 policy changes, including: "industrialization", "rural development". "egalitarian", a policy package recommended by ILO in 1973, and "population" (see Figs. 6.3A/B).

Some general conclusions can be drawn from these strategy simulations. Firstly, it was found that the distribution of income was extremely stable, though poverty might be shifted by various policies between urban and rural areas, or between groups, but without much affecting the overall pattern.

Secondly, fertility, mortality, and participation rates all responded to

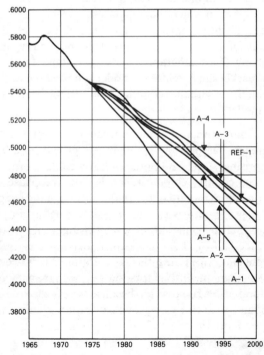

FIG. 6.3A. BACHUE-Philippines. Rural traditional employment as a proportion of all employment (A1–A5 represent the several policy runs) (ILO).

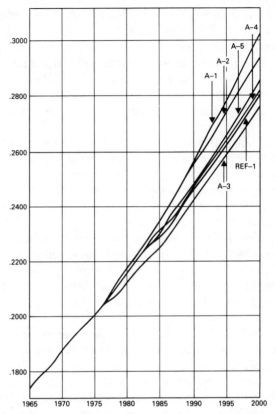

FIG. 6.3B. BACHUE-Philippines. Urban modern employment as a proportion of all employment (ILO).

change in employment, size of incomes, and income distribution. Migration, in particular, was found to play an important role in the interaction between different parts of the system. Several policies affected fertility, with movements toward income equality tending to reduce fertility.

Rural-urban interactions were found to be important: prices, migration, remittances, and movements in household expenditure playing a part. Prices fluctuated most, with changes in the terms of trade between agriculture and industry, and modifying rural-urban income ratios.

Population policies concerned with migration were found to affect employment and income distribution in the medium term more than policies relating to fertility.

Summing up, it was held that: "In analysing individual policies the model often gives unexpected results, or gives unexpected results for unexpected reasons. For example, increasing agricultural output may decrease agricultural incomes if appropriate demand policies are not followed. Rural public works reduce poverty mainly because of indirect, not direct, effects. In most cases, the expectations derive from partial analyses, and when the same policies are analysed in a system which incorporates wider interactions, feedbacks and leakages can reinforce, weaken, or reverse the conclusions." It was found also that substantial changes in income distribution could only be generated by "wide-ranging packages of complementary changes" which were unlikely to be implemented under the existing political and institutional structures.

A model of South Korea, sponsored by the World Bank, (Adelman and Robinson, 1978) reached strikingly similar conclusions to the BACHUE-Philippines model:

"Perhaps the most important lesson from our work is a more general one: immediate effects rarely reflect the overall impact of a policy intervention, and the partial-equilibrium solution is seldom quantitatively close to the final-equilibrium solution. Indeed, in many of our experiments the ultimate effect is opposite to the initial impact or partial-equilibrium effect. In addition, the total effect of combined policy packages often differs from the sum of the results of their component packages. A non-linear general-equilibrium framework, which permits any synergistic or interference effects that are present to manifest themselves, is thus basic."

The Philippines-BACHUE model is being followed by similar projects for Kenya, Brazil, and Yugoslavia. BACHUE-Brazil (de Figueiredo and Rato, 1977), will be in two versions: a demographic-economic model incorporating the dualism between rural/urban and modern/traditional sectors; and a version incorporating regionalization, i.e. presumably a broad spatial disaggregation and interaction. The former version, especially, would appear highly relevant to many developing countries.

A Population Forecasting Model

The following case study is a proposal, rather than a realized model. The model itself is not novel, and would utilize a readily available computer program of a normal kind, though with some additions. A particular feature of the model's use would be its utilization of data gained from a household and housing survey as part of a traffic origin and destination survey, together with other data normally published. The model was intended to provide inputs on a highly-disaggregated basis for other models of a very large urban system, and with specific connected submodels to provide a basis for urban policy-making.

The purpose of the model was to give projections of the population of Greater São Paulo, disaggregated by age and sex and also by zone. Some socio-economic or income group disaggregation may also be included, though this output is only likely to be relevant for shorter-range forecasts.

The model was of the cohort-survival type: a simulation model which calculated for each time period the new births and deaths and net migrants, so as to give new totals of population at the end of each period, based on the present structure of the given population.

The population is divided up into age and sex cohorts, normally 5-year age groups, and survival factors are applied to each group to determine the size of that group at the end of the time period, (again normally 5 years, to coincide with the size of each cohort). Migration rates are applied in a similar way. Fertility rates are applied to the females of child-bearing age, (10–14 to 50–54 years age cohorts), and the product of this operation becomes the next 0–4 age cohort, subdivided by sex, the ratio of male to female births being known. Thus the change of a population due to births, death and migration, over a given time period, is simulated.

Different projections may be made from the same base population, incorporating different assumptions about either fertility or mortality or migration.

If a spatial component is required for the model output, i.e. disaggregation by zones, the simulation process is carried out separately for each zone of the model, the results by zone being capable of aggregation in any desired form, i.e. combinations of zones at any higher level.

The model may also be run with a socio-economic or income group disaggregation, though such a disaggregation, being based on the present socio-economic structure, is only likely to be valid over a short term, say the first 5-year projection period.

The required inputs of the model are:

Base year population, disaggregated by age, sex, zone, and socio-economic group or income level.

Appropriate fertility rates, mortality or survival rates, and migration rates, by 5-year age cohorts.

A decision as to the time periods: normally 5-year cohorts and 5-year intervals for projections will be specified; the output cohorts can be combined as required, see later.

So far as the total range of the projection is concerned, it should be recalled that the forecasts are fundamentally less reliable when going beyond the range of births to females who are alive at the date of the base year data used as input.

A decision as to the zonal disaggregation to be used as the basis for the model forecasts.

The fertility, mortality (or survival), and migration rate inputs may take the form of single rates per cohort, e.g. the latest available rate, or a future rate implying changes due to certain policies, e.g. of birth control, or preventive medicine, or alternative migration possibilities. Alternatively, submodels may be used to produce future values of those variables from a projection from past data, using regression analysis.

There are several possibilities for the zonal system incorporated in the model—indeed the model will function for any zonal system, (within the dimension limits of the computer program for the model), for which data is available.

It was recommended, however, that the data was derived originally from the EMPLASA 1977 Origin and Destination Survey of Dwelling Units and Household Interviews. This had 243 zones, plus a further 22 external zones not surveyed. Greater São Paulo Metropolitan Area is made up of the Municipio of São Paulo and 36 other Prefeituras, and the Municipio of São Paulo is commonly divided into 56 Distritos and sub-Distritos for statistical purposes: thus a total of 92 zones might be required, though in several of the other Prefeituras some disaggregation may also be required: for example, one such area comprised 10 zones of the Origin and Destination Survey. Thus the zonal disaggregation of the model could be of the order of 100 zones, aggregated from 243 (+22) O & D zones, though for some purposes a further aggregation, e.g. into the 18 zones used for the presentation of the O & D material, may be appropriate. The need for zonal forecasts will depend, obviously, on the use to be made of them, but if the model is based on a more disaggregated input than is commonly required it will retain a greater degree of flexibility, especially as highly disaggregated data is already available. If the model were to be solely based on highly aggregated data, then, of course, no further disaggregation would be possible. It was suggested that the 1977 Origin and Destination Survey should be used as the present data base of the Population Forecasting Model, because:

(a) it was the most up-to-date information available;
(b) it contained all the required population base data;
(c) it was already available in magnetic tape form in EMPLASA;
(d) its zonal basis would be used for the 1980 Population Census, thus making the updating of the base year information a relatively straightforward task, and ensuring comparability of output for the two base years of 1977 and 1980.

The fertility, mortality, and migration information was available from the Registro Civil for the Municipio of São Paulo, for the Interior of the Estado, and for the Estado as a whole. It seems probable that information by Prefeituras was, in fact, available, though not published separately.

The migration data as published might need some further disaggregation by age/sex cohort, but this information may be available at source. It is hoped that further, perhaps more detailed, data on migration will become available from the results of the 1980 Population Census.

The normal outputs of the model were:
Base year data as input, including the fertility, mortality or survival, and migration rates used in the projections. Age and sex cohort populations

at each interval of projection, normally 5 years, by total for all zones in the system, also for each zone. The cohorts may be aggregated into larger, significant population groups, as detailed below.

A socio-economic or income level grouping may also be forecast, for the initial period only.

The age and sex cohorts are printed out as a set of population pyramids, as well as numerically, and the forecasts are printed out as a graph against time.

The forecast output may be aggregated as follows, subdivided by sex:

Children under 5 years
Children from 5 to 14 years
Children of secondary school age: 15 to 19 years
Potential working population
Population over retirement age.

These population group forecasts can then be utilized as a basis for health, welfare, and education programmes.

A submodel can be added to the Population Forecasting Model to give a conversion from population to families or households, using the household structure data incorporated in the EMPLASA 1977 Origin and Destination Survey.

A Housing Stock Model

The Dwelling Unit information of the EMPLASA 1977 Origin and Destination Survey may be utilized as a basis to reproduce the Type/Age/Size/Condition/Rental Structure of the Greater São Paulo Housing Stock. This stock can be "aged" over future periods and down-graded in condition to show future states of the housing situation of São Paulo.

These future housing stocks can be compared with the future Household or Family Structure projections derived from the Population Formulation Model, to give a picture of Housing Need at various times; such needs can be converted to Land Requirements for Housing, using a range of varying housing density assumptions reflecting various standards of housing provision.

The Housing Stock Model can also show the forecast sizes of unfit or unsatisfactory housing components of the total stock at various times, and thus, by implication, the size of programmes required to upgrade or replace unsatisfactory or unfit housing.

Some Latin American City System Models

A group of interesting spatial interaction models have been formulated over the last decade for several large Latin American cities, including Caracas in

Venezuela, Santiago in Chile, and Belo Horizonte and São Paulo in Brazil. All of these models draw upon North American or European precedents, and a large number of them represent a pioneer and very considerable line of development with which the names of Marcial Echenique and his associates of the Centre for Land Use and Built Form Studies at Cambridge are associated.

The first example, however, is a little outside the line of development of the others, being a model of Belo Horizonte, Brazil, derived from precedents in the USA.

The model originated in a desire to compare and analyse spatial alternatives for Greater Belo Horizonte, a city of 2 million people. In fact, a number of models were necessary, the principal one being concerned with the future distribution of population in the region. Auxiliary models were necessary in order to calculate future accessibility indices, the locations of basic employment, and the locations of service employment.

The main model was based on a version used in Detroit in 1967 by the Detroit Edison Company, and having similarities to W. G. Hansen's model utilized for the Washington Region in 1960.

The model, in fact, is a simple potential model, distributing population on the basis of accessibility to employment:

$$\Delta P_i = \frac{K \cdot DM_i - D_i}{DM_i} \cdot S_i \cdot A_i$$

where: ΔP_i = the increment in population of zone i for the time period considered;

D_i = residential density at the base year, of zone i;

DM_i = maximum residential density permissible at the end of the period for zone i;

A_i = an accessibility to work index for zone i;

S_i = area of land available in zone i;

K = area constant of normalization, to ensure that the total population distributed over the zones is equal to the total to be distributed, i.e.:

$$\Delta P = \sum_{i=1}^{N} \Delta P_i$$

$$K = \frac{\Delta P}{\sum_{i=1}^{N} \left[\frac{DM_i - D_i}{DM_i} \right] S_i \cdot A_i}.$$

To obtain the values of P_i, two steps of an iterative process are necessary. The first iteration calculates the value of P_i by way of accessibilities determined in relation to basic employment. The second iteration takes into consideration accessibilities in relation to total employment, (basic + service), in that the values of P_i from the first iteration are incorporated in the calculation of service employment.

The accessibility indices are calculated from data relating to the distribution of employment, by a gravity formulation:

$$A_i = \sum_{j=1}^{N} [(T_{ij} \cdot F) \cdot E_j],$$

where: A_i = accessibility to work of zone i;

E_j = attractiveness of zone j, expressed as amount of employment at the forecast year;

T_{ij} = minimum travel time between zone i and zone j;

F = a frictional factor;

N = total number of zones in the system.

The first iteration of the model used existing total employment for the calculation of the increment in basic employment for the first time period. The resulting accessibility indices were incorporated in the calculation of ΔP_i for the first run of the main model to distribute population. On the second iteration, the total employment at the end of the first time period was used to calculate the accessibility indices to be utilized in the second distribution of population. The difference between the employment figures used in the first and second calculations is equal to ΔE_s, the increment in service employment. Thus:

$$E_1 = E_{b0} + E_{s0} + \Delta E_b$$

where: E_{b0} = basic employment at base year

E_{s0} = service employment at base year

ΔE_b = increment in basic employment over the time period

And: $E_2 = E_{b0} + E_{s0} + \Delta E_b + \Delta E_s$

where: E_s = increment in service employment over the time period;

E = total employment.

The model for the distribution of the increment in service employment considers three aspects:

ΔE_{s1}: corresponding to activities producing goods and services covering the whole market area of the metropolitan region of Belo Horizonte; normally activities which would locate in the principal centres of the metropolis;

ΔE_{s2}: corresponding to those activities serving a number of zones of the metropolis, probably located in metropolitan subcentres;

ΔE_{s3}: corresponding to local activities, serving only one zone.

The values of ΔE_{s1} were intentionally distributed in the principal metropolitan centres. The values of ΔE_{s2} were distributed by determining zones z, corresponding to metropolitan subcentres, according to:

$$\Delta E_{s2_z} = K\left[\sum_{i=1}^{N} \Delta P_i \cdot Y_i\right]$$

where: ΔP_i = increment of population in zone i, calculated from the first iteration of the population distribution model;

Y_i = mean family income for the forecast year for zone i;

N = number of zones included in the area of influence of the metropolitan sub-centre z;

K = a factor of normalization, similar to the expression for K above, but here equal to:

$$\Delta E_{s2_z} \Big/ \sum_{i=1}^{N} [\Delta P_i \cdot Y_i].$$

The values of ΔE_{s3} were calculated from the expression:

$$\Delta E_{s3_i} = K[\Delta P_i \cdot Y_i]$$

—where the symbols have similar meanings to those used previously.

The total increment in service employment,

$$\Delta E_{si} = \Delta E_{s1i} + \Delta E_{s2i} + \Delta E_{s3i}.$$

In the expression for ΔE_{s2} and ΔE_{s3}, the expression $\Delta P \cdot Y$ represents a market factor indicating the potential spending power of the population.

Areas with a potential for industrial location were graded in accordance with their weighted scores in regard to access (to road and rail), the occurrence of economies of scale and agglomeration, and availability of and/or pollution effects on water supply.

A Model of Santiago, Chile

The transference of models of urban systems in more-developed countries to those in less developed countries has certain difficulties, as has been seen. The systems to be modelled may be rather different, especially in relation to the presence of dual economies and different cultural and social habits and relationships. Data is also a general stumbling block, especially in the forms and quantities required by models of any pretension. Parameter values are likely to be different.

However, in the largest cities of developing countries in some continents, these difficulties may appear not to be too adverse. Such large cities, especially capital cities, are often the most "developed" of their countries; because of their size are likely to have been the subject of censuses and other data collection exercises; to have organized transport systems; and to be the locus of bodies with an interest in forecasting future developments and in formulating ways of dealing with growing urban and regional—especially metropolitan regional—problems. It is no surprise, therefore, to find that the attempted transference of urban systems modelling methodology as been taking place at the scale of larger cities, and especially in Latin America. (And, incidentally, the transfer of any European or western technology is greatly aided where European languages are the means of communication.)

Thus, the Echenique-Domeyko model of Santiago, Chile, reported in 1970, was the outcome of several years of development work at the University of Cambridge Centre for Land Use and Built Form Studies: development work which had its origins in the well-known Lowry allocation model, (Lowry, 1964); but which had refined and improved the basic Lowry formulation by adding stocks submodels to those of activities. Although the Cambridge developments had been concerned primarily with smaller towns up to this time, the Santiago model represents also a shift in size and complexity of the urban systems modelled: Santiago had 2,700,000 population in 1967.

The Cambridge model—previously tested in Reading and other English cities—is concerned with the interaction between the physical stock of a city, i.e. channels and adapted spaces, and flows and activities; (Fig. 2.8). Such processes are interdependent: activities, e.g. residence, recreation, work, education, create demands for land and buildings; once these activities are accommodated in a usually relatively permanent form, there is an inertia to further change by reason of the fixed nature of this stock of adapted space. Thus other activities become located in the city, not merely according to their normal functional interdependencies, but also in ways which are constrained by the physical stock which exists. Such an interrelationship can be simulated to some extent by an iterative process: starting with the location of one, finding its influence on the other, reiterating back to the first relationship, and so on, until some acceptable state is approached where successive iterations make for little appreciable change.

To start the process, the basic Lowry model inputs of the location of basic employment, the stock of land available, and the transport network, are needed. Basic employment, of course, sells its goods—and services—outside the city, as distinct from non-basic, or "service" employment whose primary purpose is to service the basic employment sector.

Three interrelated submodels make up the model structure, concerned with floorspace, residence, and service location. The exogenous input of basic employment, i.e. employees, requires floorspace which is distributed by the floorspace submodel. These employees are then distributed to places of residence by the residential location submodel, which relates them to journey to work patterns, and also generates the total population dependent upon this employment. Service employment to provide for this population is located by the service location submodel, related to journey for service patterns of flow. This service employment, in turn, generates new employment and population, and the iteration continues, via floor space, residence, and service location submodels until near equilibrium is reached.

The floorspace submodel is concerned with locating floorspace according to a general demand, exogenously derived, in terms of area of floorspace per employee. The submodel distributes this space in relation to the land available, the accessibility to employment, and to the competition of all other zones are regards land availability and accessibility. The form of this submodel can be expressed as:

$$F_j = \sum_i \frac{E_i \cdot w \cdot L_j \cdot e^{-\phi dij}}{\Sigma_j L_j e^{-\phi dij}}$$

where F_j = floor space in hectares located at zone j;
E_i = employment in zone i;
w = demand for floor space, in hectares per employee;
L_j = land available in zone j;
d_{ij} = distance between zone i and zone j;
ϕ = a parameter.

The residential location submodel locates the basic employees to the floor space available in each zone, in relation to the accessibility of each zone to the employment centre and to the competition from floorspace in all other zones. The total population is derived from a participation rate which relates dependent population to employees.

The available floor space is given by:

$$F_j^r = F_j - (E_j^b p + E_j^s q)$$

where F_j^r = available floor space for residential activities in j;
F_j = total floor space in j;
E_j^b = basic employment in j;
E_j^s = service employment in j;
p, q = space standards for basic and service employment.

The journey from work and the residential location is given by:

$$R_{ij} = \frac{E_i \cdot F_j^r \cdot e^{-\phi' dij}}{\Sigma_j F_j^r \cdot e^{-\phi' dij}}$$

where R_{ij} = employees working in i and living in j;
E_i = employment in i;
F_j^r = available floor space for residents in j;
d_{ij} = distance between i and j;
ϕ' = parameter.

The total population is thus:

$$P_j = \Sigma_i R_{ij} \cdot u$$

where P_j = population living in j;
u = labour participation rate.

The service employment location submodel distributes services in relation to population via a market potential model, which covers the accessibility to the residential population, the employment in each zone, and the competition from other zones. The number of inter-zonal service trips is given by:

$$S_{ij} = \frac{R_i \cdot E_j^\alpha \cdot e^{-\phi'' d_{ij}}}{\Sigma_j \cdot E_j^\alpha \cdot e^{-\phi'' d_{ij}}}$$

where S_{ij} = service trips from i to j;
E_j = employment in j;
d_{ij} = distance between i and j;
ϕ'', α = parameters.

The service employment is derived from:

$$E_j^s = \Sigma_i S_{ij} \cdot v$$

where E_j^s = service employment in j;
v = service employment to population ratio.

The total flows are some combination of the journey to work and journey to services trips, e.g.:

$$T_{ij} = \beta R_{ij} + \delta S_{ij}$$

—where T_{ij} = trips between i and j;
R_{ij} = journey to work;
S_{ij} = journey to services;
β, δ = constants of proportionality.

In the application of the model to Santiago, no floor space distribution data was available from which to check the model's output and values from England were used. Land availability per zone data was available, and could be assessed from maps. Updated 1960 Census population was available, as was data on employment, including a five-sector disaggregation. A shortest-route program was run to obtain an accessibility between zones matrix, and an origin and destination survey was available from 1965, though trip-purpose information was not available. The ratio of population per employee (U) was found to be 3.12, and the service employment to population ratio was 0.16. The model was calibrated on the mean trip length value.

The values of the parameters finally selected are interesting as suggesting that distance was not a great impediment to travel. This may have been due to the main travel mode being public transport, on which a flat fare rate, unrelated to distance, was charged. The time cost of travel, for populations of low average income, may not be a deterrent, either. Certainly, the reliance on public transport, and the low cost of time involved in travel, are aspects of cities in developing countries which are widespread, and one must expect models of other cities elsewhere to demonstrate this characteristic, at least to some extent, depending upon the pricing policies of public transport.

The output of the model was rather better for residential location than service employment location; it was thought that service employment may adapt more slowly to changes in residential and employment locations. However, it may well be that this is also an indication that a western city-derived model does not recognize the rather different factors which lead to the existence and location of services in a dual-economy situation. The distribution of different socio-economic groups was largely undifferentiated, there being no marked travel-distance relationship for higher or lower income groups; this might have been due, again, to the particular transport system in this city.

The lesson of the Santiago model appeared to be that a transfer of this kind of model technology is possible with caveats, at least to some fast-developing, large cities in developing countries. However, it is also the case that some further modification of the theory behind such models—especially those of the Lowry type, with its emphasis on the role of service employment—is necessary for a more adequate replication of these particular urban systems.

An Urban-Regional Model for the Central Region of Chile

The Santiago Model described above was followed, in 1971–1973, by the development of an urban-regional model for the central region of Chile, including Santiago city, growing outwards, as it were, to regional and national levels from the urban stock and activity model presented in 1970 (Echenique and Domyeko). New data requirements were expressed and resulted in new surveys with a 1970 basis. The new model (de la Barra et al., 1975), thus attempted "an integration between regional planning at the inter-urban scale and urban development and transport planning at the intra-urban scale". Even with this new prescription, though, the focus of the model was at the urban level, the regional aspects acting as a context to intra-urban issues in the main in order to predict the future structure of the city. The previous activity and stock location model of Santiago was thought to be inadequate for this task, by itself. However, as the primary aim was to simulate urban structure, only those variables which were considered to act as exogenous inputs to the city structure were included. Thus population and employment were seen as the main regional input requirements to the intra-urban aspects of the model.

So far as population was concerned, birth and death rates were assumed to be affected by social and cultural factors; migration was assumed to be a function of the demand for labour in each region of Chile.

The economy of the region in future would depend on the investment made in each region and in each sector of the economy. Investment would not necessarily generate employment directly in a region or sector, as its effects would spread to various other regions or sectors: a matrix of investment flows. Thus, in general, at any period of time, investment flows would generate new

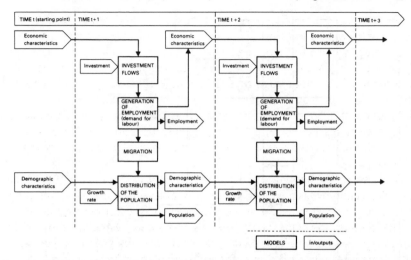

FIG. 6.4. Central region of Chile. Flowchart of the regional model showing the development in time (de la Barra *et al.*, 1975).

employment, which would cause migration, which would alter the population distribution, (see Fig. 6.4).

The basic employment model distinguished four sectors: agriculture, mining, industry, and administration. This model outputs basic employment per zone, which consists of the addition of industrial, public administration, and urban service employment generated by the rural population; agricultural and mining employment is assumed not to be urban basic employment, its employees being located in proximity to their workplace, (Fig. 6.5).

The urban stock and activity model follows the previous precedent, and requires little comment, except that, obviously, it provides a further element of service employment, (see Fig. 6.6). The transport model also is of a conventional kind. The general structure of the overall urban-regional model is shown in Fig. 6.7, (after de la Barra *et al.*).

A more detailed view of the regional aspects of the Chile/Santiago model is desirable. The regional employment generation model is based on the view that total employment will be a linear function of the investment*, or:

$$I \cdot \delta = E, \text{ where } I = \text{investment};$$
$$\delta = \text{a constant};$$
$$E = \text{employment}.$$

Investment over a period of time, t_I, is taken as a fixed proportion of the GDP:

$$t_I = t_G \cdot t_\varepsilon, \text{ where } t_G = \text{GDP at time } t$$
$$t_\varepsilon = \text{proportion of GDP invested during } t.$$

* Public investment in Chile was 77% of total investment at 1973.

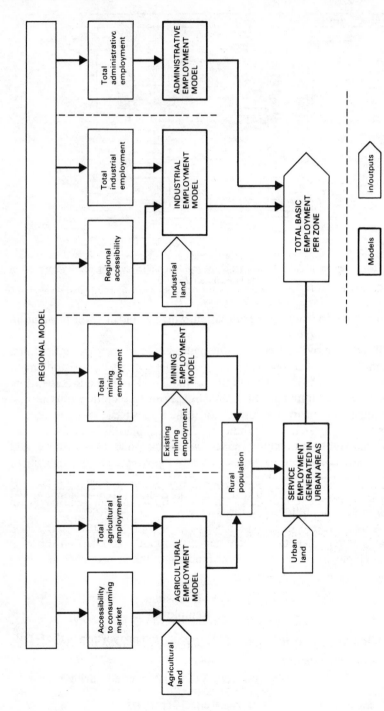

Fig. 6.5. Central region of Chile. Flowchart of the basic employment model (de la Barra, *et al.*, 1975).

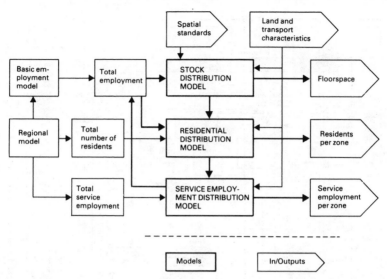

FIG. 6.6. Central region of Chile. Flowchart of the urban stock and activity distribution model (de la Barra *et al.*, 1975).

If growth rate of GDP is taken as constant,

$$t_G = (t-1)_G \cdot \alpha, \text{ where } \alpha = \text{growth rate.}$$

Investment may be apportioned between regions and sectors, so that:

$$^t I_i^m = {}^t I \cdot {}^t \gamma_i^m,$$

where $^t I_i^m$ = investment in region i, sector m, during t; and $^t \gamma_i^m$ = proportion of the investment to be spent in sector m of region i during time t.

Employment generated may not locate in the region and sector where the investment was made: it may flow from one sector to another and one region to another. This situation may be represented as a matrix F_{ij}^{mn}: the amount of money, F, that flows from region i and sector m to region j and sector n, with the following properties:

$$\Sigma_j \Sigma_n F_{ij}^{mn} = I_i^m$$

$$\Sigma_i \Sigma_m F_{ij}^{mn} = I_j^n$$

$$\Sigma_i \Sigma_j \Sigma_m \Sigma_n F_{ij}^{mn} = I \text{ (total investment).}$$

The mobility of investment can be represented by obtaining the average flow distance from each sector:

$$\bar{d}^n = \frac{\Sigma_m \Sigma_i \Sigma_j F_{ij}^{mn} \cdot d_{ij}}{\Sigma_m \Sigma_i \Sigma_j F_{ij}^{mn}}.$$

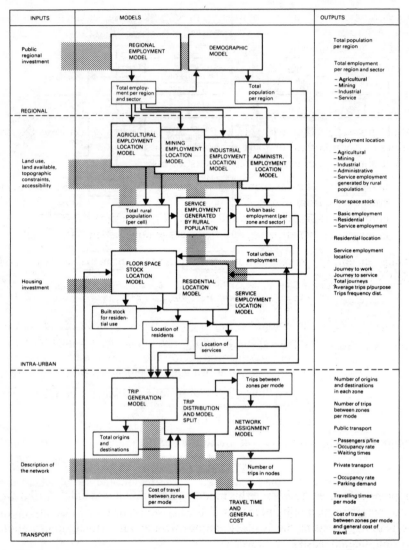

FIG. 6.7. Central region of Chile. General structure of the urban-regional model (de la Barra *et al.*, 1975).

Average flow distance for all sectors is:

$$\bar{d} = \frac{\Sigma_i \Sigma_j \Sigma_m \Sigma_n F_{ij}^{mn} \cdot d_{ij}}{\Sigma_i \Sigma_j \Sigma_m \Sigma_n F_{ij}^{mn}}.$$

The employment in each cell of the matrix, E_j^n is given by:

$$\Sigma_i \Sigma_m F_{ij}^{mn} \cdot \delta = E_j^n.$$

A second matrix, C can be obtained from matrix F. A typical element of this second matrix, C^{mn} represents the proportion of money that flows from sector m to sector n, for one unit investment in m, thus:

$$C^{mn} = \frac{\Sigma_i \Sigma_j F_{ij}^{mn}}{\Sigma_n \Sigma_i \Sigma_j F_{ij}^{mn}}.$$

It was held that, although matrix F would be constantly changing over time, C would probably be more stable as it should be dependent on longer term values of technological or socio-economic factors.

The simulation of matrix F requires as inputs:

investment policy as expressed in matrix $^t\gamma_i^m$; intersectoral investment coefficients, from matrix C^{mn};
employment in each sector and region, $^tE_j^n$; from time t;
an accessibility matrix d_{ij}, and the average flow distance $\bar{d}^n$.

Using an entropy maximization formulation, the principal equation for matrix F becomes:

$$^{t+1}F_{ij}^{mn} = {}^tT_i^m \cdot C^{mn}[{}^tW_j^n]^{\theta n} \exp(-\beta^n d_{ij})A_i^m,$$

—where $^{t+1}F_{ij}^{mn}$ = the amount of money that flows from an investment in region i, sector m, to sector n in region j, during time $t+1$;
$^tT_i^m$ = size of investment in sector m of region i during time t;
$^tW_j^n$ = the attraction of sector n of region j to investment, during t. (Determined empirically). Parameter θ represents the economies of scale.
A_i^m = a normalization factor, i.e. $[\Sigma_j \Sigma_n {}^tW_j^n \exp(-\beta^n d_{ij})^{-1}]$.

Total increase in employment is given by:

$$\Delta^{t+1}E_j^n = \Sigma_i \Sigma_m {}^{t+1}F_{ij}^{mn} \cdot \delta.$$

In point of fact, the authors of this model suggest that it was unlikely that the information needed to build matrix F directly would be found. An analytical derivation of it, using the available employment and investment information was considered feasible, however.

The basic employment submodels included in the intra-urban model were used to distribute the five different types of employment given by the regional model. A single-constraint entropy maximization model was used for these submodels, assuming that the amount of basic employment of a given type in a zone was a function of the total employment of that category, the amount of land available for it, and the attractiveness of that zone for its location. The formulation was:

$$^tE_j^n = {}^tE^n \, {}^tL_j^n \, {}^tW_j^n \, {}^tA^n,$$

—where $^tE_j^n$ = basic employment of type n, in zone j, during time t;

$'E^n$ = total of basic employment of type n during t, given by the regional model;

$'L_j^n$ = amount of land available in zone j for development of employment type n during t;

$'W_j^n$ = attraction of zone j for location of employment type n during time t;

$'A^n$ is a normalizing factor = $[\Sigma_j {}'L_j^{nt} W_j^n]^{-1}$.

For each of the five employment submodels, special factors were considered. Agricultural and mining employment were excluded from the input to the stock and activity distribution model, as having no direct involvement in the urban structure. This model and the transport model need no further comment here, and reference should be made to de la Barra *et al.* (1975) for details. It is noteworthy, however, that walking trips were included in the latter model: a fundamental need in developing country studies.

Some of the results of the simulations made using the Chile model appear below, including a simulation of regional employment for the period 1965–1970 (Fig. 6.8). The agricultural employment distribution submodel produced a particularly close fit to real data, but most of the submodels performed well. Several policy simulations, of a broad kind, were run to demonstrate the possibilities of this approach before work on it was concluded in 1973.

A Model of Caracas, Venezuela

The next development of the urban version of the Echenique model was the combination of the macro-level approach inherent in the Lowry modelling of urban systems, i.e. the modelling of aggregate behaviour, which produces a reasonable simulation of urban reality, with a micro-level approach which focuses on the behaviour of individual actors in the urban process. The micro-level approach is of importance as giving an underpinning of theory, being, of course, the normal approach to economic theory, involving concepts of rationality, perfect information, and so forth. The value of the combination of both approaches is clear: it brings to the modelling of urban systems a representation of urban market forces, including selling prices, rentals, and land values, which is an essential component in their understanding. However, a micro-scale approach does have certain problems, of which data availability —and, if available, quantity in relation to machine capacity—is one. But, additional to this, the sheer variety of urban systems, when viewed at micro-scale, enforces limiting theoretical assumptions upon the would-be-builder of theories, as well as the modeller, *per se*.

The Echenique/Feo/Herrera/Riquezes model (1973a, 1973b) thus utilizes a submodel of the land market, in addition to the Lowry structure already previously developed and seen in the Santiago case study. The overall model,

(a)

INDUSTRIAL EMPLOYMENT DISTRIBUTION SUBMODEL

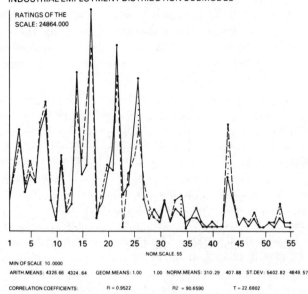

(b) Residential population distribution, real (—) and simulated by the model (- - -) (de la Barra *et al.*, 1975).

(b)

RESIDENTIAL SUBMODEL

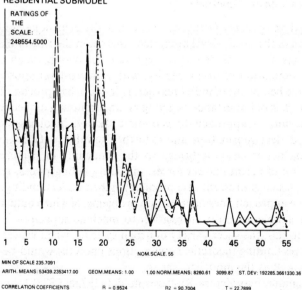

FIG. 6.8. Typical simulation runs of the Chile Model. (a) Manufacturing employment distribution, real (—) and simulated by the model (- - -).

then, consists of five submodels, concerned with: the land market, employment, residential location, service location and transport. A Flow diagram
(from Echenique, *et al.*, 1973a) is given below for the whole model; (Fig. 6.9).

The mathematical formulation of the model, utilizing the maximum
entropy formalization due to A. G. Wilson, is complex, and need not be
commented on here: details are available in the Echenique *et al.* paper (1973a),
and elsewhere.

In 1966, Caracas, Venezuela, had a population of 1,720,000 people. The city
was used as a vehicle for testing the model just outlined, in 1973. A transport
study, already available from 1966, covering a 5% sample, or 60,000 persons,
supplied base data for an aggregation to 30, from 362, zones. The distribution
of employment in 1966—the city then had 516,000 employees, or nearly 20%
of the national total—was: 51% in general services, 32% in manufacturing
industries, 16% in government services, and 12% in agricultural employment.
The socio-economic groups involved were described as: 3.8% managerial,
14.8% professional and technicians, 28.4% clerical workers, 51.5% manual
workers, 1.5% agricultural workers. The housing and transport markets were
believed to be closely related to the income levels of the socio-economic
group—a not surprising finding, in the absence of explicit or inferred (as in the
Santiago transport fare structure) subsidization. The proportion of income
expended on housing and transport taken together did not vary markedly
with incomes.

The employment inputs included the basic employment located in each
zone of the city, classified in three economic sectors: industrial, government,
and (for the perimeter zones of the city) agricultural employment. Land
available was all land of less than 60% slopes, excluding parks and certain
other uses. Shortest-route matrices of pairs of zones were available from the
transport study data.

The results of runs of the model gave a reasonable fit for land values
($R^2 = 0.8258$), see Fig. 6.10. The population in normal housing simulation was
not such a good fit ($R^2 = 0.7619$), though population in squatter housing was
better ($R^2 = 0.8849$) after adjustment of the model to accommodate a more
realistic view of location requirements, i.e. difficult-to-urbanize or marginal
land, which would not be considered suitable for normal housing. Simulated
values for income distribution for each socio-economic group showed some
examples of reasonably good fit, and some exceptions.

The model, of course, was not dynamic, and dealt with mean values of
income and expenditure, etc. A more dynamic model of this kind might
usefully incorporate an economic model of growth as one of its bases.

Based on the earlier versions of the LUBFS model, including a floorspace
location model, (Crowther, Echenique, 1972), a simple static model of the city
of Lisbon (population 1.6 million at 1970) was reported by Portes, Geraldes,
and Pereira (in Baxter, Echenique and Owers eds. 1975). Data availability was
regarded as a problem, especially on floorspace, but also regarding basic and

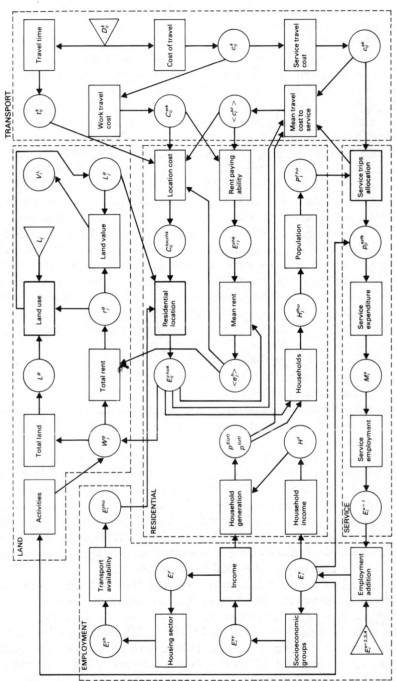

FIG. 6.9. Flowchart of the Caracas Model. (Inputs are shown as triangles; outputs shown as circles) (Echenique *et al.*, 1973).

228   G. Chadwick

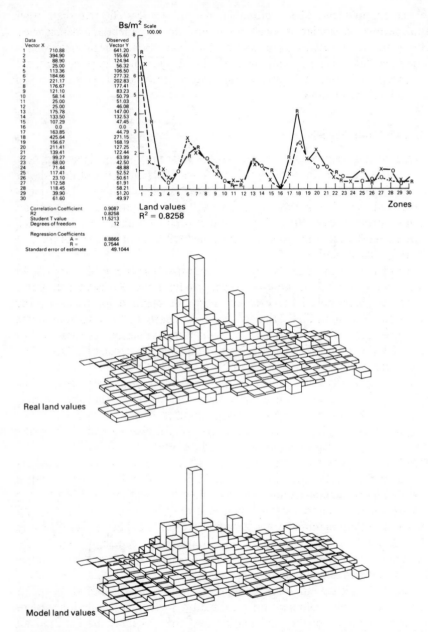

Data Vector X		Observed Vector Y
1	710.88	641.20
2	394.90	155.60
3	88.90	124.94
4	25.00	56.32
5	113.36	106.50
6	184.66	277.32
7	221.17	202.83
8	176.67	177.41
9	121.10	83.23
10	58.14	50.79
11	25.00	51.03
12	25.00	46.08
13	175.78	147.00
14	133.50	132.53
15	107.29	47.45
16	0.0	0.0
17	163.85	44.79
18	425.64	271.15
19	156.67	168.19
20	211.41	127.25
21	139.41	122.44
22	99.27	63.99
23	68.00	42.50
24	71.44	48.88
25	117.41	52.52
26	23.10	50.61
27	112.58	61.91
28	118.45	58.21
29	39.90	51.20
30	61.60	49.97

Correlation Coefficient 0.9087
R2 0.8258
Student T value 11.5213
Degrees of freedom 12

Regression Coefficients
A = 8.8866
R = 0.7544
Standard error of estimate 49.1044

Bs/m² Scale 100.00

Land values
$R^2 = 0.8258$

Real land values

Model land values

FIG. 6.10. The Caracas Model: comparisons between real and simulated land values in each zone. The three-dimensional histograms are drawn by the plotter for one kilometre cells interpolating the values (Echenique *et al.*, 1973).

service employment. The resulting simulation was less effective than other applications of similar models, no doubt due to the data deficiencies. However, the reported reasons for the discrepancies, i.e. illegal settlements, hyperspeculative legal development, and intensity of office development, are probably not the only difficulties in applying the Lowry basis to a major city of a less-developed country.

The São Paulo Models

One of the largest cities in the world, and one of those growing very fast—5.5% per annum through the 1960s—is São Paulo, Brazil. Its present population (1981) is of the order of 12 million people, and there is little doubt that it will exceed 20 million by the year 1990. The industrial sector of São Paulo represents over 40% of the national product and at least 35% of the national workforce—and this in a city which still exhibits aspects of the two circuits in its structure.

In Brazilian terms, São Paulo is a comparatively rich city, and household incomes have climbed steadily at 7% per annum in the 1970s. A result of this growth in disposable income is an enormous demand for travel by the Paulistas: 17 million daily trips in 1980, and nearly 60% of all households owning a car. As a consequence of high mobility, serious congestion has occurred which has decreased accessibility and increased transport costs. The private car, used for 36% of all trips in 1975, has been the main reason for this decline in mobility and the decreasing accessibility of the city centre. This latter factor has resulted in a large scale shift of central facilities to new locations south west of the historic city centre.

By 1974 São Paulo was faced with a serious dilemma regarding very large-scale transport investment: both an underground railway system and an urban motorway system were being constructed, but the costs of both projects were so large that the two together could not be afforded, yet investment in new transport facilities seemed clearly called for. A study, SISTRAN, was commissioned therefore by the municipal transport department (SMT) and the metropolitan planning organization (EMPLASA). The brief of the study was to create a programme for urban passenger transport within the metropolitan area, and also to create "technical and operational capabilities for the continuous planning of São Paulo".

The study set up three related systems by which transport investment policies might be evaluated: an information system, a simulation system including a model of the land market and the transport market, and an evaluation system. The basic information which was available was an origin-and-destination survey of 1968, plus a municipal cadastre covering building stock information, and network information from public authorities.

The model developed aimed at simulating the operations of the transport market; (Fig. 6.11). Firstly, the total regional growth was forecast, interpreted

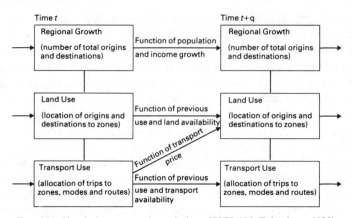

Fig. 6.11. Simulation system through time, SISTRAN (Echenique, 1980).

as a total number of origins and destinations. Then a land use model located origins and destinations to zones in the system. A transport use model allocated the resultant trips to zones, modes, and routes. Thus car-owning or non-car owning household trips were allocated from origin zones to destination zones by mode and to routes within that mode. Allocation to alternative destinations, modes, and routes, was determined by the price of transport, including the cost of time, and the location of activities or land uses, which was measured by the number of origins and destinations. The transport model was iterated until an equilibrium was reached for each part of the network between transport facility supply (in terms of capacity, speed and cost in the networks concerned), and demands as allocated. The equilibrium price of transport calculated at this time period was taken forward to the next time period, as a basis for reallocation of the locations of origins and destinations in the land use model for that time period, based on some updated totals of origins and destinations from the overall growth model.

The evaluation system was then used to compare the various outputs from the simulation model, by way of the calculation of various indices concerned with economic efficiency, distribution of social benefits, and environmental impacts.

The use of the model predicted that the continuing increase in car ownership and in daily trips (to 23 million by 1985) would give rise to further deterioration, despite the continuance of large investments in new transport facilities on certain projects: underground, surface rail, and road. Because the relative deterioration in accessibility was greater for car-owning households, an increasing number of trips on public transport would be made by these households. A shift in destination was also occurring, away from the congested city centre, towards the south west of the city.

A complementary programme of arterial roads with light-controlled intersections, rather than motorways was recommended plus an integrated bus feeder system with the existing underground railway, the suburban rail network, and a new trolley bus network, and a tax on central area parking to restrain car use in the city centre. Trolley buses were preferred for the new network of road transport facilities, as being cheaper, non-polluting, and easy to build locally. Most of these recommendations have been adopted since.

A new origin and destination survey was carried out in 1977, (EMPLASA, 1979), and a new Metropolitan Transport Authority was set up. This new authority combined with the São Paulo Municipo planning office (COGEP) and EMPLASA to commission a new study aimed at updating the transport model and amplifying the land use model. The new model, MUT, is described below, (Fig. 6.12). The fit of the SISTRAN model, compared with the actual values obtained in the 1977 O & D Survey, was good, except in the central zone, where SISTRAN overestimated the household income and the concentration there of destinations; decentralization has, in fact, overtaken the SISTRAN projections.

The new São Paulo Land Use/Transport Model was clearly derived from its progenitors in Caracas and Santiago—and, of course, in the SISTRAN experience in São Paulo itself.

Within the zoning system of the São Paulo model, zones of origin, i, were differentiated from zones of destination, f. Each kind of activity was indicated by other indices: m being an activity at an origin, and n being an activity at a

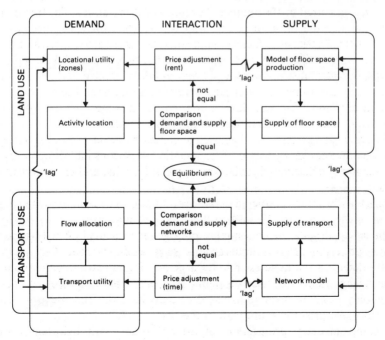

Fig. 6.12. MUT, São Paulo: general relationships (CET—Custodio, P. S. *et al.*, 1978).

destination. Relations between zones can therefore be summarized by appropriate matrices, describing, in essence, the functional structure or the spatial structure, e.g. a^{mn} might indicate an element of matrix A, showing the relationship between two activities, m and n; or a second matrix, B, might be composed of elements b_{ij}, indicating spatial relationships between zones i and j, e.g. journeys or money flows. Combining the A and B matrices would give a functional-spatial description of the urban system of São Paulo, e.g. encompassing terms such as the element b_{ij}^{mn}: the relationship between activity m located in zone i and activity n located in zone j; this relationship might be, say, that between a residential location in zone i, a family of a given income-level, and a workplace in the services supplied by the central area of São Paulo.

Such multi-dimensional matrices, however, present practical difficulties e.g. of computer capacity, and lead to too much disaggregation which is not relevant to a strategic planning model. For these reasons, seven separate matrices were evolved: four being residence/workplace matrices for families of four given income levels; one being a residence/retail services matrix for all income levels; one being a residence/education matrix for all income levels; and one being a residence/other services matrix for all income levels. These matrices could be aggregated to give the terms b_{ij}^m; summing the columns of the matrix would give the total value of production or location of activities m in a zone i: X_i^m; summing the rows would give the value of the demand for activity m in a zone j: Y_j^m. Thus:

$$
\begin{array}{ll}
\Sigma_j b_{ij}^m = X_i^m & \quad i \\
\Sigma_i b_{ij}^m = Y_j^m:
\end{array}
\qquad
\begin{array}{|cccc|}
\multicolumn{3}{c}{j} & \Sigma_j \\
b_{11}^m & b_{12}^m & \cdots & b_{1j}^m \\
b_{21}^m & b_{22}^m & \cdots & b_{2j}^m \\
\vdots & \vdots & & \vdots \\
b_{i1}^m & b_{i2}^m & \cdots & b_{ij}^m \\
\end{array}
\qquad
\begin{array}{|c|}
X_1^m \\
X_2^m \\
\vdots \\
X_i^m \\
\end{array}
$$

$$
\Sigma_i \quad | \; Y_1^m \quad Y_2^m \quad \cdots \quad Y_j^m \; |
$$

FIG. 6.13. MUT, São Paulo: Structure of the matrices b_{ij}; (CET, 1978).

These matrices, b_{ij}^m are representative of the functional-spatial relationships required in a location model: those relating activity m in zone i to a demand, Y_j^m, from zone j; the transport flow between zones i and j is also indicated.

The value of the relationship b_{ij}^m is a function of the demand of activity m in zone j, Y_j^m; the utility for activity m to be located in zone i, U_i^m; and the attractiveness of the location in zone i to the demand in zone j, W_{ij}^m. The concept of utility related to things like density for housing areas, housing floorspace, mobility, and availability of goods and services in the given location. The attractiveness index, W_{ij}^m related to the capacity in a zone to accept new activities, i.e. including the consideration of land already built up, land available for new activities.

Combining the functions of utility and attractiveness, the relationship between the demand for an activity, m, that is, Y_j^m and the functional-spatial relationships, b_{ij}^m, is:

$$b_{ij}^m = f(Y_j^m, U_i^m, W_{ij}^m).$$

In order to establish the terms, b_{ij}^m, it is necessary to solve the various systems simultaneously. In practice, though, the resolution is by successive iterations and approximations, until the systems tend to equilibrium.

The iterations take the form, firstly, of the establishment of an equilibrium market in land, and from this, the location of urban activities. Secondly, the establishing of an equilibrium for the transport market, from which the distribution of urban traffic can be evolved. The time lag for the tendency towards equilibrium of the two major systems, land use and transport, in fact, allows of the iterative procedure simulation being reasonably successful. These, of course, are the same basic systemic relationships as in the SISTRAN model system.

The land use system is initiated (cf. SISTRAN) by an initial demand model, cast in Input–Output form, which generated intermediate demand, which, for each sector, can be translated into needed new enterprises of different sizes and levels, in turn generating new families at different income levels and different demands for goods and services, etc. The matrix A, (a^{mn}) defines these relationships. The next processes are familiar from the previous models of this kind.

The full structure of the model, showing inputs required and outputs generated, is shown below, (Fig. 6.14). A full description of the mathematics and of the various subprocess is given in the references (CET, 1978).

Exogenous variables input to the model include regional income and employment projections from a model of regional growth; and planning policy variables to represent alternative projects or policies to be investigated. The latter are represented via land use and activity changes or constraints, and alterations to the public transport and street network.

The model's outputs include the location of the various urban activities, construction for these activities, use, cost, and duration of transport journeys, household incomes, and the utility and attractiveness of the zones for each activity.

An evaluation methodology is applied to the model outputs, utilizing cost-benefit analysis; measure of economic efficiency, distribution of benefits, and environmental effects are sought. The internal rate of return on capital invested is calculated.

A View on Simulation

Systems theory regards systems as having both a structure and a behaviour. A basic tenet is that system behaviour arises from, and is an expression of, the

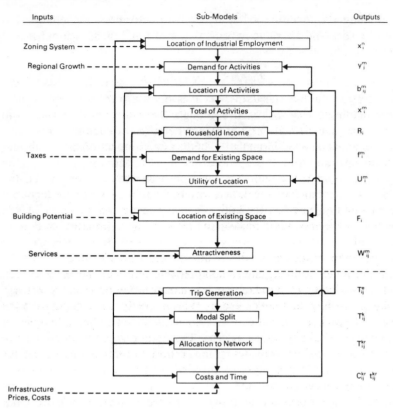

Fig. 6.14. Structure of the MUT model of São Paulo (CET, 1978).

system's structure, so that a system of certain structure will go on, through time, producing behaviour which is seen as due to, and characteristic of that structure. Thus, in system modelling, we may essay the reproduction or replication of the structure of the system being modelled—so that, if our effort is successful, the behaviour of the system model is very close to that of the system which is modelled. The alternative approach—that of simulation—is to concern ourselves with the reproduction of system behaviour, in the hope that the behaviour will be indicative of a "correct" structure. This latter approach, of course, must be subjected to many trials: the model must be capable of simulating the behaviour of the system at what are seen to be significant and representative points in time to be acceptable. Thus there is likely to be a potential source of criticism in relation to simulation modelling in general, unless the doubts about structure can be resolved: the criticism levelled at the Forrester System Dynamics models is evidence of this, no doubt.

It is true that simulation models often can be made to reproduce behaviour at a specific point in time for which real data is available, by appropriate adjustment of parameter values—which may give rise to the gibe that they are no more than "accounting machines". Thus, from this standpoint, the utility of simulation models as forecasting devices may be seen as suspect by many observers. A means of assuaging this criticism often is to essay the reproduction of a time-series of data concerning the system being modelled, e.g. to start the model at year 'x', reproduce the data series between x and $(x+10)$, and $(x+10)$ and $(x+20)$, where these years are all now history, without the need for any fundamental changes in the model over these periods of simulated time.

A model may have a structure which is deterministic or probabilistic, though, and a model of the latter sort is open to a fairly fundamental criticism—though, again, if the utility of such a model can be verified by its reproduction of behaviour in relation to time-series data, the criticism is likely to be stilled.

An important criticism of the Santiago and Caracas models, and by implication others utilizing the same approach, has been made by Mohan (1979). This relates to the use of entropy-maximization procedures in urban modelling generally, first advocated by Wilson, (1970). Proceeding from the problem of specifying a state of a system of interest, the techniques of Newtonian classical physics, i.e. microanalysis, begin to prove too difficult to use: statistical mechanics provides more appropriate approaches to questions of macroanalysis. Macroanalysis of this kind can be related to microanalysis by way of the concept of entropy.

A complete description of the system of interest is defined by Wilson as a state of the system: in fact, a microstate. A macrostate description is regarded as a distribution: many microstates can give rise to the same macrostate. If all microstates are equally probable, we can find the most probable distribution by calculating the number of microstates associated with each distribution, subject to relevant constraint. The entropy of a system is defined as the logarithm of the probability that a distribution occurs, and the most probable distribution is that having the greatest number of microstates giving rise to it: thus maximizing the entropy gives the most probable distribution of microstates.

Here, of course, the term "entropy" is being used in its very general sense as a probability measure. This is the meaning of the term as used by Jaynes (1957), as quoted by Wilson (1970):

"Just as in applied statistics the crux of a problem is often the devising of some method of sampling that avoids bias, our problem is that of finding a probability assignment which avoids bias while agreeing with whatever information is given. The great advance provided by information theory lies in the discovery that there is a unique, unambiguous criterion for the 'amount of uncertainty' represented by a discrete probability distribution, which agrees with our intuitive notions that a broad distribution represents more uncertainty than does a sharply peaked one, and satisfies all other conditions which make it reasonable . . . . in making references on the basis of partial information we must use that probability distribution which has maximum entropy subject to whatever is known. This is the only unbiased assumption we can make; to use any other would amount to arbitrary assumption of information which by hypothesis we do not have."

Thus, for any given probability distribution we can precisely measure the amount of uncertainty which it represents by calculating its entropy. This is a very *general* measure of a system's condition: applicable to its "information" or "thermodynamic" content—or any other characteristic representable as a set of probabilistic states. Maximizing the entropy of such an ensemble is arriving at the most probable distribution, subject only to those constraints which have been identified.

It is the fear that, outside such constraints, randomness will prevail, that is at the root of Mohan's criticism:

"Generating a journey-to-work distribution through the use of entropy maximization amounts to saying: If the population of a city is asked repeatedly to choose work and residence locations aimlessly (or randomly), though subject to some constraints, the distribution that results most frequently is the distribution that entropy maximization provides. The constraint set can, of course, contain information that divides people according to such things as income classes, race, and kind of employment. The journey-to-work distribution that is obtained is, in this sense, not totally random. Beyond the constraint set, however, the randomness prevails. It is this implication of the entropy maximization technique that is considered the most problematical in the context of urban modelling. Even within such classifications as employment, income, and race, people do not locate themselves aimlessly, but instead through the operation of some preference functions (implicit though they may be), and are subject to the external market forces as expressed by prevailing prices. If all this information can be included in the constraint set of the entropy-maximizing procedure, the same result is obtained as with utility maximization. In any case, in practice thus far the constraint set has seldom included information from any preference functions. Even the market information included as been rudimentary. Thus, characteristically, entropy-maximization models that use mean values to generate various location distributions can scarcely be regarded as having any predictive value".

Mohan is thus sceptical of the value of the Echenique models of Latin American cities: the Caracas model was calibrated on 1966 data, but it was not possible to update it for a later year, due to a lack of data. The Santiago model was run on 1970 data, but was abondoned after government changes in Chile, in 1973. In the case of the São Paulo models, (not mentioned by Mohan), the existence of good data sets from the O & D Surveys of 1968 and 1977 should enable a satisfactory conclusion to be drawn as to the validity of the model in its potential replicability of the 1977 situation from the 1968 data base.

A Korean Example of the Use of a Lowry-Derived Spatial Interaction Model

TOMM—Time Oriented Metropolitan Model—is a derivative of the Lowry allocation model, with greater disaggregation, and thus larger data requirements, and incorporates an attempt to change the major variables over time. The model allocates changes in employment and household location over an urban system, incrementally, using parameters which may be originally estimated by multiple regression.

The TOMM model has been summarized by Crecine (1968) as follows:

"—numbers of exogenous employees, by type (bureaucratic or industrial), and by location are taken as given. Exogenous employees support (or create) a certain number of households in the region. Households locate spatially in the urban system based partly on accessibility to particular places of employment. These households in turn generate demands for services and endogenous commercial employment. The additional endogenous employees in turn support more households, (which are then located) etc." (This, of course, is the general logic of Lowry's model, which now becomes modified.) "The location behaviour of households is said to be a function of the composite cost surface for particular household types. The composite cost surface is, in turn, a function of cost surfaces for individual households based on access to exogenous employment; access to endogenous employment (as employees and as customers), and externalities associated with various areal units or sites. The locational behaviour of endogenous commercial activities is based primarily on accessibility to customers where different types of households exert differential rates of attraction. Once a change in the level or location of employees is affected, the urban system moves toward a new equilibrium between exogenous employees, households, and endogenous employees"; (see Fig. 6.15).

The solution of the TOMM model includes the following outputs:

(a) Total number of employees by types of retail and service trades;
(b) Quantity of land in use in each of the retail and service trades;
(c) Amount of land used for residential purposes;
(d) The number of households in each income group.

The treatment of time in TOMM involves postscripting all variables to indicate their values at particular points in time; the population is also disaggregated by household types, and the service sector is disaggregated by employment in different services, with corresponding disaggregation of activity rates and population-serving ratios. The model theory recognizes that some activities are stable over longish periods, but some are more mobile: thus a "mover pool" for each category is available. The total stock of land is reallocated by the model for each time period.

Although TOMM is reputed not to have been successfully validated on real data in the USA—its data requirements are considerable—it has been used in

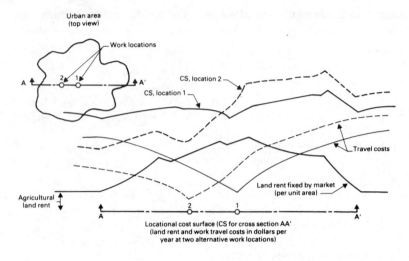

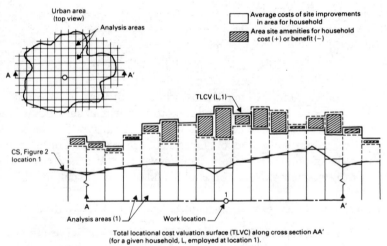

Fig. 6.15. Locational cost surfaces, as used in TOMM. (Crecine, 1968).

Korea, as part of an exercise to study the possibilities of decentralizing various kinds of employment from Seoul, (KRIHS, 1980). Seoul, 1980 population 8,366,750, is a primate city; (Pusan, 1980 population 3,160,270, is the second ranking city). The continued growth in size of Seoul, and the surrounding Gyonggi Province, is a matter of concern, though it can be argued with justification that this area represents the main engine of Korea's considerable economic growth. (R. L. Meier, 1969, quoted by Artle, 1970, suggested that the rate of growth of GRP of the Seoul-Inchon area in the late 1960s exceeded 25% per annum, after 6 years of 13 to 20% growth rates.) If Seoul does not increase in size, can it continue to increase its GRP at such a high rate: can its economic growth potential be transferred elsewhere if its physical growth is halted or even slowed down? Whether these questions have been answered, or indeed are answerable, or not, attempts are being made to hold the population of the metropolitan region at about its present level, and various decentralization possibilities are being examined; (see Kim and Bell, 1982). The aim in the study cited was to test the effects of specific policies involving the decentralization of particular types of employment and other urban functions.

The Seoul metropolitan region was divided into 36 zones as a basis for a series of regional spatial analyses involving population distributions and types of land use. Basic employment was defined for each zone, subdivided into international, national, regional and local functions, with various implications as to those functions capable of decentralization. The effects of policy decisions on employment relocation upon population distribution were tested by using TOMM in relation to four alternative broad spatial models of the metropolitan region, using data from special surveys of residential location and retail shopping in Seoul, in addition to the normal published data sources which abound in the Republic of Korea. In the general aim, then, the process of testing spatial alternatives has certain similarities to those of a number of sub-regional planning studies carried out in the United Kingdom between 1969 and 1971, which used a Lowry allocation model for the same purpose, (see Cowling and Steeley, 1973; Lichfield, Kettle and Whitbread, 1975). A similar process was adopted in the Strategic Plan for Greater Salisbury, Rhodesia, 1972–1974.

The general diagram of the Seoul study process reproduced here, (Fig. 6.16

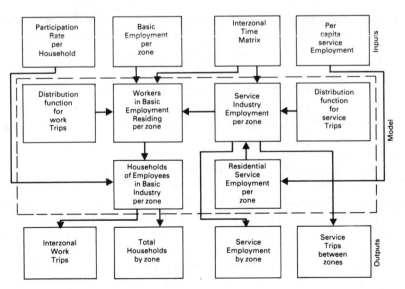

FIG. 6.16. The structure of the KRIHS version of TOMM for Seoul (KRIHS, 1980).

from KRIHS, 1980), emphasizes the data requirements and production of data for TOMM: even with a 36-zone system, (as in the Seoul region), this can be a lengthy process in a situation where original data files are sparse, (though, in general, Korean data is excellent and readily available).

As with the original Lowry allocation model, the inputs and outputs are similar, except for the disaggregation aspects already mentioned. A brief consideration of the mechanics of the model is as follows.

The sixteen equations of the model are given in the table (Fig. 6.18). Equation (1) represents the total land area as the sum of the lands allocated to the various uses; this can be recast, of course, to give the lands capable of being reallocated for residence and for housing:

$$A_{j,t}^H + A_{j,t}^R = A_{j,t}^* - A_{j,t}^V - A_{j,t}^B - A_{j,t}^P - A_{j,t}^{RS} - A_{j,t}^{HS}$$

—where the symbols are as listed, and the asterisk represents a summation. Equation (2) shows service employment to be a function of residential population, with disaggregation by income group, whilst (3) is merely a statement of summation of population over all zones at the base year, t.

The number of households, (a^k) giving rise to the employment of one person in the service sector, i.e. the population-serving ratio, is:

$$a^k = N_t^H / E_t^{RK}$$

We can also write:

$$E_t^{RK} = \sum_{l=1}^{h} a^{kl} \cdot N_{jt}^{Hl} *$$

The number of employees per zone in the service sector is proportional to the market potential of that zone, which suggests the following formulation:

$$E_{jt}^{Rk} = b^k \cdot \sum_{i=1}^{n} \frac{\sum_{l=1}^{n} (C^{kl} \cdot N_{i,t}^{Hl}) + d^k \cdot E_{it}}{Y_{ij}}$$

—where c^{kl} and d^k are weights representing the rate of use of commerce and service facilities originating from each house and workplace, i.e.

$$\sum_{l=1}^{n} C^{kl} + d^k = 1.0.$$

The total of land used can be estimated by way of an employment-density coefficient:

$$A_{it}^{R*} = \sum_{k=1}^{m} e^k \cdot E_{jt}^{RK}.$$

Only a proportion of this total area can be regarded as mobile, however, in view of the fixity of investment. Referring to equation (8) of the table (Fig. 6.18), the total of available building site area can be:

$$\sum_{k=1}^{m} l^k \cdot E_{j,t}^{RK} - \sum_{k=1}^{m} e^k \cdot E_{j,t-1}^{RK}.$$

The total number of households in the zoning system is given by the multiplier (f) on total employment:

$$N_t^{H*} = f \cdot \sum_{j=1}^{n} E_{j,t}.$$

Net housing density is thus:

$$N_{j,t}^{H*}/A_{j,t}^{H*} = g \cdot \sum_{i=1}^{n} [E_{i,t}/Y_{ij}].$$

The minimum number of households per zone is that total of "stabilized" households which do not migrate during the time period; the maximum value is the area of land available for redistribution multiplied by the maximum density allowable. The case of the maximum value is given by:

$$N_{j,t}^{H*}/A_{j,t}^{H*} > Z_j^H \rightarrow g = Z_j^H \left[1 \bigg/ \sum_{i=1}^{n} (E_{i,t}/Y_{ij}) \right];$$

—and the minimum case:

$$N_j^{H*} < N_j^{HS} \rightarrow g = \frac{N_{i,t}^{H*}}{A_{j,t}^{H*}} \left[1 \bigg/ \sum_{i=1}^{n} (E_{i,t}/Y_{ij}) \right].$$

The model differs from the Lowry formulation in that housing density, as mentioned, is used as a function of employment potential:

$$N_{j,t}^{H*}/A_{j,t}^{H*} = g \cdot \sum_{i=1}^{n} [E_{i,t}/Y_{ij}].$$

This employment potential is that related to accessibility of zonal households against the employment distribution of each zone. The work trip index used in this case was based on a work-trip function obtained from an origin and destination survey in Seoul City in 1977, i.e.

$$Y_{ij} = 1309.2(d_{ij})^{0.029352} \exp(-1313 \, d_{ij}).$$

The TOMM model is open to some criticism in that it is not completely dynamic. The model process takes the form of adding newly-formed households, preceded by a series of distributions to each zone of households which are potentially migratory. The households newly formed within the model during each simulation period may differ from those of the previous year, dependent upon their separate classification.

TABLE 6.17. *Variables Used in the Seoul Version of the TOMM Model*

A = land area in hectares.
E = employment, i.e. number of persons employed.
N = population, i.e. number of households.
Y = trip distribution index.
Z = a restraint condition.
U = land which is unable to be used for development (given exoge-
    nously).
B = exogenously generated basic industry.
R = commerce and service sector.
H = residential sector.
P = public lands (exogenously given).
S = stabilized land use or residential location.
K = facility installation groups of commerce and service sectors.
m = number of the above groups.
l = income groups, residential sector.
h = number of the above groups.
i, j = zones within the model.
n = number of zones
t = base year.
T = plan year.

Other symbols, e.g. a, b, c, d, e, f, g, r, p, w represent certain parameters or scale factors or weights. An asterisk, *, represents a summation over all zones.

Thus:
$$N_{j,t}^{H} = N_{j,t}^{H*} - N_{j,t-1}^{H}*.$$

The reorganization of the number of households in each zone is represented by:

$$N_{j,t}^{H*} = N_{j,t-1}^{HS} + N_{j,t}^{HM*} + N_{j,t}^{H}$$

or:
$$N_{j,t}^{H*} = N_{j,t}^{H*} - N_{j,t-1}^{HS*} - N_{j,t}^{HM*}$$

—where: $N_{j,t}^{H*}$ is the total number of households located in zone j in year t;

and: $N_{j,t}^{H}$ is the number of households which are newly formed in zone j between years $(t-1)$ and t, or have migrated into the area in that time;

and: $N_{j,t-1}^{HS*}$ represents non-movers who retain the same location in zone j;

and: $N_{j,t}^{HM*}$ represents the number of households which have migrated into zone j during the period from $(t-1)$ to t.

Thus both internal household movements and inwardly migrating households can be accommodated within the model.

Residential location patterns are, of course, largely treated in two groups, dependent upon, (a) the amenities of the residential environment, (b) its accessibility to workplace:

$$N_{j,t}^{Hl} = r_j \left[P_l N_{j,t-1}^{l*} + W_l \sum_{i=1}^{n} (E_{i,t}/Y_{ij}) \right]$$

Structural Equations	Total of Equations
(1) $A_{j,t}^{*}=A_{j,t}^{U}+A_{j,t}^{B}+A_{j,t}^{P}+A_{j,t}^{RS}+A_{j,t}^{HS}+A_{j,t}^{R}+A_{j,t}^{H}$	n
(2) $E_{t}^{RK}=\sum_{l=1}^{h} a^{kl} N_{t}^{Hl/*}$	m
(3) $N_{t}^{Hl*}=\sum_{j=1}^{n} N_{j,t}^{Hl/*}$	h
(4) $E_{j,t}^{Rk}=b^{k}\sum_{i=1}^{n}\sum_{l=1}^{h}\left[\dfrac{(c^{kl}N_{i,t}^{Hl})+d^{k}E_{i,t}}{Y_{ij}}\right]$	mn
(5) $E_{t}^{Rk}=\sum_{j=1}^{n} b^{k}\sum_{i=1}^{n}\sum_{l=1}^{h}\left[\dfrac{(c^{kl}N_{i,j}^{Hl})+d^{k}E_{i,t}}{Y_{ij}}\right]$	m
(6) $E_{j,t}=E_{j,t}^{B}+\sum_{k=1}^{m} E_{j,t}^{Rk}$	n
(7) $A_{j,t}^{R*}=\sum_{k=1}^{m} e^{k}E_{j,t}^{Rk}$	n
(8) $A_{j,t}^{R}=\text{Max}\left(\sum_{k=1}^{m} e^{k}E_{j,t}^{Rk}-\sum_{k=1}^{m} e^{k}E_{j,t-1}^{Rk}, A_{j,t}^{RS}-\sum_{k=1}^{m} e^{k}E_{j,t-1}^{Rk}\right)$	n
(9) $A_{j,t}^{R*}=A_{j,t}^{R}+A_{j,t-1}^{R*}$	n
(10) $N_{t}^{H*}=f\sum_{j=1}^{n} E_{j,t}$	one
(11) $N_{j,t}^{H*}=g\sum_{i=1}^{n}\left[\dfrac{E_{i,t}}{Y_{ij}}\right]A_{j,t}^{H*}$	n
(12) $A_{j,t}^{H*}=A_{j,t}^{H}+A_{j,t-1}^{H*}$	n
(13) $N_{t}^{H*}=\sum_{j=1}^{n} N_{j,t}^{H*}$	one
(14) $N_{j,t}^{Hl}=r_{j}\left(P_{l}N_{j,t-1}^{Hl/*}+w_{l}\sum_{1}^{n}\left[\dfrac{E_{i,t}}{Y_{ij}}\right]\right)$	hn
(15) $N_{j,t}^{H}=\sum_{l=1}^{h} N_{j,t}^{Hl}$	n
(16) $N_{j,t}^{Hl/*}=N_{j,t}^{Hl}+N_{j,t-1}^{Hl/*}$	hn

FIG. 6.18. Equation structure of Seoul version of TOMM (KRIHS, 1980).

—where P_l and W_l are weights. This expression can be rewritten as follows:

$$N_{j,i}^{HMl} = V_j \left[P_l \cdot N_{j,t-1}^{HSl*} + W_l \sum_{i=1}^{n} (E_{i,t}/Y_{ij}) \right]$$

—where V_j is a scale multiplier which satisfies the condition that:

$$\sum_{l=1}^{h} N_{j,i}^{HMl} = N_{j,i}^{HM*}.$$

This reformulation suggests the assumption that residential location can be seen as related, more simply, to: (a) the demand for stable households of the same location group, and (b) the employment potential inherent in the given zone.

The parameters used in the Seoul model are listed in the table (Table 6.19).

TABLE 6.19. *Major Parameters Used in the Seoul Model*

Parameter	Service facility	Income group	Input value	Description of parameter
a^k	K = 1		0.4700	Employment by income group
	K = 2		0.1350	per household per original unit
	K = 3		0.0540	
		l = 1	0.3188	
	K = 1	l = 2	0.3247	
		l = 3	0.3285	
		l = 1	0.3902	
c^{kl}	K = 2	l = 2	0.3298	
		l = 3	0.1960	
		l = 1	0.1247	Home-based trip generation rate
	K = 3	l = 2	0.2371	
		l = 3	0.3632	
d^k	K = 1		0.0280	Workplace-based trip rate
	K = 2		0.0840	
	K = 3		0.2750	
e^k	K = 1		0.00518	Original unit (ha) of land use for
	K = 2		0.00443	service employment
	K = 3		0.00131	
f			0.6536	Household support rate per capita employment
p^l		l = 1	0.8660	Environment and income-group
		l = 2	0.8160	oriented housing locational
		l = 3	0.8520	factor
w^l		l = 1	0.1340	Accessibility to workplace-
		l = 2	0.1840	oriented dwelling locational
		l = 3	0.1480	factor
Z^k	K = 1		150	Commercial and service facilities:
	K = 2		5,000	minimum scale
	K = 3		70,000	

(*KRIHS*, 1980.)

The residential mobility rates taken ranged from 72% (low) to 74% (high), based on surveys of various income groups.

The Seoul version of TOMM, with its zonal outputs, of total residential land, number of households in each income group, land used in services, and service employment by type or trade, enables the production of the changed patterns of activity and land demand associated with varied patterns of "basic" employment: i.e. the retention of certain kinds of employment in the metropolis, and the decentralization of other kinds. The evaluation of these changed patterns, of course, is another matter, although the data available on the revised interzonal trip patterns is helpful here.

An Urban Model System in Africa

Some models which have been applied to specific case situations of urban or regional systems in developing countries have been of relatively bounded pretensions: the single model embedded in some problem formulation. This is true even of path-breaking applications such as Ayeni's application of Lowry's Model of Metropolis to Lagos, or Kwon's application of TOMM to Seoul. The nearest to a comprehensive modelling programme for a given urban system with definite policy outcomes in view—and for a very large and complex metropolitan system, too—is perhaps the Echenique *et al.* model system of São Paulo, with its fundamental interactions between transport and land use changes. (Although the later Chile/Santiago model is noteworthy for its potential). Many planning efforts in developing countries, even those carried out by experienced and highly qualified consultant teams from western countries, have not attempted any kind of formal modelling as an aid to decision-making: for example, not once is there an indication in any of the most interesting and well-addressed Asian case studies cited by Taylor and Williams (1982) that formal modelling was even contemplated. The reasons for this kind of situation will be discussed later. In the meantime, a more modest application than that of São Paulo, of a comprehensive plan-making approach using a number of models, is relevant. It is also of interest as being based on the published experience of a number of British sub-regional planning studies, which may be listed here as still representing a significant contribution to physical planning methodology:

South Hampshire Study: Colin Buchanan & Partners and Economic Consultants Ltd, 1966

Leicester and Leicestershire Sub-Regional Planning Study: Leicester City Council and Leicestershire County Council, 1969

Nottinghamshire and Derbyshire Sub-Regional Study: Notts/Derbys. Sub-Regional Planning Unit, 1969

Coventry–Solihull–Warwickshire: A Strategy for the Sub-Region: Coventry City Council, Solihull County Borough Council, Warwickshire County Council, 1971

In addition, other published work (Chadwick, 1971; Lichfield *et al.*, 1975; LUBFS Cambridge, 1969) was drawn upon in this work.

Salisbury, a city of only 385,000 total population at 1969, was forecast to reach 1 million by 1995 and perhaps 1.1 to 1.3 million by year 2000. As the capital of Rhodesia it was the largest city and responsible for more than half of the economic growth of the country in the late 1960s and early 1970s.

The need for a strategic plan for Greater Salisbury appears to have arisen, firstly from work on the revision of the statutory Salisbury Outline Plan circa 1970; and, secondly, from attempts to formulate a land use/traffic plan by the City Council, also circa 1970. Despite the lack of legal powers for strategic metropolitan planning, it was seen that certain broader-scale issues required resolution as a basis for more detailed urban policy decisions. As in South Africa about that time, the transfer of advances in British planning theory and methodology of the late 1960s, including emphasis on urban and regional models, was an important stimulus.

The Salisbury approach followed closely that of the British sub-regional studies quoted: population and employment projections; development potential analysis, (based on formulation of plan objectives); consideration of alternatives; allocation modelling; retail shopping modelling; use of a suite of traffic models, based on an origin and destination survey, (trip generation, trip distribution, modal split, trip assignment); use of an evaluation model. The inter-relationships between the models are shown in Fig. 6.20.

As the technical aspects of all the models were based on well-documented British/American examples, it is unnecessary to explain their details here. However, some aspects of their use are of relevance as pointing up some of the differences ascribable to their particular application: a city of a plural society and a dual economy.

As in most of Africa, difficulties were experienced with the basic population projections, especially with those of Africans. Registration of births and deaths is not common in African countries, though many such countries have now conducted population censuses; even so, time-series data does not commonly exist in an adequate form. In Salisbury, only the European population group was covered by data sufficient for a cohort-survival model to be run for them. The only complete censuses of Africans took place in 1962 and 1969, and those two sets of data were clearly inadequate as a base for projection. However, a strong correlation was found between the numbers of Europeans and Africans in employment over a long period, and the population projections for Africans were derived, therefore, from the employment projections for Europeans.

The employment projections were derived from data which existed for the whole of Rhodesia, by sector and by race, although full data for Salisbury itself was available only for 1961, 1969, 1971 and 1972. Forecasts of national employment were made using multiple regression analysis on the yearly sets of data for the period 1957–1972. On the basis of past data for each sector of the

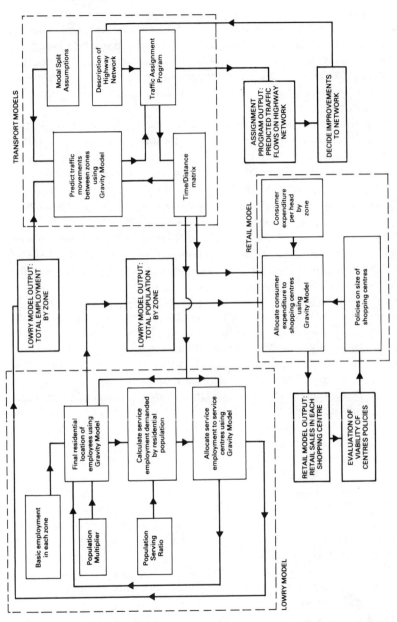

FIG. 6.20. Relationship of models and model outputs, Salisbury.

economy, trends in Salisbury's share of the national total were established and checked against what recent data was available and also by reference to surveys of demand in the city economy. The European, Asian, and Coloured populations were treated as one group for these purposes, being the population disaggregation, with Africans as a separate group, commonly in statistical use. An activity rate of 2.2 dependants per employee for this group, based upon statistics for the period 1961–1972, enabled a cross-check to be made against the population forecasts.

So far as the African population group was concerned, it was thought that European investment, employment, and population were likely to remain the basis of African employment growth for the next 20 years. This being so, African employment could be forecast by applying a ratio, varying from 2.5:1 in 1973 to 3.6:1 by year 2000, to the forecasts for European workers. (Non-urban employment was excluded. Africans in domestic employment were calculated on the basis of 0.4 domestics per person of the combined European, Asian and Coloured population group projections.) Population forecasts for Africans were based on a ratio of 2.0 dependants per employee. Some consideration appears to have been given to self-employment by Africans, but the figure quoted, of 3000 only in a forecast African employment total of 400,000 (at 2000) suggests that this is not by any means a recognition of the two-circuit economy, but rather an allowance for self-employment in the formal sector. The lower circuit of the economy, in fact, seems to have been ignored in this study, as in virtually all others known.

Migration, in this method, was treated only incidentally: African migration to Salisbury was possibly implied by the use of employment forecasts as a basis. European in-migration was considered, in view of the fact that Salisbury was the destination for 64 to 67% of European immigrants to Rhodesia during 1968–1970. However, national in-migration appeared to be a fluctuating, possibly cyclical phenomenon, and was not thought to be amenable to prediction. The difference between European population growing at its then current rate of increase, and the population projections based on the forecasts of employment demand, was assumed to be made up by in-migration in the absence of more reliable predictions of migration. Interestingly, both European and African populations of Salisbury grew at a close to exponential rate over the period 1900–1970, though the African component was about 75% of the total over most of this time. The recent (1961–1971) annual growth rates of the Asian and Coloured population groups were very high, at 4.9% and 5.6% per annum, respectively, though the total numbers involved were relatively small. The average household size in Greater Salisbury, i.e. number of persons per electricity meter supplying at the domestic scale tariff, from electricity undertaking records, at 1969, was 3.48 persons. However, for African households (also at 1969), the following size distributions was noted:

2 persons: 8.6%
3 persons: 8.3%

4 persons:	14.3%
5 persons:	16.4%
6 persons:	17.4%
7 persons:	10.6%
8 persons:	10.9%
9 persons:	7.2%
10 persons:	3.3%
11 persons:	3.0%

This may be the appropriate place to make the point that, in plural societies, disaggregation of data is essential in forecasting. At the input end of forecasts, there are commonly very large differences between the growth experiences of different racial or ethnic groups, which are masked by attempts to use averages over a total urban or regional population. Forecasts using overall averages are very unreliable, as can be seen from a comparison of the average African household size in Salisbury, above, of 5.78 persons, with the overall (all races) size which was 3.48 persons. A forecast of housing demand using the latter figure would be very seriously wrong.

At the output end, also in plural societies, disaggregation is essential in the consideration of social and cultural facilities, especially for housing and schools, probably for health facilities and recreation, also for trip-making behaviour, e.g. women rarely use public transport or drive cars in many Moslem societies.

These considerations form a considerable challenge in the modelling of urban and regional systems in developing countries which are characterized by plural societies: a challenge as to data availability, and a challenge to the mechanics of modelling—is disaggregation of the model feasible? When the plural society, as usually, has a two-circuit economy, the problem is compounded, for modelling of the lower circuit economy may not be possible at all. This point will be taken up again later.

To return to Greater Salisbury, although development potential analysis was used, and typical broad future development patterns were derived from it, a basic feature of the study was the use of a Lowry-type allocation model, based, of course, on preliminary decisions as to the location of basic industry in the metropolitan area.

As a preliminary, a matrix of minimum travel times had been prepared for the 97 zones of the regional system by appropriate past-runs of a traffic assignment program. The model was calibrated on mean trip length statistics for both work and service trips. The best fit parameter values were found to be, for residential location: 0.0525; and for service location: 0.5751. (Calibration runs cost about £10 per attempt, on an IBM 370 system). The use of an attractiveness factor for each zone, based upon the development potential analysis, as an alternative to existing zonal population as an attractiveness measure, enabled the testing of the various alternative broad development patterns, in the runs of the predictive version of the allocation model.

The logic of the Lowry allocation model is well known. From already-located basic employment, population supplying workers for that employment is located; from this population, service employment is located, and then, in successive iterations, population supplying workers in service employment is located. But the tenets of economic base theory cannot be applied to the lower circuit of a dual economy. Firstly, the population supplying those whose activities are in the informal sector is probably already located. Secondly, the work locations of this sector are probably not fixed, but mobile. Thirdly, the "work-trips" involved may well be on foot and unrecorded and costless. Fourthly, in any case, those involved in this sector may well be classified as unemployed, because not wage-earning, in any surveys or statistics. Hence, the running of a Lowry-type model for a region or a city of a developing country assumes that the underlying economic base theory of the formal sector applies to the whole population and the whole economy. If, as in the case cited—and in all others which have been investigated as Lowry model applications—the input data neglects the two-circuits economy context entirely, then obviously the model outputs will not represent that situation, and indeed cannot represent even the upper circuit situation correctly. To what extent this latter situation is a disability is not known in the case of Salisbury; it may not be material if the lower circuit is small. However, the running of a retail shopping model as part of the same study may have thrown some light on that situation.

The shopping model was of the Lakshmanan and Hansen type. Input data consisted of population per zone, and annual per head consumer expenditure per zone in 1973, both by two population groups: Europeans, Asians and Coloureds; and Africans, respectively. Retail floorspace per zone was measured from large-scale maps and direct survey and was used as a measure of zonal attractiveness. Actual sales per zone were also used. Matrices of interzonal shopping trips were available from a household interview survey, and a matrix of interzonal times had been calculated.

Calibration of the model against actual sales was attempted using a range of parameters for the distance variable. As with the Lowry model, the normal calibration method is on the mean trip length; however, the appropriate parameter of 4.8 to give MTL predicted = MTL actual = 6.85 minutes was found to give gross underestimates of actual sales in the central shopping area, whereas the best fit for actual CBD sales, though still under-reading, was with a parameter value around 1.00. Thus, either MTL was not the appropriate calibration measure, or a further explanation of attractiveness of each shopping area was needed.

However, the shopping provision in a city with several racial or ethnic groups is often a good deal more complex than that in a city which is comparatively homogeneous in its population and spending habits. One recalls the very substantial area of Indian shopping in the Grey Street area of Durban, for example, distinct from, but close to the main (European) part of the city centre. In Salisbury, a complex pattern was present also. In addition to the city centre there were a number of suburban shopping centres located in residential areas housing European, Asian, or Coloured populations; there were also small shopping areas in the African townships. Analysis of the base data used in the attempted calibration of the retail model for Greater Salisbury revealed a poor correlation between the number of service employees and the retail floorspace per zone. The latter ranged from 0.6 to 11.8 m² per service employee. It was also found that retail turnover per m² in the city centre was only Rhodesian $260 compared with $456/m² in European suburban centres (1975 figures). With substantially higher rents/m² in the city centre, this situation was unexpected, though it could be explained possibly by the inclusion of ancillary floorspace, (storage, associated offices), in the city centre data, or by the greater emphasis on sale of durable goods in the city centre.

The non-availability of disaggregation by race in the sales data, though available in population data, was also a difficulty. The African townships, with relatively high densities of population but low spending power were served by small convenience shops only: durable and specialist goods were purchased from the city centre and/or from the largely European suburban centres. Retail floorspace per head (c. 1975) was calculated at only 0.04 m² for African townships, but 0.87 m²/head for the other suburban centres, and 0.66 m²/head for the city centre. The African townships might be some distance away from the city, too, meaning long shopping trips for the African population, and thus making combined shopping trip matrices possibly rather unrealistic.

The expenditure per head was calculated from the Government Family Budget Surveys available; and zonal differences in expenditure per head (for European/Asian/Coloured populations) were established by reference to the wage distributions of E/A/C males, by place of residence, from the 1969 Census. Zonal attractiveness for the attempted calibration runs of the retail model was calculated as a direct proportion of total zonal retail floorspace. Subsequently, it was thought that either floorspace for certain specialist services, as a proxy for the relative importance of individual centres, or service employment, might have been a better measure of zonal attractiveness.

This comparative lack of success in applying the conventional logic of the retail shopping model to an African situation is interesting, especially as there was no prima facie difficulty of this kind in calibrating the Lowry type allocation model for the same situation. However, the focus of the allocation model is different and the distribution of service activity is not called into question by it to the same degree as in the retail model.

The suite of traffic models used in the Greater Salisbury study followed contemporary practice. The existing network was tested as the first future alternative, in order to ascertain where overloading or other difficulties might occur. Future public transport emphasis was on buses, and it was thought that a rapid transit system was unlikely in a city the size of Salisbury, in view of the investment involved. An evaluation program was used to test final output of all the alternative strategies. As this was virtually entirely concerned with the calculation of various future accessibility indices, e.g. how many jobs could be reached within given time bands from each zone, it may be regarded perhaps as an adjunct to the traffic models, rather than an appropriate evaluation method for all facets of the regional strategy.

Lowry in Nigeria

Attempts at the modelling of urban systems in Africa, outside Southern Africa, have been rather few, so far as is known, even in those African cities, usually the larger, capital cities, which are a continuing contribution of Colonial Government involvement. The reasons for this lack are fairly obvious, but are well stated by Ayeni (1979) in his application of a Lowry-type allocation model to Nigerian conditions:

"The empirical development of the Lowry model requires not only easily available demographic, economic and spatial behavioural data, but also an economic system that can be dichotomized into basic and service sectors. Neither such data systems, nor indeed cities, are easily obtainable in Nigeria. In the former case, there is a general lack of relevant data, while the low level of development does not encourage the collection of a wider body of data. For the latter case, it needs to be mentioned that the processes of urbanization in Nigeria do not necessarily imply a corresponding process of industrialization, or vice versa, and hence it is not in all cases that the definition of the basic and service sectors, as in Western European or American textbooks, is applicable. Nonetheless, there exists a number of cities, in particular Jos, Lagos, Kaduna and a few others, where data are not only available, but also where the division of the economy into the basic and service sectors could be done with some measure of certainty."

The data for Ayeni's model of Lagos was derived from a field survey of 1405 households, (7426 people). The resultant material was classified by income into three socio-economic groups. The person-trip data gathered was utilized in a linear formulation of generalized transport cost including distance, cost of time used, and actual fare costs. Both mean trip lengths and mean trip costs increase with socio-economic group, as may be expected, but the cost variations were found to be much greater than the trip length variations.

The model itself was calibrated on mean trip lengths, and on variance of housing expenditures, though some difficulty was found with the latter calibration. A good fit was achieved with the distributions of population, with R^2 above 0.946; however, the fit with employment distribution was less good. The latter situation is very interesting, as it is attributed by Ayeni to problems with the data on the distribution of service employment, despite his earlier statement, (above). In fact, it appears that the Lagos evidence is further proof that the Lowry logic is not at all suitable for urban systems in developing countries. This should come as no surprise: Pittsburgh and Lagos are rather different, after all. Ayeni's acceptance of the theoretic base of the Lowry model does seem rather to fly in the face of his own evidence, despite his pioneering application to Nigerian conditions. An earlier (1974) application of the Lowry approach by Ayeni was to Jos, a Nigerian city of about 100,000 population, whilst a version of Crecine's (TOMM) model was also applied by him to Jos later.

Entropy Measures in Regional Growth: Korea

An interesting application of entropy-maximization technique is provided by a Korean model which was formulated in order to test regional growth centre policies, (Kwon, 1981). The Space-Oriented Diffusion Model aims at simulating the diffusion of innovations, this being regarded in terms of the effects of particular investments in urban public services. Urban growth is regarded as being stimulated by the diffusion between cities, and the role of a "growth centre" policy is seen as increasing the capacity of national urban systems so that the entropy of diffusion can be maximized. The background of the modelling purpose was the encouragement of growth in cities away from Seoul, based on the view that Seoul was becoming too large and too congested, (cf. the earlier discussion of a TOMM application).

Robson (1973) had previously carried out simulations based on the theory that urban economic growth occurs from interaction between cities, rather than within an individual city, i.e. a diffusion of innovations as growth stimuli. This view was derived from an analysis of the spread of several innovations in England and Wales during the nineteenth century. This theory neglects the self-potential for urban growth, which is the Achilles heel of innovation diffusion theory: what happens to innovations when they cease to be new? Increased production of established manufactures and urban services is surely still possible, indeed normal, but is neglected by innovation diffusion theory. However, Kwon's model is a considerable improvement over Robson's in this respect.

Robson's model derives from traditional gravity ideas, the spread of innovation, in terms of its receiving a stimulus representing information about an innovation, being represented by a form of gravity equation:

$$P_i = h \cdot \Sigma N_i^\alpha \cdot d_{ij}^{-\lambda} \cdot S_j$$

—where $i \neq j$; and:

N_i = population of city i;
S_j = number of stimuli from city j;
d_{ij} = distance between i and j;
α = a mass exponent representing intra-urban agglomeration;
λ = a distance decay exponent;
h = a scale factor.

The Korean model introduces market potential (V_{ij}) as representing the attractiveness of a city, with the probability of market attractiveness between i and j being represented as a function of its total urban system.

Thus the previous equation is modified to:

$$V_{ij} = N_i^\alpha \exp(-\lambda d_{ij})/\Sigma_k N_k^\alpha \exp(-\lambda d_{iK}),$$

where $K = 1, 2, \ldots n$.

The negative exponential measure of the distance function overcomes the problem of retaining the self-potential of each city, i.e. the equation is valid even for $i = j$.

The investment in provision of new services is regarded in terms of stimuli sent out and is simulated as market expansion. Depending on the relative shares of market potentials, the new services will be adopted in the largest cities and follow, in succession, in the smaller cities. The relative probabilities of opportunities occurring in the various cities within the system of cities are estimated in terms of market potential:

$$P_i = g \cdot \Sigma_j V_{ij} \cdot S_i$$

—where g is a normalizing factor, and S_i is the number of stimuli from city i.

The attractiveness of a city, j, is taken as an exponential function of its population:

$$S_j = (N_j)^\beta$$

Agglomeration effects are dependent upon economic structure, as well as size, and its service area. However, in 12 out of 34 Korean cities, more than one-fifth of the total employment is associated with non-urban sectors, such as agriculture, forestry and fisheries. Hence population only is utilized as a surrogate for agglomeration economies. Thus two parameters, α and β, are used to represent intra-urban and inter-urban agglomeration economies, respectively, in the equations of the model. If $\alpha > 1$, intra-urban agglomeration economies will become larger in relation to city size, and large cities would have better growth potential than small ones: "cumulative and circular causation" would be operative. If $\alpha < 1$, the smaller cities would have a greater chance of growth occurring in them.

The simulation rules used (adapted from Robson's) were as follows:

(i) At t_0, only Seoul, the largest city, has adopted the particular innovation.

(ii) A city designated as a growth centre is given an additional and preferential number of stimuli at t_0 and also at succeeding values of t.

(iii) Adoption of an innovation is signified by the total of stimuli received from other cities reaching the value T. Having reached this threshold, they will emit stimuli to other cities.

(iv) The probability of a city receiving a stimulus is as given by the equation for P_i, in each case.

(v) Each stimulus generates Z additional population in the receptor city in that time period, plus $Z/2$ in the succeeding period.

(vi) A city which does not receive more than two stimuli over successive periods declines by Z population.

The model was calibrated by fitting α for each city at 1978, using 1973 population as a base.

The parameters used in the simulation runs were:

$$\alpha \text{ (Intra-urban agglomeration):} 0.85$$
$$\beta \text{ (Inter-urban agglomeration):} 0.25$$
$$Z \text{ (Population multiplier): } 111$$
$$T \text{ (Adoption threshold):   } 16$$
$$\lambda \text{ (Distance exponent):} 0.01$$

Z should differ for each city, in practice, and could be based, possibly, on regression of migration experience results in each city.

In using the model to evaluate policy choices—thus an extension of Robson's use—two measures of entropy were used by Kwon. The most probable state of a system is that which maximizes its entropy: this is also held to be the most efficient state in terms of a diffusion of innovation—a proposition which may be no more than an article of faith? A second criterion, of diffusion equity, is also sought, in order to reduce regional disparity.

For an urban system of n cities, its entropy, H_1 is:

$$H_1 = -\Sigma_i P_i \cdot \log P_i,$$

where $\Sigma P_i = 1$; $P_i \geq 0$; $i = 1, 2, \ldots n$.

The maximum value of this expression, equal to $\log n$, corresponds to a situation where all of the n cities have an equal value. The minimum value, equal to zero, occurs when all values of P_i are zero.

The difference between the maximum value, $\log n$, and the calculated value of H_1 for a particular city, is taken as a measure of inequality, i.e.:

$$\log n - H_1 = \Sigma_i P_i \cdot \log n P_i.$$

However, inter-regional inequality entropy (H_2) is preferably measured by:

$$H_2 = \log n - H_1 - \Sigma_g^m \Pi_g \cdot H_g$$

—where: Π_g = the total sum of adoption probabilities in region "m"; and mg = number of cities in region "m".

The policy subcriteria to be considered in evaluating the outcome of runs of the Space-Oriented Diffusion Model are thus: within the fixed amount of entropy calculated, H_1, to minimize the inter-regional entropy, H_2, and to maximize the relative decrease in intra-regional entropy, H_g. These criteria conflict: some convergence of regional differences is implied, at the same time as a given region seeks to capture "growth", which implies the existence of a large city which has "pull", and thus a difference between regions.

A run of this model as a "do-nothing" policy basis shows quite clearly the effects exerted by the present settlement structure: up to $t = 5$, all the cities adopting innovations are satellites of either Seoul or Pusan; (Fig. 6.21). At $t = 6$ this tendency is supplemented by the addition of Daejeon and Daegu, both existing major centres on the transport axis between Seoul and Pusan. Gwangju, the fifth-ranking city, and a favoured candidate as a growth centre in a backward region, does not adopt until $t = 7$. However, runs of the model with Gwangju receiving the added stimuli awarded to a growth centre show that it then adopts at $t = 3$, (a self-fulfilling prophecy?), and has the highest value out of five candidates tested for the H_g entropy measure, and the second lowest value for H_2. This comparison of the differences between the entropy

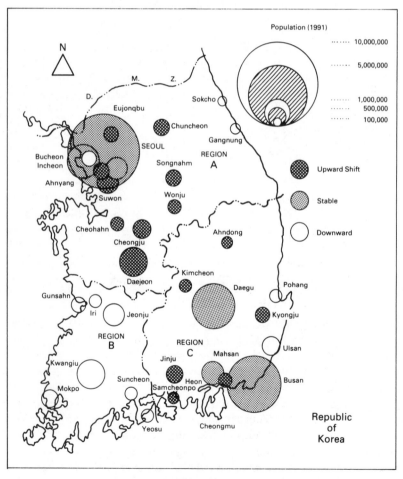

FIG. 6.21. The base run of the Space-Oriented Diffusion Model. City size distribution and rank-size shifts (1978–1991) (Kwon, 1980).

measures of a reasonable number of candidate cities may help to allay the fear at this point of a degree of circularity of reasoning: from (assumed) growth to (predicted) growth. In any case, factors other than entropy measures will no doubt enter the policy determination process beyond this point.

Dr Kwon's model is very interesting as being apparently the first of its kind anywhere: entropy-maximization as a purely statistical process involved in the various aspects of gravity modelling is by now quite well known (Wilson, 1973), but the use of entropy measurement in the simulation of innovation-diffusion is itself an innovation. The approach may well be capable of extension to other aspects of interaction modelling.

Locational-Surplus Maximization Models

The use of mathematical programming techniques has been contemplated from time to time in efforts to plan the future trajectory of urban or regional systems, and various so-called land-use plan design models have been evolved. Such approaches, however, have been subject to two very fundamental criticisms: the difficulty of specifying a realistic and acceptable objective function to be maximized, in view of Arrow's Theorem, (Chadwick, 1971, pp. 128–33); and the unfortunate fact that most of the relationships involved in urban and regional systems are inherently non-linear. Despite these considerable difficulties, a number of essentially linear programming formulations have been produced, although in the more realistic cases (Schlager, 1964, 1965; Chadwick, 1971, Chapter 10), dynamic programming has been utilized.

Since 1970, a concerted attempt has been made by a group at the Commonwealth Scientific and Industrial Research Organization (CSIRO), in Victoria, Australia, to develop a realistic "optimization" model for urban systems of various kinds and levels. (The word "optimal" is also a stumbling block in relation to models of this kind, as they do not provide a "best" solution in mathematical terms, but only an acceptably better solution, or a "best" within the limited set of solutions which is examined.)

The CSIRO model, TOPAZ, (or "Technique for Optimal Placement of Activities in Zones"), (Brotchie, Dickey and Sharpe, 1980), involves two major aspects: firstly, a statement in model form of expression of benefits and costs associated with each part of the system, together with relevant constraints on the resources of land, etc.; and secondly, a method of systematically searching for that set of decisions which maximizes total benefits less costs, subject to the resources expended. The problem of specifying an objective function in social welfare terms is thus side-stepped by moving from the area of goals, objectives, and social needs, to the calculus of costs and benefits.

TOPAZ takes benefits and costs as two components: those associated with the location of an activity, (e.g. those benefits and costs of access to existing activities and facilities, the intrinsic value of the site, and costs of development or establishment of activities there, including infrastructure provision); and those asssociated with *relative* locations of new activities, (e.g. benefits and costs of access between these activities, including transport costs, and that part of services costs which varies with dispersal of activity sites). Two constraints are imposed in the allocation: that all activity is allocated and no zone is overfilled; and that travel betweeen zones conforms to established rules.

In the early applications to the future development of Melbourne, the minimization of public service and travel costs was the main objective in allocation. Using forecasts of total land requirements over a given period, TOPAZ was used to determine how much of each land use activity should be allocated to each zone of the urban system so as to minimize public service and travel costs. Apart from such minimum-cost patterns, the development of cost-maximization allocations is also possible, showing the worst land use arrangements. In fact, as with programming techniques generally, repeated runs of such a model are valuable as showing the sensitivity of the variables included, rather than giving single "answers" (cf. Jenkins and Robson, 1974).

One measure, used initially in Melbourne, for the expected benefits of location in a particular zone was the market value of the land concerned. Travel data was obtained from a Melbourne survey of 1964, and costs of services were obtained from the relevant service authorities. The outcome of the runs of the Melbourne model showed that, on the basis used, interaction costs were dominant at A\$300 per person per year, (for 30 years), whereas establishment costs were \$2400 per additional resident. (Capital costs apparently were not discounted.) However, as in all determinations of benefits and costs, the simple numerical outputs must be seen in the light of the assumptions made, and the non-numerical, qualitative aspects of the given situation.

The mathematics and solution method of the TOPAZ model are given in Appendix A of Brotchie *et al.*, 1980, and need not be repeated here in detail.

In 1976, the TOPAZ model was applied to Tehran in Iran, alongside an application by Applied Research of Cambridge Limited of a version of Echenique's Lowry-derived model system, as a complementary longer-range modelling approach based on the same data sets as the ARC model (Roy and Crawford, 1980). The ARC model was no doubt in the line of development of models by the Cambridge group for several South American cities, described previously.

The Tehran version of TOPAZ is described as follows (Roy and Crawford, 1980):

"In TOPAZ, a balance is attempted between maximizing total net establishment and transport resource benefits over the city and maximizing the sum of individual perceived net travel benefits. The objective function for total net establishment and transport resource benefits is:

$$\text{Max } U = \sum_{ijk} b_{ijm} x_{ijm} - \sum_{ijklmn} c_{ijklmn} \cdot T_{ijklmn} \tag{1}$$

in terms of x_{ijm} and T_{ijklmn},

where $\qquad x_{ijm}$ = total amount of new activity i to be allocated to zone j in time period m;

b_{ijm} = total net benefit of locating and operating one unit of activity i in zone j in time period m; and:

c_{ijklmn} and T_{ijklmn} = unit travel resource cost and number of trips respectively of activity i interacting with activity k from zones j to l in time period m by transport mode n.

The above linear function in x and T is supplemented by linear activity allocation and zonal capacity constraints in x as well as linear origin and destination flow balance constraints in x and T (i.e. corresponding to doubly constrained trips). Note that this linear program could be readily solved to produce the cost minimizing values of x and T. However, as it would imply people's commuting to the nearest job, shopping at the nearest shops, etc., it represents a lower bound on expected cost and would usually be unrealistic in practice. The assumption is thus made that, with the trip origins x_{ijm} and trip destinations x_{klm} assumed as given, entropy-maximizing travel behaviour will occur (Wilson, 1967), according to trade-offs implied by an impedence parameter β_{ik} calibrated to each given trip type (i, k) in the urban area under study. Solution of this entropy maximization problem yields the total flows T_{ijklm} as the following implicit non-linear functions of the allocations x_{ijm} and x_{klm}:

$$T_{ijklm} = A_{ijkm} B_{ikim} (r_{ikm} \cdot S_{ikm}) (X_{ijm} + e_{ijm})$$
$$(x_{klm} + e_{klm}) e^{-\beta_{ik} g_{ijklm}} \qquad (2)$$

where e_{ijm} = existing amount of activity i in zone j at time period m;

g_{ijklm} = average perceived generalized travel cost of (i, k) interactions between zones j and l in time period m; and

r_{ikm}, s_{ikm} = origin and destination trip generation factors of (i, k) trips in time period m;

and the balancing factors A_{ijkm} and B_{iklm} are given as:

$$A_{ijkm} = [\Sigma_l B_{iklm} S_{ikm} (x_{klm} + e_{klm}) e^{-\beta_{ik} g_{ijklm}}]^{-1}$$
$$B_{iklm} = [\Sigma_j A_{ijkm} r_{ikm} (x_{ijm} + e_{ijm}) e^{-\beta_{ik} g_{ijklm}}]^{-1}.$$

Now, the above expression for T_{ijklm} is multiplied by the modal split p_{ijklmn} for mode n, computed using a cost disutility approach; we have

$$T_{ijklmn} = P_{ijklmn} \cdot T_{ijklm}.$$

When this expression, with T_{ijklmn} as defined above, is substituted back into eqn (1), U is finally expressed as a non-concave non-linear function of the reduced variable set x_{ijm}, with linear constraints."

Whereas the previous applications of TOPAZ (Brotchie, Dickey and Sharpe, 1980) had defined residential activities based on housing densities or types, the Tehran data was based on income groupings; these were predicted to change over the 20 years of the study, with higher income activities increasing and correspondingly lower income activities decreasing. This phenomenon was represented in this application of the TOPAZ model as upward movement of the population from one income group to the next higher group over time.

The transport submodel of TOPAZ utilizes two modes: public and private, although data available for Tehran covered walking, private car, bus and rail trips. Consequently, walking trips were ignored—a gross over-simplification in any city of a developing country—and bus trips were taken to represent public, and car trips to represent private transport; although in one case metro-rail trips were substituted for bus trips where rail times were shorter. Service and freight trips were not represented in the data, whilst peak-hour trips were considered as work trips and off-peak trips as shopping or social trips.

Twenty-two different scenarios were produced as basic policy parameters within which to develop model runs; these covered policies on parking, metro-building, road network, release of land, development form, building of new town, density, discount rate, mode of optimization (simultaneous or sequential), land attractiveness scores, petrol costs, bus frequencies, and travel behaviour.

An interesting outcome of the basic runs of TOPAZ for Tehran was that average trip lengths per person were reduced in the intermediate time periods, thus demonstrating that the initial land use and network patterns were less than optimal in the view of the model's structural assumptions.

The base case used presented market land release, zero discount rate, and travel impedence values calibrated to observed travel behaviour in the city. Alternative model runs included one representing indifference of travellers to time spent in either mode, as well as one run representing very high impedences. It was found that, of these two latter cases, that representing indifference to travel time was closer to the basic (calibrated) run than was the case of high impedence, thus indicating that the people of Tehran were rather insensitive to travel time. As Roy and Crawford suggested, there were many poor people in the city whose valuation of travel time was low: they do not own cars and travel on the buses, which are slow and have a long waiting time.

The results of the high impedence case suggested that there would be scope for improving the efficiency of Tehran's transport systems in conjunction with a pattern of several major centres, so as to optimize travel behaviour. A comparison of the alternatives of building a small freeway road system with that of building a small Metro rail system showed that the costs of the freeway system would be high, for low benefits, whereas the more moderate cost of the Metro system would produce relatively higher benefits, so that the Metro system is the more attractive option, (although this assumes that the Metro could be financed through the fares paid by users).

In one TOPAZ run, a perceived willingness-to-pay benefit was included, representing the intrinsic attractiveness of land in different zones to the various socio-economic groups, it being held that this should result in a more achievable allocation pattern, yet within a reasonable cost. This representation of the freedom of choice normal to the land market resulted in a less than 3% increase in unit transport costs, and suggests the near-optimal operation of the land market.

In general, the TOPAZ applications in Tehran were directed towards community cost-minimization, subject to the policy options of the various runs of the model. Included in the model parameters were: accessibility travel times, air pollution levels from traffic, energy use, the costs incurred and their distributions. Measures of economic benefit included consumer surplus for transport trips resulting from improvements to the network. Transport costs per person in Tehran are low, and infrastructure costs are relatively more important, they vary more with density than transport costs, and require more public capital, to a large extent before development occurs.

A further example of the location surplus maximization approach is that used by J. Coelho (1979) to evaluate alternative land use plans for the new town of Santo André in Portugal. The general framework of this model is:

Maximize total locational surplus (S) = user's benefit + producer's surplus, subject to:

(1) consistency conditions;
(2) economic base relations;
(3) market-clearing conditions;
(4) planning constraints;
(5) non-negativity conditions on planning and interaction variables.

In the application of the model to Santo André, the service activities are disaggregated into those associated with city-centre functions; those associated with secondary-centre functions; and those with recreational activities. The distribution of heavy industry is taken as a fixed input, but the location of light industry is subject to the optimization process. If the alternative urban zone locations are similar in geology and topography, the establishment costs for these uses have been taken as constant, and thus omitted from the final version of the model used in Santo André. The numerical computation of this model was based on its dual programme, i.e. as a convex minimization problem of smaller size. The preferred alternative for Santo André (out of 6) resulting from this procedure was estimated to give annual savings of 297 million escudos, (equivalent to US$6.5 million), in transport costs in relation to the original (and then only) plan proposed.

Coelho's model thus brings together spatial interaction concepts, utilizing entropy-maximization techniques, and mathematical programming, and provides—as does TOPAZ—a cost-benefit perspective on patterns of development. But it must be said of both approaches, that the major end-result is a set of alternative transport costs. Is this all that decisions on living environments are to be made on: hypothetical transport costs?

Spatial Interaction Models: Technology Transfer or Misconceived Application?

What is now usual to call spatial interaction models stem from basically very simple beginnings; the gravity, or mass-inverse distance relationship, and the economic base theory—though some would argue that the former relationship has now been given a more respectable percentage via the entropy-maximization technique (Wilson, 1970). It might seem that the modelling of similar sorts of relationships, e.g. between homes, workplaces, and service locations, could be essayed in developing country situations, equally with those in developed countries. Where the developing country relationships are analogous to those in developed countries—i.e. only in some parts and some aspects of the major cities of the more advanced countries —this may be true, if the required data exists or can be collected readily. But in many other developing country situations, and even, to varying extents, in most aspects of their major cities, this is not so. Although in displaying considerable ingenuity via subscripts and superscripts, it is quite possible to disaggregate spatial interaction models, at least in theory, (real data again, may be quite another problem), the crux of the matter is not primarily there, but in the basic relationships of the model.

Consider a typical disaggregated version of Lowry's spatial interaction model (Mackett, 1974). Its data input requirements are as follows:

c_{ij}: the distance, or cost of travel, between zone i and zone j;

L_i^T: the total of area of zone i;

L_i^{Hu}: the land used for housing in zone i;

L_i^B: the land used by basic industry in zone i;

I_i^S: the stock of housing in zone i;

P_{iq}: the number of people in social group q living in zone i;

E_{iq}^B: the number of workers in basic industry in social group q in zone j;

E_{jq}^R: the number of workers in retail industries in social group q in sector r in zone j;

E_{jkq}^k: the number of workers in non-retail services in social group q in sector k in zone j;

y_q: the propensity of workers in social group q not to change their job during the time period under consideration;

H_{cq}^o: the number of houses occupied by members of social group q;

L_{cr}^R: the total area of land occupied by retail sector r in the city;

K_{ck}^k: the total area of land occupied by service sector k in the city.

Firstly: is distance an impedance to travel in the "lower" circuit, or informal sector? At some level, it may well be, but let us remember that the "upper" circuit application here is derived from a vehicular journey to work perspective. The logic of the Lowry model regards basic employment as fixed, and as the determinant of residential location. If the *residential* location is fixed, as is likely to be the case for an incoming migrant in a poor country, or a secondary breadwinner in a family already housed, then the logic of the model begins to crumble. The place of employment may be very flexible, also, especially in the lower circuit sectors, and may change daily or weekly, or may rotate. Observations in many large cities in developing countries show that many "service locations" are possible: anywhere that sufficient people gather or pass by, from footpaths to underpasses, footbridges, near traffic lights, in front of orthodox shops, on stairways, outside public assembly places, and so on. And manufacturing can take place on the pavements in alleyways, on the street—there was a man who built a three-storey shack on a street parking meter bay in Hong Kong!—under bridges, and especially in one's own house, thus minimizing the journey to work completely.

Thus, although disaggregation seemingly opens the way to incorporating both of the two circuits of a dual economy in a model framework, in fact there is, as yet, no logic upon which to base the replication of the relationships in the lower circuit. This may be due to a lack of knowledge of such relationships as much as to their lack of rationality. Knowledge, in terms of actual, hard data, is conspicuously absent, due to a lack of interest, often, on the part of those who might solve the problem. Of course, officialdom is part of the "upper" circuit, and there is a feeling that the lower circuit does not really matter, or cannot be openly admitted to exist. There are also real difficulties, it must be said, in acquiring information about the informal sector, especially by officials who might be thought to be connected with taxation or legal enforcement of some kind. But until more knowledge by way of data is available, the important questions cannot be answered. It is unlikely that informal employment is located completely randomly; it is possible that it locates in associations with certain other uses or activities—but what are they, where, how, when? A beginning has been made on some studies in this field, notably perhaps by various geographers in Hong Kong, but these are as yet unrelated to residential location parameters.

In the meantime, in the absence of adequate theories derived from adequate data, the best that can be done is some heuristic modifications of, or additions to those formal models of developing country situations which have been essayed—or, the most usual treatment, the bland assumption that developed country models are quite adequate for this task also, and that the official statistical sources tell the whole story. Urban modelling, after all, is an upper-circuit activity.

As has been suggested, the residential location model, and the more general spatial interaction models formulated in the USA and Britain are unsatisfactory for application to cities and urban regions of developing countries. Whilst the dweller, or would-be dweller in such a city has some choice, it is of such a restricted nature that the western theoretical basis concept cannot be applied. The developing country migrant or city dweller, for the most part, has a very simple constraint: money. His choice of dwelling type and location is based, for the most part, on direct costs incurred, and probably also on kinship or other ethnic considerations, (Abu-Lughod, 1961; Harrison, 1967), especially in a plural society. Affordability, rather than "residential attractiveness" or "accessibility to employment", is the major factor. The incoming migrant frequently moves to a fixed location: fixed by prior location of kin, of accommodation availability at the right cost. Thus the western model logic may be stood on its head: employment follows from residential location, rather than the other way round, "attractiveness" is substituted by affordability; "accessibility" may be unimportant in a city with flat-rate bus fares, where people walk or cycle for the most part, or for the underemployed or self employed of the lower-circuit.

This, in fact, is the serious, fundamental criticism that can be levelled at very many of the published attempts at the application of western models—mainly spatial interaction or Lowry-type derivatives—to developing country situations. Putman (1980), for instance, applies his Disaggregated Residential Allocation Model to a number of cities in developing countries. Amongst the examples of data sets he used were: Natal and Rio de Janerio, Brazil; Mexico City and Monclova-Frontera, Mexico; Ankara, Gaziantep and Izmit, Turkey; Tehran, Iran; Santiago, Chile; and Hong Kong; an application of the same model to Taipei, Taiwan, is also known. However, Putman's DRAM has as its major zonal parameters the two criteria of residential attractiveness and availability already mentioned: parameters which may have explanatory validity for the North American cities to which this model was originally applied. The model is also cast in an entropy-maximizing form (Putman, 1977) and thus Mohan's strictures may be applied to it. Several of the data sets used may also have had critical deficiencies, too.

DRAM is a singly-constrained spatial interaction, i.e. gravity potential type model and has the form:

$$N_i = \Sigma_j T_{ij} = \Sigma_j E_j \cdot B_j \cdot W_i \cdot f(c_{ij}),$$

where: $N_i =$ total number of residents in zone i;

$T_{ij} =$ number of residents in zone i who are employed in zone j;

$E_j =$ total number of persons employed in zone j;

$B_j = [E_j W_j \cdot f(c_{ij})]^{-1}$, i.e. a balancing factor;

$W_i =$ a measure of residential attractiveness of zone i;

and: $f(c_{ij}) =$ a function of the travel time or cost between zone i and zone j.

The travel function used by Putman was: $f(c_{ij}) = c_{ij}^{\alpha} \cdot \exp(\beta_{cij}) \cdot$
The attractiveness measure used was:

$$W_i = V_i^a \cdot P_i^b \cdot R_i^d \cdot n_1^q \cdot in_2^r \cdot in_3^c \cdot in_4^t, i,$$

where: V_i = vacant building land in zone i;

$P_i = 1$ + percentage of land in zone i already developed;

R_i = existing residential land in zone i;

$n_{k,i} = 1$ + the percentage of residents in zone i who are type k residents (e.g. by income quartile); a, b, c, d, q, r, s, t are parameters.

Restricting comment to one case study only, that of Hong Kong, the aim of the model is to predict residential land allocation in relationship to employment and residential land availability and attractiveness to various income groups, yet in Hong Kong the location of residences is much conditioned by topography, firstly, and then by the large areas of public housing which exist and are constantly being added to, their location again related to topographic opportunities due to the severe lack of anything but steeply sloping land. Nearly 43% of all persons in Hong Kong lived in public housing, (1977 figures), whilst 48% lived in private housing, and 9% in temporary or marine housing (the original "Boat People"): thus choice of location for over 50% of Hong Kong's population is severely restricted, and, in fact, a very large proportion of private housing in Hong Kong also takes the form of high-density flats, a situation a long way away from the low-density residential land subdivision in American suburbs, which seems to be the ethos of DRAM. Also in Hong Kong, the home–workplace relationship is significant in a different way, with workplaces being closely related to home for many people (see Leeming, 1977), or with Hong Kong's excellent land-and-water public transport systems playing a role. Western views of cities in developing countries, especially of cities like Hong Kong whose superficial appearance is so western-influenced, tend to be coloured by personal experience of Europe or North America and by professional views based on theories of land use ecology and by western town planning zoning practice: such views may be less than appropriate to the cities of developing countries, even ones with the "growth" records of Hong Kong, Taiwan, Korea, or Singapore.

It is tempting to assume that a model is validated, if the data sets used in validation are adequately replicated by the model, in terms of the standard statistical tests. What such a validation cannot reveal, however, is any omission from the data sets to begin with: the model is framed in terms of a certain kind of data input set, and if that set is supplied, no error message will result. Thus, it may be assumed that an official data set of employment, disaggregated into "basic" and "non-basic", covers *all* employment, and that the disaggregation is at least adequately correct. In most developing countries this is highly unlikely to be so, and the lower circuit employment, and the dimensions of that circuit may be quite unrepresented in the statistics used. A model based on such data is quite clearly not a model of a complete urban system and, indeed, must represent the upper circuit activities also in an incomplete way, divorced from their relationships to the lower circuit.

Retail Shopping Models versus the Two-Circuit Economy

As with residential and employment location models, so retail shopping models might seem to be applicable to situations in developing countries, but again, the developing-country situation may be vastly different from those western situations in which such models have been evolved and applied.

A discussion of these differences might perhaps begin with a consideration of markets in developing countries, especially for the moment upon African countries south of the Sahara. Firstly, one should distinguish, as Bohannon and Dalton (1962) do, between the principle of the market in the sense of a method of exchange based upon supply and demand, and the institution of the market-place as a particular location where exchange takes place. In western countries the distinction is not so clear-cut, for the institution is merely the spatial particularization of the principle: of exchange taking place through the medium of money, based upon the supply of and the demand for particular goods or services, at a particular physical focus which is the representation of a general aspatial phenomenon.

As *The Economist* (2 October 1976, p. 19) has succinctly reminded us, prices set by individual markets serve:

(a) to reward sellers;
(b) to ration available supplies amongst buyers;
(c) to relay information both forwards from producers—showing relative costs of production—and backwards from consumers—showing their relative preferences, by what they are prepared to pay.

But in many African cultures, and in other developing countries, too, the principle of the market economy is not so all-pervasive as it is in western societies, where other methods of exchange are less usual, e.g. "swopping", or are simply picturesque survivals maintained for nostalgia or traditional reasons, e.g. giving a red rose as a quit-rent. The case of the Trobriand Islanders (off Papua) is well known, where there are three transactional spheres: (a) the reciprocal exchange of treasure items; (b) the exchange of some subsistence items and food on the market principle; (c) a larger sphere of reciprocal exchange of subsistence material based upon kinship obligations. Bohannon and Dalton, (op. cit.), distinguish between three categories of African market situation: those that do not have any markets; those where (as in the Trobriand case) the market is peripheral to the society, being relatively unimportant; and those where the market principle is fully established although market places vary in importance. The latter category may well be largely the result of western influences upon African societies. It is useful, though, to distinguish further between two types of African societies where the market principle prevails. Some societies may depend upon the sale of a cash crop for their major income—the cocoa crop in Ghana is such an example—which means that land, labour, and the products of these two factors become involved in the marketing principle. Other societies—probably industrializing or industrialized—are characterized by the sale predominantly of labour, producing cash wages with which to buy both subsistence, and increasingly other goods.

The effect of these very different situations might be summarized as follows. Firstly, in Africa and other developing societies there may be a lack of what to western eyes is rational economic behaviour, (cf. Berg, 1961), including exchange on a basis which ignores supply and demand factors, or on a basis from which the profit motive is absent, or where the extent of "rational" behaviour is severely limited by time or interest. Thus the "value of time" which may be important in a wholly-industrialized economy, where taking part in one activity may mean giving up an alternative activity, may be quite unconsidered, so that, for example, chickens might be brought over 400 miles to a market, or fish 200 miles, by sellers who travel perhaps by bicycle (McCall, 1962). The "friction of distance", so important in a developed economy may have quite a different level of importance in a less-developed one.

Secondly, where a monetary system exists it may be only partial: some transactions may be covered in other ways, by barter or by traditional and perhaps reciprocal gift-making. Not only may this apply to certain areas of transaction, but it may apply also to particular individuals in various societies at particular times. The case of a young man wishing to earn enough money for a bicycle or a transistor radio, or to pay a tax demanded in cash, or to raise money for bride-wealth (*lobola* in Southern Africa), and then to quit the monetary economy and return to a traditional agricultural subsistence life is well known in Africa, and probably elsewhere also. Thus situations may be judged in money terms only when certain needs are pressing, and at other times barter and traditional customs of change will take its place.

Thirdly, market places and markets may be set up not only for economic purposes, but more especially for social and cultural interchange and intercourse: attendance at the market by both sellers and potential buyers may have quite other objectives, the market being much more a meeting place than a medium of exchange, so that location size, drawing-power, sales, etc. cannot be anticipated to follow those kind of "rules"—if indeed any such are followed—which may be held to apply to developed economies in western societies.

The (partial) exceptions to the above situation may be where colonial cities have grown up, (usually capitals or primate cities), or where colonial powers have fostered the growth of market places as a deliberate policy, as seems to have been the case in Northern Rhodesia, (Rotberg, in Bohannon and Dalton, op. cit.); or where other industrial activities, as in the Copper Belt of what are now Zambia and Zaire have been the starting point of urbanized areas supported by widespread migration: "roughly half a million Africans who are largely non-self-sufficient in food production, and who have a relatively high per capita purchasing power", (Miracle, in Bohannon and Dalton, op. cit.).

Such areas have come increasingly within the orbit of western style monetary systems, and are the locus of economic behaviour which includes indigenous populations living in or near such cities as well as European settlers (who may be small in numbers in such cases, or in others may represent a large part of the urban population).

It seems clear from available evidence and from cases cited that, as a particular aspect of urban change, the provision of shops and services tends to form a series of stages, consistent with different levels of "development" of a country or city. These may begin with individual itinerant pedlars visiting villages on an *ad hoc*, then on a regular basis; aggregations of such individual salesman and women may later crystallize into a system of periodic or rotating markets, visiting key villages in a regular time pattern. The theoretical justification for such a visiting market has been stated by Stine (1962) and referred to earlier, with evidence from Korea. Of course, developments of this kind are unlikely to displace entirely the activities of pedlars and visiting craftsmen, nor would they entirely displace local exchange and barter between neighbours or other villagers.

The tendency of a pattern of rotating markets to become static ones might depend on both the size of population acting as buyers and the size of another population acting as producers for the sellers, or more properly on their aggregate demands and productivities, i.e. on both urban and rural growth, including that of agriculture and craft industries. The development of a static market function, a *souk*, into a pattern of booths and shops, and workshops, is not difficult to imagine, but is not the entire story, for the nature of economic activity is not confined to static provision.

It follows from the above discussion that mathematical representation of much developing country marketing behaviour, especially in Africa, is not feasible, because it is either absent, or is only peripheral, or otherwise does not follow the "rational" economic behaviour which lies at the basis of such mathematical formalism. The widespread use of retail shopping models in a developing country context thus cannot be justified or expected, even where "development" is rapid, for considerable lags in social behaviour are likely to continue, whilst more-developed "islands" amidst a context of rural and urban slow-or-non-development are possible, somewhat invalidating the gravitational logic of the shopping model.

Case studies of attempts to apply retail shopping models in cities of developing countries seem to be few: data as to income and spending power is available only rarely. The Salisbury, Rhodesia, example quoted earlier is the only one for which information has been found to be available, although it is understood that retail models have been run for several South African cities.

With the Salisbury example in mind, an interesting comparison may be drawn with that of Hong Kong. To the uninitiated outsider, Hong Kong seems predominantly urbanized: a great city of more-than-western appearance, and firmly based in a monetary economy. And yet appearances are deceptive: Hong Kong is—in part—highly urbanized; it has also a strong monetary economy; but it is only pseudo-western in appearance. In fact, Hong Kong is a great *Chinese* city: a large and wholly Chinese city of a Chinese and western economy: it is culturally and socially—and thus economically —quite different from the conventional western large city.

To begin with, Hong Kong, in a sense, is part of the economy of mainland China, as its entrepôt and provider of certain services to Canton and Seinkiang province. Culturally and socially, there are many ties with Mother China. As a great port and airport, too, Hong Kong is a provider of services to South East Asia to a large extent: a world-regional city like, for example, Cairo. So the layers of the Hong Kong economy are many, and their interactions complex.

At the lowest level, the New Territories of Hong Kong, including many of the islands of the Colony, show examples of more-or-less conventional central place theory: towns like Yuen Long, Tai Po Market, Shek Wu Hui, Luen Wo Market, New Sha Tin, having recognizable (though small) service areas and with only a small minority of services being obtained from Kowloon or Victoria, despite the short distance from these large centres, (Drakakis-Smith, 1971). (See also L. S. K. Wong's interesting study of the Aplichau squatter area (Wong, 1971)). This phenomenon is due not only to the mountain barriers of the territory, but more especially to the traditional Chinese shopping pattern of purchasing fresh food twice each day, so that the distance which it is convenient for the shopper to travel is quite short. Income levels in the New Territories are also lower than in the main urbanized area of the Colony, which reinforces the traditional pattern.

Turning now to the main city, in its two major parts on Hong Kong Island and on the Kowloon peninsula, it is obvious from the foregoing that, if this combined city does not largely serve the New Territories, it must, in effect, be its own hinterland or service area, (with the exception, of course, of the regional services previously mentioned). Thus Kowloon and Victoria, and the many centres within them, provide local or city-wide services rather than "hinterland" services. In fact, both of the two major parts of the city: Hong Kong Island (including Victoria) to the south of the harbour, and Kowloon across the water to the north, include quite a large number of service areas. (The expression "service centres" is purposely not used, as it suggests discrete entities, and although the Colony's shopping and service areas have recognizable focal points, there are often no clear ways of distinguishing one from another: no breaks in continuity.) Thus, on Hong Kong Island, the entertainments and services area of Wanchai becomes the entertainment and shopping area of Causeway Bay, and both are also hardly separable from the shopping area of Hennessy Road; in Kowloon, Nathan Road is also virtually a linear shopping and entertainments area of considerable length. As Frank Leeming has demonstrated in his excellent *Street Studies in Hong Kong*, (1977), many of these present "strings" have original foci of considerable age and tradition; yet he also shows that within this kind of continuity there has been, and is, much detailed and individual change. This change, of course, continues, and one of its more recent results seems to have been a tipping of the commercial scales from "Central", i.e. Victoria, across the water to Kowloon. Central is probably still the main banking and prestige office focus, (as also of government), but Tsimshatsui at the south end of the Kowloon peninsula now probably boasts the greater focus of retailing activity, with Ocean Terminal, Ocean Centre, Harbour City and the increasing concentrations of shops on Nathan Road and nearby in many new developments. And, where else but Hong Kong can you go so delightfully across the water from one to the other (and so quickly and cheaply!) as on Star Ferry?

One of the things that impresses about Hong Kong is the sheer number of retail outlets—of all kinds and sizes. This surely arises from the conviction of its inhabitants that they can well provide services of a certain kind—and make a living whilst doing so. Hong Kong is marked by the vast range of immediately accessible services—the word "service" is stressed, as there are to be found willingness to please, speed of delivery, concern with customer satisfaction, negotiability of price—all things now quite foreign to trade-union Britain. Because many businesses are family ones, staffed by families rather than employees, the relationship between takings and overheads is very different from that in many European businesses. Hence it is possible for many more businesses to survive and provide a living. One expression of this is in the number of street hawkers; another is in the informal, often illegal, use of common or public property: hallways, alleys, streets, staircases, for business use: a cobbler may set up his booth on one of the steep, stepped footways rising up to the Mid-levels on Hong Kong, or a family in Kowloon may set up a workshop in their flat, overflowing on to stairways and halls when pinched for space. McGee (1973) and others have discussed these happenings in terms of the two circuits of the economy, or distinguished between "bazaar-type" and "firm-type" activities. In Hong Kong, both kinds of activities flourish, and obviously the one is a seeding-ground for the other, but they remain mixed spatially to a great extent, and much of the attitude, economically speaking, of the earlier passes into the later form, so that a "firm" may be anything from an extended family to an international corporation.

These kinds of origins and these philosophies must be understood if one essays an explanation of Hong Kong's commercial activity—and these characteristics may well be repeated or reflected in other large cities in developing countries: certainly those with a large Chinese population such as Singapore, and possibly cities of other South Asian cultures also. Otherwise, there is no explanation, in Western European or North American terms, of the number and distribution of shops and service establishments in places like Kowloon, (cf. Chi-Sen Liang, 1973). It is possible to *describe* by multivariate techniques the land use and floor space variables of Kowloon as Liang has done; but it does not seem possible to build predictive models of such situations based on conventional gravity models such as the Lakshmanan and Hansen retail shopping model.

7. Reflections on the Theories and Models, and Their Application

There are several arguments for essaying more comprehensive models of urban and regional systems in developing countries. Major points which might be advanced in support of such a modelling endeavour (not necessarily in order of importance) are as follows:

(1) The lower circuit of the economy, in many countries and many cities and city regions, is of fundamental importance to the local population and the local economy. It offers employment, even if wages are low, thus helping family incomes. It provides goods and services suited to local needs and characteristics, also to local pockets. It makes a significant contribution to gross regional product. And in doing all these things it is reliant on self-organization instead of expensive governmental bureaucracy. It is, in fact, naturally suited, by definition, to the circumstances in which it is found.

(2) Understanding of national, regional and urban economies will be improved by having more "comprehensive" models, i.e. those which include lower circuit as well as upper circuit phenomena. "Development" should be enhanced by the addition of knowledge of what is a (presently unacknowledged) productive sector.

(3) The lot of those who live and work in the lower circuits of these urban and regional systems urgently requires improvement. A knowledge of lower circuit relationships via modelling, using realistic data and realistic theoretical bases should help towards an amelioration of life in the lower circuits, by building on existing achievements and potentialities of these circuits, rather than trying to destroy or ignore them in the name of tidy-mindedness, or planning for "development", as so often happens.

(4) Decisions regarding very large expenditure on transport systems, decentralization of population and industry, new towns, major urban utility systems, etc., are being made on the basis of models which, although representing in themselves a high degree of innovation and ingenious technology, may not include major aspects of urban activity in the lower circuits of urban and regional systems. Is it possible that these decisions and their effects can be regarded as satisfactory, both socially and economically, in view of the major omissions of urban structure and activities which they represent?

However, trenchant criticisms of current (western) endeavours in urban and regional modelling have been made by R. A. Sayer (1976). He points out that most critiques of such models concern themselves only with secondary issues: the algebra, the calibration techniques—whereas the real question is: have these models any validity whatsoever? Models, as he says, have been developed mostly as "computational devices", as techniques, that is, rather than "as embodiments of theories about the space economy". There is a minimal content of theory in such models, he avers, and what theory there is, is pretty poor.

One must accept this general criticism if one looks at those models which form the greater part of current urban and regional work. One sees the traditional gravity models, the economic base mechanism, the traffic models, the linear programmes—all applied to given situations without too much thought as to their isomorphism to the real world situation under concern. For example, there is a close analogy betwen the basic approach to transport modelling and that of drainage network or water supply design—not a surprising situation, given the genesis of such systems. In designing a drainage system, one estimates the catchment area to be drained, the rainfall conditions to be dealt with, the degree of run-off, the time of concentration, culminating in the desired quantity of water to be handled, from which the pipe size can be determined (with a certain factor of safety); other catchments are added, until the complete area is covered, and increases are made in pipe capacities as these zones are added to the network. In traffic network design, the place of pipe friction is taken by a cost and/or time or distance factor, otherwise there is a striking similarity between the calculation of "run-off" and the calculation of journey flows to be accommodated. A basic assumption is that the future is going to be like the past, only more so: as Marshall McLuhan commented: "Man walks backwards into the future, looking forwards into the past". Little regard is paid, in urban traffic network design, to changes in behaviour which are not accounted for in the "land-use plan", especially to behavioural changes in mode of travel: a situation not parallelled in pipe network design. A basic criterion seems to be that the private car driver is sovereign: he must not be kept waiting, irrespective of what is done with the time which is "saved", or of other people's convenience. Such "optimization" of driver's time is frequently at odds with the expenditure of the very large sums of money necessarily involved in providing for the same "optimum". A sensitivity analysis of the assumptions involved in now-conventional traffic analysis and design would surely be revealing? The method involves:

Future population estimates by zone.
Future employment estimates by zone, perhaps via future activity rates.
Future trips generated per household per zone for all trip purposes and all
    trip modes, probably via regression analysis of past data.
Future trip origins and destinations, by zone, purpose, and mode.

Future network geometry and times/speeds through the network.
Calibration of models on past data for future circumstances.
Calculation of volume/capacity ratios (where "capacity" is a concept
rather like pipe capacity, i.e. involving speed of flow, and thus time).

The point needs little labouring: the margin for variance is large, whilst at key points in the argument, statistical processes, e.g. regression analysis, are involved which do not necessarily indicate causality: the problem is being changed, to suit the computational methods available.

Sayer's argument is based upon a critique of neo-classical economics and its replacement by an urban political economy closely concerned with the realities of production, distribution, exchange and consumption, especially in regard to causality and the treatment of time. We need not follow his argument here: this writer is not a political economist. But, in any case, the validity of some of Sayer's criticism is apparent without any quasi-metaphysical pondering. It may be that urban and regional modellers have paid too much attention to two contextual aspects of the modelling process: the urge to have something that can be applied in the physical planning process, i.e. a "practical" outcome, a tool for use; and an urge to have mathematically tractable models. If the price to be paid for such models has been the distortion of reality, the omission of important phenomena, the making of doubtfully-defensible assumptions, then such a price may have seemed worthwhile in terms of the undoubted pioneering endeavours involved. Another factor may well have been the feeling that urban and regional models—no matter what their subjective basis—represented an objective, "scientific" step, one capable of incorporation in the practical planning process. The point is not that models are irrelevant or unnecessary, but that better models are necessary: models with a sound causal basis, which explicitly deal with time; models which can be shown to represent real situations, rather than abstract mathematical relationships. There are two major ways of setting this new direction: better theory, and—where theory is hard to verify or may land us in intractable situations—a recourse to simulation. But, first, more must be said about the real basis of urban and regional systems.

Decision-Making in Urban and Regional Systems

Almost 30 years ago, Rutledge Vining (1955), in a long paper, developed a very broad model which he described as "certain spatial aspects of an economic system". In effect, it was a simulation model which, albeit of a simple nature: stacks of poker chips on a map, enabled many empirical effects, such as the rank-size rule, to be demonstrated. Vining asserted that it was possible to describe the physical features of the spatial structure of an economic system, firstly by a distribution which describes "the density configuration formed by the loci of the individual units of the population system"; and secondly, by a distribution describing "the destinations of the value-output flows emanating from each point within the area". This is seen as a problem of analysing a time-dependent stochastic process: "of analysing a process implicit in a sequence of individual actions performed within a specified system of constraints". Importantly, there are "millions upon millions of individual choices and not a single choice of a combination of all locations"—i.e. no person, body or authority who can make an overall, comprehensive choice.

This last point is fundamental: in many urban and regional systems we wish to ascertain an overall effect, a macro-situation—but the information we have, or are likely to have, relates, by and large, to individual decisions, to micro-effects.

It is well to emphasize the micro-level of consideration: cities and regions are the aggregate effects of thousands, perhaps millions, of individual decisions made by individual decision units: families, individuals, small firms, large corporations, organizations, government bodies. Such decision units are born, change in growth or decay, beget other decision units, and die. They are linked together by all kinds of relationships—quoting the physicist, Niels Bohr, Gary Zukav (1979) suggests: ". . . the conclusion that the world consists, not of things, but of interactions. Properties belong to interactions, not to independently existing things, like 'light'".

Interactions do not necessarily involve the "friction of (physical) space" at a practical level today. For example, the conveyance of goods and people is thus subject, but information, money flows, credit, are subject to quite different considerations: it costs no more to send a TV programme 250 miles than it does to send it 20 miles. (What is the position about energy flows?). Physical space seems to be inherently logarithmic, rather than linear, in interaction terms.

An important question relates to the equilibrium position of urban and regional systems, and it seems probable that steady-state conditions will exist in them. This is possible, even with change occurring, as structure and behaviour may be maintained within certain limits*. Statistically speaking, the behaviour of very large systems is normally subject to the Law of Large Numbers, with steady-state situations characterizing its dynamics; but such large systems also include unpredictable, far-from-equilibrium situations within their ambits—and, hence, the self-organization, creation of new forms or outcomes within these systems, as discussed by Prigogine *et al.* The distinction between steady-state conditions and true equilibrium, e.g. of market situations, must be stressed: continuity within change is the keynote of the former.

General system theory appears to be very adequate as a basis for the consideration of renewed modelling of urban and regional systems—though

---

* (c.f. Ross Ashby (1956): "Even when the system undergoes a series of changes there are some parts, some things which do not change: the structure of the system").

again there is a very apposite problem in discerning whether, in a particular case or application we are seeing an example of a given theory, or merely a superficial mathematical similarity. Certainly, many aspects of system theory do seem to be demonstrated by urban and regional systems, for example:

(a) Exponential or logistic growth of population (and its decay), and of urbanized population; of population/distance effects in cities, and in the demographic transition.

(b) Competition and exclusion, as demonstrating relative feedback patterns, e.g. Hotelling, and rental/accessibility/land value patterns.

(c) The rank-size rule, and other Pareto distributions; also the Allometric law.

(d) Hierarchical order relationships, as in central-place and other patterns.

(e) The general operation of feedback; of conditions of homeostasis and morphogenesis; of conditions of stability and complexity; of threshold situations and homeostatic plateaux.

(f) The phenomenon of equifinality, shown by urban systems, for example, the growth of very large cities through migration at various historical times, or the urban/rural ecological relationship at various times and in various civilizations and cultures.

Requirements for a Theory of Systems of Cities

We can now attempt to sketch an outline of a theory of systems of cities: it should:

(1) Start from the basis of the examination of the system, *per se*, using knowledge of the stochastic behaviour of the individual elements (or sub-sub-systems) of the system (i.e. individual decision-making units), rather than focusing upon subsystem (i.e. city) relationships.

(2) See the system of cities as one in which structure and process are intertwined, with activities of individual decision-making unit behaviour, and flows from interactions between the various activities; conversely, activities being derived from flows.

(3) Include the operation of feedback loops within these systems, both negative and positive: steady rate and growth or decay taking place at the same time in different elemental subsystems (e.g. competition/exclusion), or in different attributes of the same element.

(4) Have a structure of input and output relationships between elements (seen as decision-making units, and thus subsystems in their own right), and aggregations of such elements, i.e. subsystems, such relationships being only partly determined or affected by the friction of physical space.

(5) Depict a system in which stochastic processes predominate, describ-

able as various forms of statistical distributions at various points in time.

(6) Allow of far-from-equilibrium conditions obtaining, in which self-organization and new morphological structure may develop.

(7) Essentially be a system processing and transforming information and energy, as well as food, water, air, money, goods, vehicles, and describable fully only in those terms.

(8) Have a concern for the following attributes of activity system functional relationships:

Linkages or functional interactions of a general kind, realized and potential;

Nodes or clusters of intensity of functional interaction;

Hierarchies, or relative degrees of interaction, or numbers and strengths of interaction;

Fields or "areas" of interaction, real and potential.

(Nodes, linkages, and fields are all interaction concepts, interaction depending upon function and structure. The differences between the three aspects may be one of degree, or the passing of some possibly arbitrary threshold. Hierarchy is also concerned with degree or strength of interaction of relationship).

(9) Following from (8), probably including a series of progressive behavioural patterns as the system or subsystem is carried from one steady state condition ("plateau of stability") to another, via appropriate threshold situations.

Theory or Simulation?

We can now return to the question: ought we to strive to construct new bodies of theory in order to create a sound basis for more adequate models of urban and regional systems; or must we rely on simulation as the best method of approach? In fact, the question is not so clear-cut, for the two approaches tend to overlap. As Sayer suggests, a suitable approach to building appropriate new theory may mean that we have to include in our embryo models far more than we can handle: we may start with a small subsystem and, in trying to close the system (for adequate modelling) in such a way that the correct determining relations are included, we may have to model the whole urban system. However, as Sayer seems to imply, models of major urban (or regional) processes at the macro-economic level can be essayed, and used as referents for more particular models: e.g. a general model of the land development process can be referred to in modelling part of the housing sector, or part of the retail trade sector.

But whether one wishes to start from either level, there is no doubt that the behaviour of individual decision units must be one of the principal considerations; thus this consideration, as well as the possible over-ambitiousness of a full theory-constructional endeavour, may lead one into simulation. Simulation, after all, has much to recommend it as an alternative, especially in a situation where over-concentration on algebraic formulation has occurred. Simulation, firstly of individual and small group behaviour, leading to that of large aggregations, seems to offer the opportunity of learning, of understanding, and possibly of developing new theoretical insights alongside the development of the simulation process. This may suggest that a digital simulation is the best approach, but the claims of Jay Forrester's System Dynamics method of simulation are also strong.

There is a further, highly-important reason for advocating a simulation approach: the remarks above apply to urban and regional models already in existence (as does Sayer's critique), i.e. the by-now "conventional wisdom" of urban and regional modelling; these remarks would apply also to models of developing country situations, were there any which were sufficiently embracing to cover the circumstances of both of the two circuits of their economies. However, as we do not have either sufficient knowledge of, or sufficient data for, lower-circuit situations and lower-upper circuit interactions, a direct start on a "theory-only" approach is hardly feasible, and a combined simulation-theory building process seems to be essential.

The matter of modelling the true state of affairs in urban and regional systems of developing countries is fraught with a number of difficulties, largely those which stem from ignorance as to the realities, especially expressed in terms of data, and which can only be derived from a fairly detailed level of knowlege as a basis. There can be no substitute for such knowledge at some point in an endeavour to model the lower circuits of these systems, although when a body of such knowledge becomes established in general terms, other methods may become available for particular applications. We do not know, at present, whether there is such a thing as a "typical" set of urban or regional relationships in a developing country: it is possible that there may be, but until many case studies, many data sets, have been assembled, we must remain in ignorance. We cannot expect to discover such typical systemic features, but a knowledge of systems generally leads one to suspect that it may be possible: it is possible, certainly, for the upper circuits of such urban systems (House and McLeod). However, even if some knowledge is available, perhaps of an inexact kind such as has been attempted in these pages regarding the size and significant characteristics of the lower circuits in a number of cities of developing countries, then it may be feasible to create "fuzzy" models (Zadeh, 1972) of such situations by attempting to specify plausible ranges for the parameters involved.

Two major approaches are necessary, it seems, in the attempt to replicate the operation and the interrelationships of the upper, and especially the lower, circuits. One approach, obviously, is to work with, and overcome the lack-of-data problem: no data, no models? The other approach is the development of a better body of theory—better, that is, for example, than economic base theory and its rather simplistic view of "service employment" in general, and in particular in relation to lower circuit situations.

Two kinds of models should be of interest and utility—sectoral models, which are concerned with the general processes of such systems, and spatial/locational models, which are concerned with the "where?" as well as the "how?" aspects. Sectoral models may take as a metric either employment or money: employment will necessarily include population growth and change, including migration; money flows may be in terms of value added as well as cash or credit. Disaggregation by sector or subsector—certainly below the level of the two-circuits—should be a feature. Spatial models would incorporate some of the features of sector models, but would emphasize those relationships between the activity systems and the physical fabric of the town or city, such as housing:employment; employment:transport; which are at the basis of decision-making in physical planning. Naturally, major model-building efforts, of the scale of the Chile regional/urban model, say, would encompass both aspects: a modular approach, linking submodel to submodel, would be appropriate and economical, as well as being good cybernetically.

Approaches to Simulation of the Lower Circuit

We might begin to approach an analysis of the locational parameters and sub-economies of the lower circuit of an urban economy by attempting a first principles consideration aided by empirical observations: that is, by conjecture and refutation. For example, it seems reasonable to suppose that, in selling "informal" services, be they shoe-shines or cheap artefacts, the largest market which can be dealt with is sought. A largest feasible market may imply the absence of competition or its suppression: the principle of exclusion may apply, whether reached by direct competition over price, service, quality, etc., or attempted monopoly. In the case of competition, Hotelling's principle may be seen: a larger potential market may be gained by clustering spatially with competing vendors, as with the ice-cream salesman on the beach. If monopoly is attempted, then a more solitary location is sought, but one where a large potential market can be tapped, e.g. at an approach to the location of a group of competing, but fixed, services, or where a large flow of potential customers is guaranteed as near a station or bus-terminal, or at a football match, or at traffic lights. Thus, by looking for the potential markets for such services it may be feasible to arrive at location criteria, at interdependencies, at least for some kinds of lower circuit services.

Another, and probably more difficult consideration is that of mobile services, although Stine's (1962) theory may be applicable even at the more local scale. The sales or service end of such processes may, in fact, be fixed, as with car-washers, who may congregate at particular large car parks. Street sellers, pedlars, door-to-door salesmen will seek out areas of adequately high population density consistent with the commodity they are selling: going to potential customers instead of waiting for them to come, shouting their wares (the Abacaxi Man in São Carlos, Brazil, springs vividly to mind!), knocking at doors. Others may bring their wares by cart and sell from the back of it: fresh vegetables or fish, or in winter the ubiquitous coal briquette man in Korean cities. The giving of credit, the selling of small quantities, the regularity or otherwise of such services, are all important aspects which need investigation, as does the source of such supplies, the economics of such services. (Forbes, 1981, has made an impressive start in this kind of enquiry, with his data on pedlars and trishaw riders in Ujung Pandang, Indonesia). Mobility of service has its advantages and disadvantages: range is restricted by lack of transport, though buses and trains are often seen as a good focus for sales; but different areas within the range can be served at different times, thus increasing potential coverage; no fixed premises are necessary unless stock is large, or vehicles, e.g. ice-cream carts, are needed—hiring of such vehicles can be a separate activity, also their construction and maintenance. Thus, even small, mobile vendors represent quite a complicated pattern of interactions, of stock production and keeping, of credit or other relationships, of vehicle provision perhaps, or relationship to public transport services in some cases, of customer locations, and so on. (See, for example, Sarin's (1982) account of pedlars and market traders in Chandigarh, India).

The lower circuit manufactory or maintenance service is a further category of interest. Maintenance services themselves: car repairs, tyre fitting, cart repair, refrigerator and TV repair—these may be carried out at home or on spare ground, or in the street. Manufacture, though, usually needs fixed premises, although these may vary in kind, size and location: the home often qualifies as a factory, if large enough; but almost any space near to the dwelling, or near to a potential market for the goods being made, will suffice (cf. the use of chicken sheds in parts of Hong Kong). Availability and rental cost seem to be the chief requirements (cf. V. Sit 1979). Such activities are virtually interstitial, relying on hardly-recorded small urban spaces, public or private, often for their locale—Hong Kong offers some very interesting examples. Again, as discussed in detail by Santos (1979), a more complete knowledge of, for example, relationships of lower circuit manufacturers with upper circuit companies, financial arrangements, labour employed, suppliers and markets, all are necessary to an understanding of the part played by lower circuit manufacturers in the urban, or regional, economy.

The conventional modelling approach to this manufacturing situation might be via the intervening-opportunities model. The intervening-opportunities model was first suggested by Stouffer in 1940. It proposes: "that the number of persons going a given distance is directly proportional to the number of opportunities at that distance and inversely proportional to the number of intervening opportunities". The model was originally cast in a context of migration from a given centre or centres, but in general is an attempt to modify the logic of the normal gravity model. The intervening-opportunities model can be formalized as follows:

Let: Δy = the number of persons moving from an origin to annulus width Δs, its inner boundary being $(s - \frac{1}{2}\Delta s)$ units of distance from the origin or centre of the circle, and its outer boundary being $(s + \frac{1}{2}\Delta s)$ units from the origin. Distance may be measured in space, time, or cost units.

x = the number of intervening opportunities, that is, the cumulated number of opportunities between the origin and distance s.

Δx = the number of opportunities within the annulus of width Δs.

Then:

$$\frac{\Delta y}{\Delta s} = \frac{a}{x} \cdot \frac{\Delta x}{\Delta s}.$$

If the existence of a continuous function, $x = f(s)$ is assumed, and if the above equation is recast in differential form, then:

$$\frac{dy}{ds} = \frac{a}{x} \cdot \frac{dx}{ds}.$$

Integrating: $y = a \log f(s) + c$.

Vining (1955) points out that the first derivative of this equation is of the form of a Pareto distribution.

This, the total number of movers (or shoppers or workplace locators, etc.) who stop at any point within the circle of radius S is directly proportional to the logarithm of the number of opportunities within the circle. This finding coincides with the usual personal perception of space (and time) as logarithmic: things close at hand are perceived as apparently more significant than things further away, but not in a linear fashion, the closer items being disproportionately more significant. Also, as Stouffer points out, it is only those opportunities which are perceived which are considered: the total actual opportunities cannot be considered if their existence does not reach the perceptions of the individual decision-maker.

It may be that distributions of employment in the lower circuit via an Intervening-Opportunities Model could be a fruitful approach, perhaps using a density function of opportunities for location per square kilometre.

One very important sector of the lower circuit economy is that of housing. Much has been written about squatter settlements (e.g. Grimes, 1976; Turner, 1976*) which helps to illuminate the actual mechanics of the squatting process.

* Turner (1976) has provided some very useful case studies of housing situations in Latin America, especially in Mexico City, though case numbers are limited. It must be suggested, though, that his comparison of "hierarchical" and "network" studies (i.e. of trees with lattices) is flawed. His example, of a British Rail map of services from London compared with a London Transport bus map, is a poor one; the railway map is a selection only from a more comprehensive network, i.e. it is possible to go from Glasgow to Dover in many alternative ways, e.g. via

But apart from the favelas and the tugurios, and so on, too little is known about the general provision of housing, its letting or sale, its repair, or its use in lower circuit economies: not all lower circuit housing is squatter housing. What is the actual process of getting such a non-tugurio house—or part of it—in San José, Costa Rica, or a room in Jeonju, Korea, or one in Cairo, or in Port Louis, Mauritius? Who provides the land, the building, the credit, the tenants or purchaser, who repairs it, and so on? How long does such a house last, how is it improved, if at all? Many questions of this kind remain to be answered, before even simple models of lower circuit situations can be attempted.

It should be stressed, perhaps—quite apart from Sayer's strictures on the matter—that no facile division of upper/lower circuit activities into a basic/services kind of dichotomy is possible, even though service activities are very well represented in the lower circuit. It is true that the service sector may lend itself more readily to *ad hoc* involvement, but both upper and lower circuits include examples of both manufacture and service activity. Nor is this the only reason why a Lowry model does not represent the reality of developing urban or regional systems. The simple logic of the Lowry model is that the location of basic employment (a "given") fixes the location, or the distribution of residential uses, and in turn that of service employment: this is quite at odds with the situations found in the lower circuits of cities in developing countries. (It is also an unrealistic way to express relationships in upper circuit situations). People, especially in developing countries, either have a house first and then look for a job, or look for somewhere to live first, and then find a job: there is a great deal of evidence that migrants come to a city in the hope of finding a job, but with housing of some sort already secured via kinsfolk or friends. Here, residence will tend to be the "given", and job-locations are related to residence by walking distance, or affordable bus fare.

At present, our knowledge of lower-circuit systems is fragmentary, and often limited to residual estimates of total "informal sector" employment by the ILO and others. Knowledge of operational and locational parameters, specific linkages and relationships, at the employee to firm, self-employed to market and to suppliers, firm to firm, firm to supplier or to market level, and so on, is either very generalized, or does not exist. There is a great need of first-hand knowledge of these systems, probably to be supplied mainly by social

---

Edinburgh, Newcastle and Bristol (if one wanted to). The BR map, in fact, is what a traffic engineer would call a "skim tree" for London as origin, i.e. only part of a larger network. Turner also discusses "physical" organizational networks, whereas it is the use made of networks which is important; users create their own informal networks of usefulness from the formal structures which have been set up: cf. John Power's concept of the "reticulist", i.e. he who plays the network, (Power, 1972). All human networks contain hierarchies because there are always differences between people, because competition leads to exclusion—but there will be many different kinds of hierarchies (trees) within a complex network. Perhaps what Turner is advocating is a proliferation of user's trees within a lattice structure: a variety-enhancing arrangement?

anthropologists and sociologists, and perhaps some urban economists and urban geographers, and, for example, of the kind produced by Janet Abu-Lughod (1961)* in relation to migration and residence, and Unni Wikan in relation to residence and poverty (1976) in Cairo; or by Clyde Mitchell in relation to labour circulation in Rhodesia; or at the level of Leeming's (1977) fundamental studies of street markets, McGee's (1973) of hawkers, and Sit's (1979) of domestic factories in Hong Kong. Indeed, Hong Kong seems to be one of the few cities for which we may have sufficient material from which to begin a valid explanation of its lower circuit economy. The process of assembling such data will require much patience and some time, but is essential as a basis for our knowledge of developing countries and their urban and regional systems. (Opportunities for gathering first-hand lower circuit knowledge could occur in other contexts; for example, where expensive home-interview surveys for transport modelling are still contemplated, cf. the large amounts of useful housing data collected in the São Paulo Origin and Destination Survey of 1977. Much relevant data might be collected in this way at no extra cost).

By their nature, it is difficult to identify and enumerate all the informal activities taking place in a given city or regional system, but it is a great pity that so very few attempts have been made, even on a sample basis (though a sampling procedure obviously must relate to the total size of the activity being sampled). It would appear that attempts to model activity systems in developing countries, so far, often may have been content to assume that such systems are just like those in developed countries and that the informal sector can be neglected in activity terms, that those inhabitants who do not have private motor cars, especially those who travel on foot or by bicycle, may be neglected and generally that the logic of the model is superior to the inconvenience of reality. In a sense, of course, this is only an extension of the attitude of modellers of any system, indeed of physical planners in general. The real world is of incredible variety: Nature is extravagant, untidy, wasteful, and so much of reality has to be thrown away or ignored in any model of any part of it. Man's curiosity and his feeling that he must be able to explain everything leads him to cheat by ignoring the inconvenient, by truncating the limbs of the untidy problems of reality. But if you are ignoring only 35% of the numbers involved, never mind 40, 50, 60% or more, how useful is your model?

A Schematic Model of an Urban System in a Developing Country

Milton Santos (1979) and (more schematically) T. McGee (1973), have provided probably the only attempts so far to present a model, or models, of an overall urban system in a developing country; Santos's model, though not referred to in a direct way as drawn, but elaborated at length verbally by him,

---

* See also her identification via factor analysis of the "Sub-Cities" of Cairo, 1971.

is perhaps the more complete of these. The model now sketched, a schematic model of an urban system in a developing country, owes much to Santos's exposition, but the opportunity has been taken to elaborate this precursor into a sketch of a more general urban model. Thus other sectors, e.g. housing, the construction industry, are now represented, and an external population/migration sector has been added; as a result, the model now contains many more interactions than previously. The model is intended as an initial step towards the creation of a simulation model, or more likely, a family of models, e.g. the land supply/housing demand/housing supply/construction industry sectors might be elaborated very much in the way that Sayer (1976) suggests as necessary, with a full representation of housing finance, land development process, house letting and sale, and so on. The task obviously is a big one, but bigger models of a more conventional nature appear to have been attempted. A simulation approach is intended: digital, Monte Carlo, gaming, or system dynamics—although it may be that system dynamics type formulation, possibly on the basis of initial gaming simulations, may be most favoured. (The model diagram, as drawn, might be seen as a first step towards a causal loop diagram). One of the advantages of using the system dynamics method is that many examples of system dynamics architecture are available as a stimulus and reference.

The model includes a regional sector as a context, providing the population inputs (and outputs) to the urban system. Also represented, in outline, are regional activities such as agriculture, mining, and transport. Additionally, the extra-regional modern circuit appears in outline, making the point that the upper circuit of the urban system is a subsystem of the larger modern circuit. The upper circuit of the urban system includes representation of land supply, housing demand and supply, building stock (of all types), the construction industry, modern urban industry, export industry, modern (intra-city) trading, export trading, services of all kinds, wholesaling, goods transport, and public transport. The lower circuit includes land supply, housing demand and supply, building stock, construction activities, non-capital manufacturing, services, non-modern trading, wholesaling, goods transport, public transport, and marginal activities of various kinds. The linkages between these activities are many and varied, and the system is potentially very complex with many possible states. Realistic approaches thus appear to indicate: (a) a macro-approach using large "building blocks", e.g. the two circuits only in a regional environment; (b) a micro-approach, sector by sector, e.g. lower circuit manufacturing as a subsystem, or lower circuit housing, its provision, occupation, and use.

Systems Dynamics Simulation as an Approach

In the case of simulation, the field of System Dynamics appears to offer a number of interesting possibilities, beginning with Forrester's Urban

Dynamics model (Forrester, 1969), and continuing via Hester's more embracing city-suburb model (Hester, 1969), to the sophistication of Battelle Susquehanna regional model. There is, in any case, a large literature, both of criticism and development, deriving from Forrester's original Urban Dynamics model (e.g. Chen, 1972). However, although this literature is very valuable as a source of ideas on the simulation of urban and regional systems, indeed of actual models which, with appropriate modifications, might form a basis for development into models of developing country situations, nonetheless it must be remembered that most of them have in view the specific and peculiarly North-American city, and a specific and possibly controversial perception of the way such cities operate and change. Thus there is an insistence on a fixed land area for a city, despite the American experience of suburbanization and urban sprawl; there is an insistence on urban attractiveness in terms of the job market, housing conditions, the quality of school systems, climate, and many other factors; obsolescence of structures is seen as a key process in the original Forrester model.

In contrast, the generalized model of upper/lower circuit relationships (Fig. 7.1) is concerned with two major groups, but subdivided into three or four employment situations; it is concerned with employment as a major attractiveness force to migration, but restricted choice of housing; it does not necessarily view obsolescence of higher or middle-income housing as a major source of supply of lower-income housing, nor does it view government action for such supply as a major possibility; the myth of land restriction cannot be supported in a situation where continuing urbanization is a reality, often including self-organized housing provision. However, all of these aspects, so different from the North American parentage of System Dynamics type models, can be incorporated in simulation models using S. D. approaches and formulation. There is a major caveat, of course, these progenitors can only offer ideas and techniques: major new model development must start from an appropriate theoretical formulation of relationships, and must be based on a realistic perception of the systems being modelled.

Forrester's Urban Dynamics model is illustrated as an overall concept by a simple diagram in the book of that name: just three major subsystems: industry, housing, employment, and each with three major components (levels) which are linked by flow processes over time, two of them unidirectional "ageing" flows, and one partly two-directional. True, there are several rate symbols shown to each set of three levels, especially with the employment subsystem, but the effect so far is one of relative simplicity. However, no complete flow diagram of the Urban Dynamics model has been published; a research project at the University of Newcastle upon Tyne a decade ago (Newcastle System Dynamics Group, 1973), *inter alia* attempted to derive a graphical representation (causal loop diagram) of this model from its equation structure, as also with other S. D. models. The structure of Urban Dynamics was found to be exceeding complex; the Susquehanna model was

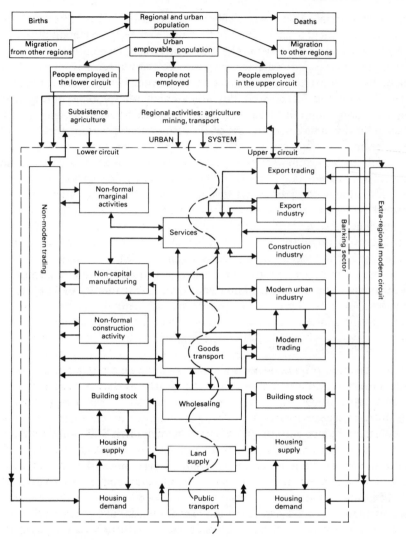

Fig. 7.1. Schematic Model of an Urban System in a Developing Country.

even more so, and a very large piece of paper was needed for it. Each level symbol in each of the three major subsystems, in fact, is at the crux of a tree-like structure, or structures, containing the multipliers and table functions applicable to it, and each veritable "Christmas Tree" of these System Dynamics symbols may be linked with others. Thus, whilst in principle a structure rather like that of the Urban Dynamics model may be suitable as a starting point for a model of an urban system in a developing country, due to its apparent simplicity, in fact any correspondence between the two is bound to be superficial. This is especially emphasized by a consideration of the axiological level of consideration of Forrester's model (Gibson, in Chen (ed.), 1972); there are also structural aspects of Urban Dynamics, e.g. the five multiplications together of linearities, referred to by Gibson, which make this model difficult to analyse and thus to accept as a basis for another elaboration. The diagram (Fig. 7.2) of an employment sector of a developing country urban system model must be regarded, therefore, as a first sketch only, a mere beginning for analysis and further thought. There are many problems in specifying the supporting "trees" of multipliers, especially in view of the needful disaggregation of the lower circuit activities in such a model. Knowledge of actual systems becomes essential at this point.

The coupling together of the several sectors of an Urban Dynamics type model occurs by way of the relationships between the individual rates and table functions, i.e. the various components of the Christmas-Tree-like structures already mentioned. To prepare such a diagram for the Developing Country Urban System Model means specifying all the components of each tree structure in detail, and then specifying their overall interrelationships, which requires more detailed knowledge of such situations than we currently possess.

An Outline Regional Model

The diagram (Fig. 7.3) shows a sketch of a regional model, using Dennis Meadows's World 3 model as a basic inspiration. In point of fact, the case study chosen as a basis is a nation, Mauritius, rather than a region, but as Mauritius is a country of two major islands, with a population a little less than 1 million and a land surface of 2000 square kilometres, it could well represent a region of a larger country—with the exception that, as islands, inputs and outputs are well documented, and migration is very limited. It might be seen as the equivalent of the regional context of the urban system model, for example. As Mauritius is essentially a grower of sugar-cane and an exporter of sugar, the representation of the agricultural industry is especially important here.

Again, as with the urban model, a sector-by-sector approach to the structure of the overall model may be useful: thus the agricultural sector, the fishing sector (including commercial fishing for tuna), the industrial sector, the population sector, etc. may be elaborated in System Dynamics form. The various sectors would be connected together as previously related for the urban system model. It may be noted that no urban sector has been indicated, apart from land for urban purposes, but this could be included, although the assumption here is that this would be one of the points of connection (the population sector, obviously, is another) with the urban system model. Housing is an important aspect of such a model (cf. the earlier discussion of the Mauritian housing situation) and a housing sector could be incorporated in the overall "regional" model, if desired.

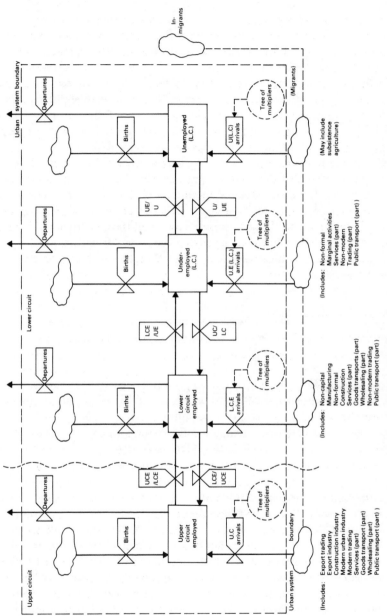

Fig. 7.2. Urban System Model: Employment Sector in System Dynamics Notation.

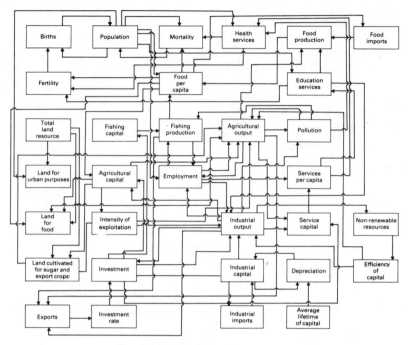

FIG. 7.3. Sketch of Mauritius Model 2.

System Theory, Planning, and Models

The idea of "system" is a simple and yet powerful one, but it is not restricted, as some commentators would have us believe, either to system analysis (in the computing sense) or to physical or mechanical systems. This narrow view is not only perverse and unwarranted, but deprives the social sciences of a much-needed means of expression. The idea of General Systems Theory was born in the biological sciences, and has much to do with life, from evolution to explaining medical phenomena: there seems little doubt that it can be helpful in explaining group behaviour of men and women, as well as that of man himself. There seems to be no evidence that socio-economic systems cannot be seen and explained in terms of system theory, whilst there is much that suggests that they can be. For example, as already pointed out, population growth and change of people can be explained in terms of feedback situations, just as with other living creatures: exponential growth or decline, the logistic curve, and so on. Monopoly situations, in business or trade unions, can be explained via competition and exclusion, as with animal populations. Stability and self-organization in human affairs seem equally comprehensible via an understanding of self-organization in the other kinds of systems. The fear—and it is as irrational as are many fears—that "systems" mean something mechanical, something antithetical to the warm humanity that social scientists see themselves as champions of; that it means men in clinical white coats with computers, forcing human beings into Procrustean environments—is perhaps understandable as an emotional reaction, but it is also absurd. What has been at fault with the application of system theory to town and regional planning has been due largely to an over-optimistic view of what planning can accomplish. (Note that many planners and social scientists shy away from the simple word "town" and use "urban" instead: why?).

Town and regional planning has been oversold, in fact, especially in Britain, but also in other countries, some of which may have borrowed unthinkingly from the British town and country planning legislation (Chadwick, 1970; Kanyeihamba, 1973). British town planning is a legal complexity concerned both with pettifogging detail and with major strategic issues. The detail: whether a woman should use a room in her house for a hairdressing business, or whether a houseowner should be permitted to have green or blue tiles on his roof, would be laughable were it not taken so seriously by the law and those concerned with enforcing it. At the strategic level, the battery of legal powers available for steering industrial and office location have begun to look rather ineffective in post-depression Britain: economics, not planning, becomes predominant. Apart from the British new towns, which have mostly avoided the excesses of a Brasilia or a Chandigarh, perhaps thanks to some extent to an insistence that they pay their way in investment terms, the only real success of British planning has been largely to conserve the country's agricultural land (and to some extent, the traditional rural landscape) from unnecessary building development. The point here, in relation to the application of system theory to planning, is that the over-detailed focus of British physical planning, its appearance of omniscience, has led to the attempt to apply very detailed expressions of system theory to physical planning situations. Thus models which are concerned with general relationships, with average probabilities, become focused on very particular issues. (Simulation models should give a warning here: it may be possible, using historic data, to simulate the past behaviour of, for example, the football teams in the English First Division: but can this be used as a basis for the prediction of behaviour of the same teams—probably composed of different players—for a new season, not only over the whole of that season, but so as to predict accurately the performance of these teams on a given Saturday?) The question of the Law of Requisite Variety must be adverted to, once again. A town, an urban system, is composed of many people, many decision-makers: it may be possible to describe the overall behaviour of such a system, the average behaviour, the typical behaviour, using the techniques of statistics and probability—but the behaviour of an individual decision-maker can be seen only in these terms: we cannot say that: "Mr Smith will do so-and-so tomorrow," but only that he may do, in the light of the average behaviour of many Mr Smiths in the past. If someone wishes to control an urban system, the only effective way, the Law of Requisite Variety reminds us, is to have the same variety in the controlling system as in the system to be controlled. Clearly, in a city of 1 million people, the only potential control system of the Requisite Variety available is that same 1 million people who live there. Thus: (a) overall control is impossible and only piecemeal control can be attempted: OR (b) the citizens must act themselves as the control mechanism, i.e. they are responsible and self-organizing and the city is a democracy. Which suggests, in most cases, that detailed control of every physical change, every activity change, is a chimera.

It follows from the above that models of the town and regional planning process as a whole, if they are to be realistic, must acknowledge the constraints of the situation: the rational-comprehensive model of this process is inapplicable and in conflict with reality; the mixed-scanning model may be more feasible, but still has an element of rationality: is it rational to attempt to be rational?; the disjointed incrementalism view of the situation seems best fitted to reality (Chadwick, 1971). Some would argue that disjointed incrementalism is a negation of "planning", by which is really meant that incrementalism and longer-range planning are antithetical. But most governmental and political decisions are made incrementally, and horizons are limited by the political process.

Thus, the question must be asked: how can models be useful in the sorts of planning that go on in developing countries? As it is considered that physical planning has a limited role to play, but that socio-economic policies have a greater relevance, the question is broadened. It seems likely that "modelling" (of kinds to be defined subsequently) might be helpful in:

(a) understanding developing country situations and systems;
(b) in probing social and economic policies in developing countries;
(c) in assisting physical planning in its limited scope.

The word "model", it is worth reminding one's self, simply means: a representation of one system by another system, usually in a less-complex way than in reality. Whilst mathematics is often involved in the business of modelling, it is by no means essential to the formulation of a model, although it is necesary for validation. Models do not necessarily mean numbers and computers: mental schemata, diagrams on backs-of-envelopes, are also essential parts of a modelling process, i.e. models themselves.

The "understanding" kinds of models in developing country situations are likely to be of two kinds. The first sort is where relationships have been perceived, say as a result of first hand experience of a village or a city, either broadly or through a detailed focus on some aspects. For example, Unni Wikan (1980) carried out a socio-anthropological study of a group of women and their households in Cairo, 1969–1972; the relationships involved, both in friendship/kinship terms, and spatially, could be shown as a series of diagrams, in addition to the text of the book, facilitating the understanding of life, kinship, poverty and physical living conditions there. A second sort of model is where numerical data is available, for example on numbers of people migrating, say to Cairo or to Ismailia and the Suez Canal towns of Egypt, from the Delta. A comparison of numbers migrating, in and out, their ages, income-levels, occupations, literacy, etc., may lead us, via the usual statistical techniques, to reach some conclusions about the present and recent-past characteristics of such migrants, which may be helpful in policy formulation rehousing provision.

The use of models in evaluating social and economic policies again has two aspects. Where policies are in existence, modelling, via the necessary fact-finding exercise, can represent the effects of the policies on the given system situations. Where policies are proposed, the possibilities of simulating the application of those policies, perhaps via gaming simulations, having firstly gained essential knowledge of the systems concerned, are relevant.

The assistance that models may give to physical development situations is probably rather obvious. The calculation of various service and utility needs takes first place traditionally via a series of very simple models, often using or implying standards of provision (which need to be looked at very realistically, and not based on western textbooks). Site layout, housing design, all rely on some kind of mental and formal models, even if non-mathematical.

Physical planning in developing cities—as the expression of socio-economic policies of governments—should be action-oriented and concern itself with the strategies of further development of those cities, rather than trying to control over-much whatever has been built already. Thus, the provision of essential services (to both existing and new areas) becomes the focus of attention, rather than absurd police measures to control trishaws or jitneys, or the number of pedlars or market stalls, or the sending-back to the countryside of the under-employed.

The traditional Public Works Department of many ex-British colonial cities might almost be an initial model, providing water, sewage disposal, electricity, footways, cycle ways, and bus routes to newly developing areas for which land has already been purchased by it, or engaging in the much more difficult task of inserting such facilities into existing built-up areas. The process should be seen as servicing community needs, and with "town planning" or "urban design" as strictly subservient to the servicing tasks in view: a limited and highly useful activity, bounded and programmed to the public budget situation. In this connection, the new urban growth areas advocated by the World Bank's Sector Policy Paper on Urban Transport (World Bank, 1975), should be related to desirable growth patterns, to urban growth strategies. These strategies may be evaluated within the urban services department by a simulation modelling process of a highly realistic kind, related to market forces, to likely public investment, and to the attractiveness of adequate urban utilities and facilities: to land suitability, accessibility, and availability—for it should be a positive duty of the urban services department to meet the demand for land as a basic urban commodity. (The Hong Kong Public Works Department comes to mind in this respect, also the British New Town

Development Corporations). Promotion—rather than restriction—of employment of all sorts within such areas should be an essential concomitant of these activities. Detailed land use would not be considered within such areas, except for obvious service needs such as school provision.

As in other aspects of life, the question as to the use of models in a given situation is not necessarily a matter of rationality, but of conviction: those who are convinced that models are useful will go on building models, others will not. There remains a role for models in the research field also, of course; somewhere, in universities, in United Nations or World Bank agencies, people will no doubt go on building models of town and regional systems in a spirit of enquiry, in hoped-for, rather than guaranteed anticipation of their usefulness. The Schematic Model of an Urban System in a Developing Country is no doubt of this kind (Fig. 7.1). But, by and large, the sort of feasible models of developing country situations, as Geraldes (1980) has described in another context, are likely to be: "Sketch-Planning models . . . of an embryonic systemic nature and thus characterized by a low degree spatial resolution, small amount of data requirements, and reduced computer support."

The elaboration of models of these former kinds is obviously a long and complex task, requiring much acquaintance with first-hand data, as has been stressed earlier. The purpose of such models must be questioned also.

It has been asserted fairly frequently by those who have studied lower circuit situations in developing countries, that government policies and actions of all kinds deliberately foster the upper circuit and restrict the activities of the lower circuit; also quite specifically, some commentators (e.g. Sarin, 1982), see physical planning controls as being applied on behalf of the upper circuit activities and against those of the lower circuit. In short, physical planning is a part of the upper circuit subsystem and, like other controls, may be aimed at circumscribing those who live and work in the lower circuit still further. Modelling, of the conventional kinds recently used in physical planning in western countries, might be seen, thus, as part of an anti-lower circuit policy for its control or suppression. The view which is put forward here, however, is that the attempted modelling of urban and regional systems in developing countries can be beneficial, especially to their lower circuit activities. Almost every treatise written on urban or regional models commends the exercise as one in which understanding of the systems concerned is greatly enhanced (in view of Sayer's strictures this may not fully be the case, in fact?). However, there is little doubt that properly conducted attempts at modelling both the upper and lower circuits of urban and regional systems in developing countries, including first-hand pursuit of appropriate data, would greatly enhance knowledge and understanding of their specific qualities and problems, so that, where indicated as helpful, properly-conceived policies can be formed and reviewed. It does not appear to be realistic to search for a planning technology which might include the use of models in these kind of situations; in fact any interference of the traditional "planning control" kinds seems to be positively unhelpful to the circumstances of the lower circuits. But greater understanding is needed at governmental and organizational levels of an international nature, e.g. the World Bank, the regional Development Banks, the United Nations Agencies, even the International Labour Office.

As Sarin (op. cit.) pertinently points out, it is not sufficient for the lower circuits, in present conditions, to continue as they are, trapped in poverty: this will not improve the situation of those who live in these circumstances, nor will it improve employment or contribute to economic growth. Only policies that will give people more money, to eat, to be housed, to be able to send their children to school ("free" education is not costless), will improve matters. Self-help may be a good beginning, but by itself it is of little practical use unless supported in other ways. In order to conceive this support, a fuller knowledge of the interaction of the two circuits is necessary, i.e. one must model the feedback loops which cross the (essentially arbitrary) boundaries between the two circuits—only then can it be seen whether some of these loops could be turned back, so that lower circuit activities might stimulate each other productively, with appropriate catalysts being introduced, e.g. small-scale credit institutions. (If millions can be "written off" in international loans, why not a few hundred rupees each to individuals?).

It has been remarked earlier that the goals of the development process are vaguely expressed and represent means only, not ends. Although indicators of various sorts are published by the World Bank and others, the laurels are always awarded to those countries with the highest growth rates of GNP per capita. Such a ratio says nothing at all about disposable incomes or living conditions, especially those of the poorest people: averages may conceal great disparities, and growth rates expressed in this way may indicate "progress" even whilst the number of very poor people is increasing. A better index of development might rather be the number and rate of change of the population below a certain minimum income datum, together with the level of the essential services available to them: food, water, housing, education, health care. The purpose of "development", surely, is to improve people's lives, most especially of those living in poverty. The problem is not one of prescribing for equality—people are not born equal, and hierarchies of many kinds are found in all societies, with people moving to different levels during their lives; the problem is rather one of providing for equity, not equality: of ensuring that no one goes without the basic necessities.

In this connection, the aims of development agencies are mostly directed at large items of spending, often of a capital investment nature; the fascination of hardware is all-pervasive: steel mills, national airlines, ports, roads, railways, power stations. The conventional wisdom is that such spending on infrastructure or social overhead capital will pave the way for overall "growth" (Koichi Mera, 1973, quoted by G. Beier *et al.*, 1975)—but how far does building a major road or a power station improve the actual income of a rural dweller or urban under-employed person? The "multiplier effects" in this respect of such investments seem to be harder to find on the ground than they are in theory, perhaps. A focus on what really happens in urban and regional systems of developing countries—upper as well as lower circuits and the relationships between them—is essential. We have a lot of (unsolicited) political theory, but not too many facts: economic policies without social policies. One must not make immodest claims, but the grass-roots knowledge essential for modelling, and adequate models themselves, seem to be a necessary part of a more realistic process of "development".

A Summary of the Main Points of this Study:

(1) "Development" is not only economic development, but has social goals. It therefore requires the prior reaching of appropriate thresholds by a number of subsystems of society: e.g. education, health, organization, logistics (e.g. transport). There is a close analogy with the process of civilization, as defined by Childe and others. Development may be a process over a longer time-scale than is allowed for in some countries. Myrdal's cumulative-causation model appears to have a broad explanatory feedback value.

(2) Now-"developed" countries are not necessarily a guide to the process taking place in other countries today. In particular, the reliance of earlier developers on manufacturing, especially heavy industry, is not usually appropriate now. The rates of population increase today are much greater than was experienced in earlier development, and agricultural and resource frontiers have shrunk in the meantime.

(3) Population growth means urbanization. Cities, especially large cities, are the locus of innovation and development, as also of many problems of poverty, housing, education, health. But, in general, cities are healthier than the rural areas and natural increase of population, in many cases, becomes a larger component than does net-migration.

(4) Cities and regions in developing countries can be discerned to have two "circuits" in their economies. These circuits are closely-interrelated subsystems, distinguished in the one case ("upper circuit") by a reliance on capital and credit, and linkages outside the city or region, and employing up to date techniques and machinery; in the other ("lower circuit") there is a reliance on self- and family labour, capital is scarce as is credit, hand techniques are usual, poverty frequent.

(5) Information about the lower circuits is scarce, and official statistics often exclude those who work in them; at best, residual calculations of lower circuit employment have been attempted, e.g. by the ILO. Much more information about circumstances in the lower circuits is needed.

(6) Those models of urban and regional systems in developing countries which have been attempted seem unsatisfactory as they are reliant on

official statistics; and on theoretical relationships derived from developed, not developing countries.

(7) There is a need, therefore, for a better body of theory regarding urban and regional systems in developing countries. In part, at least, this is expected to necessitate simulation techniques, as well as first hand enquiry, probably by social anthropologists.

(8) System Theory appears to be a useful way of organizing knowledge about urban and regional systems in developing countries. There are misconceptions about the nature of system theory and its applicability to socio-economic systems.

(9) Physical planning is seen as having only a limited role in developing countries. Policies of equity to deal with poverty, and to increase income-productive employment, are much more important. Western-type planning controls are quite inappropriate, and disjointed incrementalism is a more likely basis for policies.

(10) Models of urban and regional systems in developing countries properly framed (mainly via simulation at the moment), would be useful:

(a) to increase understanding of such systems;
(b) to evaluate social and economic policies;
(c) in assisting the limited scope of physical planning, e.g. providing utilities, schools, etc.

A physical planning technology directly using models, on the basis of recent western attempts, does not appear useful or justifiable in this field.

(11) Sketch outlines of an urban and a regional model, as potential research vehicles, are given, utilizing a System Dynamics simulation approach. These would be intended, prima facie, for the "understanding of systems" role. Case study data, e.g. for Mauritius in the regional case, would be necessary to take these models further.

8. Note on a Possible Modelling Opportunity in Hong Kong

The purpose of this note is to expand the view, expressed in the text, that data may exist in Hong Kong of a nature which could allow of some progress towards models of lower circuit activities and lower-upper circuit interactions. The published sources include:

L. S. K. Wong (1971): A Squatter Area.
D. J. Dwyer (1971): Small Industrial Units.
C. S. Liang (1973): Urban Land Use Analysis.
T. G. McGee (1973): Hawkers.
F. Leeming (1977): Street Studies.
V. Sit (1979): Factories in Domestic Premises.

Suggested Lower Circuit Characteristics

1. Manufacturing, or Servicing equipment (not mobile): need premises or space on a semipermanent basis.
   Factors: Perceived availability of premises or space for semipermanent or term basis.
   Rental or cost (most important factor, according to Sit).
   Location in relation to suppliers, markets (lesser importance).
   Location in relation to dwelling (not important, perhaps).

2. Services (Mobile), e.g. foodsellers, ice-cream/drinks sellers, newspaper boys, shoe-shiners, car washers, sellers of novelties, umbrellas, buskers, etc.: need space only on a transient basis.
   Factors: Perceived availability of space for short periods only at no cost.
   Location in relation to customers (most important).
   Location in relation to dwelling (possibly walking distance).
   Location in relation to suppliers (less important).

3. Workers in Manufacturing.
   Factors: Perceived job vacancy/availability.
   Location in relation to dwelling, i.e. cost of getting there.
   Wages offered.

4. Semi-Mobile Services, e.g. building workers, handcart and trishaw hirers, pickup truck drivers: needing some semi-permanent base or storage.

Factors: Perceived availability of openings for service trades.
Location in relation to probable work areas.
Cost/rental of premises or space.
Location in relation to dwelling.

5. Residence.
Factors: Perceived availability or vacancy of land or building.
Proximity to kinsfolk or people from same village.
Location, size, facilities (less important).

Data Requirements

1. Observed ratios of (l.c.) self-employed ⟷ manufacturing
employed ⟷ fixed location services
unemployed ⟷ mobile services.

2. Location of residence by (l.c.) income groups.

3. Known employment (l.c.) locations, by employment group:
manufacturing
fixed services
mobile services.

4. Present rentals for fixed (l.c.) manufacture/service location.

5. Model zoning system for residence, also for employment.

Simulation Methods

(a) For Lower Circuit Manufacturing (Spatial model)

(i) Assignment of employers and self-employed to employment locations by an intervening opportunities model, using rentals, not distance, as probabilities.

(ii) Assignment of employees to employment opportunities using wages related to distance from home in cost terms, possibly using the form of the intervening opportunities model used in traffic generation calculations. (This latter states that the probability of a trip from origin zone i ending at destination zone j or beyond depends upon a function of the total number of destinations (opportunities) located nearer to i than zone j. In this model only the *relative* distance affects the distribution of trips: the model does not deal with distance *per se*, but only with relative distance, i.e. whether one destination zone is nearer than another to the origin. Thus:

$$t_{i\to j}=t_i[e^{-Lt_0}-e^{-L(t_0+t_j)}]$$

where L = probability per destination of the acceptability of the destination at the zone under consideration (a constant for each zone of origin).

t_0 = present volume of destinations closer in time to zone i than zone j is to zone i).

(b) The Hawker or Mobile Salesman

The case of the hawker or mobile salesman might be seen as an analogy to that of the Marginal Value Theorem in ecology (Charnov, 1976) which deals with a mobile predator/prey relationship. This suggests that a predator implicitly calculates its present rate of gain, i.e. how fast it is finding food, and compares this with its usual rate and also with the time taken to reach the next food source. As the food source becomes depleted the present rate of gain decreases: diminishing returns set in. Travel time to the next food opportunity can be seen as time spent in that source, so that the next future rate of gain can be computed and compared with the present one. If the expected gain is higher than the present rate, then the move takes place. Apparently birds and insects carry some threshold time instinctively, and compare this with the lapse of time since they last caught a prey: if the threshold is exceeded, the animal moves on to the next probable source.

In the hawker's case, the rate of gain might be taken as the number, or, better, the value of sales made in a certain zone in a given time period, compared with some norm or threshold value: if the threshold is not reached, a move is made to the nearest or next convenient alternative sales zone not already investigated. Data necessary to explore this application does not yet seem to be available.

(c) Street Trading, including Shops

Leeming's (1977) study of a number of street "strings" of activities in Hong Kong stresses the historical continuity of many of these areas, and even of some of the trades taking place within them. Thus one hypothesis about the future location of fixed street trading would be that it will take place in, or in extension of, existing strings and nuclei. If such were to be the case, a simulation again using the intervening opportunities model would be possible, utilizing rental, first of all, and relative distance perhaps secondly. However, this would account for only a certain proportion of trading activity. Some tourist-oriented trading seems to follow Hotelling's principle and locate in, or near to, larger hotels, and specialist central shopping centres like Ocean Terminal; but some of the land use arrangements revealed by Liang (1973) appear to defy explanation.

References

Abiodun, J. O. (1967) "Urban Hierarchy in a Developing Country", *Economic Geography*, Vol. 43, pp. 347–367.

Abu-Lughod, J. L. (1961) "Migrant Adjustment to City Life: The Egyptian Case", *American Journal of Sociology*, Vol. 67, pp. 22–32.

Abu-Lughod, J. L. (1964) "Urban-Rural Differences as a Function of the Demographic Transition: Egyptian Data and an Analytical Model", *American Journal of Sociology*, Vol. 69, pp. 476–490.

Abu-Lughod, J. L. (1965) "Urbanization in Egypt: Present State and Future Prospects", *Economic Development and Cultural Change*, pp. 313–343.

Abu-Lughod, J. L. (1971) *Cairo: 1001 Years of the City Victorious*, Princeton U.P.

Abu-Lughod, J. L. (1976) "Developments in North African Urbanism: The Process of Decolonization" (1971), in: *Urbanization and Counter-Urbanization*, Sage Publications, ed. Berry, B. J. L.

Adams, E. (1966) *Evaluation of Demographic Data and Future Population Growth in Mauritius: 1962–1987*, UN, Commissioner for Technical Cooperation, Report No. TAO/MAURI/1.

Adams, N. A. (1969) "Internal Migration in Jamaica: An Economic Analysis", *Social and Economic Studies*, Vol. 18, pp. 137–151.

Adelman, I. and Robinson, S. (1978) *Income Distribution Policy in Developing Countries: A Case Study of Korea*, Stanford U.P. for the World Bank.

Aldridge, J. (1969) *Cairo*, Macmillan, London.

Allen, P. M. (1980) *Planning and Decision Making in Human Systems: Modelling Self-Organization*, Paper for the NATO Advanced Research Institute on Systems Analysis in Urban Policy Making and Planning, Oxford.

Arab Republic of Egypt/United Nations Development Programme (1976) *Suez Canal Regional Plan, Main Report*.

Arab Republic of Egypt (1982) Ministry of Reconstruction and State for Housing and Land Reclamation: *El-Obour Master Plan Study, Vol. 2: Urban Development Plan: Summary*, GOPP/GTZ, Cairo.

Artle, R. (1971) "Urbanization and Economic Growth in Venezuela", *Papers of the Regional Science Association*, Vol. 27, pp. 63–93.

Ashby, W. R. (1956) *An Introduction to Cybernetics*, Chapman & Hall, London.

Ashby, W. R. (1960) *Design for a Brain*, Chapman & Hall, London.

Asiatic Research Centre (1978) *A Study of Regional Development in Korea: Ulsan-Masan and Jeonju Regions*, Korea University.

Ayeni, B. (1979) *Concepts and Techniques in Urban Analysis*, Croom Helm, London.

Barber, W. J. (1967) "Urbanization and Economic Growth: The Cases of Two White Settler Territories", in: Miner, H., ed., *The City of Modern Africa*, Pall Mall Press, London.

Barras, R. and Broadbent, T. A. (1974) "The Development of an Activity-Commodity Representation of Urban Systems as a Potential Framework for Evaluation", in: Cripps, E. L., ed., *Space-Time Concepts in Urban and Regional Models*, London papers in regional science 4: Pion.

Barras, R. and Broadbent, T. A. (1975) *An Activity-Commodity Formalism for Socio-*

MURS – L*

Economic Systems, Centre for Environmental Studies, London, Research Paper 18.

Beals, R. E., Levy, M. B. and Moses, L. N. (1967) "Rationality and Migration in Ghana", *Review of Economics and Statistics*, Vol. 49, pp. 480–486.

Beckmann, M. J. (1957) "City Hierarchies and the Distribution of City Size", *Economic Development and Cultural Changes*, Vol. 6, pp. 243–248.

Beckmann, M. J. and McPherson, J. C. (1970) "City Size Distribution in a Central Place Hierarchy: An Alternative Approach", *Journal of Regional Science*, Vol. 10, pp. 25–33.

Beier, G., Churchill, A., Cohen, M. and Renaud, B. (1975) *The Task Ahead for the Cities of the Developing Countries*, World Bank Staff Working Paper No. 209.

Belo Horizonte (1972) PLAMBEL Report on a Structure Plan and Strategy for Greater Belo Horizonte (Original title in Portuguese), Anexo 1: Modelos de Analise e Projecão.

Benedict, B. (1961) *Indians in a Plural Society*, Colonial Research Studies No. 34, HMSO, London.

Benedict, B. (1970) *People of the Seychelles*, Overseas Research Publication No. 14, Ministry of Overseas Development, London, HMSO.

Benoit, E. (1973) *Defence and Economic Growth in Developing Countries*, Lexington Books, Boston.

Berg, E. J. (1961) "Backward-Sloping Labour Supply Functions in Dual Economies—The African Case", *Quarterly Journal of Economics*, Vol. 75, pp. 468–492.

Berry, B. J. L. (1962) "Some Relations of Urbanization and Basic Patterns of Economic Development", in: Pitts, F. R., ed., *Urban Systems and Economic Development*, University of Oregon, pp. 1–15.

Berry, B. J. L. and Barnum, H. G. (1962) "Aggregate Relations and Elemental Components of Central Place Systems", *Journal of Regional Science*, Vol. 4, pp. 35–68.

Berry, B. J. L. and Pred, A. (1964, 1965) *Central Place Studies: A Bibliography of Theory and Applications*, Regional Science Research Institute, Philadelphia.

Berry, B. J. L. (1973) *The Human Consequence of Urbanization*, Macmillan.

Birks, J. S. and Sinclair, C. A. (1980) *International Migration and Development in the Arab Region*, I.L.O., Geneva.

Blake, G. H. (1974) "Urbanization in North Africa: Its Nature and Consequences", in: Dwyer, D. J. (ed.): *The City in the Third World*, pp. 67–80, Macmillan.

Blake, G. H. & Lawless, R. I. (1980) (eds.) *The Changing Middle Eastern City*, Croom Helm.

Board, C., Davies, R. J. and Fair, T. J. D. (1970) "The Structure of the South African Space Economy: An Integrated Approach", *Regional Studies*, Vol. 4, pp. 367–392.

Boeke, J. H. (1953) *Economics and Economic Policy of Dual Societies, as Exemplified by Indonesia*, Institute of Pacific Relations, New York.

Boesch, H. (1952) "Central Functions as a Basis for a Systematic Grouping of Localities", I.G.U. 17th International Congress.

Bohannon, P. and Dalton, G. (1962) eds. *Markets in Africa*, North Western U.P.

Botswana, Republic of (1972) *Report on the Population Census*, Gabarone.

Bradley, D. F. (1968) "Multilevel Systems and Biology—View of a Sub-Molecular Biologist", in: Mesarovic, M. D., ed.: *Systems Theory and Biology*, Springer-Verlag, Berlin, pp. 38–58.

Braidwood, R. J. and Willey, G. R. (1962) eds. *Courses Toward Urban Life: Archeological Considerations of Some Cultural Alternates*, Edinburgh U.P.

Brotchie, J. F., Dickey, J. W. and Sharpe, R. (1980) *TOPAZ: General Planning*

Technique and its Application at the Regional, Urban, and Facility Planning Levels, Springer-Verlag, Berlin.

Bruckmann, G., ed. (1974) *Latin American World Model: Proceedings of the Second IIASA Symposium on Global Modelling*, International Institute for Applied Systems Analysis, Laxenburg, Austria.

Buckley, W. (1967) *Sociology and Modern Systems Theory*, Prentice-Hall, N.J.

Buckley, W. "Society as a Complex Adaptive System", in: Buckley, ed.: *Modern Systems Research for the Behavioural Scientist*, Aldive Pub. Co., Chicago.

Burle de Figueiredo, J. and Rato, H. (1977) *BACHUE-Brasil-National Version, A Demo-Economic Model*, Population and Employment Working Paper 47, ILO Geneva.

Caldwell, J. C. (1969) *African Rural-Urban Migration: The Movement to Ghana's Towns*, Australian National U.P., Canberra.

C.E.R.E.D. (1976) *Le Modèle TEMPO: Application aux données Marocaine*, Secretariat d'État au Plan et au Dévelopment Régionale, Premier Ministre, Royaume du Maroc, Publication No. 17.

C.E.R.E.D. (1977) *Projections de la Population Marocaine Totale, (Periode 1977–2002)*, Centre de Recherches et d'Etudes Demographiques, Secretariat d'Etat au Plan et au Developpement Regionale, Royaume du Maroc, Publication No. 18.

Chadwick, G. F. (1970) *Final report on Physical Planning Legislation in Mauritius*, UN Technical Assistance report to the Government of Mauritius.

Chadwick, G. F. (1978) *A Systems View of Planning: Towards a Theory of the Urban and Regional Planning Process*, Pergamon, Oxford, 1971.

Chadwick, G. F. (1978) *San José, Costa Rica: Report regarding the Preparation of a Metropolitan Strategy*.

Chapman, G. P. (1977) *Human and Environmental Systems: A Geographer's Appraisal*, Academic Press, London.

Charnov, E. L. (1976) "Optimal Foraging: the marginal value theorem", *Theoretical Population Biology*. Vol. 9, pp. 129–130.

Checkland, P. B. (1972) "A Systems Map of the Universe", in: Beishon, J. and Peters, G., eds.: *Systems Behaviour*, Harper & Row, for the Open University.

Chen, Kan, ed. (1972) *Urban Dynamics: Extensions and Reflections*, University of Pittsburgh, School of Engineering, Publication Series No. 3, San Francisco Press.

Childe, G. (1936) *Man Makes Himself*, Watts & Co., London.

Childe, G. (1951) *Social Evolution*, Watts & Co., London.

Chi-Sen Liang (1973) *Urban Land Use Analysis: A Case Study on Hong Kong*, Ernest Publications, Kowloon.

Christopher, A. J. (1976) *Studies in Historical Geography: Southern Africa*, W. Dawson, Folkestone.

Christaller, W. *Die Sentralen Orte in Süd Deutschland*, Gustav Fischer Verlag, Jena; translation into English by C. W. Baskin.

Chung, R. (1970) "Space-Time Diffusion of the Transition Model: The Twentieth Century Patterns" (1966), in: Demko, G. J., Rose, H. M. and Schnell, G. A., eds.: *Population Geography: A Reader*, McGraw-Hill.

Clark, C. (1951) "Urban population densities", *Journal of the Royal Statistical Society, A*, Vol. 114, pp. 490–496.

Clark, R. N. (1962) *Introduction to Automatic Control Systems*, Wiley.

Cléron, J. P. (1979) *Saudi Arabia 2000: A Strategy for Growth*, Croom Helm, London.

Coelho, J. D. (1979) "A Location-surplus Maximization Model of Land-use Plan Design", in: Breheny, M. J., ed.: *Development in Urban and Regional Analysis*, Pion, London.

Coleman, J. S. (1968) "The Mathematical Study of Change", in: Blalock, H. M. and Blalock, A. B., eds.: *Methodology in Social Research*, McGraw-Hill.

Condé, J. (1971) *The Demographic Transition as applied to Tropical Africa*, O.E.C.D., Paris.

Condé, J. (1973) *Some Demographic Aspects of Human Resources in Africa*, O.E.C.D., Paris.

Consad Research Corporation/Department of City Planning, Pittsburgh (1964) *Community Renewal Programme: TOMM: Time-Oriental Metropolitan Model*, CRP Technical Bulletin No. 6.

Cordey-Hayes, M. (1971) *Dynamic frameworks for spatial models*, Centre for Environmental Studies, Working Paper 76, London.

Cordey-Hayes, M. (1974) "On the Feasibility of Simulating the Relationship Between Regional Imbalance and City Growth", in: Cripps, E. L., ed.: *Space-time concepts in urban and regional models*, London papers in regional science, 4, Pion.

Cowling, T. M. and Steeley, G. C. (1973) *Sub-Regional Planning Studies: An Evaluation*, Pergamon, Oxford.

Cox, O. (1969) "The pre-Industrial City Reconsidered", in: Meadows, P. and Mizruchi, E. H., eds.: *Urbanism, Urbanization, and Change: Comparative Perspectives*, Addison-Wesley.

Crecine, J. P. (1968) *A Dynamic Model of Urban Structure*, RAND Corporation, Santa Monica, California.

Cripps, E. L., Macgill, S. M. and Wilson, A. G. (1974) *Energy and Materials Flows in the Urban Space Economy*, Working Paper 66, Dept. of Geography, University of Leeds.

Crowther, D. and Echenique, M. (1972) "Development of a model of urban spatial structure", in: Martin, L. and March, L., eds.: *Urban Space and Structure*, Cambridge U.P.

Culpin, C. and Partners (1975) *Ismailia Study: Initial Report*, UNDP, Cairo.

Czamanski, S. and Ablas, L. A. (1977) "A Model of Multiplier Effects in Maturing Economies: The Case of São Paulo", *Papers of the Regional Science Association*, Vol. 39, pp. 99–126.

de la Barra, T., Echenique, M., Quintana, M. and Guardelman, J. (1975) "An urban-regional model for the central region of Chile", in: Baxter, Echenique & Owers, eds.: *Urban Development Models*, The Construction Press, Lancaster, pp. 137–174.

Drakakis-Smith, D. W. (1971) "The Hinterlands of Towns in the New Territories", in: *Asian Urbanization: A Hong Kong Casebook*, Hong Kong University Press.

Drewnowski, J. (1970) "Measuring the level of living", *Proceedings of the Town & Country Planning Summer School, Swansea*, pp. 56–59.

Dwyer, D. J. (1971) "Problems of the Small Industrial Unit", in: Dwyer, ed.: *Asian Urbanization: A Hong Kong Casebook*, Hong Kong U.P.

Echenique, M. et al. (1969) *Development of a Model of a Town: Reading*, Land Use and Built Form Studies, Cambridge, Working Paper 26.

Echenique, M. and Domeyko, J. (1970) *A Model for Santiago Metropolitan Area*, LUBFS, Cambridge, Working Paper 11.

Echenique, M., Feo, A., Herrera, R. M. and Riquezes, J. (1973) *A Disaggregated Model of Urban Spatial Structure: Theoretical Framework*, LUBFS, Cambridge, WP8.

Echenique, M., et al. (1973) *A disaggregated model of a metropolitan area: Caracas*, LUBFS, Cambridge, WP9.

Companhia de Engenharia de Trafego, São Paulo (Custodio, P. S. and Echenique, M.) (1978) *Planejamento de Transportes e Uso do Solo Urbano: Metologia Preliminar de Modelo*, C.E.T., São Paulo.

Echenique, M. (1980) "SISTRAN: Transport Study of São Paulo Metropolitan Area", Paper to the NATO Advanced Research Institute on Systems Analysis in Urban Policy-Making and Planning, Oxford.

Eldridge, H. T. (1956) "The Process of Urbanization", in: Spangler, J. J. and Duncan, O. D., eds.: *Demographic Analysis*, Free Press, Glencoe, pp. 338–343.

Empresa Metropolitana de Planejamento da Grande São Paulo (EMPLASA) (1971) *Plano Metropolitano de Desenvolvimento Integrado Grande São Paulo*, São Paulo.

EMPLASA (1978) *Pesquisa Origem-Destino 1977: (1) Metodologia & Procidiementos; (2) Resultados Basicos*, (2 vols), São Paulo.

EMPLASA (1978) *Sumario de dados da Grande São Paulo, 1978*, Governo de Estado de São Paulo, Secretaria dos Negocios Metropolitanos, São Paulo.

Enke, S. (1957) "Speculations on Population Growth and Economic Development", *Quarterly Journal of Economics*, Vol. 71.

Enke, S. (1963) "Population and Development: a general model", *Quarterly Journal of Economics*, Vol. 77, p. 55.

Enke, S. and Zind, R. G. (1969) "Effect of fewer births on average income", *Journal of Biosocial Science*, Vol. 1, pp. 41–55.

Fair, T. J. D., Murdoch, G. and Jones, H. M. (1969) *Development in Swaziland: A Regional Analysis*, Witwatersrand University Press, Johannesburg.

Field, A. J., ed. (1970) *City and Country in the Third World: Issues in the Modernization of Latin America*, Schenkman Pub. Co. See especially: Leeds, A. & E.: "Brazil and the Myth of Urban Rurality: Urban Experience, Work, and Values in 'Squatments' of Rio de Janeiro and Lima"; and: Barraclough, S. L.: "Rural Development and Employment Prospects".

Fishlow, A. (1972) "Brasilian Size Distribution of Income", *American Economic Review*, Vol. 62, pp. 391–402.

Flowerdew, A. D. J. (1977) "An Evaluation Package for a Strategic Land Use/Transport Plan", in: Bonsall, P., Dalvi, Q., and Hills, P. J.: *Urban Transport Planning: Current Themes and Future Prospects*, Abacus Press, London.

Foot, D. (1981) *Operational Urban Models: An Introduction*, Methuen, London.

Forbes, D. (1981) "Petty Commodity Production and Underdevelopment: The Case of Pedlars and Trishaw Riders in Ujung Pandang, Indonesia", *Progress in Planning*, Vol. 16, part 2.

Forrester, J. W. (1969) *Urban Dynamics*, M.I.T. Press, Cambridge, Mass.

Forrester, J. W. (1971) *World Dynamics*, Wright-Allen Press, Cambridge, Mass.

Friedmann, J. and Sullivan, F. (1974) "The Absorption of Labour in the Urban Economy: The Case of Developing Countries", *Economic Development and Cultural Change*, Vol. 22, pp. 385.

Furnival, J. S. (1942) "The Political Economy of the Tropical Far East", *Journal of the Royal Central Asian Society*, Vol. XXIX.

Galbinski, J. (1978) *Urban Residential Density Profiles in the Brazilian Setting: A Study of the Internal Structure of Recife and São Paulo*, Ph.D. Thesis, Cornell University.

Galenson, W. and Pyatt, G. (1964) *The Quality of Labour and Economic Development in Certain Countries*, International Labour Office, Geneva.

Geraldes, P. (1980) *On the Use of Strategic Planning Models in Iberian Cities*, Paper to NATO Advanced Research Institute on Systems Analysis in Urban Policy-Making and Planning, Oxford.

Gesellschaft für Regionale Strukturentwicklung e.V. (1971) *Southern Province of Zambia: Prospects of Regional Development*, Bonn, Germany, 2 vols.

Ghali, M. and Renaud, B. (1975) *The Structure and Dynamic Properties of a Regional Economy: An Econometric Model for Hawaii*, Lexington Books.

Gibson, J. E. (1972) "A Philosophy for Urban Simulations", in Kan Chen, ed., op. cit.

Glansdorff, P. and Prigogine, I. (1971) *Thermodynamic Theory of Structure, Stability and Fluctuations*, Wiley-Interscience, London.

Goddard, A. D. and Masser, F. I. (1972) "An Approach to the Analysis of Inter-regional Migration", in: *Population Studies*.

Gould, P. R. (1970) "Tanzania: The Spatial Impress of the Modernization Process", *World Politics*, Vol. 22, Princeton U.P.

Gray, R. F. (1962) "Economic Exchange in a Sonjo Village", in: Bohannon and Dalton, eds.: *Markets in Africa*, op. cit.

Green, L. P. and Fair, T. J. D. (1962) *Development in Africa*, University of the Witwatersrand Press.

Greenberger, M., Crenson, M. A., and Crissey, B. L. (1976) *Models in the Policy Process: Public Decision Making in the Computer Era*, Russell Sage Foundation, New York, 1976. See especially Chap. 5 on System Dynamics.

Greenwood, M. J. (1969) "The Determinants of Labour Migration in Egypt", *Journal of Regional Science*, Vol. 9, pp. 283–290.

Greenwood, M. J. (1971) "A Regression Analysis of Migration to Urban Areas of a Less-Developed Country: the case of India", *Journal of Regional Science*, Vol. 11, pp. 253–262.

Greenwood, M. J. (1978) "An Econometric Model of Internal Migration and Regional Economic Growth in Mexico", *Journal of Regional Science*, Vol. 18, pp. 17–31.

Grimes, O. F. (1976) *Housing for Low-Income Urban Families: Economics and Policy in the Developing World*, Johns Hopkins University Press for the World Bank, Baltimore.

Grove, D. and Huszar, L. (1964) *The Towns of Ghana: the role of service centres in regional planning*, Ghana University Press, Accra.

Hance, W. A. (1970) *Population, Migration and Urbanization in Africa*, Columbia University Press, New York.

Hansen, W. G. (1960) "Land Use Forecasting for Transport Planning", *Highway Research Board Bulletin* 253, Washington, USA, pp. 145–151.

Hanson, D. A., Perkins, W. R., and Cruz, J. B. (1976) "Public Investment Strategies for Regional Development: An Analysis Based on Optimization and Sensitivity Results", *IEEE Transactions on Systems, Man and Cybernetics*, Vol. SMC-6, No. 3, pp. 165–176.

Hardin, G. (1963) "The Cybernetics of Competition", *Perspectives in Biology and Medicine*, pp. 58–84.

Harris, B. (1959) *Papers and Proceedings of the Regional Science Association*, Vol. V.

Harris, J. R. and Todaro, M. P. (1968) "Urban Unemployment in East Africa: an Economic Analysis of Policy Alternatives", *East African Economic Review*, Vol. 4, pp. 17–36.

Harris, J. R. and Todaro, M. P. (1969) "Wages, Industrial Employment and Labour Productivity: the Kenyan Experience", *East African Economic Review*, new series, Vol. 1, pp. 29–46.

Harrison, R. S. (1967) "Migration in the City of Tripoli, Libya", *Geographical Review*, Vol. 57, pp. 397–423.

Hart, K. (1973) "Informal Income Opportunities and Urban Employment in Ghana", *Journal of Modern African Studies*, Vol. II, p. 69.

Henshall, J. D. (1967) "Models of Agricultural Activity", in: Chorley, R. J. and Haggett, P., eds.: *Socio-Economic Models in Geography*, Methuen.

Herrera, F. (1971) *Nationalism and Urbanization in Latin America*, Paper to the Rehovot Conference, 1971.

Herrick, B. H. (1965) *Urban Migration and Economic Development in Chile*, M.I.T. Press, Cambridge, Mass., 1965.

Herrick, B. and Hudson, B. (1981) *Urban Poverty and Economic Development: A Case Study of Costa Rica*, Macmillan.

Hester, J. (1969) *Systems Models of Urban Growth and Development*, Urban Systems Laboratory, M.I.T., Cambridge, Mass.

Hirschman, A. O. (1958) *The Strategy of Economic Development*, Yale U.P.

Ho, S. P. S. (1980) *Small-Scale Enterprises in Korea and Taiwan*, World Bank Staff Working Paper No. 384.

Holling, C. S. (1966) in: Watts, K. E. F., ed.: *Systems Analysis in Ecology*, Academic Press, N.Y., pp. 185–214.

Holling, C. S. and Ewing, S. (1969) "Blind Man's Buff: Exploring the Response Space Generated by Realistic Ecological Simulation Models", in: *Proceedings of the International Symposium of Statistical Ecology*, Yale U.P.

Hoover, E. M. (1955) "The Concept of a System of Cities: a comment on Rutledge Vining's Paper", *Economic Development and Cultural Change*, Vol. 3, pp. 196–198.

Hoselitz, B. (1955) "Generative and Parasitic Cities", *Economic Development and Cultural Change*, Vol. 3, pp. 278–294.

Hotelling, H. (1920) "Stability in Competition", *Economic Journal*, Vol. 39, pp. 41–52.

Houghton, D. H. (1960) "Men of Two Worlds: Some Aspects of Migratory Labour in South Africa", *South African Journal of Economics*, Vol. 28, pp. 177–190.

House, P. W. and McLeod, J. (1977) *Large-Scale Models for Policy Evaluation*, John Wiley, N.Y.

Hutton, C. (1970) "Rates of Labour Migration", in: Gugler, J., ed.: *Urban Growth in Sub-Saharan Africa: Nkanga No. 6*, University of Makerere, Kampala, Uganda.

International Labour Organization (1970) *Employment, incomes, and equality: a strategy for increasing productive employment in Kenya:* Report of an Inter-Agency Team financed by the UNDP and organized by the ILO, Geneva.

Jefferson, M. (1939) "The Law of the Primate City", *Geographical Review*, Vol. 29, pp. 226–232.

Jenkins, P. M. and Robson, A. (1974) "An application of linear programming methodology for regional strategy making", *Regional Studies*, Vol. 8, pp. 242–269.

Johnson, G. E. and Whitelaw, W. E. (1974) "Urban-Rural Income Transfers in Kenya: An Estimated Remittances Function", *Economic Development and Cultural Change*, Vol. 22, pp. 473–479.

Kanyeihamba, G. W. (1974) "Urban Planning Law in East Africa", *Progress in Planning*, Vol. 2, pp. 1–83.

Katzman, M. T. (1977) *Cities and Frontiers in Brazil: Regional Dimensions of Economic Development*, Harvard U.P., Cambridge, Mass.

Keeble, D. E. (1967) "Models of Economic Development", in: Chorley, R. J. & Haggett, P.: *Socio-Economic Models in Geography*, Methuen, pp. 243–302.

Keyfitz, N. (1965) "Political-Economic Aspects of Urbanization in South and Southeast Asia", in: Hauser, P. M. and Schnore, L. F., eds.: *The Study of Urbanization*, John Wiley.

Kim, B. N. W. and Bell, D. S. (1982) "Managing the Unmanageable: The Case of Seoul", *Korea Journal*, Vol. 22, pp. 28–36.

Kim, J. H. (1981) *Housing Development Planning in Korea*, Korea Research Institute for Human Settlement, Seoul.

Kneese, A. V., Ayres, R. V. and d'Arge, R. C. (1970) *Economics and the Environment: A Materials Balance Approach*, Resources for the Future, Inc./Johns Hopkins U.P.

Korean Research Institute for Human Settlement (1980) *Functional Relocation in the Seoul Metropolitan Region*, KRIHS, Seoul (Original in Korean).

Kristol, I. (1978) "Seeking a 'Theory' of Growth", *Asian Wall Street Journal*, 30 November.

Korea: National Bureau of Statistics (1981) *Preliminary Count of Population and Housing Census, 1980*, Economic Planning Board, Seoul.

Kuper, H., ed. (1965) *Urbanization and Migration in West Africa*, University of California Press.

Kuznets, S. (1959) Six Lectures on Economic Growth, Free Press, Glencoe.

Kwon, W. Y. (1981) "A Simulation Model for Testing Urban Population Distribution Policy in Relation to Selecting Growth Centres in Korea", in: Chatterjee, L. and Nijkamp, P., eds.: *Urban Problems and Economic Development*, NATO Advanced Study Institutes, Series D, No. 6, Sijthoff & Noordhoff, Amsterdam.

Lea, J. P. (1972) "The Differentiation of the Rural Periphery in Swaziland: A Multivariate Analysis", *South African Geographical Journal*, Vol. 54, pp. 105–123.

Lee, D. B. (1973) "Requiem for Large-Scale Models", *Journal of the American Institute of Planners*, Vol. 39, pp. 163–178.

Leeming, F. (1977) *Street Studies in Hong Kong*, Oxford U.P.

Lewis, Sir W. A. (1955) *Theory of Economic Growth*, Unwin, London.

Lichfield, N., Kettle, P. and Whitbread, M. (1976) *Evaluation in the Planning Process*, Pergamon, Oxford.

Lindeman, H., De Hoogh, J., Keyzer, M. A. and Van Heemst, H. D. J. (1972) *MOIRA: Model of International Relations in Agriculture*, North Holland, Amsterdam.

Little, K. (1965) *West African Urbanization—a study of voluntary associations in social change*, Cambridge U.P.

Lösch, A. (1954) *The Economics of Location*, English translation, New Haven, Conn.

Lowry, I. S. (1964) *A Model of Metropolis*, Rand Corporation Memorandum RM-4055-RC, Santa Monica, CA1.

Lowry, I. S. (1966) *Migration and metropolitan growth: two analytical models*, Chandler, San Francisco.

Mabogunge, A. L. (1981) *Urbanization in Nigeria*, University of London Press.

Mabro, R. (1967) "Industrial Growth, Agricultural Under-Employment and the Lewis Model. The Egyptian Case, 1937–1965". *Journal of Development Studies*, Vol. 3, pp. 322–351.

Macfarlane, A. G. J. (1970) *Dynamical System Models*, G. Harrap, London.

Macgill, S. M. (1975) *Urban Energy Flows within a General Systems Framework: Towards the Design of New Model Structures*, Working Paper 123, Department of Geography, University of Leeds.

Mackett, R. L. (1974) *The Development of an extended Lowry Model for application at the City scale*, Working Paper 81, Dept. of Geography, University of Leeds.

Masser, F. I. (1964) "Changing Patterns of African employment in Southern Rhodesia", in: Steel, R. W. and Prothero, R. M., eds.: *Geographers and the Tropics*, Longmans.

Mathieson, R. S. (1972) "Urbanization Processes in Developing Countries: A Markov Chain Approach", in: Dwyer, D. J., ed.: *The City as a Centre of Change in Asia*, Hong Kong U.P.

Mauritius: Central Statistical Office (1970) *The Census of Industrial Production, 1967–68*, Government Printer, Port Louis.

Mauritius, Government of (1971) *4-Year Plan for Social & Economic Development*, 2 Vols., Government Printer, Port Louis.

Mauritius, Government of (1973) *1972 Housing Census*, Government Printer, Port Louis.

Mauritius, Government of (1974) *1972 Population Census of Mauritius, Volume 1, Preliminary Report*, Government Printer, Port Louis.

Mazumdar, D. (1979) *Paradigms in the Study of Urban Labour Markets in LDCs: A Reassessment in the Light of an Empirical Survey in Bombay City*, World Bank Staff Working Paper, No. 366.

McGee, T. G. (1967) *South East Asian City*, Bell, London.

McGee, T. G. (1971) *The Urbanization Process in the Third World*, Bell, London.

McGee, T. G. (1973) *Hawkers in Hong Kong: A Study of Planning and Policy in a Third World City*, University of Hong Kong.

McGee, T. G. (1977) "Rural-Urban Mobility in South and South East Asia"; and "The Persistence of the Proto-Proletariat"; both in Abu-Lughod, J. L. and Hay, R. (eds.). *Third World Urbanization*, Methuen.

Meadows, D. H., Meadows, D. L., Randers, J., and Behrens, W. W. (1972) *The Limits to Growth*, Potomac Associates, Earth Island Limited, London.

Meadows, P. (1969) "The City, Technology, and History", in: Meadows, P. and Mizruchi, E. H., eds.: *Urbanism, Urbanization, and Change: Comparative Perspectives*, Addison-Wesley.

Mera, K. (1973) "On the Urban Agglomerations and Economic Efficiency", *Economic Development and Cultural Change*, Vol. 21, p. 309 et seq.

Mesarovic, M. and Pestel, E., eds. (1974) *Multilevel Computer Model of World Development System*, Extract from the Proceedings of the IIASA Symposium, 1974; International Institute for Applied Systems Analysis, Laxenburg, Austria, 6 Vols.

Mesarovic, M. and Pestel, E. (1975) *Mankind at the Turning Point*, Hutchinson, London.

Mills, E. S. and Song, B. N. (1979) *Urbanization and Urban Problem*, Studies in the Modernization of the Republic of Korea: 1945–1975, Harvard University Press.

Mitchell, J. C. (1958) "Factors motivating Migration from Rural Areas"; in: Apthorpe, R. J., ed.: *Present Interrelations in Central African Rural and Urban Life*, Proceedings of the 11th Conference of the Rhodes-Livingstone Institute.

Mitchell, J. C. (1969) "Urbanization, Detribalization, Stabilization and Urban Commitment in Southern Africa: A Problem of Definition and Measurement"; in: Meadows, P. and Mizruchi, E. H., eds., op. cit.

Mitchell, J. C. (1969) "Structural Plurality, Urbanization and Labour Circulation in Southern Rhodesia"; in: Jackson, J. A. ed.: *Migration*, Cambridge University Press.

Mohan, R. (1979) *Urban Economic and Planning Models: Assessing the Potential for Cities in Developing Countries*, World Bank Staff Occasional Papers, No. 25, Johns Hopkins U.P., Baltimore.

Monyake, L. B. (1971) "Lesotho: Probable effect of population growth on employment and unemployment", in: *The Demographic Transition in Tropical Africa*, OECD, Paris, pp. 163–5.

Morgenthaler, G. W. (1961) "The theory and application of simulation in operations research"; in: Ackoff, R. L., ed.: *Progress in Operations Research*, Vol. 1, John Wiley.

Mountjoy, A. B. (1976) "Urbanization, the Squatter, and Development in the Third World"; *Tijdschrift voor Economische en Sociale Geografie*, Vol. 67, pp. 130–137.

Myrdal, G. M. (1957) *Economic Theory and Under-Developed Regions*, Duckworth, London.

Newcastle System Dynamics Group and IBM (UK) Scientific Centre (1973) *A Dynamic Simulation Model for Regional Planning: A Case Study of the Northern Region*, IBM, Peterlee.

Newcastle System Dynamics Group (1973) *System Dynamics Modelling Methods in Urban and Regional Planning*, SSRC Project Report, University of Newcastle upon Tyne.

Newling, B. E. (1969) "The Spatial Variation of Urban Population Densities", *Geographic Review*, Vol. 59, pp. 242–259.

Nicolis, G. and Prigogine, I. (1977) *Self-Organization in Non-equilibrium Systems: From Dissipative Structures to Order through Fluctuations*, John Wiley, N.Y.

Niedercorn, J. A. (1971) "A Negative Exponential Model of Urban Land Use Densities and its Implications for Metropolitan Development", *Journal of Regional Science*, Vol. 2, pp. 371–376.

Paelinck, J. H. P. (1972) "Alternative Methods for the Study of Urban Dynamics", in Kunck, R., ed.: *Recent Developments in Regional Science*, Karlsruhe Papers in Regional Science, 1, Pion, London.

Page, J. M. (1979) *Small Enterprises in African Development: A Survey*, World Bank Staff Working Paper, No. 363.

Parr, J. B. (1978) "An Alternative Model of the Central-place System", in: Batey, P. W. J., ed.: *Theory and Method in Urban and Regional Analysis*, Pion, London.

Patten, B. C., ed. (1972) *Systems Analysis and Simulation in Ecology*, 3 Vols.

Pike, J. G. (1968) *Malawi: A Political and Economic History*, Pall Mall Press, London.

Pirsig, R. M. (1976) *Zen and the Art of Motor Cycle Maintenance*, Bantam.

Portes, N., Geraldes, P. and Pereira, F. (1975) "A model of Lisbon", in: Baxter, Echenique, and Owers, eds.: *Urban Development Models*, The Construction Press, Lancaster, pp. 203–216.

Power, J. (1971): *Planning, Magic and Technique*, Institute for Operational Research, London.

Pred, A. R. (1966) *The Spatial Dynamics of U.S. Urban-Industrial Growth, 1800–1914*, M.I.T. Press, Cambridge, Mass.

Pred, A. R. (1969) *Behaviour and Location: Foundations for a Geographic and Dynamic Location Theory*, 2 Vols., Lund Studies in Geography Series B, Nos. 27, 28.

Pred, A. R. (1973) "The Growth and Development of Systems of Cities in Advanced Economies", in: Pred, A. R. and Tornqvist, G. E.: *Systems of Cities and Information Flows, Two Essays*, Lund Studies in Geography, Series B, No. 38.

Pred, A. R. (1977) *City-Systems in Advanced Economies*, Hutchinson, London.

Prigogine, I., Allen, P. M., and Herman, R. (1977) "Long Term Trends and the Evolution of Complexity", in: Lazlo, E. and Bierman, J., eds. *Goals in a Global Community: Background Papers for a Report to the Club of Rome*, Pergamon, N.Y., pp. 1–64.

Putman, S. H. (1977) "Calibrating a Disaggregated Residential Allocation Model—DRAM", in: Massey, D. and Batey, P. W. J., eds. *Alternative Frameworks for Analysis*, Pion, London.

Putman, S. H. (1980) "Calibrating urban residential location models, 3: empirical results for non-US cities", *Environment and Planning, A*, Vol. 12, pp. 813–827.

Renaud, B. (1977) *Economic Fluctuations and Speed of Urbanization: A Case Study of Korea, 1955–1975*, World Bank Staff Working Paper No. 270.

Renaud, B. (1979) *National Urbanization Policies in Developing Countries*, World Bank Staff Working Paper No. 347.

Renaud, B. (1981) *National Urbanization Policy in Developing Countries*, Oxford U.P. for the World Bank.

Renaud, B., Lim, G-G, and Follain, J. (1980) *The Demand for Housing in Developing Countries: The Case of Korea*, World Bank Reprint Series No. 183.

Rho, Y. H. and Hwang, M. C., eds. (1979) *Metropolitan Planning: Issues and Policies*, Korea Research Institute for Human Settlements, Seoul.

Rhodesia, Central Statistical Office (1969) *Census of Population*.

Rhodesia, Central Statistical Office (1970) *Report on the European Family Budget Survey in Rhodesia, 1968*, Salisbury.

Rhodesia, Central Statistical Office (1970) *Report on the Urban African Budget Survey in Salisbury, 1969*, Salisbury.

Rhodesia, Central Statistical Office (1972) *The Census of Distribution in 1969/70: Retail and Wholesale Trade, Hotels and Restaurants*, Salisbury.

Richardson, H. W. (1969) *Elements of Regional Economics*, Penguin, London.

Richardson, H. W. (1972) "Optimality in City Size, Systems of Cities and Urban Policy", *Urban Studies*, Vol. 9, pp. 29–47.

Richardson, H. W. (1973) *Regional Growth Theory*, Macmillan, London.

Richardson, H. W. (1973) "Theory of the Distribution of City Sizes: Review and Prospects", *Regional Studies*, Vol. 7, pp. 239–251.

Richardson, H. W. (1974) "Agglomeration Potential: A Generalization of the Income Potential Concept", *Journal of Regional Science*, Vol. 14, pp. 325–336.

Richardson, H. W. (1974) "Two Disequilibrium Models of Regional Growth", in: Cripps, E. L., ed.: *Space-Time Concepts in Urban and Regional Models*, Pion, London, pp. 46–55.

Richardson, H. W. (1976) "A Note on the Dynamics of the Population Density Gradients", *The Annals of Regional Science*, Vol. 10, pp. 15–18.

Richardson, H. W. (1977) *City Size and National Spatial Strategies in Developing Countries*, World Bank Staff Working Paper No. 252.

Roberts, B. (1978) *Cities of Peasants: The Political Economy of Urbanization in the Third World*, Edward Arnold, London.

Roberts, P. C., et al. (1978) "The SARU Model, 1976", in: Bruckmann, ed.: *SARUM and MRI: Description and Comparison of a World Model and a National Model*, Proceedings of the Fourth IIASA Symposium on Global Modelling, 1976, Pergamon, Oxford, pp. 9–39.

Robson, B. T. (1973) *Urban Growth: an approach*, Methuen, London.

Rodgers, G., Hopkins, M. and Wery, R. (1978): *Population, employment and inequality: BACHUE-Philippines*, Saxon House for International Labour Office.

Rodriguez-Bachiller, A. (1976) *Gravity Models in a Dynamic Framework*, Geographical papers No. 40, University of Reading.

Roy, J. R. and Crawford, J. R. (1980) *An Urban Land-Use Transport Study in a Developing Country*, C.S.I.R.O., Division of Building Research, Highett, Victoria, Australia.

Sahota, G. S. (1968) "An Economic Analysis of Internal Migration in Brazil", *Journal of Political Economy*, Vol. 76, pp. 218–245.

Santos, M. (1979) *The Shared Space*, Methuen.

Sarin, M. (1982) *Urban Planning in the Third World: The Chandigarh Experience*, Mansell, London.

Sayer, R. A. (1976) "A Critique of Urban Modelling: From Regional Science to Urban and Regional Political Economy", *Progress in Planning*, Vol. 6, pp. 187–254.

Schaefer, K. and Spindel, C. R. (1976) *São Paulo: Urban development and employment*, International Labour Office, Geneva.

Scott, I. (1982) *Urban and Spatial Development in Mexico*, Johns Hopkins U.P. for the World Bank.

Sethuraman, S. V. (1986) *Jakarta: Urban development and employment*, International Labour Office, Geneva.

Sethuraman, S. V. (1976) "The urban informal sector: concept, measurement and policy", *International Labour Review*, I.L.O., Geneva, Vol. 114, pp. 69–81.

Simon, H. A. (1957) *Models of Man*, John Wiley.

Sit, V. (1979) "Factories in Domestic Premises: An Anatomy of an Urban Informal Sector in Hong Kong", *Asian Profile*, Vol. 7, pp. 209–229.

Sjöberg, G. (1960) *The Pre-Industrial City: Past and Present*, Free Press, Glencoe, Illinois.

Smout, M. A. H. (1969) *Harari Shopping Survey: A Report to the Director of African Administration, Municipality of Salisbury*, Salisbury, Rhodesia.

Smout, M. A. H. (1969) *Highfields Shopping Survey: A Report to the Town Manager, Highfields African Township, Ministry of Local Government and Housing*, Salisbury, Rhodesia.

Stearns, F. and Montag, T., eds. (1974) *The Urban Ecosystem: a Holistic Approach*, The Institute of Ecology Report of the Urban Ecosystems project, Halsted Press, Wiley.

Stent, G. E. (1948) "Migrancy and Urbanization in the Union of South Africa", *Africa: Journal of the International African Institute*, Vol. 18, pp. 161–283.

Stewart, J. Q. and Warntz, W. (1958) "Physics of Population Distribution", *Journal of Regional Science*, Vol. 1, pp. 99–123.

Stilwell, J. C. H. (1975) *Models of Inter-Regional Migration: A Review*, Working Paper 100, Dept. of Geography, University of Leeds.

Stine, J. H. (1962) "Temporal Aspects of Tertiary Production Elements in Korea", in: Pitts, F. R., ed.: *Urban Systems and Economic Development*, University of Oregon.

Stouffer, S. A. (1940) "Intervening Opportunities: a Theory relating Mobility and Distance", *American Sociological Review*, Vol. 5, pp. 845–867.

Sovani, N. V. "The Analysis of Over-Urbanization", *Economic Development and Cultural Change*, Vol. 12, pp. 113–122.

Swaziland Government (1968) *Report on the 1966 Swaziland Population Census*, Mbabane.

Swaziland, Central Statistical Office (1970) *Report on a Survey of Housing in Msunduza, Mbabane*.

Taylor, J. L. and Williams, D. G. (1982) *Urban Planning Practice in Developing Countries*, Pergamon, Oxford.

Todaro, M. P. (1969) "A Model of Labour Migration and Urban Unemployment in Less-Developed Countries", *American Economic review*, Vol. 59, pp. 138–148.

Trébous, M. (1968) *Migration and Development*, OECD, Paris.

UNESCO (1976) *The use of socio-economic indicators in development planning*, Paris.

Vapnarsky, C. A. (1969) "On Rank-Size Distributions of Cities: An Ecological Approach", *Economic Development and Cultural Change*, Vol. 17, pp. 584–595.

von Bertalanffy, L. (1952) *Problems of Life*.

von Bertalanffy, L. (1971) *General System Theory*, Allen Lane/Penguin, London.

Vining, R. (1955) "A Description of Certain Spatial Aspects of an Economic System", *Economic Development and Cultural Change*, Vol. 3, pp. 147–195.

Wade, L. L. and Kim, B. S. (1977) *The Political Economy of Success: Public Policy and Economic Development in the Republic of Korea*, Kyung Hee University Press, Seoul.

Wheeler, D. (1980) *Human Resource Development and Economic Growth in Developing Countries: A Simultaneous Model*, World Bank Staff Working Paper No. 407.

Whyte, L. L., Wilson, A. G. and Wilson, D., eds. (1969) *Hierarchical Structures: Proceedings of a Symposium at Huntington Beach, California*, American Elsevier Publishing Co.

Wikan, U. (1980) *Life Among the Poor in Cairo*, Tavistock Publications, London.

Wilen, J. E. (1973) "A model of economic system–ecosystem interation", *Environment and Planning*, Vol. 5, pp. 409–420.

Wilson, A. G. (1970) *Entropy in Urban and Regional Modelling*, Pion, London.

Wilson, F. (1972) *Migrant Labour in South Africa*, South African Council of Churches, Johannesburg.

Wirth, J. D. and Jones, R. L., eds. (1978) *Manchester and São Paulo, Problems of Rapid Urban Growth*, Stanford University Press, see especially papers by Roberts, B., p. 77 et seq; and Katzman, M. T., p. 107 et seq.

Wong, L. S. K. (1971) "The Aplichau Squatter Area: a Case Study", in: *Asian Urbanization*, op. cit.

World Bank, The (1981) *Annual Report*.

World Bank, The (1980–1982, 1984) *World Development Reports, 1980, 1982, 1984*, Oxford University Press.

Zadeh, L. A. (1972) "Simple Models for Complex Systems?", in: *Third Annual Pittsburgh Conference on Modelling and Simulation*, University of Pittsburgh.

Zipf, G. K. (1949) *Human Behaviour and the Principle of Least Effort*, Addison-Wesley.

Zukav, G. (1980) *The Dancing Wu Li Masters: An Overview of the New Physics*, Bantam Books, New York.

Acknowledgements

The permission of the following to quote or reproduce tables or diagrams is gratefully acknowledged:

The World Bank, to quote from:

World Development Report, 1984, published by Oxford University Press, New York;

Staff Working Papers, Nos. 209/1975; 252/1977; 363/1979; 366/1979; 384/1980; by Beier, Churchill, Cohen and Renaud; H. W. Richardson; J. Page; D. Mazumdar; and S. Ho, respectively.

The Johns Hopkins University Press for the World Bank, to reprint material from:

I. Scott: *Urban and Spatial Development in Mexico*, 1982;

O. F. Grimes: *Housing for Low-Income Urban Families*, 1976.

The Organisation for Economic Cooperation and Development, to reproduce tables from:

M. Trébous: *Migration and Development*, Paris, 1968.

Marcial Echenique & Partners, Cambridge, to quote the various equations and reproduce diagrams of model relationships and results shown in Chapter 6.

The RAND Corporation, Santa Monica, California, to reproduce two figures from:

J. P. Crecine: *A Dynamic Model of Urban Structure*, 1968,

The University of Hong Kong, Centre of Asian Studies, to reproduce a diagram from:

T. G. McGee: *Hawkers in Hong Kong*, 1973.

Hong Kong University Press, to reproduce a figure from:

D. J. Dwyer (ed.): *Asian Urbanization: A Hong Kong Casebook*, Centre for Asian Studies No. 3, Hong Kong U.P., 1971.

The Council on East Asian Studies, Harvard University, to reproduce one table and one quotation from:

E. S. Mills and B-N Song: *Urbanization and Urban Problems*, Studies in the Modernization of the Republic of Korea, 1945–1975, distributed by Harvard U.P., 1979.

Cambridge University Press, to reproduce a table from:

K. Hart: "Informal Income Opportunities and Urban Employment in Ghana", *Journal of Modern African Studies*, Vol. II, 1973, p. 69, published by Cambridge University Press.

Australian National University Press, Canberra, to quote from:

J. C. Caldwell: *African Rural-Urban Migration: The Movement to Ghana's Towns*, A.N.U. Press, Canberra, 1969, pp. 54–55.

The International Labour Office, Geneva, to reproduce and/or quote from:

W. Galenson and G. Pyatt: *The Quality of Labour and Economic Development in Certain Countries*, 1964, pp. 88–89, paras (1) to (4); Copyright 1964, International Labour Office, Geneva.

I.L.O.: *Employment, incomes and inequality: a strategy for increasing productive employment in Kenya*, 1972, pp. 506–508; Copyright International Labour Office, Geneva, 1972.

S. V. Sethuraman: "The Urban Informal Sector", *International Labour Review*, Vol. 114, 1976, p. 81, Appendix; Copyright 1976, International Labour Office, Geneva.

S. V. Sethuraman: *Jakarta: Urban development and employment*, 1976, Table 70, p. 128. Copyright 1976, International Labour Office, Geneva.

K. Schaefer and C. R. Spindel: *São Paulo: Urban development and employment*, 1976, Table 10, p. 22; Table 17, p. 32; Tables 37 and 38, p. 69. Copyright 1976, International Labour Office, Geneva.

G. Rodgers, M. Hopkins, and R. Wery: *Population, employment and inequality: BACHUE-Philippines*, Saxon House for ILO, 1978. Copyright 1978, International Labour Office, Geneva.

J. S. Birks and C. A. Sinclair: *International Migration and Development in the Arab Region*, 1980, Tables. Copyright 1980, International Labour Office, Geneva.

Drs. J. R. Roy and J. R. Crawford, Victoria, Australia, to quote from:

An Urban Land-Use Transport Study in a Developing Country, CSIRO, Highett, Victoria, 1980.

The University of Chicago Press, to reproduce:

Two figures from: C. Vapnarsky: "On Rank-Size Distributions of Cities: An Ecological Approach", In: *Economic Development & Cultural Change*, Vol. 17, 1969, pp. 584–5;

Three tables from: J. Abu-Lughod: "Urbanization in Egypt: Present State and Future Prospects"; *Economic Development & Cultural Change*, 1965, pp. 324, 328, 338.

Princeton University Press, to reproduce Figures 2 and 5 from:

Peter Gould: "Tanzania 1920–63: The Spatial Impress of the Modernization Process"; *World Politics*, Vol. 22, No. 2 (January 1970). Copyright © 1970 by Princeton University Press. Reprinted with permission of Princeton University Press.

The Macmillan Press Ltd., London and Basingstoke, for permission to reproduce:

Fig. 4.1, p. 75, from: G. H. Blake: "Urbanisation in North Africa: Its Nature and Consequences", in: Dwyer, D. J. (ed.): *The City in the Third World*, 1974.

Schenkman Publishing Company Inc., to quote from:

S. L. Barraclough: "Rural Development and Employment Prospects" in: A. J. Field, Ed.: *City and Country in the Third World: Issues in the Modernization of Latin America*, 1970.

The Editor, *Economic Geography*, Clark University, Worcester, Massachusetts, to reproduce:

Fig. 8 and Table V from: J. O. Abiodun: "Urban Hierarchy in a Developing Country", Vol. 43, 1967, p. 347 et seq.

The M.I.T. Press, Cambridge, Massachusetts, to reprint:
Fig. 4.1, p. 178, A. R. Pred: *The Spatial Dynamics of U.S. Urban-Industrial Growth, 1800–1914*, 1966.

The School of Law, Stanford University, California, to reproduce quotations from:
pp. 78 and 99, B. Roberts: "Agrarian Organization and Urban Development", and:
p. 118, M. T. Katzman: "São Paulo and its Hinterland";
both in: J. D. Wirth and R. L. Jones, eds.: *Manchester and São Paulo: Problems of Rapid Urban Growth*, Stanford University Press, 1978.

The American Geographical Society, to reproduce an adaptation of:
Figs. 8 and 9, from R. S. Harrison: "Migration in the City of Tripoli, Libya", in: *Geographical Review*, Vol. 57, 1967, pp. 397–423.

McGraw-Hill Publishing Co. to reproduce a diagram and note from:
R. Chung: "Space-Time Diffusion of the Transition Model: The Twentieth Century Problems", (1966), in: G. J. Demko, H. M. Rose, and G. A. Schnell, eds: *Population Geography: A. Reader*, 1970.

The Publishers of *Asian Wall Street Journal*, to quote from:
"Seeking a 'Theory' of Growth" by Irving Kristol, 30th November 1978.

The Macmillan Press Ltd., London and Basingstoke, and Barnes and Noble Books, Totowa, New Jersey for permission to reproduce:
Figure 42, page 77, from G. H. Blake "Urbanisation in North Africa: Its Nature and Consequences", in D. J. Dwyer (ed.) *The City in the Third World*, 1974.

Dr Victor Sit for permission to reproduce:
Two diagrams and data from his paper on "Factories in Domestic Premises", *Asian Profile*, Vol. 7, No. 3, 1979.

Duckworth (Gerald) & Co. Ltd., London, for permission to reproduce:
A schematic diagram, "Myrdal's Process of Cumulative Causation", from G. M. Myrdal *Economic Theory and Under-Developed Regions*, 1957.

Index

318   Index

Madras 186 et seq.
Malaysia 68
Malawi 49, 50, 129
Mali 35
Manama, Bahrain 32
Manchester 144, 146, 147, 197
Manila 132, 136
Maringa, Brazil 147
Mauritius 26–29, 31, 115, 117, 126, 129,
    130, 131, 158, 177–179, 182, 281, 286,
    288, 295
Maya 18
Mazumdar, D. 61, 133, 135
Mbabane, Swaziland 199
McGee, T. G. 155, 157, 158, 270, 282, 296
McLuhan, M. 272
Meadows, D. H. et al. 177, 178, 203, 286
Meier, R. L. 238
Melbourne 258
Mesarovic, M. 2, 10, 177, 203
Mera, K. 293
Meso-America 18
Mesopotamia 18
Mexicali, Mexico 76
Mexico 11, 76, 79, 177, 264
Mexico City 72, 76, 77, 79, 183, 196, 280
Middle East cities 198
Migration 41 et seq
Migration models 54 et seq
Mills, E. S. and Song, B. N. 74–76,
    111–113, 190 et seq
Minas Gerais, Brazil 146, 166
Mitchell, J. C. 43, 50, 282
Models, particular
    Adams, Jamaica migration 56, 57
    Ayeni, Lagos Lowry 245, 252, 253
    BACHUE-Philippines 203–208
    Beals et al., Ghana migration 55, 56
    Belo Horizonte, potential 212–214
    Berry & Barnum, central place 101
    Christaller, distribution of centres 96–99
    Chung, demographic transition 30–32,
        176–178
    Cobb-Douglas 92, 93
    Coelho, location surplus 261, 262
    Crecine, TOMM allocation 237, 238
    de la Barra et al., Chile regional 218–225
    Demographic-economic 27, 29, 30
    Echenique et al., Caracas urban 224–228
    Echenique et al., Santiago
        urban 214–218
    Greenwood, India migration 57–58
    ILO/Galenson & Pyatt
        development 172, 173
    ILO Kenya informal sector 123, 124
    ILO/Wheeler development 173, 174
    Intra-urban growth 110, 111
    Ismailia local economy 37, 38

KRIHS, Seoul TOMM 238–245
Kwon, Korea innovation
    diffusion 254–257
Lowry migration 54, 55
Markov, urban growth 94
Mackett/Lowry allocation 262
Mills & Song, Korea housing 190–192
Mills & Song, Korea urban density
    111–113
MUT São Paulo, land use/transport
    231–234
Myrdal, cumulative causation 160,
    161
Outline regional 286–288
Paelinck, population/employment 103
Population 25, 26, 34
Pred, cumulative causation 162
Portes et al., Lisbon urban 226
Putman, DRAM interaction 264, 265
Rank-size 84, 85, 92
Renaud, Korea migration 64, 65
Renaud et al., Korea housing 192, 193
Richardson, income potential 105, 107
Robson, innovation diffusion 253
Rural-urban migration 66
Sahota, Brazil migration 59, 61
Salisbury, metropolitan series 246–252
Santos, two circuits 119
São Paulo, population forecast 208–211
schematic urban system 282–286
SISTRAN, São Paulo transport 229–231
stocks and flows 43
Stouffer, intervening opportunities 279,
    280, 297, 298
TEMPO, Morocco 30
Tinbergen, urban hierarchy 91
Todaro, urban labour market 61
TOPAZ, Melbourne and Tehran location
    surplus 257–261
Von Thünen agricultural allocation 95,
    96
World Bank, urbanization 69, 71
Zambia, dual economy 124, 125
Modernization surface 63
Mohan, R. 235, 236, 264
MOIRA model 177
Monterrey, Mexico 76
Monyake, L. B. 128
Morrison 45
Morocco 30, 32, 36, 76–78, 131
Moseley, M. J. 160
Moslemization of urban life 76, 249
Mountjoy, A. B. 126
Mozambique 49
Multiplier effects 34, 36, 37, 161
Muth, R. 192
MUT model, São Paulo 231 et seq.
Myrdal, G. M. 160, 161, 294

Other Titles in the Series

FALUDI, A. K. F.
Essays on Planning Theory and Education (Volume 20)
BLOWERS, A.
The Limits of Power: The Politics of Local Planning Policy (Volume 21)
McAUSLAN, J. P.
The Ideologies of Planning Law (Volume 22)
MASSAM, B. H.
Spatial Search: Applications to Planning Problems in the Public Sector (Volume 23)
HOYLE, B. S. and PINDER, D. A.
Cityport Industrialisation and Regional Development (Volume 24)
TAYLOR, J. L. and WILLIAMS, D. G.
Urban Planning Practice in Developing Countries (Volume 25)
SPENCE, N. *et al.*
British Cities: An Analysis of Urban Change (Volume 26)
PARIS, C.
Critical Readings in Planning Theory (Volume 27)
STARKIE, D.
The Motorway Age (Volume 28)
HEALEY, P. *et al.*
Planning Theory: Prospects for the 1980s (Volume 29)
O'RIORDAN, T. and TURNER, R. K.
An Annotated Reader in Environmental Planning and Management (Volume 30)
HEALEY, P.
Local Plans in British Land-Use Planning (Volume 31)
COPE, D., HILLS, P. and JAMES, P.
Energy Policy and Land-Use Planning: An International Perspective (Volume 32)
BANDMAN, M.
Regional Development in the USSR: Modelling the Formation of Soviet Territorial-Production Complexes (Volume 33)
BROMLEY, R.
Planning for Small Enterprises in Third World Cities (Volume 34)
de BOER, E.
Transport Sociology: Social Aspects of Transport Planning (Volume 35)

The terms of our inspection copy service apply to all the above books. A complete catalogue of all books in the Pergamon International Library is available on request. The Publisher will be pleased to consider suggestions for revised editions and new titles.